Chicago before the Fire

Chicago before the Fire

An Economic History

LOUIS P. CAIN

UNIVERSITY OF ILLINOIS PRESS
Urbana, Chicago, and Springfield

Manufactured in the United States of America
1 2 3 4 5 C P 5 4 3 2 1
♾ This book is printed on acid-free paper.

Some of what appears in this book is based on material previously published by the author. The relevant pieces are:

Sanitation Strategy for a Lakefront Metropolis: The Case of Chicago, Northern Illinois University Press, 1978.

"William Dean's Theory of Urban Growth: Chicago's Commerce and Industry, 1854–1871," *Journal of Economic History,* June 1985.

"From Mud to Metropolis: Chicago Before the Fire," *Research in Economic History* 10, 1986.

"A Canal and Its City: A Selective Business History of Chicago," *DePaul Business Law Review,* Fall/Winter 1998.

Library of Congress Cataloging-in-Publication Data
Names: Cain, Louis P., author.
Title: Chicago before the fire : an economic history / Louis P. Cain. Description: Urbana : University of Illinois Press, [2025] | Includes bibliographical references and index.
Identifiers: LCCN 2024056880 (print) | LCCN 2024056881 (ebook) | ISBN 9780252046582 (cloth ; alk. paper) | ISBN 9780252088698 (paperback ; alk. paper) | ISBN 9780252047893 (ebook)
Subjects: LCSH: Business enterprises—Illinois—Chicago—History—19th century. | Entrepreneurship—Illinois—Chicago—History—19th century. | Businesspeople—Illinois—Chicago—History—19th century. | Chicago (Ill.)—Commerce—History—19th century. | Chicago (Ill.)—Economic conditions—19th century.
Classification: LCC HF5068.C4 .C35 2025 (print) | LCC HF5068.C4 (ebook) | DDC 338.7/40977311—dc23/eng/20250206
LC record available at https://lccn.loc.gov/2024056880
LC ebook record available at https://lccn.loc.gov/2024056881

My maternal grandparents both died before I was born. My maternal grandfather, a doctor, was born in Chicago in 1856, shortly after his parents arrived from England. Family lore says that they lived on Noble Street in the old Twelfth Ward, west of the river and just west of the fire. In the days following the fire, my fifteen-year-old grandfather picked up what had been a box of tacks. The metal was fused into the shape of the box, but the box itself was ash. After this object served as a family paperweight for well over a century, my cousin recently placed the tacks in a shadowbox frame to help preserve them. My maternal grandmother, born in 1867, moved to Chicago from St. Catherines, Ontario, following the advice of a sibling who had made the move earlier. My paternal grandfather, whom I did know and for whom I am named, was born in Danville, Illinois, on the last day of 1866. He attended seminary in Chicago in the early 1890s but did not become a permanent resident until 1900, when he answered the call of the four-year-old Edgewater Presbyterian Church. My paternal grandmother was born in 1871 in a log cabin on land her father homesteaded north of Abilene, Kansas, following his discharge from the Union Army. It was still the frontier; she told stories of neighboring Indians gathering around her family's dining table when, say, the Thanksgiving turkey was being cooked. She died in 1968 having watched astronauts prepare to go to the moon. All four grandparents witnessed decades of economic growth and development in Chicago and the world. This book is dedicated to their memory and to all the Dales and Cains.

Contents

Chicago before the Fire

Introduction

The economic growth and development of Chicago in the middle decades of the nineteenth century were astounding. The secret to this success was that one of the lowest divides between the Great Lakes and the Mississippi River watersheds lay a short distance upstream from the mouth of the Chicago River. The fur trade, which had a 150-year run on Lake Michigan, used this divide, as had generations of Indigenous natives, but it was not an easy trip. As a young man, Gurdon Hubbard was part of the American Fur Company's "Illinois brigade," which each autumn made its way from Mackinac Island to the lower Illinois River valley across this divide, the Chicago Portage. In his autobiography Hubbard provided an account of a trip via the portage in October 1818.[1] Roughly a dozen empty boats were pulled through the narrow, winding channel that connected the Chicago River's South Branch to Mud Lake. Much of this channel had dried, and there was no water. In such areas the boats were placed on "short rollers" (tree trunks and branches) as they made their way southwest. Mud Lake itself generally was without water in the dry seasons, but there was always an abundance of mud. Four men would remain in the boat with forked tree branches fastened to boat poles or oars. Another six to eight men were in the mud alongside the boat. The men in the boat would place their extended pole up against a tree, a mound of earth sticking above the mud, or whatever they could find to push against. The men in the mud lifted and shoved the boat. On occasion, the mud was waist-deep or deeper. The mud was filled with bloodsuckers, the air with mosquitoes. After three days of dawn-to-dusk labor, all the boats reached the Des Plaines River. The trip down the Des Plaines to Cache Island (near present-day Romeoville) was relatively smooth, although some portaging and rolling of the boats was necessary. From Cache Island to the confluence of the Des Plaines and Kankakee Rivers (the start of the Illinois River), the goods were mostly carried on men's backs while the boats were pulled where there was shallow water and dragged on poles where there were rocks. The entire trip from the South Branch to the mouth of the Fox River (near present-day Ottawa) took almost three weeks.

At the time of Hubbard's journey, indeed, through most of the first half of the nineteenth century, travel in the Midwest was more efficient on water than on land. That had been true for centuries. The idea of building a canal across the divide was of long standing and presumably dates from the Marquette-Jolliet expedition of 1673. Yet it remained just an idea into the 1830s. In 1830, as the fur trade in the Chicago area was winding down, fewer than one hundred people lived on the site of the future city, then an unincorporated corner of Peoria County. Travelers still faced the obstacles that had hindered Hubbard. When the canal idea finally moved toward reality in the early 1830s, Chicago's population surged. When the site was incorporated as a town in 1833, its population was 350. Four years later, when it was incorporated as a city, its population had grown to 4,170. In 1871, the year of the fire, it was 325,000. This is an average growth rate of just under 17 percent per year, roughly a doubling in size every four years. Those who came west were anxious to speculate, either on the value of land or on their own ability to earn a living in whatever Chicago would become. The latter was still attracting migrants when the Great Fire burned much of the city to the ground.

This book is an economic and business history of Chicago before the Great Fire that stresses how its early growth and development determined its meteoric rise as the Midwest's dominant city. Given that the fur trade was the area's principal economic activity before Chicago's initial incorporation as a town, that is where the story begins, even though the fur trade's contribution to what came afterward was negligible. Growth proved rapid in the fledgling town. Between Chicago's incorporations as a town and as a city its population increased almost by a factor of twelve, but then the Panic of 1837 slowed that progress for almost a decade.[2] Chicago's growth was spectacular in the panic's aftermath, and it continued at a high rate before and after the fire. Although Chicago started to grow later than older Midwestern cities such as Cincinnati and St. Louis, it surpassed both before 1871.[3] How it did so is the subject of this book. By 1871 Chicago had come to occupy such an important place in the national economy that the net benefits of rebuilding after the fire far exceeded those of leaving the site an ash heap. The groundwork for the city's growth was firmly in place, so the fire proved little more than a brief interruption, a much shorter one than that caused by the Panic of 1837.

This book applies the economic location theory of William Dean Jr., a pioneering Black economist, to help examine these initial decades of Chicago's growth.[4] A short discussion of his theory appears as the second section of this introduction. According to Dean, the development of a site's commercial agglomeration results from three interrelated variables: trade routes, position, and nodality. The term *trade routes* relates to the transportation and communication infrastructure. *Position* involves what must be done so that a site can accommodate commerce and industry. *Nodality* encompasses the properties of a site through which it commands an area where trade routes converge, the financial system that facilitates commerce and industry, and the labor force that performs a variety of tasks.

Given the important roles played by position and nodality, the place itself needs to be explained. (Chicago's geographic assets and liabilities are discussed in the section of this introduction titled "Portages.") To put it simply, Chicago is located on a glacial lakebed. The ground once held water above it and is quite flat. This means that from its very beginning, drainage was a major issue; mud, a serious problem. Any solution to the drainage issue had to consider the interdependency problem faced by cities on freshwater lakes: The lake is simultaneously the logical water supply and wastewater disposal resource. The Americans, unlike the French or the British (or even the Native Americans) developed a permanent site on the shoreline where the Chicago River empties into Lake Michigan.

Geography and topography gave Chicago advantages that other market sites lacked, but those advantages define a potential, not a reality. How that potential is developed depends on many other factors, such as economics and luck.

As noted, the low divide is Chicago's most critical geographic feature. Robert Morrissey in his brilliant *People of the Ecotone* points to the fact this was more than a divide between two watersheds; it was a divide between eastern woodlands and western grasslands (the tallgrass prairie), between trappers of beaver and hunters of bison.[5] On his return to Quebec in 1674 Louis Jolliet related that a canal could be constructed across the divide. Historians of Chicago have long assumed that the canal to which Jolliet referred was across what we know today as the Chicago Portage.[6] Historically, that portage was an important component of Chicago's position. The area's flatness facilitated the construction of trade routes; the Illinois and Michigan Canal (hereafter the I&M Canal) and several railroads traversed the portage before the fire. Since the fire, a new, larger canal and an interstate highway have been constructed on the flat terrain. In addition, Chicago's sanitation infrastructure is tied to the portage. As we can see from Hubbard's experience, many French, British, and American traders preferred to avoid that route and made use of alternatives. Nevertheless, in the 1795 Treaty of Greenville, the United States gained a six-mile-square piece of land at the mouth of the Chicago River for the purpose of controlling access to the Chicago Portage and protecting American interests. In 1803 the U.S. Army constructed Fort Dearborn.

Outline of the Chapters

The balance of the book is arranged topically, from the fur trade to finance. The first chapter, "The Fur Trade and Chicago," involves a subject, the fur trade, that is much discussed in accounts of Canadian economic history but little mentioned in American economic history. By examining the trade between Frenchmen and Indigenous people one can see how the site was utilized in the years before a city was located near the Chicago Portage. Unlike the English, who established factories (trading posts) to which the Native Americans came to trade, the French went to the Natives, lived with them, and intermarried. That trade created the initial conditions from which Chicago grew. It ultimately established a node on the trade route between the Great Lakes and the Mississippi River valley. The fur trade is the reason why Chicago's "founders," Jean Baptiste Point de Sable and John Kinzie, came to live at the mouth of the Chicago River. And it is one reason why the U.S. government built, then rebuilt, Fort Dearborn. Although economic development was not explicitly one of the fort's missions, by protecting the trade route the fort facilitated the fur trade and the other economic activity that developed there. It was not until Fort Dearborn was constructed that a factory belonging to any government existed at Chicago. Throughout most of the 1700s the site was for the most part a point on the route between French villages in Michilimackinac and the Illinois River valley. After the American Revolution, Chicago was largely empty. The decision to build Fort Dearborn increased the importance of the site's position and its nodality. Given that the site was relatively ignored or avoided during much of the fur trade era, this is a surprising development.

The second chapter, "Pioneers and Boosters," focuses on four men in whose careers the 1830s transition from a muddy fur-trade outpost to an evolving metropolis can be observed. The pioneers are two men who began in the fur trade. Jean Baptiste Beaubien was one of Chicago's early prominent citizens. It was he who purchased the remaining physical assets of the American Fur Company when it left town. In the end, he chose to live in exurban Chicago. Gurdon Hubbard, whose career began as an American Fur Company apprentice assigned to downstate Illinois, moved to the city the year after its incorporation and was still involved in the city's commerce at the time of the fire. The boosters are two men who promoted the growth of Chicago in word and deed. John S. Wright was a prolific writer of enthusiastic reports predicting great things for the city. He became known as the "prophet of the prairies" because many of his predictions came true. William B. Ogden, Chicago's first mayor, helped produce those great things. He came to Chicago to deal with his family's real estate holdings and had an implicit understanding of the requisites for urban growth and the amenities citizens needed in order to support that growth. He understood what was needed to improve the site's trade routes, position, and nodality. His investments were not limited to infrastructure for transportation (by canal, railroad, and ship); he invested in diverse activities that developed the city's commerce and industry (e.g., the Board of Trade, education, healthcare, reapers, and breweries). He was Chicago's first venture capitalist, and most of his ventures were growth-producing. Taken together, these four biographies produce an impressionistic picture of how the Chicago economy first evolved; the chapters that follow fill in the details.

The transportation and communication infrastructure centered on Chicago is the subject of the third chapter, "Assembling Trade Routes and Establishing Position." It addresses the construction of the trade routes that dramatically increased Chicago's nodality. The keys were the portage and then the canal. Chicago's initial development took place when waterways were the most economical means of travel. Had the area developed a decade or so later, when railroads were in competition with canals, the principal node at the southern end of Lake Michigan likely would have been located closer to the bottom of the lake, with a straight run from east to west. As it was, because early railroads were built as spokes centered on a node, the railroads came to a site defined by the river's mouth and a canal, even if it was several miles north of the bottom of the lake. When the canal finally opened in 1848, it was clear from the experience in the East that railroads would be the preferred mode for passengers and most types of freight. Consequently, railroads have the more prominent place in Chicago's transportation history as they brought an ever-widening area's rapidly expanding commerce to Chicago. Further, because many telegraph lines were located on railroad rights-of-way, transportation and communication routes had similar economic effects on the city. Although the canal, railroad, and telegraph all date to 1848, it was the location of the former that determined that the latter two would be built to the junction of Lake Michigan and the Chicago River.

The fourth chapter, "How Chicago Grew," first presents statistical data that provide concrete evidence for how the city's commerce and industry developed. The discussion in the section titled "The Commercial Data" centers on commercial data from two important sources. The first is Judge Jesse B. Thomas's statistics from the River and Harbor Convention of 1848, which provide insight into Chicago's trade balance (imports and exports) and the composition of exports (wheat, flour, beef and pork, and wool) for the years before 1848 (the trade balance data begin in 1836). The second is the annual reports of the Chicago Board of Trade. These chronicle the arrivals and departures of a wide variety of goods and are arranged by mode of transport. These data identify three industries as being of primary importance to Chicago's growth. The chapter concludes with short histories of the grain, meat, and lumber industries, those that are featured in most histories of Chicago, most notably that of William Cronon.[7] Cronon does a superb job of explaining Chicago in a regional context; the emphasis here is on how Chicagoans devised and ran the institutions and the procedures responsible for transforming the region. Unlike most histories of these industries, the discussion is limited to the period before the Great Fire.

Like the second chapter, the fifth chapter, "Those behind the Growth," presents brief biographies of several entrepreneurs responsible for the growth highlighted in the data presented in chapter 4. These biographies provide insight into the human dimension of economic growth. Archibald Clybourn was a jack-of-all-trades who opened the city's first stockyard. George Dole is generally credited with being the city's first meatpacker and was considered the father of the shipping, warehouse, and elevator systems. George Craigin, Nelson Morris, and George Hammond were important packers in this pre-refrigeration era. J. Young Scammon and Walter Newberry were both financiers and longtime associates of William Ogden in the Galena and Chicago Union Railroad, among other pursuits. John Wentworth, editor of the *Chicago Democrat*, represented the city's interests in Washington and Springfield in addition to serving two terms as the city's mayor. Potter Palmer and Marshall Field were merchants who sold goods to Chicago's ever-widening market; Cyrus Hall McCormick produced the reapers that harvested midwestern grain. Finally, George Pullman, before building his Palace Cars, arrived in Chicago to help lift it out of the mud.

Chapter 6, "Creating Position: Sanitation and Health," focuses on the development of the city's sanitation infrastructure and its early healthcare efforts and medical infrastructure (medical schools and hospitals). As previously noted, the site's flatness was a major issue. In order to create position, Chicago had to confront the problems created by its topography. The development of a sanitation strategy in general, and a drainage strategy in particular, was a major problem to be solved before the site could accommodate commerce and industry. Consequently, in the 1850s Chicago was the first city in the United States to adopt a comprehensive sewer system. Using Lake Michigan for both water supply and wastewater disposal created another problem. In the main, the wastes were directed toward the river, and this meant that in the 1860s steps had to be taken to conserve the city's water supply. Thus, all three dimensions of a city's sanitation requirements (water supply, sewerage, and drainage) were eventually solved. If they had not been, the city's growth would have been severely constrained. Chicago's approach to these problems was unique. At the end of the 1860s work began to reverse the flow of the Chicago River by sending it southwest through the I&M Canal to minimize the quantity of wastes entering the lake. For this, the Chicago Portage was a benefit. Chicago's earliest healthcare history can be traced through records from Fort Dearborn. As expected, waterborne diseases were particularly lethal; typhoid fever was known to have been present quite early. The city's first two nonmilitary physicians, Josiah C. Goodhue and Daniel Brainard, began pushing for what became the Rush Medical College. It is through that institution that the first hospital, Mercy Hospital, was opened in the 1850s. The first Board of Public Health was formed, and it produced reports that tracked epidemics and mortality. Cholera, brought to the city by soldiers coming to fight the Black Hawk War in 1832, was a common visitor in the years before the first major sanitation works. The *Chicago Tribune* blamed cholera deaths on "the foreign population"; one has the sense this includes free Blacks as well as immigrants.

Chapter 7, "Population and Labor," first provides insights into Chicago's growth through census data. The age and sex of the city's White and free Black population are reported, as are the sources of the native- and foreign-born populations. Population growth measured in per capita terms is a two-edged sword for economic growth: There are more laborers to produce goods and services *and* more mouths to feed. Pioneer cities such as Chicago had a large excess of young adult males. Consequently, during their early working years, there often was but one mouth to feed, and that facilitated growth. The census also reported the nativity and occupational breakdown of the labor force in 1870, which provides a picture of the Chicago economy on the eve of the fire, complementing the picture of growth in the fourth chapter by exploring who was working in the commercial and industrial sectors. Following the discussion of the available statistics, the chapter focuses on two large groups that were at the bottom of the occupational/income ladder and faced discrimination: the Irish and the free Blacks. The former largely came to work on the I&M Canal and took up residence all along the canal's route; in Chicago, that primarily meant the greater Bridgeport neighborhood. Once the canal was completed, the Irish competed with Blacks for jobs as servants, stevedores, and so on. The city's Black population increased despite what Bessie Pierce termed the "kindliness and intolerance" of their White neighbors as well as the "Black codes" that used the law to restrict the rights of free Blacks.[8] Nonetheless, there are several success stories such as that of John Jones, a gentlemen's tailor who was also (arguably) the city's leading abolitionist.

Chapter 8, "The Lubricant of Growth," is an examination of the banking system that financed commercial and industrial firms and supplied much of the money that facilitated transactions. Developing an economy requires a well-functioning financial system, but that does not describe the situation in Illinois in general, or Chicago in particular, during most of the pre-fire years, a time known as the "wildcat banking" era. The history of banking in Illinois before the fire can be broken into four cycles. Two involved major panics (1837 and 1857); all four followed a similar pattern. The initial upturn was triggered by an increased demand for money and credit. The state then passed a law permitting the formation of a bank or banks allowed to issue notes, typically notes that were inadequate in number and safety. These became the primary medium of exchange in the city and led to an initial period of prosperity followed by a downturn that first led to a suspension of note redemption and then to the failure of the issuing bank. At the bottom of the cycle, there were hard times coupled with strong anti-bank sentiment until such time as the demand for money and credit increased once again. Eight years before the fire, the creation of the national banking system provided a better-functioning system, one that would prove useful in the resumption of growth following the fire.

The final chapter, "Where Things Stood," draws the story together in terms of trade routes, position, and nodality. The two keys to the city's success—before and after the fire—are Chicago's geographic location and the infrastructure, in particular the transportation routes, put in place before 1871. The hinterland's agricultural pursuits turned the port of Chicago into an important commercial node, one that expanded concurrent with the railroad network. This, in turn, attracted industry (e.g., reaper production, meat packing). Additional industry arose in and near the city after the fire (e.g., the production of steel, railcars, boxed meat), but it was part and parcel of a process that had been put in place before the fire. The pre-fire economy nurtured Chicago's later growth. The phoenix is an oft-summoned metaphor in histories of the city, but relative to the city's growth, it would be more to the point to say that the fire caused a painful interruption rather than a cataclysm necessitating a rebirth. Its trade routes remained; its position was unchanged; and its nodality only required new bricks and mortar.

William Dean's Location Theory

One important question that must be confronted in this study is whether it made economic sense in the early 1800s to locate a city on a glacial lakebed where mud was all too common. The answer, not surprisingly, is that there were pluses and minuses. In order to assess those assets and liabilities, it will be useful to have a conceptual framework. William H. Dean Jr. offered a dynamic approach to the creation and development of commercial and industrial functions at a given site. For example, when he first came to Chicago, Cyrus McCormick built his reaper factory on the north side of the Chicago River near its mouth, giving him access to both ships and railroads. After the fire, when McCormick rebuilt elsewhere, what the U.S. Supreme Court described as "the gateway of commerce" included his original site.[9]

Dean simultaneously corrected and extended the economic location theory of Alfred Weber, a theory that "can provide a great deal of insight into the spatial structure of cities that developed in the nineteenth century."[10] Before Weber, economists such as Charles Cooley argued that major cities were likely to develop at a place where primary land routes met primary water routes, what Dean referred to as a *node*.[11] To Dean, a node was a site that is intensively involved in marketing processes.

Most location theorists, beginning with Johann Heinrich von Thünen, have assumed that they are starting from a featureless plain with evenly distributed resources.[12] That assumption does not, however, lead to the conclusion that per-unit transportation costs will be equal in all directions, that cities can emerge anywhere. As Cooley argued, a definite hierarchical system of transport lines and marketing sites must evolve:

> The solution must be found in some complexly branched system. Each neighborhood would collect what it has to send at some central point whence the movement would proceed by a common road. . . . The roads from them would concentrate at other points. . . . Finally, we should have the greatest movements traversing a few great roads of which a number of the most important would meet at the center of the country.[13]

As Paul Vidal de la Blanche argued, the agglomeration of commercial activities and a commercial population become inevitable at a break-in transport—the transfer of goods from one mode to another, the storage of goods in transit, a change in ownership:

> A study of city growth in the past shows that what made the seed spring to life and guaranteed its growth was usually an obstacle. At the borders of mountain barriers, at river crossings, on the edge of deserts, in short wherever it is necessary to halt and find new methods of transportation, there is the opportunity for city growth.[14]

Thus, geographic and historical variables are as important as economic variables in determining location. Whereas canoes traversed both rivers and lakes, the same would not be true of canal and lake boats.

The location of a commercial site depends on access to population and resources. Dean argued that nodes bear on the relative importance of commercial sites:

> A "node" is far more than a site considered from the point of view of its relation to the relief, contour, and drainage of an area. It is rather a site considered from the point of view of utilization in the marketing structure. Geographic

> superiority relative to other points furnishes a potentiality, but the employment of this capacity depends on economic forces and as such is historically conditioned. While the transport system is always adapted to the topographic and hydrographic structure of the earth, the technology of the system, the locus of population and the nature of traffic are socioeconomic phenomena.[15]

Dean viewed the evolution of the transportation infrastructure and transport rate structure as augmenting the importance of some sites and reducing that of others. It was clearly augmenting in the case of Chicago. He first analyzed the forces that determined the significance of a site's commercial function, then considered the forces that attracted industry to a commercial site. In particular, he argued that the development of a commercial function at a node was a result of three interrelated variables: trade route, position, and nodality.

A *trade route* is a line of passage. Its economic importance depends primarily on population density, the size of the tributary area, and the area's dependence on trade per capita. It is not necessarily the case that a trade route's importance depends on how readily a transport technology can be adapted to the physical geography, although this can be a significant factor.[16] Most important, "Improvements in the technology of transport, whether by land or by water, increase the relative importance of primary nodes and diminish the relative significance of others through selection of routes and sites depending upon special features incidental to the improved technology."[17] One specific feature is geographic obstructions, which vary in importance depending on the transport technique: "The precise elements of physical selection are often small, but their implications to the traffic obtained by routes and nodes is often decisive."[18] In the case of Chicago, the confluence of river and lake provided a break-in transit, especially once the I&M Canal was completed and steamboats plied the Great Lakes. Railroads helped further widen Chicago's growing hinterland, which with the canal included a large portion of the Mississippi River valley.[19]

In the 1820s a sandbar blocked the entrance to the Chicago River for most vessels larger than a canoe. Soldiers at Fort Dearborn cut through the sandbar to enable their boats to reach Lake Michigan, but nature soon refilled the cut. As construction on the I&M Canal began, a more permanent solution was recommended by the Corps of Engineers. In 1833 Congress appropriated $25,000 to dredge a new channel and make other improvements. The Chicago River thus became a harbor under federal jurisdiction before Chicago became a city. Fifteen years later the canal began bringing cargoes from inland, and the amount of freight handled at the port multiplied dramatically when railroads joined the canal.

Before the canal and the railroad were created, long-distance transport over land was difficult. The consequences of this fact for market structure were important. Each new mode of land transport intensified the hierarchy of urban places around a node; they increased the efficiency of travel and fostered movement over ever-longer distances. Although the effect of natural obstacles varied by transport technology, route differentiation was strengthened in general as land transport became increasingly sophisticated. Where the transport system was not well developed, distance proved a greater problem relative to cost than did road gradients. A flatter route was more important to mechanical-based than to animal-based land transport.[20]

Railroads, like canals, were topographically selective, but they placed greater emphasis on the construction and maintenance of their routes, as well as their utilization of motive power. They had a greater choice of routes and the ability to move a greater volume of traffic. Early railroads were constructed as spokes from a major node, often an existing node located on a waterway, to a lesser one in the hinterland. Hence, the development of Chicago's railroads did not change the location of the city.

Dean's second variable, *position*, is defined as the properties of a region with respect to the convergence of trade routes. There are two aspects. First, a region possesses *primary qualities of position* when its location is either intermediate or terminal to major trade routes. At the southwest corner of the Great Lakes, with its connection to the interior, and, somewhat later, with a railroad network that brought cargo to the port, Chicago was a terminal node on major trade routes. Second, position also depends on the *degree of immediacy* for cargoes involved in trade with other areas. Chicago was the point of transshipment for trade between the Midwest and the East. Position, therefore, is an economic, not a geographic, concept. It is crucial to the development of a commercial agglomeration within a region. Population and resources create markets, and those markets change as population and resources grow and move. Both the nature and the geography of commerce are sensitive to changes in a region's commercial and industrial pattern, which means that the properties of position vary with changes in the total geography of settlements, route, and economic activities, not simply the changes within a city. One contribution to the growth of Chicago was the growing number of trade routes centered on the city. That, in turn, proved attractive to industry.

Dean's final variable is *nodality*, which encompasses the properties of a site through which it commands the area where trade routes converge; nodality is "the marketing significance of a site emerging from its properties at an intersection of trade routes."[21] The commercial significance of sites varies greatly; the quality of attraction to a trade flow is a function of preferences for other routes, areas, or points. Every factor that alters a trade route or a region's significance also alters a site's nodal importance. Route competes with route for traffic, region with region for position, and site with site for nodality. In the fur trade era, the St. Joseph and the Chicago Rivers provided access to the Mississippi watershed. Saint Joseph, Michigan, and Chicago were located at the mouths of these rivers, respectively. During much of the fur trade era the city of St. Joseph, Michigan, was as active a site as Chicago. Early on, St. Joseph thought it might become the primary node at the bottom of Lake Michigan, but it was not to be. A canal was built across the major portage from the Chicago River, but none was built at the portage on the St. Joseph near what is now South Bend, Indiana. Chicago became the primary node for a very large region, while St. Joseph (and South Bend) became subsidiary to Chicago. Not only did a single event affect the primary node, but the effect was also transmitted backward to smaller subsidiary nodes and even small towns whose main function was the collection and shipment of agricultural goods or timber. Life in these small towns was highly correlated to the life of the route on which the town was located. The growing number of trade routes centered on Chicago enhanced its nodality.

Before the nineteenth century, Chicago's nodality was based on trade between Natives of the eastern woodlands and the western grasslands. Once Europeans penetrated the area, what mattered was the location of beavers and bison and the Natives who hunted them. During most of the fur trade years, Chicago was a minor point on a trade route between the interior and the east—Quebec or New York and ultimately Europe.

Portages

The seed that blossomed as the city of Chicago was nurtured by the promise of a canal. The I&M Canal is customarily traced to Louis Jolliet, who, when he returned to Quebec from his 1673 trip with Father Jacques Marquette, allegedly reported, "We can quite easily go to Florida in boats, and by a very good navigation. There would be only one canal to make by cutting only half a league of prairie, to pass from the lake of Illinois into the St. Louis River."[22] Historians of Chicago have cited these sentences from the first histories of the city, but it is far from certain that Jolliet is referring to what is now known as the Chicago Portage, the link between the Chicago and Des Plaines rivers.

It seems clear that "the lake of Illinois" refers to what is now called Lake Michigan, but what of "the St. Louis River"?[23] Given what seem to be normal naming protocols, one might expect the St. Louis River to be one that involves a route leading to St. Louis, Missouri, but what we know today as St. Louis was not yet in existence. The "St. Louis River" is most likely what is now known as the Illinois River. La Louisiane, the administrative district of New France including New Orleans, was often anglicized as "Saint Louis." Fort St. Louis was the name LaSalle gave the post he built in 1683 atop what is now known as Starved Rock

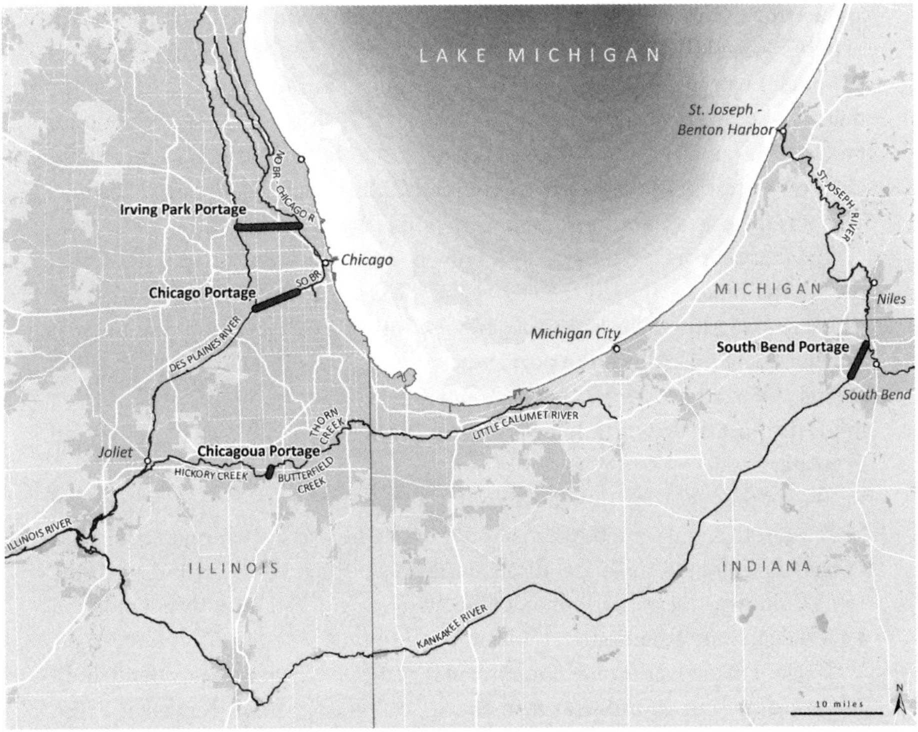

Map 1. The four portages from the Great Lakes to the Mississippi River drainage areas near Chicago. Two are within today's City of Chicago, one is in the southwestern suburbs, and the final one is near South Bend, Indiana. The three near Chicago lead to the Des Plaines River, and that near South Bend, to the Kankakee River. (Produced by Méch Frazier, Digital Scholarship Department, Northwestern University Libraries.)

ten years after Jolliet and Marquette's trip.[24] Lest the "St. Louis River" be thought to be the Mississippi, Marquette's journals refer specifically to the "Missisipi."

There were multiple portages connecting the Great Lakes and the Mississippi River drainage areas over the divide in the greater Chicago area. It seems advisable to examine them all rather than jump to the conclusion that Jolliet was referring to the one the Americans chose to develop more than a century later.[25]

The Great Lakes drainage area contains what were the northern (as opposed to central or southern) North American colonies, while the Mississippi River drainage area contains at least parts of thirty-one states and covers the vast majority of the area between the Appalachians and the Rocky Mountains. At a time when water routes were the most efficient ways to move people and goods, the ability to make use of such portages increased potential commerce. At least three portages crossed this divide in the immediate Chicago area, and there is one other that merits consideration (see map 1).

The northernmost of the three Chicago portages connected the North Branch of the Chicago River to the Des Plaines River along what today is Irving Park Road (through Portage Park). As Ann Durkin Keating has noted, this was so swampy that a person in a canoe could paddle across the divide in wet weather.[26] It is a much longer portage than the others, longer than Jolliet's "half a league." If the goal was to travel from Quebec to Louisiana, other routes dominated this one. This was the portage for those headed to points north of Chicago.

The middle portage, the one now known as the Chicago Portage, connected the South Branch of the Chicago River and the Des Plaines River across what the British called Mud Lake. Here, too, in wet weather, a person could canoe across the divide. Because this is the portage across which the I&M Canal (along with several railroads and an interstate highway) was constructed, regardless of whether this is the portage to which Jolliet's sentences refer, it is (and must be) discussed in greater detail.

The southern portage was known as the Portage de Perches (Pole Portage), but for reasons that will soon be clear, it is referred to here as the Chicagoua Portage. Largely forgotten in historical discussions, this portage from a tributary of the Little Calumet River to a tributary of the Des Plaines River recently has received a good deal more attention.

The fourth portage is one hundred miles east of Chicago at South Bend, Indiana, and entails a two-mile trek from the St. Joseph River to the Kankakee River, which becomes the Illinois River at its confluence with the Des Plaines River. In the early 1780s La Salle (or, at least, some of his men) took this route to Fort St. Louis. But, like the northernmost passage, it involves a much less direct route to the Illinois River.

The unit of length to which Jolliet referred was the French league (*lieue*), which varied over time. Its mean length was roughly the same as the metric league that emerged in France in the early 1800s. That league was exactly four kilometers, approximately two and one-half miles. It is uncertain whether the portage at South Bend, at eight tenths of a league is too long to be considered what Jolliet was describing. It does not appear that Jolliet was referring to this portage or to the one through Portage Park. Of the remaining two, the Chicagoua Portage seemingly comes closer to Jolliet's estimate than does the Chicago Portage; his "half a league" wildly underestimated the length of the I&M Canal, which proved to be ninety-six miles (thirty-eight and four tenths leagues) long.[27] Both of these portages need to be examined a bit more closely.

CHICAGO PORTAGE (PORTAGE DES CHÊNES)

The Chicago portage (the French name refers to the oak trees lining the path from the lake to the prairie) lies on an extremely flat part of the divide between the Great Lakes and the Mississippi River drainage areas. That flatness is a product of the ice age. As geographer Paul Goode explained, the site of Chicago was "determined by the little, inconsequential Chicago River, a glacial after-thought, which gave a channel across the sandy shoreline, supplying a haven for lake boats."[28] In wet seasons, especially with melting snow and spring rain, it was a bit more substantial. In dry seasons, the riverbed could be more marsh than river. What accounts for such a topography?

Polar ice moved south across northern North America on four occasions, covering it with ice to a depth of at least one mile. As the glaciers moved south, they picked up small rocks that acted like sandpaper to smooth the land. When the climate warmed, the meltwater formed "Lake Chicago," the ice age ancestor of Lake Michigan (see map 2). A channel for the lake water, the "Chicago outlet," developed to the southwest through a much-enlarged Illinois River valley. During these periods the southern end of the lake lay much farther to the south than it does now. Today's Chicago was mostly underwater.[29] As the glaciers receded, Lake Chicago did as well.[30] During the first three occasions, the water drained to the southwest as the receding glaciers remained an ice barrier blocking a northern outlet through the Great Lakes.

After the glaciers receded for the fourth time, after Lake Chicago disappeared, the flow of water through the Chicago outlet slowed, then stopped. It was during this process that the modern Chicago River and the Chicago Portage (see map 3) appeared, and Lake Michigan began to drain to the northeast. Initially, the upper Des Plaines River flowed out to Lake Michigan, but a ridge formed between today's Kedzie and California Avenues, which became an extremely low spot (ten and one-half feet above lake level) on the divide between the Great Lakes and Mississippi River drainage systems.[31] This ridge backed up the waters of the Des Plaines River, forcing it to the southwest. A small lake called Mud Lake developed in part of the portage. It was a slough, one and a half miles wide and five miles long. Four miles to the southwest it divided into two shallow channels (the North and South Arms) with a land mass one mile long and half a mile wide (Cache Island) between them. The two channels rejoined at the west end and flowed to the Des Plaines via Portage Creek.[32]

In fact, Lake Michigan was roughly seven feet below the level of Mud Lake when there was little water covering the latter. Even then, there was still a great deal of deep mud, which provided the name. As Hubbard reported, it did not afford easy passage. The argument supporting the Chicagoua Portage as the route of Marquette and Jolliet in no way reduces the importance of the Chicago Portage; it played a critical role in Chicago's economic history. As John William Nelson argues in *Muddy Ground*, it and the other portages were important avenues of trade among the Indigenous peoples who lived near a divide. Nelson quotes Pierre-Charles DeLiette, who arrived in 1687, describing the Chicago Portage as "the route usually taken to go to this country [the Illinois]."[33]

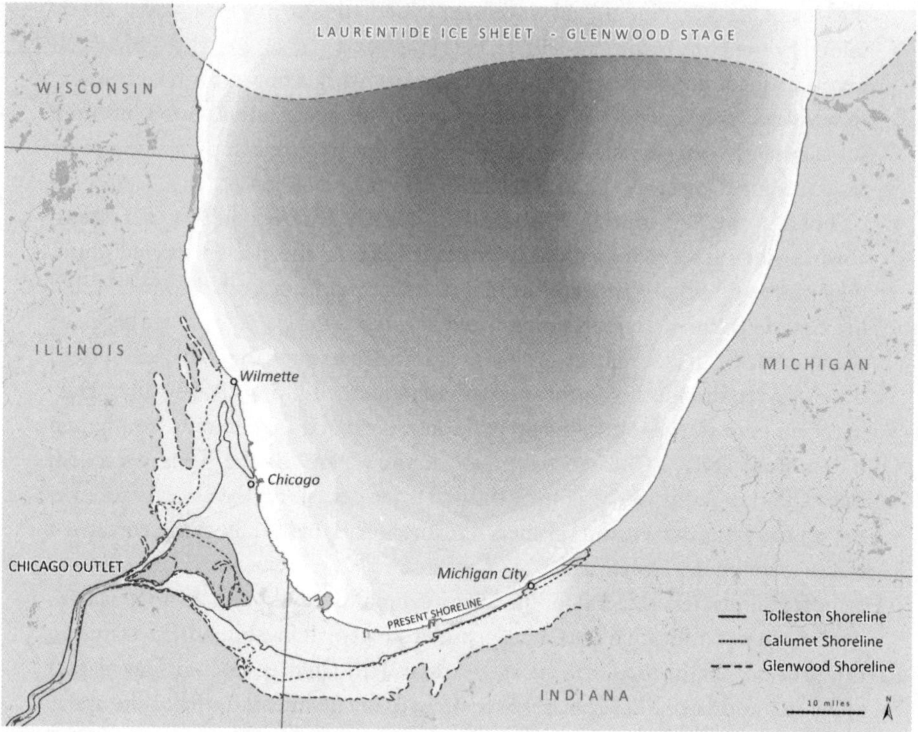

Map 2. The shoreline of Lake Chicago in the Chicago area at three glacial stages: the Glenwood, Calumet, and Tolleston stages. Lake Chicago involved a greater amount of water at the southern end of today's Lake Michigan. In all three stages, today's City of Chicago was underwater. (Produced by Méch Frazier, Digital Scholarship Department, Northwestern University Libraries.)

CHICAGOUA PORTAGE (PORTAGE DES PERCHES)

The champion of the Chicagoua Portage (the Portage of Poles) being the route of Marquette and Jolliet is John Swenson, lawyer and student of Chicago history.[34] For the past four decades he has found and read seventeenth- and eighteenth-century documents in French and Algonquian that discuss early European involvement in the Chicago area.[35] He believes there are many errors in the traditional story of Chicago's origins. His revision answers many questions that seemed puzzling before, but it simultaneously raises new ones.

Swenson believes that the original Chicago, or Chicagoua, was located forty miles south-southwest of the Chicago River's mouth.[36] Chicagoua was a Native American civic and cultural center dating from circa AD 1100 marked by a platform mound (located in Olympia Fields's Spirit Trail Park).[37] Swenson refers to it as "Marquette's mound" because he believes that this is where Marquette moved

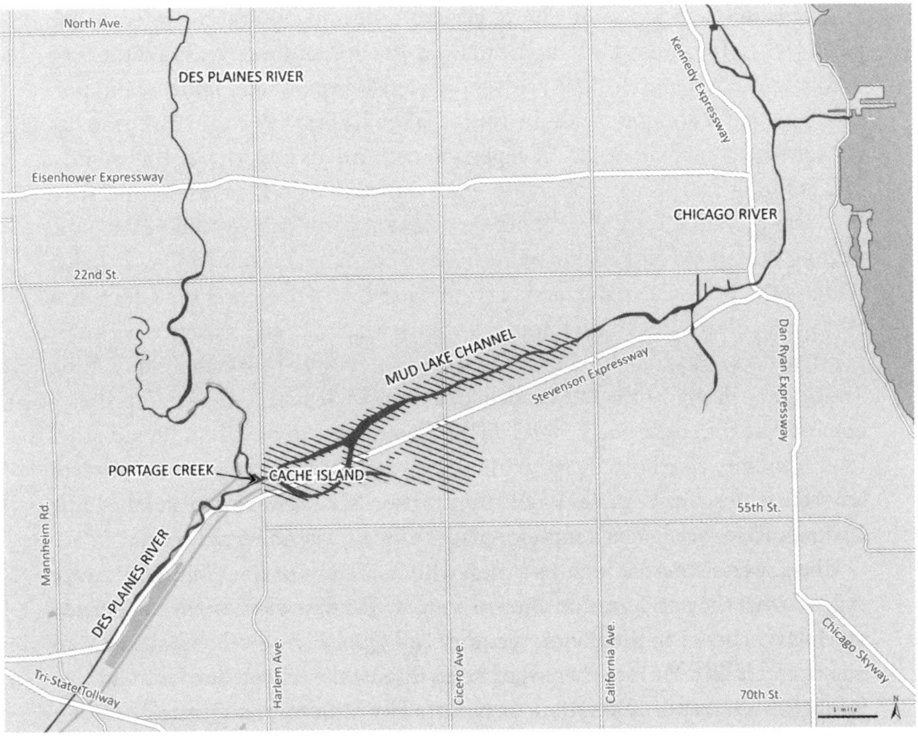

Map 3. The Chicago Portage across the Mud Lake Channel connecting the south branch of the Chicago River and the Des Plaines River. This is a detailed drawing of one of the portages depicted in map 1. (Produced by Méch Frazier, Digital Scholarship Department, Northwestern University Libraries.)

when floods visited his camp in the late fall of 1674 and forced him to seek higher ground.[38] The Chicagoua Portage is two leagues from Marquette's mound. From Lake Michigan, one enters the Little Calumet River and continues into Thorn Creek and then into Butterfield Creek. The portage is between Butterfield Creek and Hickory Creek (just west of I-57, between the towns of Frankfort and Matteson off the Old Plank Road Trail). Hickory Creek flows into the Des Plaines River south of Joliet.[39]

Two strong pieces of evidence stand out in Swenson's argument. The first is the journal of Marquette from his 1674–75 return trip to visit, and possibly convert, the Illinois Indians living near Starved Rock.[40] Swenson believes that the description of the area where Marquette and his party camped from December 1674 to March 1675 fits Chicagoua perfectly. The same is true of the area described in Henri Joutel's journal. Joutel, an associate of La Salle, passed through the Chicago area on his way back to Quebec following La Salle's assassination in Texas in 1687.[41]

Swenson's description of Chicagoua as a civic and cultural site refers to the period when the mound was built, but what was the nature of the site at the time of Marquette and Joutel? If the Natives directed Marquette and Jolliet to this portage, how did it compare with the route via the Chicago Portage? Swenson has consulted with a wide variety of experts to confirm his hypothesis. But would a canal of "only half a league of prairie" have sufficed? Would such a channel (and the various creeks) only allow for the movement of canoes? Would a canal connecting Butterfield and Hickory Creeks have been capable of handling as much trade as the I&M Canal did, and, if so, at what cost? Given that the Chicagoua Portage involved a more circuitous path, such a canal would have to have lower construction costs than the I&M Canal in order for it to be a viable competitor. The original design of the I&M called for a channel deep and wide enough to accommodate the larger boats found on the Great Lakes in the 1820s. Would other improvements have been necessary in the various creeks to permit lake boats to cross the Chicagoua Portage? Would the junction of Lake Michigan and the Little Calumet River have been a superior place to locate a commercial center?

The experience of at least two men who made use of the Chicago Portage suggests that they preferred an alternative to it. The first was La Salle, who made several trips between the Illinois territory and Quebec a decade following Marquette and Jolliet. He is perhaps the first to discuss the downside of the Chicago Portage as a transportation route, as reported by Milo Milton Quaife:

> From the lake one passes by a channel [the Main and South Branches of the Chicago River] formed by the junction of several small streams or gullies, and navigable about two leagues to the edge of the prairie. Beyond this at a distance of a quarter of a league to the westward is a little lake a league and a half in length, divided into two parts by a beaver dam. From this lake issues a little stream which after twisting in and out for half a league across the rushes, falls into the Chicago [Des Plaines] River, which in turn empties into the Illinois.[42]

La Salle figured that there might be "but fifteen or twenty days at most" when the Des Plaines–Illinois route had sufficient water to paddle a canoe all the way from Chicago to La Salle's Fort St. Louis. Those days generally came before the ice had melted at the northern end of Lake Michigan. Indeed, the distance that had to be portaged at Chicago varied from "nothing at all to fifty miles or, at times, to even twice this distance."[43] Recall that the I&M Canal was ninety-six miles long.

The second was Gurdon Hubbard, one of early Chicago's longest-lived citizens. His compelling testimonial of a trip in October 1818, more than a century after La Salle, opened this introduction. Given his experience, it is little wonder that six years later, when he was promoted to head of the American Fur Company's Illinois River posts, Hubbard ordered that pack horses be used to transport goods between the Chicago and Illinois Rivers. He was anxious to avoid "the long, tedious, and difficult passage" across the Chicago Portage.[44] In sum, there are good reasons to believe that Swenson's argument has merit. Had Marquette and Jolliet passed through the Chicago Portage, one suspects, they would not have reported that one could travel "quite easily."

Finally, even with a canal across the Chicago Portage, one might ask whether the land at the confluence of the river and lake was the best location for a large commercial center. The location's potential as a commercial site was long established by the Indigenous population. The Potawatomi, who with the Ojibwa and Odawa (Ottawa) were part of a long-term alliance called the Council of Three Fires, gathered there to trade, but they mostly lived inland from Lake Michigan along rivers and streams in locations that afforded superior shelter.[45] There was little hint of Chicago arising where it did.

As a former glacial lakebed, the site was on land intended to hold water, not absorb it. An urban area built on such land was sure to suffer from a surfeit of mud, a problem the new local government confronted almost immediately after incorporation. Conversely, the flat land and low divide facilitated construction of the transportation infrastructure that would cross the portage and traverse the glacial river valley. A great deal of imagination would be needed to successfully drain the city that grew atop the former lakebed, and the portage would again prove crucial.

Looking back, the Chicago Portage was of much greater importance to the Americans than to the French and the British, the two powers that had claimed the area earlier. There is evidence of Indigenous villages near St. Joseph, Michigan, and Lake Calumet, but, in the course of time, there were but few villages at the mouth of the Chicago River. In his book about the history of Chicago's portages, John William Nelson says of the site, "Chicago came to serve more as an intersection of movement rather than as a site of permanent settlement."[46] Although the portage was used by the French and the English, its potential was generally ignored. The Americans, on the other hand, chose to build a fortress at the Chicago River's mouth and planned for a canal even before Illinois achieved statehood in 1818.[47] Canal-building technology in the early nineteenth century was little more than men hand-digging a ditch. It appears to be the case that, though it may have been simpler to dig a canal for canoes to traverse the Chicagoua Portage, the plan to dig a canal for boats to traverse the Chicago Portage made more economic sense. The presence of fur traders at the river's mouth may have played a role in the Americans' decision to protect the Chicago Portage, but that decision had its greatest impact once the Erie Canal opened in 1825 and brought new settlers to Chicago.

CHAPTER 1

The Fur Trade and Chicago

At the close of the eighteenth century, beaver hats were in high demand among the upper and middle classes. A fine beaver hat was not cheap; it has been estimated that its price was approximately equal to the weekly wage of a skilled worker and more than double the weekly wage of an unskilled one. The European beaver had been hunted to near extinction when the first American colonies were founded, so attention turned to the North American beaver. Over time, Indigenous North Americans, those who trapped the animals, became more and more dependent on the trade goods they received as compensation for pelts, hides, and grain. When beavers in the Great Lakes area approached the same fate as their European namesake, Natives found themselves with debts they were unable to repay. When the American Fur Company pulled out of Chicago in the early 1830s, all accounts were settled. For this and many other reasons, Native Americans were forced to cede Illinois land and move west of the Mississippi River.

For roughly 150 years before Chicago was incorporated as a town, the fur trade was the principal economic activity in what Richard White referred to as "the Middle Ground."[1] The European traders have been described as sowing the seeds for urban growth and development. This contains a kernel of truth. Paradoxically, it is also true that fur trading was (and is) incompatible with urbanization because the presence of humans repels the animals on which the trade depends. A discussion of Chicago's early economic history must include the fur trade that occupied a large portion of the time Europeans traversed Lake Michigan. If its ultimate contribution to Chicago's economic growth and development was relatively minor, it did shape the initial conditions from which Chicago grew; it created a small but critical node on a major trade route connecting the Great Lakes and the Mississippi River valley. The prospect of an improvement of that trade route, a canal, accelerated the node's growth.

To understand Chicago on the eve of incorporation, it helps to understand how the French organized the area's trade and why their influence persisted after the British, and then the Americans, claimed the area. In the early 1830s half the population of Chicago was still French (or French-related). It was the fur trade that brought its two "founders" to Chicago: Jean Baptiste Point de Sable and John Kinzie. It was the fur trade, at least in part, that led to the construction of Fort Dearborn. Neither the first nor the second fort had economic development as part of its mission, but urbanization sprouted in the shadow of the rebuilt fort.

This chapter first presents a basic outline of the area's trade until the beginning of the eighteenth century. Beaver pelts came from the Great Lakes watershed, while bison hides came from the Mississippi River watershed. Other furs and grain (corn and wheat) were also traded. It then discusses the three Frenchmen who first explored the greater Chicago area: Marquette, Jolliet, and La Salle. The chapter then returns to the beginning of the eighteenth century and continues the story, focusing on the Chicago area. It discusses the founders of Chicago, the node they created, the destruction of the first Fort Dearborn, and the decision to rebuild it after the War of 1812. Finally, the American Fur Company, which dominated Chicago's economy for the two decades before incorporation is considered; it vacated Chicago shortly thereafter—as did its Indigenous suppliers in what Claudio Saunt referred to as a "deportation."[2]

The Beginning of the French Fur Trade

In order to understand the economic activity in Chicago before the 1820s, one needs to understand how the French ran the Great Lakes fur trade. It changed little over the years, at least from the perspective of those trading in the area. At the end of the eighteenth century the traders were still mainly French. The Potawatomi dominated the area around the bottom of Lake Michigan, trapping furs and growing grain. The Illinois and others shared the Illinois River valley with the bison. Frenchmen traded with all the Native tribes.[3]

In 1534 Jacques Cartier explored the St. Lawrence River in a search for a northwest passage to China. Two years later, he claimed the river and its entire drainage basin for his homeland. The French already were fishing the Grand Banks of Newfoundland, and a minor trade in furs had developed with the mainland.[4] The Indigenous economy of the lower St. Lawrence River valley at that time, dominated by the Wendat (Huron) and Iroquois, was based more on fishing and agriculture than on hunting. Some contact had been made with hunting populations (the migratory Algonquin-Montagnais), but there was little reason to do so; beaver hats had yet to come into fashion in Europe. Cartier's failure to find a passage to the Far East or easily exploitable precious metals caused the French crown to lose interest in the area.

When beaver hats did come into fashion, the North American beaver quickly became a profitable commodity, and the French regained interest. Sponsored by Pierre Dugua, Sieur de Mons, Samuel de Champlain with a company of twenty-eight men founded Quebec City in 1608.[5] This is usually taken as the year the North American fur trade transitioned from a seasonal coastal trade to a permanent interior trade. Colonization in New France proved slow at first; many settlers died because of the harsh weather and disease. Things began to change in about 1630, when there were approximately 100 colonists living in New France; within a decade the number grew to 355.[6]

Directly south of New France was the Iroquois Confederacy. Map 4 shows the range of the confederacy (or Five Nations—the Mohawk, Onondaga, Oneida, Cayuga, and Seneca) during the colonial period in North America.[7] For most of that period, furs from this area made their way to Europe mainly through New Amsterdam (later named New York).[8] This forced the French to search for furs from areas to the north and west of the confederacy, including the three western Great Lakes. The proximity of the St. Lawrence River to the Iroquois forced the French to make use of the Ottawa River as the main route west. As more European weaponry found its way to the St. Lawrence valley, and hunting activity increased, eastern beavers began to disappear, and the trade inevitably moved west toward the Great Lakes.[9] The Iroquois tried to gain a monopoly of the fur trade by invading lands outside the range shown on the map. During the long period known as the Beaver Wars (1629–1701), battles were fought with some regularity in the Great Lakes area.

Early on, Champlain allied himself with the Wendat and the Algonquins. This created relationships that proved essential to New France's fur-trading interests.[10] When the Beaver Wars erupted, the French offer of assistance during a period of intertribal warfare cemented these connections and increased the supply of furs headed toward Quebec. As the number of western traders grew, however, competition among them increased operating costs as wages rose, along with the amount of trade goods that needed to be offered. Concurrently, traders' costs grew as distances increased. The return on investing in the trade took a long time to be realized; at least four years passed between the shipment of European trade goods to Quebec and the proceeds from the sale of furs in Europe returning to Quebec. As the payout period lengthened, the North American end of the trade became increasingly concentrated, dominated by a few large merchants.[11]

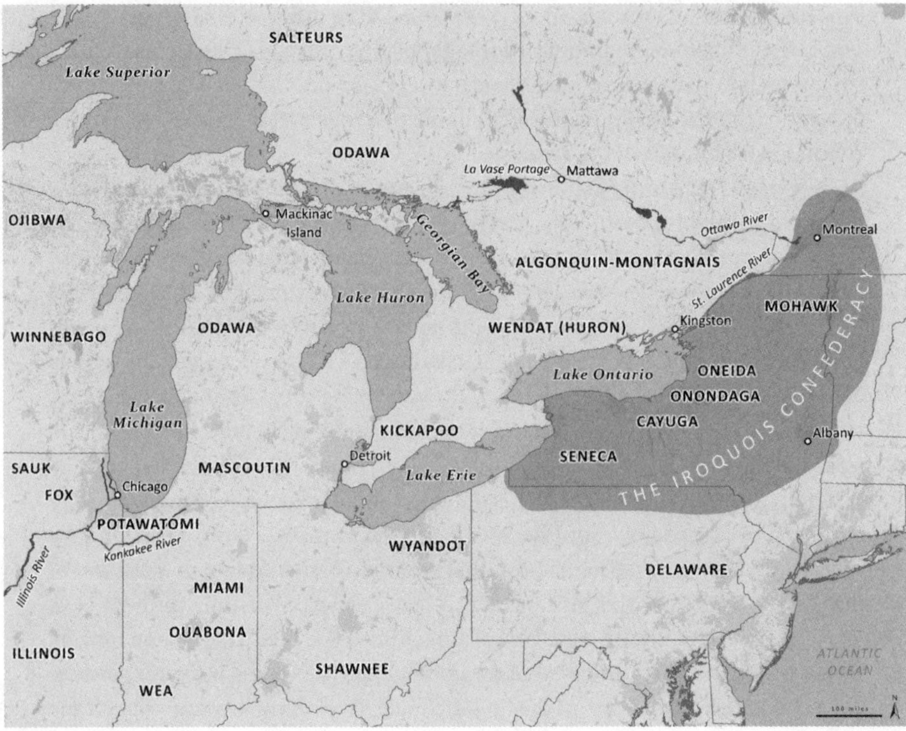

Map 4. Indigenous tribes and the Chicago fur trade. (Produced by Méch Frazier, Digital Scholarship Department, Northwestern University Libraries.)

The essential link in the French trading network was the existence of a personal relationship between the trader and the Native fur trapper.[12] Such connections took a long time to develop, especially when the Natives with whom the French traded were involved in protracted war. A monopoly headquartered in Quebec had to rely on local traders who worked out of small boats or canoes, and this weakened the ability of the monopoly to control the trade. William L. Marr and Donald G. Paterson characterize the structure of the trading network as a monopoly that "was operated as a multi-plant firm with a weak central organization."[13]

Beginning with Champlain's group, and with his encouragement, young Frenchmen began living with local Indigenous people, learning their language and customs and helping the French adapt to life in North America. Later, many young men sent to New France as settlers became traders, in part because the lack of European women in the colony meant that there was little hope of starting a "family" farm; it has been argued that until the early eighteenth century the odds of finding a European wife in New France were one in seven.[14] On the other hand, in many of the Indigenous villages involved with the fur trade, the men were the hunters; the women, the farmers. The French traders paired with or married Native women, and they often lived in or adjacent to the villages of their wife's family.[15] Indeed, many early Chicagoans—Point de Sable, Ouilmette, Beaubien—had Native wives.

Robert Michael Morrissey points out that French colonial officials initially saw intermarriage as a way of assimilating the Indigenous population. He quotes Champlain as telling the Natives that his hope was that "our young men will marry your daughters, and we shall be one people."[16] Champlain believed that what separated the two races was culture and that the Native people would be improved by exposure to French civilization. To that end, "the charter of the Company of New France defined Indians as full subjects, on the same legal footing as European-born colonists of New France."[17] However well-intentioned this aim, by the end of the seventeenth century it was becoming clear that the policy of "Frenchification" had failed in most of New France. As Harold Innis notes: "The fur trade was a phase of a cultural disturbance incidental to the meeting of two civilizations with different cultural traits."[18] Even at the end of the fur trade on the Great Lakes, Frenchmen with Native wives were more likely to follow their wives' families than vice versa.

Over time, tribes trading with the French, and the French themselves, came into contact with ever more remote tribes and introduced them to European goods. As Innis writes:

> This demand of Indian tribes in the western territory for European goods occasioned a rapid increase in trade. The tribes of the territory adjoining Lake Michigan, which were not familiar with the canoe, such as the Sauks, Fox, and Illinois, became the hunters of beaver to be traded with middlemen who were thoroughly acquainted with the Ottawa [River] route and expert canoemen like the Ottawas and the Saulteurs (who were even better canoemen than the Hurons). The Miamis and the Sioux ceased roasting the beaver for food, and began a search for skins. Indian tribes limited to the restricted returns incidental to trade with middlemen who held a monopoly were obliged to search far afield and to war on other tribes for a supply of beaver.[19]

Unlike the English model of a single monopoly company (e.g., the Hudson's Bay Company), the French trade had been primarily accomplished through small partnerships. Regulations limiting the number of traders were first issued in 1673, and in 1681 the French initiated the congé system (requiring a license to trade), whereby a license was issued to three men with a single canoe that permitted them to be involved in the fur trade. No more than twenty-five licenses were to be issued each year in an attempt to limit the total manpower involved in the fur trade to seventy-five individuals. At about this time, however, unlicensed independent traders, known as *coureurs des bois* (runners of the woods) entered the business;

many of them were métis (French-speaking mixed-race individuals). With the entry of the coureurs des bois, the number of pelts arriving in Montreal increased. As Marr and Paterson note, the French were unable to "assert private-property control over the resource and inevitably depletion of the resource followed."[20]

Over time, the idea that seventy-five licensed men in twenty-five canoes would be adequate proved derisory. Nearly four hundred men became involved in the fur trade directly, and additional men were required as troops to man the system of fortresses and to fight the battles. All this restricted the supply of labor available for agriculture. Innis quotes a 1685 letter to describe how the trade took place.[21] By that year the congé permitted two canoes and six men. Goods worth about 1,000 crowns were packed in the outgoing canoes and were priced at 15 percent more than the cash price in Montreal.[22] The return cargo commonly brought what was described as "seven hundred per cent clear profit." The logic of this exchange is that the six men returned in four canoes, each with forty packs of skins worth fifty crowns each, for 8,000 crowns total. The letter also spoke to the distribution of the profit. The merchant received 600 crowns to cover the cost of the license and 1,000 crowns for the trade goods. The merchant then took 2,560 crowns for 40 "bottomree," a loan to cover the operation (payroll, supplies, and so on), using the ship as collateral. The balance was split equally among the six voyageurs (those who transported the furs by canoe), who received 640 crowns each. This was at least double what they could earn by remaining in eastern agriculture.[23]

As W. Thomas Easterbrook and Hugh Aitken note, the rate of return depended mainly on the trader in the interior, so a merchant and a financier normally partnered with a trader for a fixed amount of time.[24] Most companies consisted of three or four men to whom the authorities granted a three-year lease on the trade at a specific place. Trade goods (e.g., muskets and ammunition, cloth and blankets) were usually obtained on credit (at 30 percent interest) from a small number of Montreal merchants whose agents in France marketed the furs.

While beaver hats remained in vogue, the demand for beaver pelts proved relatively inelastic (i.e., the quantity demanded was not very responsive to price changes) because the French traders generally felt they had to purchase all the pelts they were offered lest they lose the allegiance of the Natives and encourage them to trade with the competition (not to mention creating friction in their own families). As a consequence, prices varied with supply. A large increase in supply would significantly depress prices. To a colony whose economy was based on the export of furs, this could prove quite harmful. The move west caused such an increase. The French tried to mitigate the problem by limiting the number of traders and controlling prices.[25] Neither policy proved successful. It was impossible to enforce such arrangements because traders had the option of heading to Albany as well as Montreal. Any attempt to limit supply was doomed as long as fur-bearing animals remained abundant.

Marquette, Jolliet, and LaSalle

Jean Nicolet is considered the first known European to explore Lake Michigan. John Swenson's reading of the French texts leads him to believe that Nicolet was the first European to visit the Chicago area. In this section we consider several who came later. Nicolet was sent in 1634 by Champlain along with seven Wendats to explore the Great Lakes. In Nicolet's wake, missions and forts were erected around the western Great Lakes. One such mission was founded in 1668 by Father Jacques Marquette in Sault Ste. Marie, where Lake Superior drains into Lake Huron via the St. Mary River at the north end of Michigan's Upper Peninsula. Another was founded in 1671 at what is now known as Point St. Ignace, immediately west of Mackinac Island at the south end of the Upper Peninsula.[26] French traders built a small village at the latter. The advantages of this co-location were clear to all. Natives attracted to the goods available at the trading post were fair game for missionaries seeking converts. A year later a fort was erected to protect both the traders and missionaries; later it was moved south to the opposite side of the strait between Lakes Huron and Michigan, near present day Mackinaw City, and renamed Fort Michilimackinac.[27]

Marquette was born in France in 1637, joined the Jesuits at seventeen, and was assigned to New France in 1666. Some time later he met Native Americans at La Pointe, Wisconsin (on Lake Superior's Madeline Island), who told him about the Mississippi River and their use of it as a trade route. He requested permission from his ecclesiastical superiors to explore the river and was granted leave to do so.

In 1673, Quebec-born Louis Jolliet arrived at Marquette's mission. He was eight years younger than Marquette and had studied for the priesthood but chose to become a trader like his stepfather. Since the Indigenous population was a part of the day-to-day life of New France, it is likely that Jolliet was fluent in several local languages. Marquette and Jolliet began their famed expedition on May 17, leaving from St. Ignace with two canoes and five métis voyageurs.

They traveled south through Green Bay, portaged from the Fox River to the Wisconsin River, then traversed the upper Mississippi from the mouth of the Wisconsin River near Prairie du Chien, Wisconsin, to the mouth of the Arkansas River, north of Arkansas City, Arkansas, making them the first Europeans to explore whether the Mississippi River could connect New France and La Louisiane.[28] Friendly Natives, who were in possession of European goods that came up the river from Louisiana, warned them about hostile Natives farther south as well as the Spanish, who still had a claim to the area. They returned to Lake Michigan via the Illinois River, but their route from the confluence of the Kankakee and Des Plaines rivers remains in dispute. Traditional histories suggest that it was via the Chicago Portage; Swenson argues that it was via

Fig. 1a. Louis Jolliet. (Chicago History Museum, ICHi-010889.)

the Chicagoua Portage. In late October 1674 Marquette made a return trip to the Illinois, fulfilling a promise he had made to them on his way north the previous year. Because they had started so late in the year, when Marquette and his group reached the southern end of Lake Michigan, they thought traveling farther south was unwise, so they became the first known Europeans to winter in the area; Swenson believes it was near Chicagoua.[29]

A third French explorer, René-Robert Cavelier, Sieur de La Salle, visited the Great Lakes region, the Mississippi River, and the Gulf of Mexico, claiming the entire Mississippi River basin for France. Born in Rouen in 1643, La Salle joined the Jesuits in 1660, but rather than pursue ordination, he left for New France in the spring of 1666.[30] René-Robert received a seigneurie (a land area governed by a seigneur) at the western end of the Island of Montreal (the current borough of Lachine) and established a village. He learned the language of the Mohawk, and they told him about the Ohio River and how it flowed into the Mississippi. La Salle thought these rivers might flow into the Gulf of Mexico, so he conceived of a plan for an expedition to find a western passage to China. He sought and received the government's permission, selling his seigneurie to finance the trip.[31]

Fig. 1b. Portrait of Father Jacques Marquette by Jules M. Gaspard. (Chicago History Museum, ICHi-060010.)

In 1673, while Jolliet and Marquette were exploring the west, La Salle and the governor of New France, Louis de Buade, comte de Frontenac, met with Iroquois leaders at what is now Kingston, Ontario, to encourage them to trade with the French. Concurrently, Fort Frontenac was constructed at Kingston (where Lake Ontario empties into the St. Lawrence River) to assist New France's effort to control the Great Lakes fur trade. After commanding the fort for a year, La Salle returned to France in 1674–75, where, with Frontenac's assistance, he acquired letters of nobility for himself and his heirs that included a fur trade concession with the right to establish frontier forts.

Fig. 1c. René-Robert Cavelier, Sieur de La Salle. (Chicago History Museum, ICHi-066068.)

Jean-Baptiste Colbert, France's first minister of state, with responsibility for New France, wrote to the colony in 1666, saying, "It would be better to restrict yourselves to an extent of land which the colony could protect by itself, than to claim too vast an amount, part of which one might perhaps be obliged one day to abandon."[32] Claiborne Skinner notes that Frontenac and La Salle, who he called "a turbulent pair," would "drive New France into a new and dangerous future" by expanding the area it claimed.[33]

By 1677 La Salle had ordered four barques (three-masted sailing ships) that operated on Lake Ontario. In early 1679 members of his expedition constructed Fort Conti at the mouth of the Niagara River on Lake Ontario and built *Le Griffon* (thought to have been a barque) at the Lake Erie end of the river.[34] La Salle and his lieutenant Henri de Tonti sailed on *Le Griffon* to Michilimackinac and then to Wisconsin's Green Bay.[35] They traveled down the western shore of Lake Michigan by canoe, rounding the southern end to the mouth of the St. Joseph River, then known as the Miami River, where Fort Miami was built. Following the St. Joseph River to South Bend, Indiana, the group portaged to the Kankakee River. In January 1680 they built Fort Crèvecoeur at the southern end of Lake Peoria.[36]

In the winter of 1682–83 two of La Salle's men, André Eno Hunault and Jean Filatreau, were briefly in a small shelter "at the portage of Chicagou." They enlarged the shelter in the spring to accommodate approximately twenty of La Salle's men. In most sources, this is described as an "unnamed fort" located along Hickory Creek, suggesting that they used the Chicagoua portage.[37]

By the 1680s the largest concentration of Indigenous people in the greater Chicago area lived in the Grand Village, to the west of Starved Rock on the Illinois River.[38] This was a large Kaskaskia (Illinois) village. In addition, there were many smaller villages in the same area including those of the Miami, Ouabona, Shawnee, and Wea to the south and those of the Kickapoo and Mascoutin to the north. Morrissey calls these peoples "pedestrian bison hunters"; hides and buffalo meat were major products of the hunt.[39] La Salle obtained a monopoly of the bison trade and ordered de Tonti to construct Fort Saint-Louis-des-Illinois there to be a place where hides could be traded. He did so in 1682—atop Starved Rock.[40] La Salle visited in the spring of 1683, then returned to the unnamed fort on Hickory Creek. In a letter dated June 4, 1683, La Salle noted that it was thirty leagues (seventy-two miles) from Fort St. Louis and about twenty miles south of the Chicago portage, which La Salle generally avoided. By all indications, this is near John Swenson's Chicagoua Portage.

In 1684, during the Beaver Wars, the commandant at Fort Michilimackinac and sixty of his men came south. A Jesuit mission and a French army post were built in 1685 on the South Branch of the Chicago River near its intersection with today's Damen Avenue (just north of the Stevenson Expressway). It is generally believed that the Iroquois destroyed both the following summer.[41] Whether these were the first European-built structures is unclear; if there were earlier ones, they likely met the same fate.[42]

In 1696 the Jesuit priest Pierre François Pinet founded the Guardian Angel Mission (La Mission de L'Ange Gardien) on the north bank of the Chicago River's main branch west of present-day Michigan Avenue. The mission served two Miami villages of perhaps three hundred cabins. In addition to the mission, there were French traders who lived nearby. A trading post near the site of the former Tribune Tower building was run by two men associated with La Salle. Several other traders and helpers, most with Indian wives, were associated with this post. In 1702 the mission and trading post closed when the Miami started to move to the Maumee and Wabash valleys in Indiana because of raids. At least some of these raids were likely to have been what Morrissey refers to as "mourning war," in which lost kinfolk were replaced by kidnapping a person from elsewhere. When the Beaver Wars between the French and the Iroquois ended, wars between the French and the Fox began and lasted until 1730.[43]

One consequence of these later wars was that access to the Chicago Portage was blocked. Commerce shifted eastward, away from Chicago and toward where the Miami moved. Even after the Fox Wars ended, raids by Natives continued to create problems for the balance of the century, well after the English claimed the area in the 1760s.[44] As a consequence, there is not much evidence of a European presence in the Chicago area for most of the eighteenth century. The site of Chicago was still just a point on a route between Michilimackinac and villages in the Mississippi River valley. By the end of the century the trade for furs, hides, and grain returned to the area, and Chicago attracted new European settlers.[45]

Point de Sable and Kinzie

Following the French and Indian War (1754–63), the victorious British faced a problem: The area's Indigenous population had mainly sided with the French.[46] Because of intermarriage, the kin and trade networks often overlapped. The British could not gain acceptance if they did not honor those networks. As Keith R. Widder notes, lower-level officers were, therefore, sent "to travel throughout the region, meet some of the people, make surveys and maps, and write reports describing the inhabitants, waterways, and terrain."[47] For this reason, a British lieutenant named Dietrich Brehm was in the Chicago area in 1761 to map the village. He found several settlers who were still there two years later. There is no indication of who they were, but they likely were French or métis. In this section we'll examine the development of Chicago under the British and the transition to the Americans after the Revolution.

In 1770 Jean Orillat, the wealthiest man in Montreal, a merchant and trader, financed the voyage of two canoes from Montreal to Chicago under Jean Baptiste St. Cyr.[48] The unique feature of this voyage was that the only cargo other than provisions was two hundred pounds of chocolate. No one knows the reason for this, but it has been speculated that Orillat and St. Cyr were checking whether Chicago was ready for a new trading post. It was not.

The English and Scottish merchants headquartered in Montreal who assumed responsibility for the Great Lakes fur trade after the French and Indian War accepted all the traders working in the west. Operating in the Chicago area were both the short-lived General Company of Lake Superior and the South and the Michilimackinac Company.[49] Unlike the Hudson's Bay Company, the other English-controlled companies accepted intermarriage between traders and Natives, which led to a certain stability. By the early nineteenth century, métis populations existed around almost all the company's trading posts and in remote locations such as Chicago.

On his 1718 map of Louisiana and the Mississippi River, cartographer Guillaume Delisle, working for the French Crown, noted a property on the west bank of the North Branch just north of its confluence with the South Branch.[50] No one knows who owned it. There is speculation that it might have been owned by Simon Guillory, owner of a well-known Michilimackinac trading company. Gurdon Hubbard described the vacated site as he observed it in 1818 as containing gardens and adjoining cornfields. It had to have been in use within a decade or so of 1818. Hubbard learned from Antoine des Champs, Louis Bisson, and other early residents that the property existed before 1778. Simon Guillory died c. 1744, but his son Joseph carried on the family business.[51] Joseph married a woman from St. Joseph, Michigan, and it is known that Jean Baptiste Guillory (likely his son), a resident of St. Joseph, carried on a trade in St. Joseph and the Chicago area at the time of the American Revolution. In the late 1770s William Burnett, also a St. Joseph resident, traded furs and grain there and in the Chicago area. In 1779 Guillory became the proprietor of a general store in Mackinac. It is reasonable to think that Guillory made use of the site, then abandoned it, and it became available to Burnett and those he allowed to use it. (Burnett, unknown to most Chicagoans, is a man who should play a more prominent role in histories of the city.)

As the eighteenth century ended, the residence of Jean Baptiste Point de Sable stood on the north bank of the Chicago River.[52] The first record of his being in Chicago is in the journal of a visitor from Detroit named Hugh Heward who in 1790 purchased supplies at Point de Sable's trading house. Still, many date his arrival as early as 1784. Point de Sable is described as being of African descent, but little else is known about him.[53]

At present, one theory is that he was born in 1746 in Kaskaskia, Illinois, to a woman named Catherine who was of Haitian ancestry. They were slaves owned by Jean Brunet-Bourbonnais and his wife Elizabeth Deshayes, the richest property owners in the French "Illinois Country," and were freed by them in 1748.[54] It should be noted that Indigenous people were also held as slaves by the French in Illinois. Jean Baptiste later married a Potawatomi woman named Kitiwaha (also known as Catherine) with whom he had two children (Suzanne and Jean Baptiste Jr.). The normal date given for their marriage in a Catholic ceremony in Cahokia is 1778, but there likely was an earlier Native American ceremony.[55]

Another theory of his origins points to Quebec on the basis of a listing in the records of 1768 of a "Jean Baptiste, nègre," a native of Vaudreuil (just west of Montreal), a contract laborer working for Montreal-based traders in the northwest Great Lakes region.[56] Both theories could be correct if Catherine and her son moved to Vaudreuil once they received their freedom.

In 1775 Jean Baptiste and Pierre Durand, an experienced trader, left Montreal for Cahokia, Illinois, under the trade license of Michel Bellau. Durand referred to Jean Baptiste as a "free negro," which meant his mother was also a free woman.[57] By 1779 Point de Sable was operating a satellite trading post for Durand at the mouth of Trail Creek (in what is now Michigan City, Indiana); Durand was then based in Detroit. It was at Trail Creek that Point de Sable was arrested by the British on suspicion of having anti-British sentiments.[58] The officer under whose command he had been captured, Major Arent Schuyler de Peyster, ultimately concluded that this was an error and introduced him to the British lieutenant governor of Quebec, Captain Patrick Sinclair. Point de Sable subsequently managed Sinclair's estate, the Pinery, near St. Clair, Michigan, until 1784, when it was sold.

Why the Point de Sable family moved to Chicago is unknown. Whether William Burnett had anything to do with the move is unknown, but it is likely; the two men knew each other before the move. Ann Keating notes that "Point de Sable was part of Burnett's successful trading enterprises," while Benjamin Sells writes: "Burnett also had a business relationship with Point de Sable and may have been instrumental in facilitating Point de Sable's move to Chicago sometime between 1784 and 1788 to establish a farm and trading post at the mouth of the Chicago River."[59]

Burnett (sometimes described as a Frenchman) was born in New Jersey and, in the early years of the American Revolution, made his way to Detroit, where he began his career as a trader. Such a move would suggest that his sympathies lay with the British at that time.[60] After leaving Detroit, he spent a short time in Mackinac before moving to St. Joseph and trading with the Potawatomi. Point de Sable could have met Burnett, who traded in furs as well as agricultural goods (especially corn and wheat), in any of these places.[61] In time, Burnett's posts would include Mackinac and Chicago in addition to St. Joseph. Burnett married Kakima, daughter of Nanaquiba (a great chief of the Potawatomi) and sister of Topinbee (who became a great chief) in 1782. His sympathies thereafter were very pro-Indian.[62] Burnett and Kakima employed a wide variety of individuals—Anglophones, Francophones, and métis—who traded on their behalf.

In Chicago, Point de Sable appears to have performed work similar to that he had done for Durand, running a trading post and maintaining a warehouse and other outbuildings, including accommodations for visiting fur traders. Based on Robert Morrissey's discussion of Indigenous activity in the Illinois River Valley, it is quite likely that buffalo hides, grain, and other goods were brought to Point de Sable's post and traded along with furs.[63] In the tradition of the Potawatomi, Catherine Point de Sable and her daughter would have been the ones to cultivate the fields that supplied fresh produce to the post.[64] The Point de Sables grew corn and wheat as well as vegetables and fruits. They raised livestock including cows, pigs, chickens, and horses. They ground wheat into flour, then baked bread. They cured meats in a smokehouse. It also is likely that other Potawatomi women produced goods that they supplied to Point de Sable's post. Philip Vierling argues that it is reasonable to believe the Point de Sables made use of the Guillory land on which crops had been grown previously.[65] There is no discussion as to whose (if anyone's) permission they had, but Burnett is the most likely candidate. To quote Nelson:

> Point de Sable's business interests represented the local nexus of a far-flung transnational trade that stretched from the lower Mississippi to Upper Canada. Passing brigades of fur traders relied on Point de Sable to broker relations with Chicago's Potawatomi headmen, who continued to facilitate movement through the portage.[66]

Burnett supplied the financing that underwrote the efforts of traders who are better known than he (e.g., John Kinzie). Though it is most likely that Point de Sable's business was seasonal, the presence of a trading post with someone in residence year-round suggests the development of a minimal urban function in an area with a very small year-round population. It seems likely that the European economic activity at the mouth of the Chicago River would have been initiated by a trader, and it is doubtful that Point de Sable held a trading license. So his motivation for settling there remains unclear. Nonetheless, the fact there was economic activity at the site appears to be a factor in the American demand for title to that land in the Treaty of Greenville.

Living in a place now visited by American loyalists and soldiers as well as British and French traders, Point de Sable would not have wanted to be suspected of having strong leanings toward any of the three powers in the difficult times that followed the American Revolution.[67] Although the Americans had gained title to the land, the British still controlled the area's fur trade, and many of the area's traders were French. His neighbors were mainly French traders with Indian wives. The local economy in which Point de Sable worked was one based on barter; what he grew was traded as furs were traded. His farm was known (reputedly as far away as the nation's capital) as the only source of fresh produce in the area. It appears that Chicago was becoming a node in Dean's sense of the term.

Indeed, a small métis community developed in Chicago during the 1790s. Beginning in July 1790, the Point de Sables' next-door neighbors were the Ouilmettes. Little is known of Antoine Ouilmette's early years. The traditional claim is that he was a French Canadian who may also have had Native American ancestry; "Ouilamette" was a name associated with a Potawatomi prominent in the Lake Michigan region beginning in the 1680s, decades before Ouilmette's birth sometime around 1760.[68] Ouilmette erected a log cabin just to the west of Point de Sable's post. He married Archange Marie Chevalier, a French-Potawatomi woman, in about 1796; her father belonged to one of the most powerful métis fur-trading families on the Great Lakes.[69] The wedding took place at Grosse Point, to the north of Chicago.[70] When John Kinzie, another associate of Burnett's, arrived in Chicago, Ouilmette went to work with him, and both became among Chicago's most prominent citizens. François and Marie-Therèse Le Mai (he most likely from Cahokia and she a Potawatomi), Louis and Angelique Pettell, and Louis and Suzanne Buisson (he a French Canadian and she Archange's sister Sheshi) were other traders living in Chicago. Finally, there was Jean La Lime, a Quebec-born trader, and his Potawatomi wife Nokenoqua, who were also Point de Sable's neighbors. La Lime arrived in Chicago in 1792 to be William Burnett's agent.

What would become the site of today's Chicago is tied to the 1795 Treaty of Greenville (Ohio) that ended the war between the U.S. forces led by "Mad" Anthony Wayne and a confederation led by Miami chief Little Turtle. The treaty followed a decisive victory by the U.S. forces the previous year at the Battle of

Fallen Timbers near present-day Maumee, Ohio, ten miles southwest of Toledo. The main thrust of the treaty was a redefinition of the east-west border between the U.S. and Indian land. On the north, the border was where the Cuyahoga River joined Lake Erie (Cleveland) and, on the south, where the Kentucky River joined the Ohio River at Carrollton, Kentucky, roughly halfway between Cincinnati and Louisville. In addition, several parcels of land west of the revised border were ceded to the United States, including what would become present-day Toledo, Ohio, Mackinac Island and Detroit, Michigan, Fort Wayne and Lafayette, Indiana, and Peoria, Illinois. Most important, in article 3, item 14, the Natives ceded "one piece of land six miles square at the mouth of the Chikago [*sic*] River emptying into the southwest end of Lake Michigan, where a fort formerly stood."[71]

The Indians told the Americans there was no such fort, and there is no eighteenth-century record of such a fort.[72] Why the Americans believed otherwise is unclear. Whatever their belief, this and the other parcels were viewed as strategic locations where the Americans planned to build military fortifications and trading posts. John William Nelson argues that Wayne was advancing "a new geographic solution to control the untaxed and unmonitored movement through the lakes at a crucial overland bottleneck."[73] Given that the site of Chicago had been relatively ignored or avoided for a century or more, this was a somewhat surprising development. Then again, it was a way to try to control access to the northeastern Mississippi River valley and, in a few years' time, the western part of the valley following the Louisiana Purchase.

In 1800 Point de Sable sold his property to La Lime for 6,000 livres ($1,200).[74] The money for the purchase was guaranteed by Burnett. The bill of sale for the purchase (written in French), discovered in a Detroit archive in 1913, revealed that the sale included a twenty-two-foot by forty-foot cabin containing fine furniture and paintings, a house, two barns, a horse-powered mill, a bake house, a poultry house, a dairy, and a smokehouse.[75] The bill of sale did not mention the land. For the ten years or more that Point de Sable spent in Chicago, this was a remarkable accumulation of capital. It is why he is normally credited with being one of the city's founders. How he was able to accumulate this much capital from farming is a mystery.

Fig. 2a. Jean Baptiste Point de Sable, by Raoul Varin. (Chicago History Museum, ICHi-012166.)

There is no shortage of theories about why Point de Sable left Chicago, but, given that he moved to St. Charles, Missouri, which was part of Spanish Louisiana (and not all that far from Cahokia), those that suggest he was anxious to

Fig. 2b. Chicago's first house, depicted in 1827 by Raoul Varin. (Chicago History Museum, ICHi-092930.)

avoid the American government have a good deal of credence.[76] But Point de Sable was, in fact, a paid interpreter for the U.S. government.[77] In 1798 Burnett had information that led him to believe that construction of the Chicago fort was imminent.[78] There was no doubt that the Americans, like the British, hoped to obtain land for settlers. The first Fort Dearborn certainly wasn't constructed to protect the mostly French and Indian residents and their claims to the land.

Most scholars believe Point de Sable's wife and daughter had died of typhoid before 1800.[79] Given that maintaining the farm was considered women's work by the Potawatomi, for the now fifty-something man to do the work largely on his own would have been an onerous task. He was likely to have felt a bit footloose. Perhaps he was more a supporter of the British than of the Americans. That was certainly true of the Potawatomi, his wife's tribe, who began their westward migration following the Treaty of Greenville. It was also true of John Kinzie, who would come to live in what is considered to be Point de Sable's house. Further, the government might not have considered him to be a landowner. He was essentially a squatter living on land for which he had no U.S. title. Point de Sable legitimately could have expected the American government to apply the Land Ordinances of 1785 and 1787 to those already living within the ceded lands, although the issue didn't arise in the Chicago area for several more decades.[80]

The first Fort Dearborn was constructed on the south bank of the Chicago River in 1803.[81] When the U.S. schooner *Tracy* arrived, there were, according to Julia Whistler, daughter-in-law of Major John Whistler (the officer sent to build

Fort Dearborn), "four rude huts, or traders' cabins, occupied by white men, Canadian French with Indian wives."[82] Perhaps the Point de Sable farmstead was not as grand as the bill of sale made it appear because the sixteen-year old Mrs. Whistler had spent time in Detroit, still a frontier city.

The decision to build Fort Dearborn increased the importance of the site's position and its nodality. The fort, whose primary purpose was to "control river traffic, exact tariffs, and pacify the local Indians," elevated the role of the portage in Chicago's economic history.[83] Its second purpose was to advance the new country's economic interests by facilitating commerce. The Revolution had driven the English merchants in New York to Montreal.[84] In general, they and the French fur traders in their employ attempted to impede American efforts to enter the Great Lakes trade. The United States constructed a factory (the first trading post) adjacent to Fort Dearborn, but it had to compete with what by then were well-established non-American interests in the Great Lakes region. The United States factory would always be at a competitive disadvantage because it was prohibited from trades involving alcoholic beverages. Traders such as Burnett became dissatisfied with the U.S. approach to the trade because it restricted the activities of American traders without limiting the activities of their rivals. This was due, in part, to the fact the officers of Fort Dearborn were primarily concerned with questions of survival.

The other founder of Chicago, John Kinzie, was born in Quebec in 1763 to Scots-Irish parents.[85] Apprenticed as a silversmith in Quebec, he practiced his trade in Detroit when his mother and stepfather moved there. While in Detroit he began working for William Burnett, trading with the Natives, and becoming familiar with the people and, most likely, their languages.

Kinzie established trading posts for Burnett in the interior, including one near Fort Wayne, Indiana, among the Miami tribe, in 1789–90. As time passed, the U.S. government attempted to exclude Canadians from trading on American lands. As American settlement moved westward, traders such as Burnett and Kinzie tried to keep ahead of them, as did the fur-bearing animals. Kinzie operated a post at the St. Joseph–Kankakee River portage site from 1796 until Burnett sent him to Chicago. As Ann Keating notes, Kinzie, as well as a majority of those living in "Indian Country," was more concerned with the preservation of that country and its way of life than with whether the French, the British, or the Americans were in charge.[86]

Sometime in 1803 or a bit later, Kinzie arrived in Chicago with a new wife and child.[87] He acquired Le Mai's trading business and operated a general store. He also acquired the Point de Sable property from La Lime in 1804. La Lime has been described as Kinzie's "frontman," but it is unclear what that role entailed. Both men were associated with Burnett. That same year, Kinzie was appointed a justice of the peace by the territorial governor, and Fort Dearborn was completed. La Lime became a government interpreter at the fort, filling a role Point de Sable had played before there was a fort.

The Kinzie home became the center of nonmilitary hospitality in the area; its outbuildings included living quarters for the French Canadians in his employ.[88] Many of these would have been engagés, essentially indentured servants.[89] There were also four Black slaves, although slavery was forbidden in the territory by the Northwest Land Ordinance of 1787.[90]

Kinzie's general store sold provisions to Fort Dearborn and traded with the Natives in competition with the government factor (agent) at the fort. Kinzie and his half-brother and business partner Thomas Forsyth had a reputation for fairness and trustworthiness, even among the Natives, who were often at odds with the government's factor.[91] Area residents brought goods they could produce at home (e.g., bread, clothing, corn, and whiskey) and acquired goods Kinzie and Forsyth obtained in what literally was international trade. Given that the soldiers were paid in cash, and the Natives received cash from annuity payments arising from their land cessions in various agreements (e.g., the Treaty of Greenville), there was a little cash circulating in a world normally characterized by barter with those close to you and credit with those at a distance, all of which was recorded in the traders' account books. Kinzie was considered a bourgeois trader, a skillful veteran of the business with access to credit.[92]

On June 17, 1812, Kinzie and La Lime quarreled. Although they were neighbors in a tiny community, there was reputed to be bad blood between them.[93] Phillip Vierling argues that La Lime borrowed the money to purchase the Point de Sable property from Burnett, who in turn sold La Lime's promissory note to Kinzie. Kinzie, according to Vierling, foreclosed on La Lime, which was how the property came to be in his hands.[94] Kinzie, who allegedly was a volatile person, stabbed and killed La Lime, then fled to Milwaukee, which at that time was little more than a trading post.[95] He claimed the killing was self-defense, that La Lime shot at him first. Ann Keating believes it was premeditated murder. She cites a witness who said:

> We saw the men come out together; we heard the pistol go off, and saw the smoke. Then they fell down together. I don't know as Lalime [*sic*] got up at all but Kinzie got home pretty quick. Blood was running from his shoulder where Lalime [*sic*] shot him.[96]

If indeed it was self-defense, and that is what it was officially ruled to be, it is unclear why Kinzie ran. There seems little doubt that he was pro-British in a time just before war was to break out between the former mother country and her newly independent former colonies. It has been alleged that, while in Milwaukee,

Kinzie met with pro-British Indians who were planning attacks on Chicago and other American settlements.[97]

Little more than a month after the declaration of war in 1812, Fort Michilimackinac fell to the British, and the occupants of Fort Dearborn were ordered to evacuate and travel overland to Detroit. Even as the Natives became increasingly unruly, they continued to trade with Kinzie. On August 15, 1812, Fort Dearborn was destroyed as the evacuating troops and their families were attacked by a force of five hundred British-incited Indians. Fifty-three died, including women and children, in what is referred to as "the Battle of Fort Dearborn."[98] Kinzie had been warned by Billy Caldwell to avoid marching with the column from the fort, and he did send his family in a small boat that followed the land party a small distance from the shore.[99] He himself marched with the soldiers thinking that his relationship with the Natives would afford the soldiers some measure of protection. He was wrong.

Kinzie escaped injury and managed to return to his home and collect a few possessions. He and his family were officially the prisoners of Topinbee, Potawatomi chief and Burnett's brother-in-law. This enabled the family to make its way back to Detroit. Many view this as confirmation that Kinzie was pro-British. In 1813, however, the British arrested Kinzie and Jean Baptiste Chandonnai, who was also living in Detroit, and charged them with treason.[100] They were accused of having corresponded with the enemy (the army of the U.S. general Harrison) while supplying gunpowder to Tecumseh's forces, who were allied with the British. Kinzie was to be transported to Britain but, when the ship on which he was imprisoned put into port for a second time, Kinzie was returned to Quebec, where, after several months of confinement, he was released; Chandonnai is alleged to have purchased his freedom in Detroit with ten gallons of whiskey. Kinzie was back in U.S.-held Detroit by 1814 and, now claiming to be an American, was in Chicago in 1816, the year Fort Dearborn was rebuilt. The loss of the trade goods Kinzie and Forsyth held in Chicago before the battle, the debts that were owed in St. Joseph, Detroit, and elsewhere, and the sale of almost everything they owned to pay those debts left the Kinzies almost penniless. The opportunities in a rebuilding Chicago seemed more promising than remaining in Detroit.[101]

Archange Ouilmette and her sister Sheshi remained in the Ouilmette home during the Battle of Fort Dearborn.[102] The Ouilmettes hid the wife of a lieutenant, a sergeant, and métis trader Alexander Robinson in their house.[103] After the battle, when the Natives returned to burn the fort, they warned the Ouilmettes to leave Chicago, which they did. They returned a month later. Their house had been looted; their animals were missing; but they carried on. They were among the few residents of Chicago in the four years between the battle and the rebuilding of the fort.

Not simply a trader in furs, Antoine Ouilmette was a "progressive, energetic man of good business ability" for those times; he accumulated considerable property. He had a store in Chicago, and a farm at Racine, Wisconsin, which he frequently visited while living in Chicago. He also made occasional business trips to Milwaukee and Canada." He is known to have had a fine lot of horses, cattle, sheep, and hogs. Ouilmette was "known as a kind, whole souled, generous man of remarkable energy and perseverance, who made friends with everybody, both Indians and whites, and he in turn was universally liked and respected."[104] The larger share of his income was derived from guiding people and goods across the Chicago Portage.[105]

In 1829 Ouilmette helped persuade the Ojibwa, Odawa, and Potawatomi to sign the second Treaty of Prairie du Chien. As a result, Archange Ouilmette received 1,280 acres in present-day Evanston and Wilmette (named for the family). Shortly thereafter, the family moved to a cabin on this land. In the late 1830s Ouilmette accused Joseph Fountain of Evanston and others of trespassing and illegally harvesting timber from his land. He lost the suit and had to pay substantial court costs. He also lost two Indian ponies that were his special pride. Shortly thereafter, the Ouilmettes moved to Council Bluffs, Iowa, where many Potawatomis had relocated.

The American Fur Company

Following the War of 1812, economic activity in Chicago increased because John Jacob Astor's American Fur Company, established in New York in 1808, gained control of the U.S. fur trade.[106] Chicago's being the locus of a unit of the company marginally increased the site's nodality and position. Though it was but a baby step, Chicago's civilian population increased roughly sixfold from the early years of the nineteenth century to the departure of American Fur in the early 1830s. Those years are the subject of this section.

When the (Canadian) Michilimackinac Company dissolved in 1810, two of its constituent companies joined with Astor in 1811 in forming the South West Fur Company, which was to operate in the United States with trade goods from both the United States and Canada.[107] In 1817 Astor bought out his Canadian partners and began doing business as the American Fur Company. He had entered the trade with the thought of competing with the British on the Pacific Coast and trading with the Chinese. Eventually, Astor's trading posts would stretch from the Great Lakes to Astoria, Oregon, at the mouth of the Columbia River. Pelts would be loaded on Astor-owned ships headed for Guangzhou, China, where they would be sold. Chinese goods would then be acquired for resale in American and European markets.

The company's regional headquarters in the Great Lakes area was on Mackinac Island, from which it competed against Great Britain's North West and Hudson's Bay companies. The American Fur Company was known for its hard-nosed practices of purchasing competitors or driving them out of business, as Chicago-based traders soon discovered. This would be the final chapter of the fur trade in Chicago.

On his return to Chicago, John Kinzie unsuccessfully sought appointment as the U.S. Indian factor. He consequently returned to the fur trade, whereupon he was hired by Astor's company in large part because of his close ties to the area's Indian tribes. Kinzie and Antoine Deschamps were appointed agents of the Chicago unit in 1817. Kinzie traded in the Chicago area, while Deschamps operated in the Illinois River valley. In 1819 Jean Baptiste Beaubien was brought in to assist Kinzie and eventually became head of the unit. By the early 1820s the American Fur Company was the economic (and social) life of Chicago, the principal employer other than the U.S. government.

Astor's major competition in the Chicago area came from British firms operating out of Canada. In 1815, prior to Kinzie's return to Chicago, the governor of the Michigan Territory, Lewis Cass, hired Kinzie to visit the tribes living around Chicago to learn what an appropriate policy might be. The tribes were still generally hostile to Americans. Kinzie's advice, which echoed that of other frontier officials, was to rebuild Fort Dearborn in order to reduce British influence. Cass recommended this course to the secretary of war, who was aware of Britain's actions.

In addition to constructing the second Fort Dearborn, the government forbade British traders from operating within the United States, a policy that displeased the American Fur Company. Although it had hoped that British firms would be barred, it wanted the right to hire experienced British (and French) traders. Astor wrote President James Madison requesting that his company have the right to determine who received a license to trade. Madison vested that power in the territorial governor and the Indian agents in Mackinac, Green Bay, and Chicago.

This policy created a problem for the agents because they were also charged with restoring the government factory system at sites such as Fort Dearborn. Those factories were to buy goods from the Natives at fair prices and to sell the (government-approved) goods at cost. This meant an agent was to license the traders (such as the American Fur Company) with whom he was to compete as factor.

The position of factor at Chicago went to Jacob Varnum.[108] He was appointed in 1815 and for the first two years had a limited amount of success before having to compete against Astor's Kinzie and Deschamps. The American Fur Company opposed the idea of government factories and campaigned for their removal. The competition between the two entities was uneven because the government factories were forbidden to provide liquor to the Indians. It has been asserted that the American Fur Company would have preferred not to trade liquor but recognized its value in competition against the government factories.[109]

Within a year or two it was clear to many in Washington that its factory system was going to lose the competition. The House of Representatives requested that Secretary of War John Calhoun, whose responsibilities included the Indian Bureau, report on an alternative way of conducting the Indian trade in the absence of a factory system. He recommended that the factory system be phased out. In 1820 the Reverend Jedidiah Morse was dispatched to tour western tribes and factories. He found a strong preference for the American Fur Company because of its experienced traders and its trade goods. The following year, Congress passed a bill that would close the factories over time in a manner that would minimize the loss to the government. Senator Thomas Hart Benton, a Missouri Democrat, member of the Indian Affairs committee, and friend of the American Fur Company, persuaded the government to close the factories within two months.[110] This almost certainly meant the government would take a loss; the problem was confounded when those appointed to oversee the closing were found to be unacquainted with the factories and their business and had no way of collecting debts owed by the Natives.

With its main competition eliminated, the American Fur Company turned its attention to private traders. In many cases, American Fur hired such traders. Jean Baptiste Chandonnai, who by then was an independent Chicago trader, was hired in 1819, and Antoine Bourbonnais, a former competitor of Gurdon Hubbard, was hired in 1821. Hubbard at that point had but two years left on his indenture and was trading at the confluence of Big Bureau Creek and the Illinois River, where the Illinois River turns south just west of Starved Rock, not far from where the Grand Village stood.[111]

Some traders were forced out owing to losses in competition with the firm. John Haeger reports the case of the Chicago operations of the Conant and Mark Company of Detroit. Their local agent, John Crafts, arrived in 1816, did well competing against American Fur and, after 1817, its agent John Kinzie. As a result, American Fur moved Jean Baptiste Beaubien from Milwaukee to Chicago in 1819 to increase the competition against Crafts. By 1822 Crafts was losing money, and he became an employee of American Fur.[112]

At about this time, Kinzie left American Fur and was appointed Indian subagent in Chicago under (and serving as interpreter to) Varnum's replacement, Alexander Wolcott. The following year, Crafts was appointed to replace Kinzie, but Kinzie remained in close contact with the firm.[113] When Crafts moved to Mackinac in 1824, his replacement was told by management in Mackinac that, if needed, Kinzie would provide assistance. This could have been an awkward position for Kinzie, who was to protect the Indians' annuity payments from the traders' "inflated" prices.

With Crafts's departure, the American Fur Company needed a new factor. Hubbard would have been a logical successor to Crafts, but the firm believed that Hubbard's work downstate was more valuable to it at that time. The firm's choice was Kinzie, who knew the job and who was on good terms with Wolcott, a man who had fought American Fur on a number of fronts during his tenure.[114] Jean Baptiste Beaubien was appointed his assistant, but conflict arose between the two men. In time, Hubbard would move to Chicago to replace Beaubien.

Beginning with the rebuilding of Fort Dearborn, the U.S. government sought more and more land cessions, eventually resulting in less and less hunting ground for the Indians and fewer and fewer animals. With the opening of the Erie Canal in 1825, increased settlement around the Great Lakes played a part in the increasing scarcity of fur-bearing animals. By 1827 this contributed to a situation in which the Natives could not repay the credit that American Fur had extended them. Kinzie resigned, and the firm began contracting its Chicago operations.[115] Anticipating the canal's effect, Astor in 1822 had joined forces with the Pierre Chouteau family of St. Louis to concentrate the efforts of the American Fur Company in the Missouri River valley and up into the Rocky Mountains.

By the late 1820s, the value of Chicago's fur trade had decreased from thousands of dollars annually to hundreds. The Treaty of 1833 ended all Indigenous land claims in Illinois and marked the end of the fur trade in Chicago.[116] The treaty included arrangements for the purchase of Indigenous lands and compensation to settlers and traders for damages, including property stolen at the time the first Fort Dearborn was abandoned. The majority of claims were from traders trying to earn one last payment from the Natives. The largest share of the payments went to the American Fur Company, which received $17,000.[117] Gurdon Hubbard received more than $6,000, and the family of John Kinzie, who died of a stroke in 1828, received $20,000. But most of the money owed to individual traders immediately went elsewhere. Hubbard was in debt to American Fur for $6,000; the Kinzie family was faced with debts that the late John Kinzie had incurred early in his career and in the Battle of Fort Dearborn. Jean Baptiste Beaubien, who received nearly $3,000, owed $2,000 to the company.[118] Both Hubbard and Beaubien settled in Chicago. Hubbard, who speculated on the area's future, received $80,000 in 1835 by selling land for which he had paid $5,000.

Following the distribution of claims, in 1834 Astor sold his interest in American Fur to Ramsay Crooks, who reorganized the company and focused on areas in the west. The following year the firm concluded its affairs in Chicago by selling its buildings and property to Beaubien for $500.

All through this period, the village around Fort Dearborn was beginning to grow. In 1818 Major Stephen H. Long visited the Chicago area and found, apart from the fort, roughly five dozen men living in a dozen log huts he characterized as "low, filthy, and disgusting."[119] Bessie Louise Pierce, one of the foremost historians of the city, noted that by the mid-1820s Chicago had fourteen taxpayers and thirty-five voters.[120] The majority of the roughly $8,000 of taxable property

Fig. 3. A view of Chicago from Lake Michigan in 1830. (Chicago History Museum, ICHi-183705A.)

belonged to the American Fur Company, the area's only major business. Before 1831, when Cook County was created, the area was part of Peoria County. Records from that county show that there were 155 people living in the Chicago area in the late 1820s, more than half of whom were French or métis.[121] Nelson describes Chicago in the 1820s as "a multicultural and multiracial space as a trading outpost in which Indigenous headmen, métis middlemen, leading merchants, and government officials cooperated as power brokers in an intimate community that still revolved very much around the fur trade and waterborne traffic through the portage."[122]

After the Treaty of 1833, the site boomed with the promise of a canal across the Chicago Portage. From perhaps 350 inhabitants when it was incorporated as a village in 1833, the city grew to approximately 3,500 in 1835 and two years later reached 4,170 when it was incorporated as a city.[123] Other activities blossomed to replace the fur trade as Chicago's economic engine, while land speculation became the local pastime. The wee node of the fur trade years became a city in less than a decade. The trade route across the Chicago Portage became a good deal busier. Those who had lived near the portage for generations were not present and did not participate in the site's future growth and development.

CHAPTER 2

Pioneers and Boosters

At a memorial for John Wright, "the prophet of the prairies," more than a decade after his death, his son asserted:

> "A set of men superior to the early settlers of Chicago were never brought together." Only the most enterprising and energetic ventured upon the long and trying journey to the then "Far-West," and those early settlers have left their impress upon every profession every occupation in the life of this great metropolis![1]

Behind such hyperbole is a simple truth: Opening a business at the mouth of the Chicago River in the late 1820s and 1830s involved a great deal of risk, not to mention the hardships involved in traveling there from the east. Several of Chicago's pioneer citizens were already there; they were former fur traders who envisioned what the site could become. Two of the few hardy souls who lived there around 1830 were Jean Baptiste Beaubien and Gurdon Saltonstall Hubbard, both employees of the American Fur Company when it closed shop in Chicago. Both stayed to become part of whatever it was that the site was to become. Beaubien became frustrated and moved to Chicago's hinterland; Hubbard persevered and prospered until the fire.

Other early citizens such as John S. Wright and William B. Ogden were boosters, not in a derogatory sense, but in the sense that they helped attract settlers and economic activity to the growing area. *Booster* is derived from the real estate industry term to describe a person with land to sell who takes actions likely to "boost" the price of land. Whether pioneers or boosters, most of Chicago's early settlers were engulfed by the land speculation that took hold in the mid-1830s and made many of them rich—if only for a year or two. Both Wright and Ogden were involved in real estate. Wright was also a newspaper editor—a "prophet"; Ogden, a real estate tycoon, investor, and politician—Chicago's first mayor. By the end of the nineteenth century boosters were being lampooned. In many cases, their optimism may have been warranted, but economic growth was negligible because they had an incomplete vision of what was required. In Chicago, on the other hand, growth was substantial. Ogden implicitly understood the necessary conditions for urban growth. What both men had that many other boosters lacked was an understanding that creating a city requires a great many things, not merely a promising location and a few investors. Those "great many things" must be considered in the context of the network of urban places into which any specific node fits. These two boosters enhanced Chicago's nodality.

There were others, of course. Work on the I&M Canal, which began in earnest in the 1830s, attracted people to the area. In addition to those who sought work on the canal, there were those who established businesses that would benefit from the completed canal. For instance, John Calhoun shipped his printing press and type from New York; the *Chicago Democrat*, the first regular newspaper, appeared in 1833. The medical officers at Fort Dearborn maintained private practices as well, but, in 1833, William Egan was one of the first physicians to arrive on his own account. By looking at the careers of Beaubien, Hubbard, Wright, and Ogden, all among the new town's most influential citizens at one time or another, one can get a sense of how Chicago's economy first grew, a sense that will be confirmed by statistics in later chapters.

Jean Baptiste Beaubien

Beaubien was born in 1787 into a large French Canadian family living in Detroit.[2] His mentor was Joseph Bailly, a French Canadian allied with the British. Bailly's trading posts ranged from the Grand River in Michigan to the Calumet River in Indiana. He took on Jean Baptiste as an eight-year-old apprentice in 1795. He learned the fur-trading business alongside Alexander Robinson, a métis who would also become a resident of Chicago.[3]

Jean Baptiste married four times and possibly had as many as twenty children. His first two wives were Odawas. He moved with his first wife (whose name has been lost) to Chicago in 1804, the year of their marriage, to represent Bailly's interests there. She died giving birth to a daughter two years later. Beaubien's second wife was Mahnobunoqua, the sister of Shabbona, a Potawatomi chief.[4] At the time of this marriage in 1806, he and Robinson were working at the Calumet River site. Sometime before 1812 Robinson built a house on the east side of the Chicago River's south branch. Like Ouilmette, Robinson was living and farming in Chicago during the period before the fort was rebuilt.

Fig. 4. Jean Baptiste Beaubien. (Chicago History Museum, ICHi-040647.)

Following the death of his second wife in 1811, Beaubien married Josette LaFramboise, a métis, on Mackinac Island in March 1812. She was from a fur-trading family that moved from Milwaukee to Chicago in 1803 and did work for the Kinzies.[5] Beaubien purchased land in Chicago in 1812, but most of the LaFramboise family returned to Milwaukee just as the hostilities between the Americans and the British-supported Natives began to escalate.

In 1823 Beaubien purchased what had been the Fort Dearborn factory (trading post) from his employer, the American Fur Company, for $500. When Chicago's first tax roll was assembled in 1825, Beaubien's property was evaluated at $1,000, the most of any in the area. His home, a large frame structure just south of the fort, hosted the first town election in 1825 and the first general election a year later. In that same year his younger brother Mark arrived; he achieved notoriety as the fiddle-playing proprietor of the Sauganash Hotel on Wolf Point.[6] The hotel replaced Jean Baptiste's home as the place where important civic functions were held. Chicago was gaining nodal characteristics.

In 1827 a renewal of Indian attacks led Beaubien to assemble a citizens' militia like one put together before the War of 1812. According to the federal census of 1830, there were 500 people in the area from whom a militia could be drawn.[7]

Beaubien's friend Alexander Robinson and Billy Caldwell, also known as Sauganash, the son of a Mohawk mother and a British officer, became chiefs and helped convince other chiefs to sign the second Treaty of Prairie du Chien in 1829. Their reward included large tracts of land. Caldwell received sixteen hundred acres on the north branch of the Chicago River; Robinson received sixteen hundred acres on the Des Plaines River that adjoined Caldwell's reserve on the east.[8]

In April 1832 the Black Hawk War began when Black Hawk, a Sauk warrior, left the Iowa Indian territory and attempted to reclaim Illinois land that the United

States believed the Sauks had ceded to them in the Treaty of St. Louis (1804). Black Hawk and others argued that tribal leaders lacked the full tribe's authorization when they signed the treaty. Beaubien raised a militia of about twenty-five men and became their captain. The company worked with a group of Potawatomi scouts during the short-lived war, which ended that August. The Treaty of Chicago (1833) was negotiated by Caldwell, Robinson, and others who endorsed the concept of compensated removal, as did Beaubien. Chicago was incorporated as a town that year. Beaubien ran for election as one of the new town's trustees but lost. The following year he was elected the first colonel of the Cook County militia. Saint Mary's Catholic Church, the first of that denomination in Chicago, was built on two lots he donated.[9]

In 1835, after land in the Chicago area was surveyed, the General Land Office put it up for sale. Provision was made for "preemption rights," but houses still had to be within the property lines the surveyors created.[10] If one's house happened to have been built across what would become a property line, then either the house would have to be moved to one lot or the other, or two lots would have to be purchased, if allowed. All this, however, lay in the future when the Chicago economy began its uncertain transition from the fur trade. What was more certain was that the land was likely to be valuable once land sales began and the proposed canal was under way.

Beaubien became involved in the land speculation that soon occupied many Chicagoans. Twice in the early 1830s he attempted to purchase the site of the largely abandoned second Fort Dearborn (seventy-five or more acres), and in 1835 (the year he purchased American Fur's remaining Chicago assets), it appeared that the third time was the charm. The local government land agent sold it to him for $94.61, but the General Land Office in Washington did not respond to his request for a land patent, though he submitted the certificate of registration from the Chicago land office. When Beaubien's lawyer attempted to evict the fort's commander, a lawsuit over Beaubien's claim made its way to the U.S. Supreme Court, which found the claim invalid. Subsequently, his payment was returned, the fort closed, and most of the land was sold after the Panic of 1837 for $106,042.[11]

The Michigan Avenue land on which Beaubien's home was located was surveyed and sold as six lots, with Beaubien only allowed to purchase one. The land on which his trader's cabin was located was a narrow strip of lakefront land south of the fort. The canal commissioners who oversaw land allocation chose to mark this potentially valuable land as "Public Ground—A Common to Remain Forever Open, Clear, and Free of Any Buildings, or other Obstruction Whatever."[12] Feeling cheated, Beaubien moved in 1840 to a farm in what is now Bridgeport. Following his fourth marriage, to seventeen-year-old Louise Pinion in 1855, he moved to the city's West Side, then three years later to what has become Naperville, where he died in 1864.[13]

Gurdon Saltonstall Hubbard

Hubbard was born in Windsor, Vermont, in 1802. After suffering financial losses in Vermont, his family moved to Montreal in about 1812. His father hoped to work as a lawyer for fur companies but was barred from that work because he was an American. The family ran a boarding house instead. When Hubbard turned sixteen he began a five-year indenture to the American Fur Company. For the first summer he worked in the company's Mackinac Island factory with another young apprentice, John H. Kinzie, who, when Hubbard left for Chicago, gave him letters of introduction to his extended family. This included his father John Kinzie, who had returned to his house across the river from Fort Dearborn.

Hubbard seems to have been one of the few traders in Illinois who foresaw the impact of increased settlement. Through his involvement with the Natives, he became the adopted son of Chief Waba of the Kickapoo and, for a short time, the husband of Watseka, niece of Chief Tamin of the Kankakee Potawatomi. In the mid-1820s he moved to Danville, Illinois, and opened a store in order to trade with white settlers. In 1826 he wrote to Astor requesting goods for his new venture. Those in charge of the Mackinac headquarters were reluctant to move toward retailing, lacked a supply of goods suitable for such trade, and refused to trade with whites. Two years later, as the Indian fur trade continued to falter, they relented, but, in exchange, Hubbard was required to purchase the company's interests in the Illinois Territory, much as Beaubien had done in Chicago. From his home in Danville he began to haul produce and to drive hogs up to Chicago. He also established several trading posts along the route, which became known as the "Hubbard Trace."[14]

Fig. 5. Gurdon Saltonstall Hubbard. (Chicago History Museum, ICHi-059718.)

In 1831 Hubbard married Eleanora Berry, who died seven years later after giving birth to a son, Gurdon Jr.[15] In 1834 they moved to Chicago and purchased a cabin from Billy Caldwell near Lake Michigan. He already was a provisioner of meat to Fort Dearborn. After the move he expanded his operations. Allegedly, the first winter was so cold that pig carcasses could be stored on the banks of the Chicago River, but Hubbard soon built a large brick warehouse (the largest in the West) on the river's south bank at LaSalle Street; it came to be known as "Hubbard's Folly." Unperturbed, he and two partners formed a trading company, built a second warehouse, and established a line of lake steamers serving Buffalo, New York, and the upper Great Lakes.[16] He and his partners, primarily John H. Kinzie, also constructed the city's first modern hotel, the Lake House, a three-story brick building on the north side of the river at what is now Rush Street.[17]

Bessie Pierce notes that Hubbard may have set off the land speculation that swept Chicago. In 1835, shortly after canal construction was authorized, Chicagoans received news that Hubbard had sold an addition (parcel) that had originally cost $5,000 for $80,000. Land values rapidly rose thereafter, while speculators started to arrive from several eastern and southern states. This escalated the speculative fever. Landowners were earning more than a 100 percent return on an investment of a few months, and the town was "jammed full of people and the excitement about property . . . tremendous."[18] By the time the sale of government land along the proposed canal route began in Chicago, there was not a vacant room to be had.

Shortly after moving to Chicago Hubbard became one of the town's first trustees, having served in the Illinois General Assembly during his time in Danville. Hubbard had the honor of turning the first shovel full of dirt as one of the commissioners of the I&M Canal. In 1835, acting on his own, he ordered and paid for Chicago's first fire engine, and later that year he became one of the directors of the branch of the State Bank of Illinois established in Chicago; his friend John H. Kinzie was its president. Along with Kinzie, Hubbard helped organize St. James Episcopal Church. He served as an alderman, helped raise the money for Chicago's first convention center (the Wigwam), and saw combat in the Civil War.[19]

With the money he earned in furs, meat, and land speculation, Hubbard entered the insurance business and became Chicago's first underwriter. The Great Fire nearly bankrupted him. Although his company paid all claims, Hubbard's business interests never recovered completely. Nonetheless, as Alfred Andreas noted,

> He stands prominent as one of the foremost merchants for the succeeding twenty years, during which period, besides carrying on one of the largest shipping, commission, packing, and forwarding trades in the city, he held nearly every office of trust and honor that his fellow-citizens could thrust upon him.[20]

A century later, Lloyd Wendt commented that Hubbard was responsible "as much or more than any other man" for what the city Chicago had become at the time of Hubbard's death in 1886.[21]

John Stephen Wright

John Stephen Wright was born in 1815 in Sheffield, Massachusetts. His father was a storekeeper; his mother, a former schoolteacher. About the time of John's birth, his father spent a year traveling in the West, including the site of Chicago, hoping the fresh air would improve his health. The family moved in 1822 to Williamstown, Massachusetts, where responsibility for John's education fell to his uncle, a professor at Williams College.[22] Father and son headed west in 1832 as a result of what has been described as "a family calamity." They intended to set up shop in Galena, Illinois, the Black Hawk War having just ended. They arrived in Chicago in late October, stayed at Mark Beaubien's Sauganash Hotel, and rented a storeroom in one of his buildings. The father then purchased a horse and surveyed a wide area. At Plainfield, Illinois, he met a man who owned a lot in Chicago on the north side of Lake Street a little east of Clark. He purchased the lot for $100, and father and son built a log merchant house that came to be known as the Prairie Store.[23]

While his father was away, John began selling their wares at a minimum 100 percent advance, or markup, consistent with that charged by George Dole, John H. Kinzie, and other merchants he befriended. Mark Beaubien's wife was nominally responsible for John in his father's absence, but the boy moved out of the noisy hotel and slept in the rented storeroom. Independently, he decided that, given the economic activity he observed and the prospect that a canal would be built, Chicago was the place for them to locate their store.

On his father's return, John reported that his friend Philo Carpenter had proposed that they get the surveyor to carve out a quarter-section (160 acres) that they could buy at $1.25 per acre.[24] That piece, later known as Wright's Addition, was just west of the South Branch and included what today is Union Park. The purchase was contested, and by the time the Wrights survived the adverse claim in 1836, the speculative boom had inflated the price from $1.25 to $1,000 per acre.

That first fall, the father returned to Massachusetts to inform the family that they would be moving to Chicago. When he returned in the spring of 1833, John had sold their inventory of goods, and having become a proficient marksman with a rifle, had converted their store into a gunnery. He did not ask his son what had happened but inquired of George Dole, who told him, "Never you fear for John."[25] During his father's absence John had helped build Chicago's third frame building (P. F. W. Peck's store) and had begun a census of Chicago. In 1834, when the entire Wright family moved to a home at the southwest corner of Michigan and Madison, John published a lithograph map of the area, and, just before land speculation really took hold, opened a real estate business. By 1836, when he turned twenty-one, his real estate holdings were estimated to be worth $300,000, at least $7.5 million today.[26] At one point he owned more than seven thousand acres of I&M Canal lands, and John's son remarked years later that he believed

Fig. 6. John Stephen Wright, c. 1870, by Susan Hely St. John. (Chicago History Museum, ICHi-064467.)

his father may have "owned a greater portion of Chicago than any other person."[27] Much of Wright's real estate wealth disappeared (as did Carpenter's and John H. Kinzie's) when the Panic of 1837 burst the speculative bubble.

Beginning in 1836, Wright handled grain and merchandise on commission and traveled extensively around the area. While this business also fell victim to the panic, his familiarity with the area's farmers and their practices led to Wright's next job as general manager/secretary/trustee of the Union Agricultural Society and editor of a newspaper entitled the *Union Agriculturist*.[28] Shortly after its start, the paper merged with one titled the *Western Prairie Farmer*. Wright bought the rights to the amalgamated paper and, in 1843, changed its name to the *Prairie Farmer*. He relinquished the job of editor that same year, but he retained a connection to the paper for the next fourteen years. Such was life on the western frontier; a man who had never worked on a farm or written anything for publication assumed such positions.

During the early 1840s Wright traveled by buggy throughout the Midwest trying to persuade influential farmers to write for the paper, particularly on the subject of common schools. He regularly met with the educational reformer Horace Mann, secretary of the Massachusetts Board of Education, on his trips east. Wright built Chicago's first public school in 1835 with his own funds. In 1844 he was largely responsible for the first state convention to promote common schools and later made a presentation to the joint committee of the Illinois senate and house on common schools. Ultimately, a school law was passed in 1845 that gave voters the choice of levying taxes for such purposes as building and repairing schoolhouses. Wright also was a prominent advocate for a state normal school and an agricultural college. He understood that in order to grow a city one needed more than homes and shops, that infrastructure was essential.

In the mid-1840s Wright wrote articles about the economics of a variety of midwestern agricultural outputs and mineral deposits and about the outlook for manufacturing, especially once the construction of the I&M Canal and the Galena and Chicago Union Railroad were completed. His advocacy of transportation improvements became national in scope. In the aftermath of President James K.

Polk's veto of a bill providing for federal funds for river and harbor improvements, the River and Harbor Convention was held in Chicago in 1847 to express support for such expenditures. This national convention drew twenty-five hundred people from nineteen states.[29] Notable delegates included Abraham Lincoln, Millard Fillmore, and Horace Greeley. In his memorial to Wright, his son noted that "he could name each State's representatives in the procession as it passed by, personal acquaintances."[30] One attendee, Joseph Buckingham, editor of the *Boston Courier*, later that year published a series of articles informing "business men and capitalists of Boston" of the desirability of investing in western railroads such as the Galena and Chicago Union.[31]

A year later Wright published a series of letters advocating the construction of railroads, in general, and the Illinois Central Railroad, in particular. Wright cooperated with his friend Senator Stephen Douglas to obtain the land grant for the railroad. He wrote, printed, and distributed at his own expense six thousand copies of petitions to Congress (two thousand each were sent to easterners, southerners, and westerners). Douglas commented on their influence as the second-earliest external push for the grant.[32] Wright went to Washington and lobbied for the bill in person, and, in September 1850, it became law.

Author Lloyd Lewis, who subtitled his biography of Wright *Prophet of the Prairies*, noted that while there was a self-serving dimension to these writings because Wright was once again active in the land market, there was more:

> Frankly, in his letters to newspapers, and in the series of circulars on railroads and Western real estate opportunities which came flying from his presses, he confessed that he expected to make money through Chicago's growth. He prophesied his own prosperity, and begged all who had faith to join him in his march to glory. But above and beyond his self-interest there was beginning to glow, in his writings, a belief for and love of Chicago that verged on the mystic. There was ecstasy in his vision of the city. It was the Promised Land.[33]

Wright was also an advocate for public parks; in 1847 he proposed a coordinated system for the city's three divisions to be connected by boulevards that was consistent with what the city ultimately did. Wright was an early example of Daniel Burnham's turn-of-the-century exhortation, "Make no little plans."

With respect to Wright's unfailing optimism concerning Chicago's destiny to become the preeminent midwestern city, his friend Judge John Dean Caton wrote that Caton "without hesitation, gave John S. Wright the credit of seeing more clearly than anyone else he had known, the possibilities of this part of the country and just what measure must be taken and how to make those possibilities."[34]

Wright returned to the real estate market following his marriage in 1846 and again did well. His holdings a decade later were estimated to be worth $600,000

($18.7 million today using the Consumer Price Index), but once again he would lose much of it. Almost from the beginning of the publication of the *Prairie Farmer*, Wright had been intrigued by agricultural machinery. In 1851 he became a partner of Obed Hussey, expecting the inventor to move to Chicago as Cyrus McCormick had.[35] Instead, Wright found he had the rights to produce the Hussey reaper for seven midwestern states. Wright continued looking for a reaper project to join, one to which he could contribute his ideas. In 1852 he believed he had found it: the Automaton Self-Raking Reaper.[36] The inventor, Jearum Atkins, a bedridden Evanston, Illinois, mechanic, gave Wright a half-interest to patent and introduce it. The inability to get necessary materials to Chicago, faulty construction, and the Panic of 1857 all helped doom the project. The start of the Civil War provided the final blow.

When the economy began its recovery from the panic, Wright again attempted to profit from his real estate expertise by creating a land company that provided a link through which eastern capitalists could invest in the Midwest. The Illinois legislature issued a charter in 1861, but Wright believed that this company would have little chance of success during the Civil War. In 1867 Wright obtained an option on thousands of acres in a belt surrounding Chicago at prices between $65 and $450 per acre. On the eve of the fire, some of that land was worth $20,000 per acre. In order to promote his land, he planned a pamphlet that would present the case for investing in Chicago property, but his mind was becoming "disordered" (as his son put it), and the pamphlet grew into a book titled *Chicago: Past, Present, and Future*, which has been variously described as "jumbled" and containing "much irrelevant to the subject."[37] Indeed, shortly after the fire of 1871, his family was forced to commit him to an asylum. He died at age fifty-nine in October 1874; among his pallbearers were Gurdon Hubbard and Philo Carpenter.

Alfred Andreas's history offers a fitting summary of the life of one of Chicago's principal boosters:

> Although a born trader and a bold speculator, he was a man of rare virtues, and during his long residence in Chicago, was identified with nearly every enterprise and measure calculated to promote its prosperity or elevate the educational, mental, moral, or religious standards of the city. The benefactions of this wonderfully energetic citizen permeated nearly every channel of the life and shewed in every phase of her early growth. The building of the early railroads, the development of manufactures, the first Presbyterian church, Sabbath-schools, and the common-school system of the State, the Press; to all these he devoted his energies and gave in no stinted measure.[38]

One presumes that Andreas's list of Wright's successful promotions would have included references to Chicago's position, trade routes, and nodality had Dean's dissertation been available.

William Butler Ogden

Fig. 7. William Butler Ogden, c. 1855. by George P. A. Healy. (Chicago History Museum, ICHi-037333.)

The person who plays the most prominent role in enhancing Chicago's position, trade routes, and nodality was William Butler Ogden. In no small part, his vision was formed from lessons learned in his youth. It was Ogden's Chicago that burned in the fire of 1871; what rose from the ashes was claimed by others. That Chicago did rise is in no small part attributable to what Ogden had done. To paraphrase Charles Wilson's infamous 1952 remark, "What was good for Chicago was good for Ogden, and vice versa."[39]

Ogden's father, Abraham, was born in New Jersey in 1771.[40] Abraham left home in 1790, shortly before his nineteenth birthday, with the expectation of moving to Washington, DC, just as it was being designated the nation's capital. While in Philadelphia, he visited family friend Mahlon Dickerson, who convinced Abraham of the opportunities the pine forests of the upper Delaware River valley held to supply that city with lumber.[41] Abraham joined a company that built the Federal Mill (named in honor of the Constitution) in what is now Cannonsville, New York. By 1797 Abraham had moved to the west branch of the Delaware near Walton, New York, where he and his brother Isaac built a sawmill. Within three years, each had a house, and two other brothers had joined them in running the mill. Its power was also used to operate a carding machine, and later a fulling mill was added so that they could produce functional woolen goods. Abraham successfully managed both businesses until 1820, when he became paralyzed, likely as the result of a stroke.

William Ogden, the first son of Abraham and his wife Abigail (Weed), was born on the fifteenth of June in 1805.[42] The few accounts of Ogden's childhood in the Delaware Valley suggest that he was intelligent and athletic, planning a career in the law. His father's disability meant that at age fifteen William was called on to perform the tasks his father could not. While this call to familial duty prevented him from studying law, it must have provided him a significant commercial education.[43] Abraham had regularly gone to New York and Philadelphia on business, and one assumes it became William who now performed those duties. And, foreshadowing what would transpire in Chicago, William learned the demands of a growing city (Philadelphia) by attending to his father's businesses. One important element was transportation, as the lumber had to get downstream to Philadelphia. Trees typically were cut in the winter, dragged to the river, then formed into rafts so the spring thaw could transport what would become boards, shingles, masts, and spars downstream.[44] It could not have escaped Ogden's attention that the presence of shipbuilding and other lumber-using industries contributed to Philadelphia's growth.

At age twenty-one Ogden joined a partnership in what proved to be a moderately successful mercantile firm. Three years later, the local girl to whom he became engaged, Sarah North, died before they could be married, causing a melancholy that remained with him thereafter and loosened his tie to the Delaware Valley.

Another element of Ogden's early education in city building likely came from another branch of the family. There is no hard evidence to indicate that the two branches of the family communicated, but it seems reasonable to assume that William would have been aware of his cousins' activities. One cousin, also named Abraham Ogden, was a distinguished lawyer whom President Washington appointed U.S. Attorney for New Jersey in 1792.[45] Washington also appointed him to a commission that was charged with bargaining with the Iroquois for a portion of northern New York State. The knowledge he gained from successfully completing this commission led to his purchasing a large tract of land in conjunction with his brother Samuel and others. Wherever they owned land, they attempted to create a system of privately financed internal improvements, including harbors, mills, and turnpikes that would promote economic development and attract settlers. A quarter century later their young cousin William would adopt a similar approach in Chicago. He would have learned that owning land in a good location was important to promoting growth, but it was no guarantee.

In 1834 Ogden was elected as a Democrat to the New York legislature from his native county.[46] There were two legislative sessions in 1835. Ogden resigned his seat shortly before the end of the early term to go to Chicago, but, before he left, he was selected the legislative leader of a bill to provide state aid to support the finances of the New York and Erie Railroad, much like the support given to the Erie Canal. His speech, which extended over three days, is suggestive of the lessons he had learned about the importance of transportation in urban development. Ogden envisioned "continuous railways from New York to Lake Erie . . . through Ohio, Indiana, and Illinois, to the waters of the Mississippi, and connecting with railroads running to Cincinnati and Louisville in Kentucky, and Nashville in Tennessee, and to New Orleans." It would be, he argued, "the most splendid system of internal communication ever yet devised by man."[47] Ogden believed that the position New York occupied because of the Erie Canal would be threatened if it did not embrace the newer technology. Indeed, the Erie Canal itself had altered the economic landscape of the state.[48]

In 1833 Ogden's brother-in-law Charles Butler and his friend Arthur Bronson visited Chicago. The following year, Bronson paid $20,000 for nineteen town blocks and eighty additional acres adjoining the town, a total of 182 acres on the north side of the Chicago River including what was known as Kinzie's Addition. Bronson hired agents, including John H. Kinzie, to deal with legal problems, improve the property with both commercial and residential structures, and arrange for the sale of lots. For his part, Butler organized a group of investors into, and became president of, the American Land Company. A year later he purchased the town lots from Bronson for $100,000 and convinced his brother-in-law to go to Chicago to manage the property even though this meant resigning his seat in the New York legislature.[49] In May 1835 Ogden arrived in Chicago less than two months after his speech to the New York legislature.

The company's plot was covered with oak and brush and was muddy from a recent rain; Ogden thought it was not worth the purchase price. He wrote his brother-in-law, "You have been guilty of the grossest folly. . . . Nothing could be more unattractive, not to say repulsive in its surface appearance."[50] Nevertheless, Ogden hired surveyors, laid out blocks and streets, had maps and plans drawn, and established a loan and trust agency just as government land sales, including sales along the route of the I&M Canal, brought easterners to the Midwest.[51] The land craze was under way. Ogden held an auction at which he sold roughly a third of the property for more than $100,000. After wintering in the East he returned to Chicago in 1836. By June of that year Ogden could write to one North Side landowner that his property would return a minimum of 400 percent on the investment, but he expected a return of "6 to 800 per cent & possibly over a thousand per cent."[52] He extended credit to purchasers of land who agreed to erect homes and office buildings. And, in August 1836, he was named fiscal agent for the town of Chicago.[53]

Ogden had a home built by John van Osdel in the center of the block bounded by Ontario, Rush, Erie, and Cass (now Wabash).[54] One of Ogden's many associates, Walter Newberry, built a home nearby, as did Ogden's brother Mahlon, an attorney. Real estate remained a good investment throughout 1836, and Ogden attracted a significant amount of eastern money to the Midwest. Notes Patrick McLear:

> The results demonstrate that an able man might serve each of those groups [eastern investors and western businessmen] and his own interests as well, and that no essential conflict need exist. In short, Ogden's ability to serve both eastern and western interests at the same time demonstrates that regional am-

> bitions could harmonize quite well with those of other regions and that business cooperation across regional lines could be markedly improved by skillful entrepreneurs like Ogden.[55]

Ogden ran for and was elected to a one-year term as Chicago's first mayor (1837–38), running as a Democrat. His opponent was John H. Kinzie, running as a Whig.[56] The Kinzie family also was involved in what Henry Binford describes as "scrambling" to profit from the growth of the city.[57] Kinzie was as well known as Ogden; both belonged to the St. James Episcopal Church. Indeed, the Kinzies had donated the land on which the church stood. Their views concerning the future of the city were remarkably similar. But, while the Kinzie forces attempted to paint Ogden as an outsider ("a transient speculator"), most eligible voters were as much outsiders as Ogden. Although Kinzie was "the first born of Chicago," his party was less well organized.[58]

As the city's fiscal agent, Ogden had built the city's reputation as creditworthy at the same time he was building his own, for he understood how important credit would be to the growth of the city.[59] As mayor he managed to keep the new city financially solvent through the initial year of the Panic of 1837, a most difficult period. As the panic began to grip the city, several citizens espoused suspending the law concerning debt collection. Mayor Ogden spoke against the suspension, arguing that it would lead to the dishonor of the individuals and the city: "Above all things, do not tarnish the honor of our infant city."[60]

The land boom ended with the panic, an episode that embarrassed Ogden. He assumed the liabilities of many friends and did not fully resolve them until the resulting depression reached its end in the early 1840s. He wrote Butler in 1839 that "One fourth of 1836 prices can hardly be obtained for much business property . . . at this time, and one 10th or a 20th is about all out [*sic*] town property will bring or is worth compared to sales in 1836."[61] Ogden's reputation in Chicago was based on real estate. Many, including Ogden, believed Chicago would become a great city by virtue of its location. Others, consistent with the stereotypical "booster," believed that destiny would be achieved with relatively little work. Ogden did not share this view. He and his partners knew they needed to build residential neighborhoods and business districts, streets and bridges, transport infrastructure generally, and much more to promote economic growth.

BRIDGES AND CANALS

As Ogden and his group attempted to stimulate the economy of the north side, it was clear that a good bridge that connected the north and south sides of the river was essential. Warehouses on the north side needed access to goods coming from the south side, and vice versa. The river as harbor would prove inefficient otherwise, and growth would be stunted. Nelson Norton erected the Dearborn

Street drawbridge, the first to span the Main Branch, in 1834. Joseph Kirkland pointed out that such bridges were controversial for two reasons:

> One [objection] was by the jealous South-siders who wanted to keep all the trade from crossing the river; another by people of all sides who preferred ferries. The "prairie schooners," covered wagons, had begun coming in great numbers, often 500 a day, bringing grain [to be shipped east] in what seemed then large quantities.[62]

In 1837 both the Dearborn Street Bridge and a rope ferry erected at the site of today's Rush Street Bridge proved necessary because most of the grain warehouses were built on the north bank of the river. When the City Council ordered the removal of the Dearborn Street Bridge in 1839, south-siders chopped it to pieces before the council had a chance to change its mind. Yet the south bank west of the Fort Dearborn military reservation was unsuitable for warehouse construction. It soon became clear that a connection was needed, but the council remained divided. At this juncture, in order to influence the vote on the bridge issue, Ogden and Walter Newberry gave Roman Catholic authorities the land on which to build Holy Name Cathedral.[63] The ploy was successful. Ogden convinced the city council to erect a bridge funded by a bond issue. A total of $3,000 in bonds was issued, with Ogden subscribing approximately a third of the total in the names of people for whom he was land agent. The following year, a float bridge was constructed at Clark Street. Ogden himself designed and built the bridge, the first floating swing bridge over the Chicago River, even though he had not seen one previously.[64] The fact that the easterners for whom Ogden was the agent approved this use of their money testifies to the esteem in which he was held by those who entrusted their money to him.

In 1836 Ogden and Harry Smith signed a contract with the State of Illinois to perform roughly $200,000 of work on the I&M Canal. During the panic, Ogden and Smith attempted to maintain their crews after the state was forced to suspend payments in 1840. Ogden and George Barnett (another contractor) were elected to negotiate with the governor. Some funds were generated, but the respite was short-lived. Ogden's relative success helped maintain the Chicago economy for a few years, so the worst effects of the panic were not felt until the early 1840s. When work on the I&M Canal ceased, Ogden found economic conditions frustrating. He wrote to one correspondent, "Our Canal is stopped, the country beggered, the state disgraced, & Bankrupt. But partys [*sic*] rules, tho' the state be ruined."[65] And to another,

> The whole Western Country, and States, have all gone to the Devil together & the Legislatures & particularly that of Illinois ought to go there. The wisdom of a generation cannot repar [*sic*] the damages and remove the cause that Knaves & asses have fastened upon us.[66]

To Ogden and others, recovery would be facilitated if work on the canal resumed, and he was one of many who did all they could to revive construction. The River and Harbor Convention held in Chicago in 1847 helped emphasize the expected impact of the completed canal.[67] At the same time, Ogden knew that attention had to be paid to railroads, even if part of the reason for the state's bankruptcy could be tied to its overly ambitious involvement in railroad schemes.[68] One technology was needed to jump-start the city's growth; the other, to carry it into the future.

RAILROADS

Ogden was one of the major promoters of Chicago's first railroad, the Galena and Chicago Union Railroad, which made its inaugural run on October 25, 1848, six months after the canal was completed, when less than ten miles of track had been laid. A locomotive (the *Pioneer*, which arrived in Chicago by boat), a tender, and two cars traveled five miles out of Chicago and returned.[69] Not only would this road shorten the journey between Galena and the East Coast, but it would also attend to the needs of farming communities along its way.[70] Ogden resigned as president of the Galena and Chicago Union in 1851, at least in part because of continued skepticism from a minority of the directors about whether his primary business interest was the railroad or real estate.

The Galena and Chicago Union was the first of many railroads with which Ogden was involved. In 1850 he served as president of the National Railroad Convention in Philadelphia, organized to plan for a transcontinental railroad to the Pacific, a plan Ogden viewed as long-term. In the short term, his intent was to connect Chicago with the most promising markets of the Old Northwest. To that end, he envisaged two additional lines. One would head north; the other, west.

It was also at this time that Ogden, among others, began thinking about railroad consolidation. He merged the two small lines of which he was president with two others to form the Chicago, St. Paul, and Fond du Lac Railroad. Following the Panic of 1857 he reorganized it into the Chicago and North Western Railway Company and served as its president.[71] It was that road that completed the link northward to Green Bay.

As the first step toward completing the western link, Ogden and a longtime associate, New York attorney Samuel Tilden, put together sufficient proxy votes to absorb the Galena and Chicago Union into the Chicago and North Western in 1864.[72] Indeed, with this merger, Ogden controlled 836 miles of midwestern railroads.[73]

Shortly after the Civil War, journalist James Parton published a pamphlet arguing that Ogden and Tilden oversubscribed the road by $20 million and diverted more than $2 million. Ogden was accused of using the railroad company to boost his investments in coal and lumber, but evidently not real estate. Compounding

Parton's concern was the fact that other directors of the Chicago and North Western owned steamboat companies, grain elevators, and other investments that would tie in to the Chicago and North Western. Yet these potential synergies were exactly what Ogden envisaged. The Chicago and North Western completed Ogden's short-term plan of connecting the area north and west to Chicago.

As to the longer-term plan for railroad consolidation, Ogden had helped secure a charter for the 1852 extension of the Michigan Central Railroad from Michigan City, Indiana, to Chicago. This was but one step in a planned direct and continuous line from New York to Chicago, then to the West Coast. In 1853 he became a director of the Chicago and Fort Wayne Railroad. Six years later, as the road's receiver, Ogden combined it with two other roads to form the Chicago, Fort Wayne, and Pittsburgh Railroad, which proved to be a profitable part of the Pennsylvania Railroad system to the east.

To the west, Ogden was elected the first president of the Union Pacific Railroad in September 1862.[74] He held that position for a year until the press of his other business interests contributed to his retirement from the presidency. Indeed, the golden spike was driven in 1869 at a place named after him, Ogden Flats, Utah. Although less heralded as a railroad tycoon than were his eastern and western counterparts, Ogden clearly was a member of their group. But railroads and real estate were only a part of Ogden's involvement in building Chicago. He knew that the hinterland needed to become productive and supply the railroads with needed cargo. He had built a transportation network centered on Chicago—trade routes—which would ensure the city's growth for decades to come.

OTHER VENTURES

Ogden's involvement in pursuits other than real estate and intercity transportation began shortly after his arrival. While he would not have described it in this way, it was clear to him that for a city to become a principal node, a central place, a wide variety of activities were required. To that end, the following is but a partial discussion of the many activities in which he became involved to promote Chicago and enhance its nodality.

LOCAL TRANSPORTATION The Chicago and Michigan City Steamboat Company was formed in 1836 with Ogden as president to provide passenger, freight, and mail services among the four major ports of southern Lake Michigan: St. Joseph, Michigan; Michigan City, Indiana; Chicago; and Milwaukee. Although the firm failed, it did foster growth in shipbuilding and related industries.

In the 1850s Ogden created what became known as Goose Island by digging a canal across a large bend in the North Branch of the Chicago River between Chicago and North Avenues. The additional waterfront sites drew tanneries, breweries, and soap factories. Irish workers moved to the island, which got its name from the geese they kept.[75]

In 1857 Ogden and several partners founded the Chicago Dock and Canal Company. This company developed an industrial area at the east end of the land Ogden owned on the north side of the river. In his day, it was used as a heavy industry and shipping facility near the original McCormick works, but it ultimately fell into disuse. In time, this land became home to the North Pier Terminal, which is located on what is known today as the "Ogden Slip."[76]

Ogden also became involved with the North Chicago Railway Company, a horse railway that was approved in 1859 for operation in the North Division of the city. Five years later, this company linked its tracks to those of the Chicago City Railway, completing horse railway connections between the city's three divisions.[77]

MANUFACTURING As early as 1838 Ogden was a silent partner in a brewery. Because he had no particular knowledge of the industry, he may well have wanted to limit his liability. Whatever the reason, Ogden hired William Lill and William Haas to run the brewery while he attended to the finances. As the only brewery in town, the Lill and Haas enterprise did well. By 1840, in the midst of the panic, Ogden wrote that the brewery was "the only thing that makes money without trouble."[78]

One example of the trouble to which Ogden referred was provided by Isaac Arnold. While head of the Galena and Chicago Union Railroad, Ogden also served as a special partner in the firm of McCagg, Reed, and Co., a lumber firm.[79] Since the railroad had little money, the lumber firm, at his request, provided ties for the road on credit. When Ogden retired from the presidency of the railroad, it still had not paid for the ties. The railroad's new officers refused to pay, arguing that Ogden had contracted with himself. Arnold, acting as attorney for the lumber company, demonstrated that the price charged for the ties was below market and that the financial position of the railroad made it unlikely that the ties could have been obtained in any other way. Continued construction of the railroad would have ceased without access to ties. Arnold obtained judgment for the amount due.[80]

In 1845, Charles Gray and S. P. Warner of Chicago obtained the contract to manufacture the McCormick reaper. It proved so popular that McCormick entered a partnership with Gray, and they began constructing a factory on the north side of the river that was to open in 1848. That year, Gray became financially embarrassed and turned to Ogden for help. Ogden convinced Cyrus McCormick to move his operations from Cincinnati to Chicago to take advantage of Chicago's location and transportation relative to the emerging wheat-growing region to the west. Ogden offered to help finance the move, complete the construction of the Chicago factory, and enter into a sales agency agreement with McCormick.[81] After all, McCormick's presence in Chicago was good for the city and good for Ogden's railroad.[82]

In 1848, W. H. Scoville in partnership with his sons opened the Scoville Iron Works on land supplied by Ogden. The Scoville firm produced freight and flat cars for the Galena and Chicago Union Railroad, the first cars to be built in Chicago. Ultimately, the firm produced passenger cars and locomotives. At that point, the firm was incorporated as the Chicago Locomotive Company with Ogden one of the many stockholders.[83]

In 1856, Ogden purchased two hundred thousand acres of pineland in northern Wisconsin on the Peshtigo River, forty-five miles north of Green Bay, to supply timber to Chicago as his father had supplied Philadelphia.[84] Peshtigo was home to the Menominee and Ho-Chunks. The first sawmill, built in 1838, firmly tied the town to the lumber industry. The northern forests of Wisconsin and Michigan, once home to Indigenous peoples, like eastern forests, became inputs in the construction of urban places. For Ogden, Peshtigo was to play a disquieting role as his business career wound down.

SERVICES As the *Chicago American* noted in 1837, "The benefits resulting from the establishment of literary and scientific institutions in a community are very great."[85] Ogden was elected in 1837 as the first president of Rush Medical College, a position he held for many years. The first such institution in the area, it is discussed in detail in Chapter 6. Because of the financial panic of that year, a building was not opened until 1844; the first annual course of lectures began in December 1843 in rented facilities. There was but one graduate the first year, but the college quickly grew to become one of the city's most important institutions.

Ogden was also involved in founding the first University of Chicago. In 1856, Senator Stephen Douglas offered ten acres of land at Thirty-Fifth Street and Cottage Grove Avenue to the Presbyterian Church for a seminary.[86] When it proved unable to raise the requisite funds, Douglas offered the land to the Baptist Church, which also faced difficulties owing to the Panic of 1857. Rather than reclaim the land, Douglas chose to deed it to the school's trustees so that they could mortgage it and get the funds to complete construction. At the first board meeting, Douglas was named president; Ogden, one of the trustees. When Douglas died in June 1861, Ogden succeeded him as president of the board of trustees and retained the position until he died. Shortly after that first board meeting, in the fall of 1858, the university opened. During the first year, three faculty members taught six students. In short order, the school began training men for medicine and the law. It also offered agricultural education on an experimental farm. The Dearborn Observatory of the Astronomical Society, another recipient of Ogden's largesse, was affiliated with the university. The Baptist Union Theological Seminary began as part of the university but moved to Morgan Park in 1877 following financial problems.[87] Indeed, the university itself closed in 1886 because of its growing debt.[88]

Ogden was one of the twenty-five Chicagoans who formed the Chicago Board of Trade in 1848 to promote Chicago's commerce and to bring order to the city's chaotic grain market. It, too, is discussed in greater detail in a later chapter.[89] The Board of Trade standardized bushel sizes and developed a system for identifying different grades of grain. Official inspectors of fish and provisions were appointed. In addition, it promoted harbor improvements, tolls on the I&M Canal, and a land grant for the Illinois Central Railroad.

From the beginning, the grain trade involved speculation. During the harvest season supplies were plentiful, and prices fell. In the winter supplies were scarce, and prices rose. If the harvest was late, by the time farmers shipped their crop to Chicago, water transportation on the upper Great Lakes might have come to its seasonal end. This meant that much of the grain would not be shipped until the spring. Some farmers believed they were not receiving a fair price for their crop and that paying to ship it for sale in Chicago was a losing proposition. By offering "to arrive" contracts ("futures"), the board provided farmers with a way to negotiate at planting time the price they would receive at harvest time; buyers gained by assuring themselves a supply in advance. Consequently, Chicago became an international market for agricultural commodities.[90]

Ogden was named president of the Chicago Branch of the State Bank of Illinois, and, following the Free Banking Act of 1851, Ogden, Kinzie, and Hubbard, among others, chartered the Illinois Savings Institution in 1857. At its peak, it had $4 million in deposits. Ogden also served as a trustee of the Merchants' Savings, Loan, and Trust Company.[91]

Ogden was one of the incorporators and one of the first vice presidents of the Chicago Historical Society, which was organized in 1856. The society's principal objective was to provide the city with a documentary library, and, within the first fifteen years, it collected more than fifteen thousand volumes.[92] After the fire of 1871, Ogden was one of many who subscribed generously to rebuild the society.

In 1847, Ogden was a delegate from Illinois to the North Western Education Society convention in Milwaukee. This society attempted to establish organizations in each state and groups in every town and county to advance common school education and attract qualified teachers. Ogden was named chairman of the convention and elected president of the society.[93]

In 1844, the *Chicago Democratic Advocate and Commercial Advertiser* was started by two printers, William Ellis and Robert Fergus. It was a weekly paper that lasted for two years. Although it had no nominal editor, many of the leading men of Chicago, including Ogden, contributed editorials.[94]

What became the Chicago Club, a private social club for gentlemen, had its origin in 1861 as the Dearborn Club with Ogden as its president. After struggling for two years because of the war, it closed its doors. For five years the city lacked such a venture, but it essentially reopened as the Chicago Club in 1868 after Ogden had moved to New York.[95]

At best, this is a partial listing of Ogden's many activities in areas other than real estate and intercity railroads. All were part of his vision for a thriving, multidimensional city, and he was involved financially and in executive positions in institutions ranging from the Chicago Nursery and Half-Orphan Asylum to Rosehill and Graceland Cemeteries.

By 1866, Ogden's business interests had become such that he spent much of his time in New York. He purchased and improved a home named Boscobel on a hundred-acre plot on a ridge overlooking the Harlem and Hudson Rivers at Fordham Heights. It was there, on October 8, 1871, that he received word of the fires burning in both Chicago and Peshtigo, Wisconsin. The Great Fire burned Ogden's Chicago home and many of the enterprises in which he had invested. The forested ground to which Ogden had moved thirty-five years earlier was scorched earth.[96]

At the same time, fire destroyed the town of Peshtigo, the site of several of Ogden's lumber companies. More than three hundred died in the Chicago fire, but one thousand died in Peshtigo, many of them friends and employees of Ogden's.

He returned to Chicago on October 10 and spent four days attending to his personal and business affairs in the city. He then traveled north to Peshtigo, where he would spend the next two months rebuilding that city by day and planning the logistics of its renewal by night. It has been estimated that he lost $2 million ($52.4 million today using the CPI) in the two fires.[97]

In February 1875, at age sixty-nine, Ogden married Mary Anna Arnot, a long-time companion, at Boscobel. One reason for the long delay was that Ogden never forgot his first fiancée, Sarah North.[98] He died at Boscobel in August 1877 at age seventy-two.

Following the fire, the new Chicago rewrote its history; none of the four men discussed in this chapter played even a featured role. Beaubien and Hubbard stayed when the fur industry departed. Beaubien was a leader in the city's formative years, then retired to the life of a farmer. Hubbard became involved in many activities and became one of Chicago's most long-lived and celebrated citizens. Wright was a prophet, a man whose vision came close to what Chicago became. Ogden was Chicago's first venture capitalist, a peerless entrepreneur, and an urban booster who put his money behind his boast. As a result of their efforts, Chicago's position was established, trade routes were established, and its nodality was enhanced.

CHAPTER 3

Assembling Trade Routes and Establishing Position

Chicago is a canal town. It grew from a frontier outpost at its incorporation as a town in 1833 to a major city in roughly four decades. Its initial growth was largely a function of geography (the connection of lake and river and the low continental divide), but momentum created by the promise of a canal attracted an energetic entrepreneurial class that contributed to the infant's recuperation from the Panic of 1837. Between 1830 and 1840, Chicago's population increased from 50 to 4,470. The beginning of construction of the I&M Canal before the panic attracted men who hoped to find work on the canal or to speculate on appreciation in land values because of the canal. It was the beginning of many trade routes that would develop on both water and land. Initial railroads were constructed outward from the port created by the lake, river, and canal. As the city's position developed, its nodality increased. So, in the aftermath of the fire, given the critical role Chicago's transportation infrastructure had come to play in the nation's economic life, the city was quickly rebuilt.

The Land Ordinance of 1787, the Northwest Ordinance, divided the Old Northwest (the land west of the Appalachians, north of the Ohio River, and east of the Mississippi River) into three to five states. If there were but three, they would have corresponded to today's Ohio, Michigan and Indiana combined, and Wisconsin and Illinois combined. If there were to be more than three, the north-south dividing line was to be at the bottom of Lake Michigan. This line, a line tangent to the minimum point of a parabola, made little sense because it meant, theoretically, that the two states south of the minimum point would not have access to

Lake Michigan. Consequently, in 1818, when Illinois became a state, its northern boundary was moved approximately sixty miles north.[1] The new boundary was the work of Judge Nathaniel Pope, Illinois's territorial delegate in Washington. On his own initiative, Pope offered an amendment to change Illinois's northern boundary; Congress adopted the change without exception and without recorded debate. His principal objective was to gain a Lake Michigan coastline for Illinois and an outlet for the proposed canal that would connect the Illinois River and Lake Michigan. If the only commercial avenues available to the new state were to be the Mississippi River and its tributaries, then, Pope noted, "There is a possibility that her [Illinois's] commercial relations with the South may become so closely connected that in the event of an attempted dismemberment of the Union, Illinois will cast her lot with the Southern States."[2] It also seems reasonable to surmise that, if canal construction had to be financed without federal government resources, as was true of the Erie Canal, it would be wise to put the entire area benefited by the canal in one state. Hence, Chicago became part of Illinois rather than Wisconsin, as would have been the case had the boundary been drawn as originally legislated. Once the Erie Canal was completed, a steamboat route between Buffalo, New York, and Chicago helped connect the fur-trading village with the East Coast. In 1832 the first steamboat arrived in Chicago carrying troops for the Black Hawk War who were stricken with cholera.[3]

River, Harbor, and Canal

A node's growth necessarily depends on the growth of its transportation and communication facilities. A competitive advantage accrues to the commercial node with the best facilities. Connections between nodes are necessary but not sufficient; there must be contact with productive areas that furnish food and raw materials. For Chicago, the problem was how best to develop trade routes to tap its rich agricultural hinterland and, in return, to furnish the hinterland with the goods it demanded. To this end the canal, the railroad, and the telegraph all became part of Chicago's economy, and, coincidentally, all three began their Chicago operations in 1848 (as did the Chicago Board of Trade). Almost two decades earlier, when boats much larger than a canoe had begun to ply the Great Lakes, steps had been taken to make the Chicago River a viable harbor.

In 1830 there was no harbor on Lake Michigan south of the Manitou Islands. It was customary for ships arriving in Chicago to anchor at least a half mile offshore. The river itself curved around Fort Dearborn and entered the lake several blocks to the south. Before Chicago was incorporated as a town, the river became a federal harbor, and improvement work was begun under the auspices of the Army Corps of Engineers.[4] In 1832 construction began on a lighthouse. A year later the federal government appropriated $25,000 to improve the Chicago harbor. Most of these monies were expended on dredging through the sand to straighten the mouth of the Chicago River.[5] This proved a continuing problem as, within a few years, new sandbars developed to replace the dredged ones. Regular improvements became necessary, but, once past the sandbars, shelter and good harbor facilities were available. By the 1840s lake-going vessels of one hundred tons entered the Chicago River. Chicago became the leading western port on the Great Lakes, the logical end of the line for lake-going ships from the East, a major improvement in its position.

The idea of a canal across the Chicago Portage was brought before Congress by Representative Peter Buell Porter of New York State in 1810, and President James Madison acknowledged its importance in his inaugural address.[6] In 1816 the United States negotiated with the Potawatomi and obtained title to a twenty-mile strip of land between Chicago and Ottawa, Illinois, the navigable water route across the Chicago Portage.[7] Economic location theory predicts that a metropolitan node is most likely to develop at a break-in transport.[8] With the canal tying the river (Illinois) and the lake (Michigan), Chicago would have such a break, which was Dean's position. The site's potential was clear, but it developed slowly.

Shortly after Illinois became a state (1818), one of the first items discussed was a survey of the lands obtained from the Natives. On March 30, 1822, Congress gave Illinois permission to cut a canal through public lands and donated a strip of land for the canal along with an additional ninety feet on each bank. A $10,000 appropriation was approved for the survey. In the following legislative session, the House authorized an inquiry by the Internal Improvements Committee as to the practicality of such a canal.[9] All this encouraged Illinois's governor to hire engineers to visit the Chicago portage and estimate the construction costs of a canal. On Valentine's Day 1823 a bill was passed that created a commission to survey the route, prepare cost estimates, and report to the next legislature.

The commission surveyed five potential routes and estimated the cost of each. The construction plan was analogous to that of the Erie Canal, then still under construction. The commissioners made their report in January 1825, and a few days later the I&M Canal Company, a private venture, was incorporated with a capital stock of $1 million. This company proved unable to sell its stock, however. Consequently, the next legislature annulled the act of incorporation so that no future company would be encumbered by the failures of its predecessor. This was just as well because there were public fears of monopoly, and politicians hoped that federal aid would be forthcoming if the canal were to be a public venture.

To that end, in January 1826 Illinois sent a memorial to the U.S. Congress requesting a further grant of land because fluctuating conditions in the money market prohibited arranging a long-term loan. A year later, on March 2, 1827,

Congress donated alternate sections in strips five miles wide on either bank of the proposed canal. The remaining land was held by the federal government in the hope that an increase in the price of land attributable to the canal would more than cover the value of its donation. It is notable that this land grant has many similarities to land grants that were made to railroads in future years. Alfred T. Andreas in his encyclopedic history of early Chicago was unabashedly enthusiastic in assessing the grant:

> The obtaining of this magnificent land grant made the building of the canal a certainty, and in after time was the means of lifting the State from the slough of financial despair. It made possible and necessary the survey of Chicago Town, and flourishing villages were eventually born along the route of the proposed improvements.[10]

In 1828 a bill was passed that provided for the sale of lots and land, for the appointment of a new set of canal commissioners, and for the start of work. But the only results of this act were the sale of a few lots plus a new survey and cost estimates. The following year, a second state commission was appointed and empowered to raise money by selling lots, making a loan, or other means.

The new survey established that the highest point of elevation along the proposed route between the Chicago River and the Des Plaines River (which becomes the Illinois River at its junction with the Kankakee River) was fourteen feet above the level of Lake Michigan; the average height, ten feet. Thirty-four miles downstream, the level of the Des Plaines was identical to that of Lake Michigan. The plan was to connect Lake Michigan and this point via a deep-cut channel. Downstream, however, the rock was so near the surface that it became evident that the cost would be much greater than originally thought. Even so, the expected benefits still exceeded the re-estimated costs. The higher costs led the Illinois legislature to appoint additional commissioners to see whether the Calumet River could be used as a feeder. These commissioners were also to determine whether a railroad might be a more efficient approach. James William Putnam reports that the commission concluded that a railroad was the preferred alternative, but the Illinois legislature decided to build neither. In March 1833 it repealed the acts of 1829 and 1831 when it learned that the latest cost estimates had increased considerably.[11] At the time Illinois had hardly any money and less credit, so it made little sense to go forward with this second attempt to construct the canal.[12]

On the other hand, by this time the federal government had accumulated a surplus, and discussions about what do to with it had begun. One widely discussed alternative was to divide the money among the states to fund internal improvements. For some this would be a railroad; for Illinois, it was to be a canal and railroads. With the thought that money might be forthcoming, on February 10,

1835, Illinois launched its third attempt to build the I&M Canal. The governor, a staunch canal supporter, was to negotiate a $500,000 loan for construction costs, to issue stock, and to appoint a new board of canal commissioners. The canal was to be deep-cut, its depth to be such that boats with four-foot draughts could pass through it unimpeded. The canal was to be forty-five feet wide at the surface and thirty feet wide at the bottom. Because it would be deep-cut, a supply of water would be drawn directly from Lake Michigan through the South Branch.[13]

It took time, but a loan was arranged in the East.[14] This loan, which assured that construction would finally begin, brought "new life to everything" in Chicago. Property values, already considered high, rose rapidly. When navigation opened on the Great Lakes in the spring of 1836, many people traveled to Chicago ready to engage in land speculation. The effects of available credit and currency were amplified when the U.S. Treasury distributed its surplus to the states.[15]

The new commissioners wanted construction to begin as soon as possible because they felt this would benefit the financing of the project. It soon became clear that the cost of the project was significantly underestimated. The estimate of $4 million proved to be too little to build a canal of the desired dimensions. Consequently, because costs would be larger in any event, the commissioners chose to build an even bigger canal. The new plan called for a deep-cut canal that was sixty feet wide at the surface and thirty-six feet wide at the bottom, with a minimum depth of six feet. Their logic was that the benefits of the bigger canal would exceed the increased construction costs, and that it was likely to be cheaper in the long run to have built such a canal in the first place than having to enlarge the smaller canal when it proved inadequate.[16] Given that East Coast railroads were proving superior to many of the older canals there, this was a remarkable argument.

The commissioners anticipated that construction would begin in the spring of 1837, but little labor was available, and the labor scarcity continued into the summer even after immigrants, many of them Irish, arrived from the eastern United States and Canada (see chapter 6).[17] In addition, the commission's construction plan was under investigation by the Illinois House Committee on Internal Improvements, which believed the plan was beyond the state's financial capability. The claim was that the engineering estimates severely underestimated some expense items and entirely omitted others. The committee's estimate of $13.25 million was half again the revised estimate of the commission. The committee, therefore, recommended that the deep-cut canal be replaced with a shallow-cut one.

The financial situation was another problem. Under the terms of the 1836 act, the full faith of the State of Illinois was placed behind canal stock certificates, and canal bonds were marketable securities. The governor had easily negotiated a loan for $500,000 in 1837 and was authorized to borrow an additional $500,000. With the first installments from September 1836 land sales and the second installment due a year later, the canal's finances seemed secure.

Based on its expected share of the federal surplus, the Illinois General Assembly passed an Internal Improvement Act in 1837. The act incorporated "plans for a system of railroads and river improvements which, together with the canal, would give her [Illinois] an unsurpassed system of transportation and communication."[18] The railroad system, much of which appeared later as the Illinois Central, was to supply the thinly settled western portion of the state with rail services sufficient to meet the needs of the eastern portion. The act also authorized an additional $4 million loan for canal work. These were all a reflection of overly optimistic expectations, given the state's finances. Once the Panic of 1837 began to tighten its grip, both the canal loan and the internal improvement funds failed when the state temporarily lost its credit. The act was repealed.

Work on the canal continued, and, by the fall of 1837, the pace of work was as planned. This despite the fact that Chicago was also in the midst of a building boom, and the canal had to compete for materials and provisions. By the end of 1838 all but twenty-three miles of the canal was under contract, and several sections were at or near completion, even as the panic's grip continued to tighten.[19]

On March 1, 1840, the canal commissioners issued scrip bearing 6 percent interest, payable when the funds became available, because the canal's treasury was depleted. They tried to sell more bonds and land, but sales were small, and payment was often in previously issued canal scrip.[20] Land prices had fallen, and the commission felt that selling the land at a low price was not a good idea. Contractors (e.g., Ogden) recognized what a work cessation implied, so they offered to take $1 million of authorized bonds at par and bear the discount if they had to sell them. The commission accepted, thus allowing construction to continue, albeit at a slower pace, for several months. This was an attempt to buy time for the state legislature to resolve the financial problems. It spent much of the winter of 1840–41 trying, and failing, to find a solution. One problem was that so many states had issued bonds to finance internal improvement projects spawned by the distribution of the federal surplus that the market for that type of security was now severely depressed. By March 1841 the canal's treasury was empty once again.

The failure of the Illinois legislature to generate needed funds was taken to mean it was leaving the canal to its fate. Contractors who were able to abandon the work without undue financial loss did so. When all means of payment to contractors failed at the end of the 1841 work year, construction was suspended except for the contractors who bore their own burden. The following February, when the Bank of Illinois failed, the difference between a completed and uncompleted canal seemed to be the difference between a solvent and insolvent Illinois. What was needed was an additional $3 million, and, while there was consensus that a completed canal would be a godsend, there was general agreement that the state's insolvent condition meant that raising the necessary funds would be impossible.

When Illinois's economy entered the upswing, the canal was the only internal improvement project near its end. Homer Hoyt noted that three groups formed a coalition to see the canal through to completion:

> These were, first, the citizens of Chicago, who fondly expected that the canal would make the city a great emporium; second, the bondholders, who had already sunk their money into the enterprise and who by putting in a little more might recover their entire investment; and, third, the state, which by opening up a profitable market for the products of the Illinois River Valley would enable farmers to pay the taxes that would enable the state to meet its obligations.[21]

The most likely way to complete the job was to reconsider the shallow-cut canal. It was estimated that it would require $3 million more to complete the canal as planned, but only half that to complete a shallow-cut canal. The bondholders, commissioners, and state legislators believed it would be possible to raise the smaller sum on a pledge of the canal lands, future revenues, and the canal itself. In February 1843 the legislature passed an act authorizing the governor to negotiate a new $1.5 million loan and to secure payment by a deed of trust. This satisfied American creditors who subscribed to their portion of the new loan, but foreign creditors were less forthcoming.

The commissioners then agreed that Baring Brothers, a London investment house representing European bondholders, could prepare a report on the canal's financial condition. This was done over the winter of 1843–44. The report found the canal was a "safe financial proposition" and recommended that the European creditors subscribe to their portion of the loan.[22] The report also showed that the total debt borne by the canal as of January 1, 1844, was $5.4 million; the net debt, $4.85 million. The assets included, in addition to the canal, 230,476 acres of land worth $10 million if the canal were to be completed and 3,491 town lots in Chicago, Lockport, Ottawa, and LaSalle worth $1.9 million.[23] It was estimated that waterpower rentals would gross between $75,000 and $100,000 per year and that tolls during the second season of operation would bring $300,000. The first portion of the European loan was due in September 1845.

The 1843 act required that the canal be completed within three years of the time it was turned over to the commissioners in 1845. Throughout that summer, necessary preparations for the resumption of the work took place. Sections that had been preempted by contractors were reassigned to them. New contracts were issued on the remaining sections to the "lowest responsible bidder." Given that two years had passed since the work cessation, many completed sections needed to be restored.

The change from a deep-cut to a shallow-cut canal created a water supply problem that would require several additions. That problem was yet unresolved as the work resumption neared. Engineers at the Chicago Mechanics' Institute recommended in 1843 that water be supplied to the canal by a set of steel pumps designed to lift Chicago River water above the level of the Des Plaines River.[24] After considering alternatives, this plan was adopted as the most effective and least expensive. In addition, a series of locks was necessary to overcome the elevation of the low divide at the Chicago Portage. Three feeders became necessary because a shallow-cut canal could not generate a sufficient flow of water during dry seasons.[25] Although flooding and worker sickness slowed progress, the I&M Canal opened for business in April 1848.

Chicago's commercial potential with a completed canal had been sufficient to draw a significant population while work was under way. The Erie Canal was crucial in this regard. Both its success and the rapid increase in land values along its route gave rise to similar expectations for the I&M Canal. New settlers arrived throughout the 1830s, looking beyond the squalid village of log huts to the large city that would rise when the canal was completed. The I&M Canal became Chicago's first great commercial feeder, an important trade route, if only for a time; its effect on Chicago's commerce was immediate. The canal enabled Chicago to become the dominant node for a large part of the Illinois River valley, which earlier had shipped its agricultural surplus to St. Louis.

The economic development of its hinterland was not the only benefit Chicago received from the canal. Wyatt Winston Belcher commented:

> It was noted that more and more steamers descended the Upper Mississippi to the mouth of the Illinois River, and then turned up that stream with their cargoes to be forwarded to New York *via* Chicago. Every shipment of this kind was a commercial gain for Chicago and represented an equal trade loss for St. Louis.[26]

By 1854 the Rock Island Railroad competed with the I&M Canal along its entire route. Even when the railroad captured the larger share of the traffic, the canal still had the important effect of lowering freight rates on the Chicago–St. Louis route.[27] The expansion of rail facilities in this area accelerated the trends established by the canal and widened the city's effective hinterland. Chicago's position as the transshipment point on this trade route significantly enhanced its nodality.

As Eric Monkkonen writes, despite all that was made of the competition between St. Louis and Chicago for business, immigrants, and railroads, the fact remained that the competition proved a benefit to both, presumably because of the area-wide growth it engendered: "Chicago and St. Louis also needed one another. In the long run, Chicago's port and market benefited St. Louis, even though St. Louis no longer occupied its preeminent frontier position."[28] While that was small consolation for St. Louis, this mutual benefit is especially clear in the interconnected network of farms and towns that grew on the water- and railways connecting the two cities. Those sites benefited from the growth of the two cities, and vice versa. To this day, there is no clear dividing line between the two cities' hinterlands.

Railroads

Before the I&M canal was completed, it was clear from the experience back east that railroads were winning the competition for traffic between the two modes of transportation. Chicago's future depended as much on railroads as on the canal. As we have seen, Ogden began promoting a railroad before the canal was completed. The initial railroads were built as spokes that connected two nodes (e.g., Galena and Chicago).

The relationship between commercial development and transportation lines was observable as the number of railroads—and railroad miles—grew. Previously, the major nodes had been located along water routes. The railroad removed commerce's dependence on waterways; roads could be built almost anywhere to facilitate commerce. The first railroads, however, were the servants of nodal cities located on water. As David Young put it, Chicago's railroads were "built to function as an overland extension of the Great Lakes."[29] Thus, an eastern railroad headed to Chicago had to come up from the bottom end of the lake to the confluence of lake and river, adding several miles to its journey. As spokes were assembled into systems, Chicago became the western terminus for the most important eastern routes and the eastern terminus for the most important western routes. Railroads created the opportunity to trade perishable commodities over longer distances. Finally, the initial railroads left little doubt that they could provide dependable year-round service as opposed to the suspension of water transport caused by summer droughts on the rivers and winter ice on the lakes and rivers. Railroads were not subject to the usual bottlenecks involved in river transport (such as sandbars and rapids). There was little doubt that railroads would bring an ever-widening area's rapidly multiplying commerce to Chicago.[30]

Railroads created opportunities for broadening the hinterlands of cities at critical junctures on the rail network. The area north and west of Chicago could still ship its surplus to Lake Michigan ports for movement by water, but eastward shipment by rail required travel through Chicago. Noted Belcher, "As long as Lake Michigan remained a 'fixed fact,' every railroad or town that was built and every farm that was settled north and west of the city would only increase the trade and prosperity of Chicago."[31] If railroads had become competitive with canals before the completion of the I&M Canal, one suspects that a major city would have developed at the very bottom of the lake, say, at what is now Gary or Michigan

City, Indiana. The confluence of the Chicago River and Lake Michigan would have been far less important. A cost-minimizing rail system would have preferred a straight east-west run. This, however, is not the way the railroad system developed, and, consequently, Chicago retained its role as a transshipment point even for trips made entirely by rail. While much of the traffic moved to the railroad, the competition between canal and railroad constrained freight rates. As the rail technology evolved, the city expanded, but its foci remained at the site dictated by waterborne transportation. The canal that initiated Chicago's economic growth thereby played a significant role in the siting of its railroad network.

The I&M Canal had reversed the flow of goods over much of the Illinois River valley. Railroads had the potential to do the same over a large portion of the upper Mississippi River valley. Many of the important western roads, beginning with the Rock Island Railroad in 1854, utilized the glacial Illinois River valley, the Chicago Outlet, as a place to lay their tracks. Chicagoans were aware of the tie between city and hinterland and were anxious to exploit the city's advantage in railroad construction. The new city did so in spectacular fashion.

Chicagoans felt that it was necessary to expand transport lines for the dual purpose of continuing existing prosperity and providing for future growth. At the most basic level, a growing city needed to obtain greater quantities of foodstuffs. As the canal era gave way to the railroad era, Chicago became a break-in transport (node) between (1) rail and rail, (2) rail and water, and (3) river and lake. Many individual railroads were involved, and several important issues become clear by looking at the history of individual roads—first those headed west, then those coming from the east.

WESTERN RAILROADS

GALENA AND CHICAGO UNION RAILROAD On October 25, 1848, six months after the I&M Canal opened, the Galena and Chicago Union Railroad made its first trip. Less than ten miles of track had been laid, but by January 1850 the road reached Elgin, forty-two miles west of Chicago. The main purpose of this line was to shorten the eastward journey of the lead mined in and around Galena in the northwest corner of Illinois.[32] Rather than travel the length of the Mississippi River and around Florida to New York City or down the Mississippi to the Illinois River and then north to Chicago via the I&M Canal, the railroad would carry it directly to Chicago. It could also carry crops grown and goods produced at either end of its route or along its route. The railroad could seriously alter the commercial situation in the upper Mississippi valley, for it reduced the travel time between nodes and expanded the area of nodal competition.

The road had originally been chartered in 1836, but it soon became a victim of the panic. As the economy began its recovery, the plan once again gained currency. In January 1846 a convention was held at Rockford to discuss reviving the railroad. Chicago interests recognized that there was some potential competition with Milwaukee, so the issue of regional supremacy was at stake. William Ogden did not attend the convention; his interests were represented by William Jones, J. Young Scammon, Isaac Arnold, and Walter Newberry.[33] For the Ogden group, all north-side property owners, also at stake was the fact that economic development on the north side of the Chicago River was not as rapid as on the south side. They believed that this road, and in particular a terminal on the north side, would prove helpful.[34] To that end, Jones went to the convention to report on the negotiations to buy the charter. The delegates passed resolutions favoring the revival of construction. At the time of the convention, Ogden was in New York meeting with the majority stockholder. A month later he was elected president of the revived company. The trustees purchased the charter and authorized the issuance of one thousand shares of stock. The shares were to be $100 each, but they were sold for $2.50 down.

At this juncture, reports McLear, "The directors sought to build the railroad more rapidly than the subscribers could pay."[35] Some skeptical directors accused Ogden of being involved only because of his real estate business, though there were potential spillover benefits to all from a growing Chicago. The skepticism derived from the panic's negative impact on many internal improvement projects, and this made attracting additional investors difficult. Therefore, in 1847, Ogden and Scammon promoted the railroad among those who lived along the proposed route. Many farmers borrowed money to help fund the railroad, confident that it would be superior to the muddy roads.[36] Most farmers could only pay their subscription a little at a time. Regardless, in May 1848, Ogden went east to purchase the necessary materials. In the absence of sufficient cash, Ogden used company stock. By January 1850, when the track reached Elgin, the road began to be profitable, but it was a close call. A year earlier, George Smith, the only Chicago banker in a position to make a loan to the railroad, had refused. He had, however, made a personal loan of $20,000 for a six-month period to Scammon, chair of the directors' committee seeking the loan.[37] Smith's loan assured the first step toward Chicago's becoming the nation's railroad hub. It was local funding, and the determination of men like Ogden and Scammon were responsible for the initial tracks headed west.[38]

ILLINOIS CENTRAL RAILROAD The major problem facing Chicago's railroad promoters was that the most populous area of Illinois, the area to the south and west, was economically tied to other cities, in particular St. Louis. One of the first railroads to be planned in the state was what became the Illinois Central Railroad. As originally conceived, it was to connect the area around Galena in the Upper Mississippi Valley with the area around Cairo in the Lower Mississippi Valley. In between, it would run through the middle of the state. The initial proposal contained no mention of a connection to Chicago. It was marketed as an all-weather alternative to the Upper Mississippi River that would circumvent the navigational hazards; the Lower Mississippi River was open year-round. Chicago's interest in the Illinois Central Railroad had little to do with its stated purpose; Chicagoans hoped it would cut off traffic headed for St. Louis.

A Chicago branch line first appeared in a bill sponsored by Senator Stephen A. Douglas; his proposal for a federal land grant needed backers. With the railroad's southern terminus extended to New Orleans, opposition developed from those who preferred not to promote north-south trade. Douglas and his colleague Senator Sidney Breese, with the assistance of John S. Wright, were able to draw enough backers for the bill to pass Congress in September 1850 by including grants of public land for rights-of-way in Mississippi and Alabama as well as Illinois, and by nurturing the South's desire for stronger economic ties with the emerging Northwest. According to Andreas,

> It was significant that this change secured more backers for the measure, especially in the Northwestern and Middle Western states, where there had been much opposition to the original bill because of its tendency to keep trade moving from the Upper Mississippi toward New Orleans.[39]

The Illinois legislature granted the railroad a charter in 1851, and the entire 704-mile road was completed in September 1856. It had a major effect on the state's development because it was the longest road and passed through the least-settled areas.[40] From Cairo the track came north to Centralia, where one branch headed northwest to Dunleith, near Galena, and the other headed northeast to Chicago. The land along the branch line to Chicago was exceptionally fertile. The Illinois Central mainline had agreements with the principal western railroads, and it brought a large amount of produce into Chicago from these other railroads, although some crops were shipped east on railroads that passed to the south of Chicago. Ironically, although the Illinois Central was built north to south, it made a significant contribution to transforming Midwestern trade to an east-west axis, to tie Chicago and the Midwest to New York City and the East, as its congressional opponents feared and its backers expected.[41]

CHICAGO AND ROCK ISLAND RAILROAD While western railroads were less competitive with one another than were those in the east, they faced a common competitor in the steamboat traffic on the Mississippi River. The first Chicago road to reach the Mississippi was the aforementioned Chicago and Rock Island Railroad. Chartered in 1847 and opened in April 1852, it reached Rock Island, 181 miles to the west, in 1854. The route paralleled the I&M Canal to LaSalle, then headed west. Much of the commerce that came up the Illinois River by steamboat then transferred to the railroad rather than the canal. The loss of this monopoly position is one reason the canal ultimately proved relatively unprofitable. Further, just as the Illinois Central found the southwestern part of the state to be extremely fertile, the Rock Island found the area west of LaSalle to be the same.

One of the more interesting features of the Rock Island story is that, despite its obvious contribution to Chicago, its promoters were not Chicagoans. They were mainly individuals from Rock Island, Illinois, and Davenport, Iowa, on the opposite bank of the Mississippi. Chicagoans foresaw these efforts as the opening of a new area, rich in corn and other grain, that would use Chicago as its market. Their intent was not merely to connect Chicago with the Mississippi but, in fact, to bridge the Mississippi to reduce the cost of bringing eastern goods to Iowa markets. The concept of a bridge was critical. It would extend Chicago's hinterland beyond what could be construed as its natural limits in an era of waterborne commerce.

The first group to consider bridging the river consisted of the backers of the Mississippi and Missouri Railroad, a road that was to run due west from Davenport. Rock Island is directly across the river from Davenport, and a bridge would connect the two roads. With the authorization of the State of Illinois, but without federal sanction, a bridge was constructed between 1853 and 1856. Indeed, the two companies consolidated into the Chicago, Rock Island, and Pacific in 1866. By 1869 its track reached Council Bluffs, Iowa, across the Missouri River from Omaha, the eastern terminus of the Union Pacific Railroad. Once the Missouri was bridged, through rail connections were available from the Atlantic to the Pacific—via Chicago.

Given the bridge's obvious ability to divert even more traffic to an east-west axis, steamboat owners looked for a way to prevent it. They argued that such a bridge required federal authorization since it would introduce a hazard to navigation. There was merit in this argument. In fact, in order to minimize construction costs, the bridge had been built at a narrow point in the river, a point where cross currents and concealed rocks made navigation difficult even in the absence of bridge supports. It was claimed that the bridge pilings were placed so close together that they presented a hazard in a strong wind. But these safety considerations were not the major preoccupation of the steamboat operators. If land-based transport overcame the natural barriers posed by major watercourses, there would be significantly less business for steamboats. The competition between canal and railroad provided a clear set of expectations as to what would happen in the competition between steamboat and railroad.

The City of St. Louis, which opposed the bridge for reasons similar to the steamboat industry's, led the legal fight. As stated by the St. Louis Chamber of Commerce and quoted by Belcher:

> The railroads reaching the east bank of the Mississippi . . . are clamoring for bridges, but the firm stand taken by St. Louis has deterred them from doing anything more than making their normal commencement which was rendered necessary to save their State charters. If we are beaten in this suit . . . two years will not pass . . . before we shall see the Mississippi bridged in at least three additional places, and perhaps more. A half dozen bridges in the rapid current and changing channel of this river, would render navigation extremely hazardous . . . and the commercial position of St. Louis . . . would be counted among the things that were. The city always has been and must necessarily remain dependent upon her rivers for the bulk of her trade, and it well becomes her to watch with a jealous eye all attempts to encroach thereon. We do not propose to decry the importance of railroads, nor shut our eyes to the immense benefit they have been to the country; but we cannot consent that our noble rivers should be obstructed just when and where it may suit the interest of those corporations.[42]

Chicago, on the other hand, argued that St. Louis was defending an outmoded technology:

> We tell St. Louis once and for all that not Chicago but the genius of the age demands the bridging of the Mississippi and the Missouri and the removal of every obstacle to the great central railway of the continent. It must soon bind the states of the Atlantic and the Pacific in one brotherhood forever. . . . Chicago offers her best wishes to her anxious sister, and asks only a fair field and an honorable struggle for the prize of commercial supremacy.[43]

The attempt to enjoin construction of a Mississippi River bridge failed. Shortly after the bridge was completed, a steamboat collided with one of the pilings, caught on fire, and was lost. The boat's owners filed a damage suit, but the suit was settled in favor of the bridge company. Nonetheless, following the Civil War, in 1872, the federal government built a new bridge at a less hazardous site; the old bridge was razed.

OTHER WESTERN RAILROADS The Chicago, Burlington, and Quincy and the Chicago and Alton Railroads were also active in tapping the Mississippi valley. The former was tied to the ownership of the Michigan Central; the latter erected the most direct line to St. Louis.

To the north and west of the city were the Chicago, Milwaukee, and St. Paul and the Chicago, St. Paul, and Fond du Lac Railroads.[44] The former started as a short line out of Milwaukee with the hope that it would allow Milwaukee to effectively compete with Chicago. The latter was Chicago promoters' attempt to counter the former; it failed in the Panic of 1857 and was ultimately completed by the Chicago and Northwestern Railroad, a consolidation of the Galena and Chicago Union and several other distinct Illinois, Wisconsin, Iowa, and Michigan railroads controlled by William B. Ogden and his partners.

EASTERN RAILROADS

MICHIGAN CENTRAL AND MICHIGAN SOUTHERN RAILROADS Eastern railroads were extending their tracks to Chicago at the same time as the western roads were being built. Competition between two of the roads created several interesting problems that had to be resolved. The Michigan Central from Detroit and the Michigan Southern and Northern Indiana from Toledo were extending their tracks to the Illinois-Indiana line in close proximity to the lake. Each was desirous of becoming the first eastern railroad to enter Chicago. State policy, however, prohibited granting charters to out-of-state companies, a simple extension of the idea that these railroads were spokes emanating from a city.[45] Time and effort would be saved if an arrangement could be made with a railroad that Illinois had chartered. Consequently, the Michigan Central entered into an agreement with the Illinois Central, and, similarly, the Michigan Southern entered into an agreement with the Rock Island Railroad. The surveyed plan was to bring the Michigan Central and Illinois Central together near Lake Calumet's western shore, then run due north to the Chicago River to a point where there were docks, grain elevators, and connections with the Galena and Chicago Union. The Michigan Southern–Rock Island group, however, owned much of the land involved in their rival's surveyed plan. No such obstacle appeared along the lakeshore.[46] When the lakeshore plan became the recommended alternative for the Michigan Central and Illinois Central, it contributed to a bitter local controversy.

Residents of the North and West divisions of Chicago, seeking relief from the tax burden incident to maintaining the lakeshore, allied themselves with the Michigan Central–Illinois Central group to silence the protests of wealthy South-division landowners along Michigan Avenue, who feared depreciation of their property and sought to defend the scenic beauty of the shore.[47]

Not until 1851 did the city and state governments accede to the Illinois Central's request. In exchange for building a breakwater that would protect property along Michigan Avenue from waves, the railroad was given the right to enter the city on a trestle in the lake.[48] That is to say, the Illinois Central tracks were roughly where they are today, but in those days the Lake Michigan shoreline extended to Michigan Avenue.[49] The railroad terminus was on a spit of land near the river's mouth that was once part of the Fort Dearborn reservation.

The competition between the two eastern railroads led to a second bitter fight. Because the Michigan Southern arrived to the west of the downtown area and the Michigan Central to the east, the two railroads had to cross. The

Fig. 8. A bird's-eye view of Chicago from Lake Michigan. (Chicago History Museum, ICHi-005656.)

right of one railroad to cross the tracks of another was not yet established in law, but that right emerged as a result of an accident on April 25, 1853, at what is now known as "Grand Crossing." The Michigan Southern attempted to get an injunction to prevent the Michigan Central from crossing its tracks. Throughout the time when its request was pending, both roads ran as if the other did not exist, passing the crossing at full speed. On the day of the inevitable collision, eighteen people were killed and another forty were injured. Because the trains ran at street level, it is not clear whether all the victims were on the trains. Rules regarding train crossings were quickly promulgated. Finally, the fact the Michigan Central and the Michigan Southern initially competed against one another and with Great Lakes steamboat routes meant that rates were lower than if there were only one route. Later the two roads would become part of the New York Central Railroad system. All this enhanced Chicago's position and nodality.[50]

OTHER EASTERN RAILROADS The other major eastern railroad was the Pittsburgh, Fort Wayne, and Chicago, formed by the merger of three separate lines in 1856; the first through train between Pittsburgh and Chicago ran two years later. At Pittsburgh, there was a connection with the Pennsylvania Railroad. After the Civil War, when the Pennsylvania gained control of the Pittsburgh, Cincinnati, and St. Louis Railroad, a parallel route, the Pittsburgh, Fort Wayne, and Chicago, signed a 999-year lease with its former rival.[51]

All the railroads discussed, and others that weren't, created new trade routes or enhanced old ones that centered on Chicago.[52] Even where existing water routes were located, the railroad decreased the amount of time goods were in transit, which had the effect of widening Chicago's market. That these railroads were initially built as spokes out of the city enhanced its position and its nodality. And it should not be forgotten that the center point was not defined by the railroads, but by the canal.

The Telegraph

The first telegram received in Chicago was sent from Milwaukee on January 15, 1848. A connection with Michigan City, Indiana, was made late that same month. The first through telegram from the East was received on April 6, 1848. Competing lines soon expanded the network, putting Chicago in contact with many cities. Expansion into the hinterland tied rural communities ever more closely to Chicago. The price of a telegraphic message on the Chicago–Milwaukee wire was twenty-five cents for the first ten words and two cents per additional word, a common charge for a message sent less than one hundred miles. Transmissions over longer distances were priced correspondingly higher: A twenty-word message on the Chicago–New York route was approximately $2. Such prices generally limited the use of the telegraph, particularly the long-distance wire, to business and news.[53] Telegraph connections between North America and Europe were first established in 1858, but reliable service was not available until 1866.

In the opposite direction, the line to San Francisco was completed in 1861. Shortly thereafter Chicago was made the eastern terminus of the transcontinental line. Thus, the telegraph, like the steamboats, the canal, and the railroads, enhanced Chicago's nodal significance and contributed to the agglomeration of commercial activities in the city. In 1871 the telegraph carried news of the Great Chicago Fire quickly to most of North America and Europe.

The main railroad network centered at Chicago was relatively complete by 1857. This network combined with the I&M Canal and the Great Lakes–Erie Canal route to shift the major midwestern trade route from St. Louis and the South to Chicago and the East. What remained was the consolidation of existing roads into the large rail systems that ran between Chicago and the Atlantic Coast and between Chicago and the Pacific Coast. In particular, the railroads greatly facilitated immigration through Chicago to the West. No longer was westward travel limited to the times of the year when the stagecoach paths were dry or when the upper Great Lakes were free of ice. Passenger traffic data from 1856 suggest that westbound passengers outnumbered eastbound by more than 150,000. The westbound traffic alone was estimated to be 3.5 million passengers. The gross earnings of Chicago-centered railroads increased from approximately $40,000 in 1851 to approximately $18.6 million in 1857. As Belcher observed, "The effect of Chicago was electrifying: within a single decade it ceased to be a frontier town and became a great mart of trade."[54] It is interesting to note that while Chicago became the principal midwestern node primarily because of the railroads, Chicago "in her corporate capacity . . . never invested a dollar in railways or loaned her credit in any one instance to them."[55]

Timothy Mahoney in his study of midwestern river towns downplayed the rivalry and emphasized that all benefited from these developments. He observed that the railroad network c. 1858 and the shifts in production patterns

> should not, however, be taken as evidence that one integrated regional urban economic system centered at a new entrepôt (Chicago) simply moved in and replaced the old system. Such a description would oversimplify the economic confusion caused by such intersections. Alongside Chicago merchants in the towns along the upper [Mississippi] river were also merchants from Cincinnati, New York, and even Boston, each trying to establish for their cities a foothold in a market in which they once had, or would like to have, direct contacts.[56]

By 1858, with the new transportation infrastructure in place, the competition among those merchants was enhanced, and Chicago grew because of that competition.

CHAPTER 4

How Chicago Grew

The impact of Chicago's expanding trade routes on its economic growth is documented quite clearly in the statistical record. The city's nodality, in addition to its growth and development, correlates highly with the infrastructure expansion discussed in chapter 3. That the city's position grew stronger can be inferred from the growth that the record reveals. In this chapter we will explore that record as well as the three largest industries to emerge before the fire: grain, meat, and lumber. That they all should involve primary production (agriculture, fishing, forestry, and mining) is no surprise.

The Commercial Data

Before 1848 farmers sent their surplus to Chicago via wagons or unimproved waterways. Chicago was a net importer throughout these years. The import and export data shown in table 4.1 suggest that the city's commerce grew faster than its population. Between 1836 and 1847 population more than quadrupled, while imports increased slightly more than eightfold. Exports increased by a factor of ten between 1840 and 1847 though they were practically nonexistent before 1840.

The composition of Chicago's leading pre-canal exports, given in table 4.2, reveals the tributary area's growth and the variety of agricultural products for which Chicago provided a market. Such growth is quite remarkable when it is recalled that it was aided not by canal or railroad but only by expectations of their impact once completed.

Table 4.1. Chicago's trade balance before 1848

Year	Population	Imports	Exports	Balance
1836	3,820	$325,204	$1,001	$324,203
1837	4,170	373,677	11,065	362,612
1838	4,000	579,175	16,045	563,130
1839	4,200	630,980	38,843	600,137
1840	4,470	562,106	228,636	333,470
1841	5,000	564,348	348,862	215,486
1842	6,000	664,348	659,305	5,043
1843	7,589	971,850	682,211	289,639
1844	8,000	1,686,416	785,504	900,913
1845	12,088	2,043,446	1,543,520	499,926
1846	14,169	2,027,150	1,813,468	213,682
1847	16,859	2,641,853	2,296,299	345,589

Sources: Yearly population—Hoyt, *One Hundred Years of Land Values*, 44n; trade balance data—Judge Jesse B. Thomas's statistics, cited in Fergus, *Chicago River and Harbor Convention*, 184.

Table 4.2. Composition of exports before 1848

Year	Wheat (bu.)	Flour (bbl.)	Beef & Pork (bbl.)	Wool (lbs.)
1842	586,907	2,920	16,209	1,500
1843	628,967	10,786	21,492	22,050
1844	801,891	6,320	14,938	96,635
1845	956,860	13,752	13,268	216,616
1846	1,459,594	28,045	31,224	281,222
1847	1,974,304	32,538	48,920	411,488

Source: Judge Jesse B. Thomas's statistics, cited in Fergus, *Chicago River and Harbor Convention*, 184.

Once they were completed, Chicago's growth accelerated. The population of the area flanking the I&M Canal, which had grown from a few hundred in 1830 to 30,000 in 1840 and 81,000 in 1850, reached 171,000 in 1855, more than doubling in five years. Between 1848 and 1854 Chicago's population more than tripled, from 20,023 in 1848 to 65,872 in 1854.[1] Chicago's trade increased concomitantly over the course of those years. According to Putnam: "The grain exports grew from 3,001,740 bushels to 13,132,501 bushels, the shipment of corn alone increasing from 550,460 bushels to 4,837,890 bushels."[2] By 1851 the value of exports increased 233 percent over its 1847 level; the value of imports, about 225 percent. The excess of imports can be explained by the fact that Chicago itself had become the major market of this rapidly growing area. Although the I&M Canal and the first railroads had greatly expanded the city's hinterland, especially when one considers the reach of the upper Mississippi River, the node was its own best customer.

Owing to conscientious record keeping, in particular the annual reports of the Chicago Board of Trade, there exist substantial data attesting to Chicago's commercial growth. The yearly receipts and shipments of selected items for four distinctive years are displayed in tables 4.3 through 4.6. These figures show the commerce carried on Lake Michigan, the I&M Canal, and Chicago's expanding railroad network, divided between eastern and western railroads. Remember that Chicago was the western terminus for eastern railroads and the eastern terminus for western railroads. These tables report the vast majority of the trade which Chicago handled. Only the relatively insignificant quantities transported by wagon and other such conveyances are omitted from this analysis.

The four selected years represent four distinct periods in Chicago's development before the Great Fire.[3] The I&M Canal was in full operation by 1852 (table 4.3); thus, 1852 can be said to be representative of the pre-railroad years even though some data for the Galena and Chicago Union and a few other western railroads were reported. By 1859 (table 4.4) the railroad network was established and actively competing with the other transport modes; this represents Chicago's transport network on the eve of the Civil War. The years 1864–65, near the war's end, demonstrate what effect, if any, the war had on Chicago's commerce (table 4.5). Chicago was fortunate to be geographically removed from the battles, but its firms increased production for the war effort although a significant proportion of its labor force joined the Union Army. The postwar economy was in a business cycle expansion in 1871 (table 4.6). Although the Panic of 1873 would mark the national peak, the Great Fire of October 1871 marked Chicago's peak as well as marking the end of an era. Chicago rebuilt and resumed its growth, but industrial relocation turned the city away from the port and toward the railroad. Thus, 1871 represents Chicago's commerce in the final year of an era that began in 1848. Together, these four years tell a remarkable story about Chicago's commercial and industrial growth.

As expected, the important items in Chicago's commerce in the four selected years are principally agricultural, in particular grains. Cattle, hogs, fresh and cured meats, hides, and wool are among the products that reflect the development of Chicago's packinghouses and subsidiary industries. Coal was Chicago's primary fuel; lumber, its primary building material. The merchandise and sundries category leads directly to some consideration of Chicago's industrial function. This category includes groceries, hardware, and dry goods, as well as larger items. To the extent that these items were produced externally, Chicago's function was solely commercial. If some were produced internally, Chicago's role was both commercial and industrial. William Dean suggested that an industrial agglomeration would be attracted to the site of an existing commercial agglomeration. If true, one would expect an excess of goods received in the earlier years, reflecting a commercial function only, and an excess of goods shipped (or at least a smaller excess of goods received) in the later years, reflecting the city's increased internal production and an increasing industrial function.

Table 4.3. Receipts and Shipments of Goods in Chicago, 1852

		Receipts				Shipments		
		Lake	Canal	Railroads (western)		Lake	Canal	Railroads (western)
Barley	bu.	1,687	8,785	90,248	bu.	70,818	508	
Corn	bu.		1,810,830	671,961	bu.	2,737,011		
Oats	bu.		833,703	674,941	bu.	2,030,317		
Wheat	bu.	129,251	108,597	504,996	bu.	635,196	807	
Flour	bbl.	2,857	1,846	44,316	bbl.	61,196	2,901	
Wool	lbs.		525,632	244,662	lbs.	920,113		
Hides	lbs.	11,000	887,318	396,312	lbs.	47,875	40	
Hogs, live	no.	280			no.	4,508		
Hogs, dressed	lbs.		86,800	10,881,510	lbs.			
Beef	bbl.	11	1,178		bbl.	49,856	175	
Pork	bbl.	960	2,310		bbl.	9,938	38	
Cured meats	lbs.	3,300	303,576	1,836,084				
Lard	lbs.		67,793		bbl. & kgs.	4,638		
Butter	pkgs.	866	2,818	9,587	pkgs.	9,062	90	
Salt	bbl.	91,674			bbl.	4,259	27,457	22,248
Salt	tons	185			sacks		402,746	
Sugar	tons		1,604		tons		384	
Molasses	lbs.		746,564		lbs.		254,000	
Whiskey	bbl.	1,783		5,658	bbl.	14,021	2,868	
Lumber	feet	149,419,482	163,548	759,894	feet		49,095,181	21,645,090
Merchandise & sundries	lbs.	8,892,000	408,000	1,962,000	lbs.	6,528[a]	14,477,564	34,061,600
Agricultural implements	tons		72		tons		274	
Iron	bdls. & bars	122,555	5,100					
Iron	lbs.	32,336,000			lbs.	138,000	20,146,000	3,936,000
Coal	tons	42,933	3,310		tons		196	1,245
Lead	lbs.	11,323	642,027	715,300	lbs.	2,036,000	2,000	

Sources: *The Daily Democratic Press, Annual Review, 1852*, adapted from Pierce, *History of Chicago*, 2:492; Chicago Board of Trade, *Second Annual Report*, 83–104, adapted from Pierce, *History of Chicago*, 2:493–94.

[a]This figure is in pkgs.

Table 4.4. Receipts and Shipments of Goods in Chicago, 1859

		Receipts				Shipments			
		Lake	Canal	Railroads		Lake	Canal	Railroads	
				Eastern	Western			Eastern	Western
Barley	bu.	25,198	26,068	832	599,640	380,364		90,040	12,817
Corn	bu.	5,146	1,949,187	31,477	3,416,060	3,967,852		356,233	25,275
Oats	bu.	9,472	405,297	9,419	933,508	989,586	7,830	133,918	54,369
Wheat	bu.	2,638	453,059	76,847	7,428,222	6,764,695	35,088	301,507	65,408
Flour	bbl.	5,456	45,779	32,202	642,894	365,309	54	306,523	14,465
Cotton	lbs.				5,113,630	80,000		1,190,360	
Wool	lbs.	9,000		662	746,557	106,900		147,759	
Hides	lbs.	91,716	140,548	259,780	12,193,402	4,382,022		11,930,042	101,256
Cattle	no.	9		2,159	78,535	1,005		34,591	1,990
Hogs, live	no.	4		4,601	184,070	88		85,821	1,345
Hogs, dressed	no.			5,341	77,192			22,392	599
Cured meats	lbs.		714,502	80,143	7,147,795	3,180[a]		9,854,557	29,256
Pork	bbl.	87	6,413	90	17,943	21,430	31	60,023	10,734
Beef	bbl.	166	533	869	4,655	51,331		65,881	4,557
Lard	lbs.		1,311,570	11,140	2,593,541	1,410,514		4,030,424	332,007
Butter	pkgs.	89,300	41,257	384,820	942,279	1,395[b]		232,974	126,360
Salt	sacks							17,175	
Salt	bbl.	316,291				7,058	17,418		216,196
Sugar	hhds.	837			15,151	423	13,456[c]		5,529,389
Sugar	bbl.	683	1,066,344[c]		7,726	189			5,303
Molasses	bbl.	783	102,650[c]		5,296	147	200[c]		7,030
Liquors	bbl.	337	1,236	2,083	27,475	11,369	67	11,212	12,382
Lumber	ft.	297,438,000		6,146,148	101,840	698,000	64,824,186	3,250,795	162,367,408
Merch. & sundries	lbs.	79,104,000	208,509	557,584,960	83,850,041	6,156,000	865,312	37,351,774	315,673,228
Iron & nails	lbs.	27,344,000			214,526		39,787	1,097,189	5,486,404
Pig iron	tons	89,034[d]			8	1,571			12,135
Iron	lbs.		187,332		4,816,053	6,818,000	451,081	25,100	47,663,018
Lead	lbs.		127,083		14,224,096	6,666,690		1,654,750	413,307
Coal	tons	111,506	7,932		11,766	158	1,317	565	17,848

Source: Chicago Board of Trade, *Second Annual Report, 1859*, 83–104, adapted from Pierce, *History of Chicago*, 2:493–94.

[a] This figure is in bbls.

[b] This figure is in kegs.

[c] This figure is in lbs.

[d] This figure is in bars.

Table 4.5. Receipts and Shipments of Goods in Chicago, 1864–65

		Receipts				Shipments			
		Lake	Canal	Railroads		Lake	Canal	Railroads	
				Eastern	Western			Eastern	Western
Barley	bu.		26,741	845	570,284	173,425	2,588	34,359	117,026
Corn	bu.		4,310,864	13,540	8,810,936	11,993,475	48,760	615,577	82,231
Oats	bu.		2,015,125	7,710	14,352,516	12,098,000	647,525	3,023,164	702,612
Wheat	bu.	22,861	404,639	329,336	10,085,326	9,983,567	93,067	116,075	56,619
Flour	bbl.	12,414	84,715	38,242	1,033,953	1,034,793	1,133	209,917	41,702
Cotton	lbs.				815,280	13[a]		5,187,338	
Wool	lbs.	49,000	23,950	35,801	5,152,685	1,786,500		4,987,790	15,040
Hides	lbs.	113,625	23,820	606,521	19,313,659	10,205,700	200	17,062,980	387,921
Cattle	no.	103		2,499	306,334	397		222,462	39,587
Hogs, live	no.	13		26,786	1,243,538	690		569,799	10,071
Hogs, dressed	no.			139,701	129,585			56,001	786
Cured meats	lbs.		1,097,924	5,700	13,857,253	3,651,500	62,910	46,263,132	77,750
Pork	bbl.		9,756	49	31,434	106,935	65	171,166	32,373
Beef	bbl.		521	45	8,648	91,131	2,015	40,028	7,453
Lard	lbs.		987,835	1,700	12,270,693	10,183,500		31,791,534	367,936
Butter	pkgs.		17,825	754,193	8,800,017	1,869,000	3,479	3,596,211	458,379
Salt	sacks	30,404			2,203		10,080		20,887
Salt	bbl.	675,649	54	2,551	38		32,500	12,360	438,583
Sugar	hhds.	7,131	300[b]				24,937	565,203	
Sugar	bbl.	51,517							4,721
Molasses	bbl.	14,950	900[b]				800		
Liquors	bbl.	9,985[c]	9,696	4,951	107,385	43,990	69	75,711	15,139
Lumber	feet	480,165,000	695,076	16,886,391	3,845,939	599,000	53,612,045	8,613,576	209,671,958
Merch. & sundries	lbs.		42,516	181,222,385	62,740,626		469,783	69,578,954	33,063,664
Iron & nails	lbs.	18,341[d]				680			
RR iron	bars	97,132				1,017			
Iron	lbs.	42,478,000	3,044,832	70,243,932		306,000	407,990	9,368,677	6,263,376
Lead	lbs.			2,700	10,696,378	3,265,125		3,428,968	119,549
Coal	tons	251,038	28,244	5,491	38,491		1,488	1,808	15,799

Source: Chicago Board of Trade, *Seventh Annual Report, 1864–65*, 26, 48, 50, 57, 65, 74–104, adapted from Pierce, *History of Chicago*, 2:495–96.
[a] This figure is in bales.
[b] This figure is in lbs.
[c] This figure is in casks.
[d] This figure is in bdls.

Table 4.6. Receipts and Shipments of Goods in Chicago, 1871

		Receipts				Shipments			
		Lake	Canal	Railroads		Lake	Canal	Railroads	
				Eastern	Western			Eastern	Western
Barley	bu.		160	3,080	4,060,410	1,397,048		1,295,293	215,772
Corn	bu.		5,521,143	153,748	35,405,118	34,200,876		2,435,225	79,934
Oats	bu.	1,750	1,128,086	142,098	13,253,080	8,797,599		3,312,421	41,227
Wheat	bu.	77,540	11,289	99,216	14,203,861	12,120,923		576,468	110,108
Flour	bbl.	47,673	13,586	33,622	1,317,296	488,705	97,950	694,274	102,811
Cotton	lbs.				2,399,000		1,784	2,267,300	
Wool	lbs.	194,100	5,661	34,904	26,791,956	174,700		23,909,660	266,810
Hides	lbs.	203,680	4,382	1,756,806	23,061,166	1,783,240		19,769,744	909,910
Cattle	no.			8,425	524,534			370,426	31,501
Hogs, live	no.			65,308	2,295,911			1,159,078	3,208
Hogs, dressed	no.			9,539	262,927			167,684	1,058
Cured meats	lbs.			135,022	30,068,596	155,600		155,759,074	11,760,386
Pork	bbl.	127		527	68,295	34,207		90,869	24,646
Beef	bbl.	50		13	53,239	5,603		83,235	614
Lard	lbs.			127,549	16,535,339	384,550		58,936,122	1,709,181
Butter	pkgs.	1,093,795	515	510,446	9,126,696	528,330		9,790,064	710,974
Salt	sacks	668,410		19,354		4,778			
Salt	bbl.				1,025		11,536	6,641	427,183
Sugar	hhds.				11,666				
Sugar	bbl.								45,034
Molasses	bbl.			185,989	5,137		9,990[a]		3,483
Liquors	bbl.			37,216	83,753			126,606	44,425
Lumber	feet	984,758,000	62,605	43,112,200	11,395,570	5,993,000	37,421,522	120,003,466	397,376,628
	miles	186,507	12	8,165	2,158	1,135	7,087	22,728	75,261
Merch. and sundries	lbs.		762,592	847,761,388	368,867,023		201,791	293,993,569	1,176,800,616
Iron & nails	lbs.			281,448,439	5,047,674		17,950	16,250,643	576,830
Pig iron	tons			14,291	8,268			2,739	39,660
Iron	lbs.		932,273				1,122,825		192,596,139
Lead	lbs.			1,365,189	12,910,586			5,804,551	190,100
Coal	tons	515,253	4,176	186,356	373,945		2,890	3,083	191,031
Agricultural implements	lbs.		2,400	14,777,635	4,642,481		443,555	2,241,815	39,666,739

Source: Chicago Board of Trade, Fourteenth Annual Report, 1871, 86–109, adapted from Pierce, History of Chicago, 2:497–98.

[a] This figure is in lbs.

AN OVERVIEW BY CARRIER BY YEAR

In each year, the area's grain surplus was exported eastward via Lake Michigan. The railroads made incursions into this trade, and by 1871 most of the flour left Chicago by rail. Meat and byproducts such as hides and wool were initially shipped on the lake, but the railroad was preeminent as early as 1859. By 1871 the share of this traffic shipped on lake vessels was inconsequential. Lake boats brought lumber and, to a lesser extent, coal westward. The 1871 lumber receipts reflect the fact that it was easier for the lumber towns of Michigan and Wisconsin to ship their wares via the lake than by rail. On the other hand, a majority of the coal received in Chicago arrived by rail. Lumber and coal shipped from Chicago left by rail. Receipts for 1852 indicate that all the iron and a majority of the merchandise and sundries arrived via the lake; 1852 shipments indicate most of the lead departed via the lake. These patterns hold true in 1859, but the railroads greatly increased their share of merchandise and sundries receipts. By 1864–65 the largest share of iron arrived by rail, and by 1871 none of the iron received in Chicago arrived via the lake. No merchandise and sundries were reported to have arrived by lake in the last two selected years. Some lead was shipped east via the lake in 1864–65, but in 1871 it was all handled by rail.

Increasingly large quantities of grain, lumber, and coal were transported on the lake each year, allowing for the large wartime oats and flour shipments in 1864–65. The grain shipments are indicative of Chicago's growing commerce; the lumber and coal receipts reveal growth in the city's physical dimensions as well as its commerce (and perhaps even its industry). The quantity of beef and pork shipped by the lake route increased through 1864–65, then rail was used. These figures are indicative of the growth of Chicago's packing industry. It is reasonable to expect that many of these shipments were headed for the mill towns on Lake Michigan, given the perishability of fresh meat. The other items are goods one expects will be shipped by water, that is, nonperishable goods with high bulk-to-value ratios.

As expected, the I&M Canal did not fare well in competition with the railroads. By 1871 the canal transported northward significant shares of only corn and oats and southward significant shares of only lumber and coal. As with commodities shipped via the lake, these are goods one expects to be moved by water. To the extent that corn and oats were the principal crops of the Illinois River valley, and lumber and coal were the building and heating materials demanded by valley residents, the canal continued to perform its historic role throughout the period, a role on which the railroads consistently encroached. Comparable data are not available for the railroad traffic generated in the same exact area, but the likely pattern is self-evident. Though not directly comparable, the case of sugar and molasses is illustrative. Shortly after the canal opened, sugar and molasses were shipped eastward from Louisiana via the canal; this was more efficient than the old water route around Florida. By 1871 the sugar and molasses received in Chicago arrived from the South (or from the East!) via rail. The small amount of sugar and molasses still carried on the I&M Canal was carried southward!

The railroad network grew tremendously in these years, extending its influence in all directions. The railroads quickly captured the more valuable and perishable commodities. At an early date the railroads became the primary carrier of merchandise and sundries because of their generally smaller size and greater value per volume. Turning to the livestock industry, the initial shipments to the East Coast were either live animals or cured meats; fresh meat was too perishable to make a long trip. Shipping live animals via rail was superior to shipping via water because the greater variability of conditions aboard a ship increased the risk of bruising the animals and reducing their value as fresh meat. On the railroad, animals could be unloaded and loaded at various points along the way and given food and water. Shipping cured meats via rail was faster. Shortly after the fire, Gustavus Swift introduced refrigerator cars, enabling Chicago packers to ship fresh meat all the way to the East Coast. The data reflect these notions; in almost every case there is an across-the-board increase in receipts and shipments for each item. As such, the data mirror both the growth of rail facilities in Chicago and its hinterland and the growth of Chicago's commercial agglomeration. Given that such items as reapers and meat (as opposed to live animals) were being shipped, the growth of Chicago's industrial function is also revealed.

AN AGGREGATE VIEW

Table 4.7 aggregates the receipts and shipments information in each of the four preceding tables as well as the balance of trade (receipts minus shipments). Table 4.8 presents figures for the growth rates of receipts and shipments. For almost every item both receipts and shipments grew substantially throughout the four selected years. The figures for 1871 are typically many times those of 1852. These results give a clear indication of Chicago's commercial growth and development plus the beginnings of its industrial growth. Simultaneously, for most items, the size of the difference between receipts and shipments also grew over the period. This difference admits of several possible interpretations. Where receipts exceed shipments, consumption within the city probably was growing, reflecting the city's growing population. Where shipments exceed receipts, production within the city probably was increasing. This argument abstracts from the amount of an item inventoried or shipped from storage in any given year, but in general these quantities are a small proportion of the total and tend to cancel each other. The mere presence of inventories argues for the presence of a developed commercial function. Thus, the overall picture provided by these two tables is that of a city that was growing with respect to both its commercial and its industrial agglomerations.

In general, the grains behaved as one would expect, with receipts and shipments increasing over time as the hinterland developed.[4] The excess of receipts over shipments grew because Chicago was a net consumer of grains. The balances shown in table 4.7 for 1852 are underestimated. Receipts for that year actually contained a significant amount of grain (in comparison to the other three years) that had been transported by wagon and were not included in the tabulated figures. As noted, most grains were shipped eastward via Lake Michigan and would be included in the tabulation of shipments.

Thus, the excess of shipments over receipts for corn, oats, and flour in 1852 is surprising. The Civil War years were abnormal as well. The area's grain production was greater in absolute terms; receipts at Chicago were larger in 1864–65 than in 1859, but shipments were a larger proportion of receipts than the trend would suggest. Oats and flour both report an excess of shipments over receipts. Barley shipments in the war years were less than in 1859, but this may reflect the growth of Chicago's brewing industry.

Over the entire period receipts and shipments of barley, oats, and flour all grew at a greater rate than Chicago's population (9.383 percent annually). The greater growth of shipments indicates the growth of Chicago's commercial function. The growth of production in the city's hinterland was extremely rapid, much faster than the growth of demand within the city, with the result that shipments were an increasing percentage of receipts. Corn exhibited a similar pattern but with growth rates less than that of population. This may reflect the fact that much of the corn grown in Chicago's hinterland was used for animal feed and arrived in the city in the form of livestock. Wheat demonstrated the lowest overall growth, reflecting the growth of the western milling industry. Wheat receipts grew faster than shipments over the years 1854–1871. Chicago's 1871 receipts of wheat were the same approximate percentage of U.S. production as corn and oats, and the 1871 data were not atypical. The slower growth of shipments may simply reflect the growth of flour manufacture in the city.

The growth of Chicago's livestock and meat industry is clearly sketched in these data. From extremely low starting levels, the number of live cattle and hogs shipped to Chicago increased at a rate greater than that of population. In this era before refrigeration, live animals were shipped eastward for slaughter near the ultimate consumption point. The difference between receipts and shipments reflects the consumption of fresh meat in the city and the surrounding area plus the demand of the Chicago meat industry for inputs. A similar pattern is present for dressed hogs, that is those already slaughtered. Cured meats could be shipped long distances without refrigeration, and the growth of cured meat shipments was truly remarkable. Beef and pork, as fresh meat products, would not have been transported over great distances in these years. Nonetheless, the absolute

Table 4.7. Summary totals and balance of trade, 1852–1871

	1852			1859		
	Receipts	Shipments	Rec–Ship	Receipts	Shipments	Rec–Ship
Barley, bu.	100,720	71,326	29,394	652,278	483,218	169,060
Corn, bu.	2,482,791	2,737,011	–254,220	5,401,870	4,349,360	1,052,510
Oats, bu.	1,508,644	2,030,317	–521,673	1,357,696	1,185,703	171,993
Wheat, bu	742,844	636,003	106,841	7,960,766	7,116,698	794,068
Flour, bbl.	49,019	64,097	–15,078	726,321	686,351	39,970
Cured meats, lbs.			2,142,960	7,313,977	9,883,813	–2,569,836
Cattle, no.		77	–77	86,703	37,584	49,119
Live hogs, no.	280	4,508	–4,228	188,675	87,254	101,421
Dressed hogs, no.	10,968,310[a]			82,533	22,992	59,541
Beef, bbl.	1,189	50,031	–48,842	6,223	121,769	–115,546
Pork, bbl.	3,270	9,976	–6,706	24,533	92,218	–67,685
Hides, lbs.				12,685,446	16,413,320	–3,727,864
Wool, lbs.	770,294	920,113	–149,819	756,219	934,595	–178,376
Coal, tons	46,243	1,441	44,802	131,204	19,888	111,316
Lumber, feet	150,342,924	70,740,271	79,602,653	303,685,988	114,140,389	189,545,599
Lumber, miles	8,474	13,398	15,076	57,516	21,617	35,899
Iron, lbs.	32,336,000	24,220,000	8,116,000	32,577,911	25,580,579	6,997,332
Lead, lbs.	1,368,650	2,038,000	–669,350	14,351,179	8,725,717	5,625,462
Merchandise & sundries, lbs.	11,262,000	48,539,000	–37,277,164	151,927,510	80,987,214	70,940,296
Merchandise & sundries, tons	5,631	24,270	–18,639	75,964	40,494	35,470
Agricultural implements, lbs.						

continues

Table 4.7. *Continued*

	1864–65			1871		
	Receipts	Shipments	Rec–Ship	Receipts	Shipments	Rec–Ship
Barley, bu.	823,644	327,398	496,246	4,063,750	2,908,113	1,155,637
Corn, bu.	13,195,340	12,740,043	455,297	41,080,009	36,716,035	4,360,974
Oats, bu.	16,365,441	16,470,929	−103,488	14,525,014	12,151,247	2,373,767
Wheat, bu	10,888,436	10,249,328	639,108	14,391,906	12,905,449	1,486,459
Flour, bbl.	1,170,244	1,287,545	−117,301	1,412,177	1,287,574	124,603
Cured meats, lbs.	17,020,877	50,055,292	−33,034,415	31,203,618	167,675,060	−136,971,442
Cattle, no.	343,726	262,446	81,280	532,959	401,927	131,032
Live hogs, no.	1,270,337	580,560	689,777	2,361,219	1,162,286	1,198,933
Dressed hogs, no.	269,286	56,787	212,499	272, 466	168,742	103,724
Beef, bbl.	9,214	140,627	−131,413	53,302	89,452	−36,150
Pork, bbl.	41,238	310,439	−269,201	68,949	183,931	−114,982
Hides, lbs.	20,057,625	27,656,801	−7,599,176	25,026,034	22,462,894	2,563,140
Wool, lbs.	5,261,426	6,789,330	−1,527,904	27,026,621	24,351,520	2,675,101
Coal, tons	323,264	19,095	304,169	1,079,730	96,833	982,897
Lumber, ft.	501,592,404	272,496,579	229,095,895	1,039,328,375	534,884,543	504,443,832
Lumber, miles	94,999	51,609	43,389	196,842	101,304	95,539
Iron, lbs.	115,766,764	16,346,043	99,420,721	332,546,386	295,362,387	37,183,999
Lead, lbs.	10,699,078	6,813,633	3,885,445	14,275,775	5,994,651	8,281,124
Merchandise & sundries, lbs.	244,005,527	103,112,401	140,893,126	1,217,391,903	1,470,995,976	−253,604,073
Merchandise & sundries, tons	122,003	51,556	70,447	608,696	735,498	−126,802
Agricultural implements, lbs.				19,422,515	42,352,109	−22,909,593

Sources: *The Daily Democratic Press, Annual Review, 1852,* adapted from Pierce, *History of Chicago*, 2:492; Chicago Board of Trade, *Second Annual Report, 1859*, 83–104, adapted from Pierce, *History of Chicago*, 2:493–94; Chicago Board of Trade, *Seventh Annual Report, 1864–65*, 26, 48, 50, 57, 65, 74–104, adapted from Pierce, *History of Chicago*, 2:495–96, Chicago Board of Trade, *Seventh Annual Report, 1864–65*, 26, 48, 50, 57, 65, 74–104, adapted from Pierce, *History of Chicago*, 2:495–96.

[a] This figure is in lbs.

numbers grew, albeit at rates that are not as high (nor as statistically significant) as those for the other goods considered.

The stockyards represent the development of an industry consistent with Chicago's initial agricultural bias. Its expansion depended on the development of a transportation network that brought animals to the yards and of a fast mode of transportation that could service distant points. The network that developed to meet the hinterland's commercial needs, in particular to carrying the farmers' produce to market, helped develop Chicago's industry as well. The refrigerated railroad car opened more distant markets to the city's perishable fresh meat products and thereby ensured the Chicago-based meat industry's growth.

The quantity of hides that Chicago received increased throughout the four selected years, with shipments increasing through 1864–65, then decreasing in 1871. Receipts were greater than shipments for the first three years, and the difference increased over the course of those years. In 1871, however, shipments were more than five million pounds less than those of 1864–65, whereas receipts were approximately five million pounds greater than in 1864–65. That Chicago changed from a net exporter to a net importer of hides is consistent with the development of the city's boot and shoe industry and the harness and saddle industry, both of which were established at about the time of the Civil War and both of which experienced remarkable growth after the war. These data clearly support the development of secondary industry through utilizing the byproducts of the packing industry.

Table 4.8. Growth rates, 1854–1871

	Absolute (%)		Per Capita (%)	
	Receipts	Shipments	Receipts	Shipments
Barley, bu.	19.154	23.202	9.771	13.819
Corn, bu.	8.975	9.123	-0.408	-0.260
Oats, bu.	13.090	10.687	3.707	1.304
Wheat, bu.	5.525	5.182	-3.858	-4.201
Flour, bbl.	13.389	15.992	4.006	6.609
Cured meats, lbs.	5.694	21.209	-3.689	11.826
Cattle, no.	14.126	17.836	4.743	8.453
Live hogs, no.	16.327	17.860	6.944	8.477
Dressed hogs, no.	10.128	17.357	0.745	7.974
Beef, bbl.	13.621	3.089	4.238	-6.294
Pork, bbl.	6.300	8.551	-3.083	-0.832
Hides, bbl.	15.534	11.923	6.151	2.540
Wool, lbs.	19.949	22.143	10.566	12.760
Coal, tons	16.186	14.332	6.803	4.949
Lumber, feet	8.900	7.379	-0.483	-2.004

Source: Chicago Board of Trade, Annual Reports, 1854–1871.
Notes: Chicago's rate of population growth over this period was 9.383 percent. Only the growth rate for beef shipments is not statistically significantly different from zero.

The pattern for wool follows that for hides, indicating the development of wool-using industry in the years after the Civil War. In the 1840s flocks were driven from New York and Pennsylvania to midwestern farmers as farmers saw wool as another staple product they could ship east. Woolen factories like those at Elgin and St. Charles, Illinois, often engaged in direct exchange with sheep farmers. The level of wartime prices led many communities to promote woolen manufacturing. As Arthur C. Cole noted, "At the end of the decade [the 1860s] the census enumerators found twenty-four wool carding and cloth dressing establishments and eighty-five woolen mills in Illinois."[5] Many of these had disappeared a decade later, yet Andreas notes that, by 1885, Chicago was the third-largest woolen market in the United States.[6] Much of that wool went to the city's clothing manufacturers.[7]

Coal receipts increased each year, but shipments show a slight drop in 1864–65. An increasing excess of receipts over shipments gives a clear picture of Chicago's physical growth throughout the period. Coal was the area's principal fuel, and a growing population plus industrialization increased the demand for it. The railroads were large coal consumers, and, as the distances out of the city grew longer, the demand for coal at Chicago increased.

Lumber was Chicago's principal building material in the years before the fire. In its aftermath, Chicago's City Council severely limited frame construction. Receipts and shipments grew continually throughout the period at a rate slightly less than population. The excess of receipts over shipments also increased over the period. Chicago's lumber consumption was approximately one-half of the period's total receipts. These lumber receipts, like those of coal, reflect the city's physical growth as well as the growth of the commercial agglomeration supplying the city and its hinterland.

The data for iron are composed of receipts and shipments of many different iron products: iron bars, iron nails, pig iron, and railroad iron, to name but a few. Consequently, interpretation of the difference between these receipts and shipments is difficult. Since the area's steel production was minimal until after the Civil War, the iron that Chicago received was mostly in final form. Railroad construction proceeded throughout the period, and iron rails passed through Chicago. During the Civil War, much more iron was received than ever before, but shipments fell from previous levels. One possible inference from these data is that Chicago was involved in processing iron for the war effort. After the war the data show the city to be a net iron consumer, suggesting that Chicago processed iron for more than war needs. The manufacture of railroad equipment (particularly locomotives) and agricultural implements (such as McCormick's reaper) represent Chicago-based industries that had a strong demand for iron and that dates from just before the Civil War. These industries transformed iron into a form that was then shipped elsewhere and that was not entered as an iron shipment. The growth of these iron-processing industries was evidently the result of the growth of Chicago, its hinterland, and the area's transportation facilities, which had developed originally in response to the city's agricultural orientation. The excess of lead receipts over shipments for each year following 1852 suggests that Chicago was involved in lead processing as it was in iron processing.

A large excess of shipments over receipts for merchandise and sundries more than likely represents the growth of small industries. It is doubtful that Chicago was well endowed with export-producing small industry and manufactures before 1859. Between 1859 and 1864–65 receipts and shipments grew rapidly, as did the excess of receipts over shipments. Consumption increased as the city's marketing forces transshipped a large portion of these receipts to the hinterland. It could be argued that before the Civil War there was a significant commercial agglomeration without a significant industrial agglomeration. By 1871 the situation was radically different. Receipts increased fivefold in seven years, but shipments increased fourteenfold. The city became a net exporter of merchandise, indicating significant production within the city. The commercial agglomeration was greatly increased, but now it attracted a fast-developing industrial agglomeration. The continually increasing demands from a dependent hinterland make it unlikely that the 1871 excess of shipments came from inventories and even more unlikely that this excess would be reversed in the years to come.

Three Prominent Industries

Three commodities stand out from the statistical summary: grain, meat, and lumber. Each of these is discussed in turn.

GRAIN

Agricultural crops dominated Chicago's commerce in the years before the fire, and not simply because a growing city needed an increased supply of food. Indigenous people and the occasional European who lived in the area during the fur trade era planted crops, particularly corn, some of which was intended for the market. As discussed in chapter 1, there was a trade in grain involving such places as southwestern Michigan. By the early 1830s, crops were being planted in and around Chicago for export to the East—wheat for bread and corn for man and beast. Following the Civil War, production of oats grew as the number of urban workhorses increased. Given the uncertainty of weather and other risks facing prairie farmers, most planted multiple grains. Wagons and boats, then the I&M Canal and the railroads, began bringing crops from an expanding hinterland. Chicago, the principal node, became one of the nation's, if not the world's, most important agricultural markets.[8] Improvements in transportation are one part of the story of Chicago's prominence in the grain trade. Another major part is the development of grain elevators, often owned and operated by railroad companies. The third part, overarching the other two, is the watchful eye of a body designed to police the market: the Chicago Board of Trade. The board introduced grading standards and a futures market. Two members of the board with interests in elevators unwittingly helped define the regulation of grain and many other markets. The grain trade was such that the U.S. Census of 1860 noted that the board was the "leading agency in the opening up of seven-eighths of our settled territory."[9]

TRANSPORTATION IMPROVEMENTS In the 1830s and '40s, farmers typically traded their surplus production with the merchant who operated the local (general) store. Such merchants were also a source of credit, extending supplies for spring sowing and being repaid with a portion of the fall harvest. The first grain to arrive in Chicago came via wagon, with the grain placed in sacks for safekeeping. Throughout the early 1840s, it was not unusual for hundreds of wagons to arrive each day in season. Wabash Avenue got its name from teamsters who brought goods to Chicago from farms near the Wabash River. The quantity of wheat increased when the I&M Canal was completed in 1848, with the grain still shipped in sacks because of the large number of potential transshipments that could be involved in waterborne transportation and the need to carefully balance vessels of irregular shapes. A farmer in northwestern Illinois might take the grain to a merchant by wagon. If there was local demand, some of the grain might be sold there; any surplus would be taken to a navigable river, where it would be shipped downstream by raft, flatboat, or the like. When it reached the Mississippi River, it might head south by steamboat or continue on its original vessel. When it reached the mouth of the Illinois River, it might be moved to a different steamboat to go upstream to the I&M Canal, where it would be moved to a canal boat.

When it reached Chicago, it would either be sold to a dealer for local use or it would be put under the care of a commission merchant to move it to, say, Buffalo. This merchant did not own the grain; he received a commission for the marketing services he provided. The risks remained with the owner, either the farmer or the local merchant. It is for this reason that insurance brokers, many of them agents of eastern companies, became a major source of business in Chicago as early as 1840; fire, marine, and commercial insurance were all popular products. As William Cronon observed, "Sacks and ships seemed an ideal combination."[10]

The quantity of grain increased with the opening of western railroads. The journey from farm to Chicago was reduced from something measured in days by wagon to something measured in hours by railroad. The railroads, their hopper cars, and in particular the adoption of grain elevators rendered the use of grain sacks an inefficient way of proceeding. By the start of the Civil War, approximately thirty interstate lines had a hub in Chicago. Three favorable harvests centered on 1850 also contributed to the growth of Chicago's nodal importance.

Grains became, and remain, the heart of the city's agriculture heritage. Ceres, the Roman goddess of agriculture, especially grain, has stood atop the current Board of Trade building since it opened in 1930. Wheat was the first to be planted, but barley, corn, oats, and rye all filled ships departing from Chicago's harbor in addition to becoming food for midwesterners and their livestock. Production on Illinois's fertile prairies led the nation in the Civil War era before even greater quantities were grown farther west in the years thereafter. As the prairies were transformed for grain production, Cyrus McCormick's reaper, John Deere's plow, and other planting and harvesting machinery made their mark. And the climate provided what proved to be ideal growing conditions. The result was crops that provided an exportable surplus that passed through Chicago.

GRAIN ELEVATORS When the grain arrived in sacks, as it did when shipped by wagon or on the canal, it was possible to identify a specific farmer's crop. Sacks were a far less efficient technology on the railroads, and the whole approach from farm to market had to change to deal with grain in bulk. The first eastbound bulk grain shipment left the port of Chicago in 1839, having been loaded via a chute from the upper floor of Newberry & Dole's warehouse.

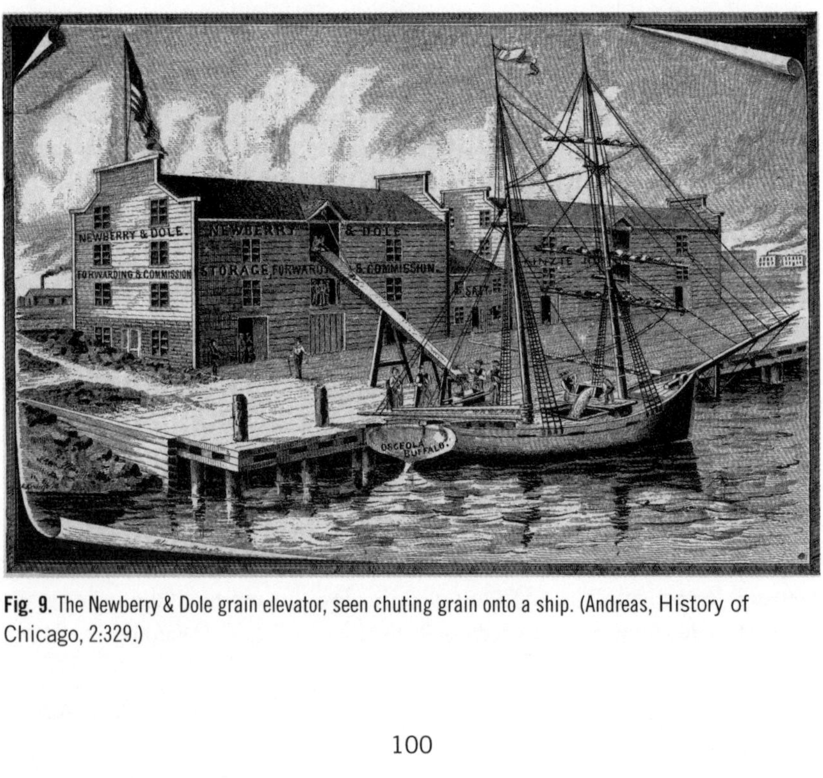

Fig. 9. The Newberry & Dole grain elevator, seen chuting grain onto a ship. (Andreas, History of Chicago, 2:329.)

The major innovation that led to the emergence of grain elevators was the introduction of steam power, which took place in Buffalo, New York, in 1843. Buffalo was the most common recipient of grain from Chicago because it was at the western end of the Erie Canal. In the 1830s, increasing quantities of grain, largely wheat, arrived in Buffalo via Lake Erie from farms in Ohio and Indiana. The Chicago shipments increased the volume tremendously. All of this was handled as it had been for centuries, first in Europe, then in the United States. Stevedores using a block and tackle would lift sacks of grain stored on a pallet in a ship's hull or simply lift and carry sacks stored on deck. It was a time-consuming process to unload one boat.

The American inventor Oliver Evans designed a grain mill by 1790 in which steam power was used to lift buckets of grain several floors so that gravity could be used to move the raw material from the top floor of the mill through various stages of production on succeeding floors, ending with the finished product on the bottom floor. A Buffalo engineer named Robert Dunbar modified Evans's work to design a steam-powered "grain storage and transfer warehouse" for Joseph Dart Jr., a grain merchant of the city. A marine leg scooped bulk grain from a ship's hull and raised it to the top of a tower for transshipment onto an Erie Canal barge or conveyed it to one of the many flour mills that were built in Buffalo. What is now generally known as "Dart's Elevator" went into operation in 1843. It cut the time required to unload a boat to one-seventh of what it had been. This enabled the city to keep up with the number of boats arriving in season.[11] Chicago's first steam-powered grain elevator was built in 1848 for Captain Robert C. Bristol. The four-story building could hold more than eighty thousand bushels of grain, but it was soon dwarfed by others. On the eve of the Civil War, elevators ten times the size of Bristol's had been constructed and were owned by (or tied to) the railroads.[12]

To the west, steam elevators began appearing in important grain markets such as Peoria, Minneapolis, Duluth, and Kansas City. The development of the telegraph network, with its ability to send and receive information quickly, reduced price differentials between cities, and Chicago prices became important data everywhere. In these outlying cities there were large elevator companies that built hundreds of branch elevators throughout their areas. A farmer's grain would be weighed and graded, then placed in a local grain elevator with that from other farms.[13] If there were multiple elevators, the different grades could be separated, but to get to such a site, a farmer would likely incur greater transportation costs. From the elevator, gravity would simplify the loading of railroad cars (or ships). In many wheat-growing areas, however, there were no elevators, and grain was brought to the railhead and piled along the tracks, potentially spoiling before the railroad could get a hopper car there. So it was that the railroads began to build their own elevators as well as purchasing many built by others, further solidifying their monopsonistic power. Farmers were often hard-pressed for cash when they arrived at the railhead and sold as quickly as possible to the elevator company most readily at hand. They returned home feeling cheated, but with no information to confirm their feeling. Farmers and elevator companies had access to the same price information, but the company seldom rated a farmer's wheat as highly as he did. The farmer had the choice of accepting the buyer's rating or hauling his wheat home. What the farmers desired was impartial grading by public officials.

BOARD OF TRADE In 1841 a notice appeared in a Chicago paper suggesting that it would be a good idea to develop a board of trade similar to those in other cities. It was not until 1848, however, that Thomas Richmond, a grain elevator operator, and W. I. Whiting, a grain broker, assembled a volunteer body. Eighty-three Chicago business leaders (including William Ogden) formed the Chicago Board of Trade. As articulated at its second meeting in 1848, the board's objectives were

> to maintain a Commercial Exchange; to promote uniformity in the customs and usages of merchants; to inculcate the principles of justice and equity in trade; to facilitate the speedy adjustment of business disputes; to acquire and to disseminate valuable and economic information; and generally to secure to its members the benefit of cooperation in the furtherance of their legitimate pursuits.[14]

The board was incorporated in 1850 under an 1849 state law. The board's members, each of whom paid annual dues of $2 for the privilege, promoted Chicago's trade. They appointed inspectors of fish, provisions, and flour; had committees on activities such as banking and grain measurement; and promoted harbor improvements, tolls on the I&M Canal, the land grant for the Illinois Central Railroad, and the Welland Canal.[15] By 1857 most merchants in the city considered membership in the Chicago Board of Trade a desirable thing.

Andreas summarized its first years of existence as "uneventful and uninteresting." Yet, he went on to note, "nearly all the modern means, methods and facilities for transacting business . . . had their inception in the Board." The list is instructive. The board's activities included

> The inspection, warehousing and shipping of grain, in well-defined and standard grades; the standards of inspection of flour, pork, beef, lard, butter, lumber, etc. . . . The rapid dissemination and interchange of reliable commercial news and market quotations, . . . The system of gathering of all important commercial statistics . . . [and] an essential agency in the direction of State and national legislation on all commercial questions.[16]

During the 1850s the Chicago Board of Trade developed a grading system for grain that the Illinois Legislature approved via a special 1859 charter that granted the board the authority to impose its regulations for grain handling and to arbitrate merchants' disputes. These applied once the grain arrived in Chicago, but title to the grain that arrived in Chicago was seldom held by the farmer who grew it. As time passed, an increasing proportion of the arriving grain was owned by the railroads, the farmer having sold at a point much closer to the family's farm.

Over the same period, grain arriving in Chicago was mixed according to its grade rather than by its ownership, as previously had been the case with sacks. This meant that the identity of a particular farmer's grain was lost as that grain was intermixed in the elevator with grain of the same grade from other farms. Beginning in 1857, the owner (or his agent) received a receipt from the warehouseman that entitled the bearer to a given quantity of that grade of grain. The use of warehouse receipts has a long history, but generally they were simply proof of ownership of a specific good or goods stored in a warehouse. Guy Lee likened this to the operation of a bank wherein the dollar you deposit is not necessarily the dollar you receive when you make a withdrawal. When the grain was in sacks, until the final sale the dollar you withdrew was the dollar you deposited.[17] One consequence of constructing grain elevators was an enormous quantity of negotiable warehouse receipts tied to a grading standard that was known to and recognized by a large market. These contracts created an option for buyers or sellers with respect to future delivery of grain.

This system spread to other markets in Chicago and elsewhere and, in turn, made marketing more efficient, created credit, and supported speculation. What the receipt represented became widely known and enabled Chicago grain to be marketed in Buffalo, where it was milled into flour, in New York City, whence it was exported, and in British ports such as Liverpool, where it was imported. The receipts were used as collateral for the issuance of credit providing the capital for growth in Chicago and the Midwest. They represent one reason why Chicago became the Midwest's financial center.

A substantial fraction of the grain traded in the years before the Civil War was for future delivery, but it was not until October 1865 that the board officially recognized this as a separate activity and developed a standardized futures contract to address a straightforward problem.[18] From the beginning, especially at the beginning, the grain trade involved speculation. In the 1840s, grain was sold "to arrive." Well before the grain arrived in Chicago, the buyer knew whence it would come and more than likely had contracted to buy it from the farmer. As noted, since most of the grain went east via Lake Michigan before 1871, there was a closed season of transport and a speculative opportunity. Grain was bought and sold for cash, for storage, or for the future. By the time farmers were able to harvest their crop and ship it as far as Chicago, water transportation on the upper Great Lakes was coming to an end for the winter. Much of the wheat purchased in Chicago was for shipment in the spring. Lee reports that in the winter of 1861–62 in excess of six million bushels were stored in Chicago elevators awaiting the opening of navigation on the lakes.[19] Then, during the Civil War, Union Army purchase contracts had provisions for delaying delivery of grain until it was needed. Other things being equal, one expects prices to be higher in planting season than in harvest season, but that differential was not pure profit for Chicago's grain traders. One part was compensation for storage; another was compensation for risk. Other things were not necessarily equal.

Speculation in grain, in the sense of holding on to a supply hoping for a rise in the market, is a very old practice. Trading in grain futures was something new. The rules and regulations governing speculative purchases and sales were adopted by the Board of Trade in 1865, and by the late 1870s a "futures" market was a regular part of the board's operations. Speculation as we now understand it was impossible prior to the system of grades and receipts because there was no way to sell short (i.e., someone would sell grain for future delivery at one price and hope to purchase that amount later at a lower price). This developed in the Chicago market because of the large supply of grain that flowed through the market, both buyer and seller knowing what was being exchanged, the ability of the elevators to store and maintain that good over time, and the credit facilities that developed as a result of the receipts.[20]

THE MOVE TO REGULATE It made little difference to the farmer whether the elevators close to the farm were independently owned or owned by a railroad company. In either case, the farmer faced an entity with monopsony power that demanded a division of the receipts. Whether the producer stored his grain for a few days in the elevator or not, even if it did not pass through an elevator, he had to pay an elevator toll to the carrier or his grain would not be shipped. In the central markets, such as Chicago, a similar system was used. All the agencies pooled their interests. Unless the farmer had already sold his grain at the offered price, it was dumped in whatever warehouse the railroad agent designated and held for storage at ruinous charges. If the owner did not sell quickly, he might as well donate the proceeds of his year's effort to the railroad and the elevator companies.

Farmers' clubs in Illinois inaugurated a movement for railroad regulation in the years before the Grange became prominent.[21] In 1867 Illinois adopted the Warehouse Act, which compelled railroad companies to handle grain from independent elevators. In 1870 a constitutional amendment (Article 13) that permitted state control of railroads and public elevators was included in the new state constitution. The following year the legislature fixed a scale of maximum freight and passenger rates.

In 1856 Ira Munn, who would become president of the Chicago Board of Trade in 1860, and several partners owned a 200,000-bushel Chicago grain elevator. Two years later, George Scott became a partner, and the company that owned the elevator became Munn & Scott, one of five major elevator firms in Chicago.[22] By 1865 it owned four elevators with a total capacity of 2.3 million bushels, approximately one-third of Chicago's total. Munn's speculation in the grain market bankrupted the company in 1872, the same year it was charged with violating Illinois regulations. Munn & Scott had refused to take out a license to operate a public warehouse as Illinois law required, and, moreover, its elevator charges were above the official rates.[23] It argued that the state did not have the right to regulate privately owned enterprises. Its position was identical to that of the railroad companies, which were also facing state regulation. The carriers refused to abide by these regulations and ejected passengers who insisted on paying only the legal fare. The railroad cases would be tied to that of Munn & Scott and decided as one.[24]

By 1874, fourteen Chicago elevators handled the business of inspection, grading, and mixing the grain. These were owned by about thirty persons but

Fig. 10. A view of the Chicago River showing a Munn and Scott grain elevator. (Chicago History Museum, ICHi-06853, Jevne & Almini, publishers.)

controlled by nine firms that agreed closely on storage charges. Nearly all the marketed wheat of seven or eight states passed, sooner or later, through the hands of this monopoly. The US Supreme Court found in favor of Illinois. Munn & Scott's enterprise, the Court noted, connected rail and lake transport, stood astride the very "gateway of commerce," and charged a toll, and thus had monopoly powers by virtue of its location. The power of Parliament, it was argued, had devolved upon the states after the American Revolution, apart from those powers specifically given to the federal government in the U.S. Constitution. The powers of the states included the traditional economic controls, the "police powers."[25] The power to regulate was inherent in the common-law rule that charges must be "reasonable." This set events on a path that in 1889 led to the creation of the Interstate Commerce Commission, the first federal regulatory commission. While this was almost two decades after the fire, its origins in large part lay in Illinois grain markets well before the fire, and as Cronon argues, its specific origins lie in

> the original decision to remove grain from its sacks was undoubtedly a pragmatic one, driven by the technological possibilities of the grain elevator. Probably no one foresaw that so simple an act would have such complex consequences, imposing a new symbolic order on Chicago's marketplace and distancing it from the physical universe of fields and crops and rural nature. The shift from sack to elevator enabled grain traders to come indoors, to a market called 'Change [Exchange] where sheets of paper would stand as surrogates for grain bought and sold in millions upon millions of invisible bushels. The shift to standard grades meant that those sheets of paper represented not real physical grain but abstract conventions whose homogeneity was the condition that made them interchangeable. Interchangeability in turn made it possible to sell grain not only over great distances of space but over extended periods of time as well, for the futures market depended for its existence on the standardized fictions that enabled traders to buy and sell grain they had never seen, because it did not yet exist. Those who dealt in futures extended the abstraction of Chicago's market by dealing not in grain, not even in elevator receipts, but in the prices that *future* elevator receipts would bring when they finally came into being several weeks or months later.[26]

MEATPACKING

The Board of Trade was similarly involved with the meatpacking industry, but quite a bit later. The modern oligopolistic meatpacking industry did not emerge until about 1875 with the development of the refrigerated railroad car and continuous-processing plants.[27] Chicago had become the nation's primary corn market in 1851 and its primary wheat market in 1854. Although most farmers also kept livestock, Chicago did not become the nation's primary hog market until 1862.[28] Before the advent of refrigeration, most of the animals arriving in Chicago were either consumed locally or shipped as live animals or cured meat to the East via the railroads. The animals consumed locally were often slaughtered by the neighborhood butcher. Those shipped east usually went via rail because travel by ship was more than likely to bruise the meat, and something akin to a cattle drive was impractical given the distances involved.

At the beginning, Chicago's small meat market was based on the needs of Fort Dearborn. Much of this meat was supplied by ship, the only viable mode of conveyance at the time. Animals were brought from Buffalo, Erie, or Cleveland via the lakes or from St. Louis via the rivers, and there were a few from the upper Wabash valley that arrived on the hoof such as the hogs that the young Gurdon Hubbard drove to Chicago. In the early 1840s, most of the slaughtered hogs were consumed locally; Howard Hill reports that in 1844 slightly more than seven thousand barrels of pork were shipped from Chicago.[29] By the late 1850s, 40 percent to 45 percent of the hogs and 40 percent of the cattle arriving in Chicago were shipped to the East, primarily by rail.[30]

At first, most hogs were penned in the city, while cattle were allowed to fatten on the contiguous prairie. Many of the small stockyards were attached to boarding houses and taverns that provided accommodations for the drovers. Pierce identifies Myrick's Tavern, at Cottage Grove and 29th Street, as having such facilities as early as 1837.[31]

Cattle were slaughtered and sold as fresh beef throughout the year; this was largely because preserved beef (salted or smoked) was not popular with consumers. Hogs, on the other hand, were much easier to preserve and, consequently, were slaughtered only during the cold season. Hog fat was converted into lard, and the meat was packed in salt or smoked. Animal hides were a profitable byproduct of these operations. The blood and offal were simply dumped, creating a nuisance. The live animals were also a potential nuisance; in early years some simply roamed the city feeding on the wastes that residents threw into the streets. For obvious reasons, most cities tried to relegate meatpacking operations to their periphery.

There is some uncertainty about how large the early packing industry really was. Its seasonal nature raises questions as to whether those involved in the industry at any given time of year would be present at the time of year the census collected data. What does exist in various censuses suggests that hog production in the 1820s and 1830s centered on Cincinnati, the original "Porkopolis." As production spread westward, the corn-hog cycle developed, in which the number of hogs produced would fall when corn was scarce and expensive and would rise when corn was abundant and cheap.

The emergence of cities created a demand for meat. The coming of the railroad, especially during the 1850s, enhanced the nodal significance of existing cities by expanding their hinterlands. As the rail network grew larger, packing plants at principal nodes grew in number and size.[32] All this was attributable to the greater speed, all-season availability, and flexibility of route development the railroad enjoyed by not being as tied to geography as waterways, natural or artificial. Given that animals traveled by rail, as trade expanded the railroad companies all constructed their own yards. As Chicago grew, these yards, once located adjacent to the prairie, became surrounded by the city. The geographical dispersion of the yards made buying and selling difficult. Further, in these early years, many animals simply passed through Chicago on their way to eastern markets because the only way to assure fresh meat was to slaughter locally. This meant that live animals had to be moved from the yard of the railroad on which they arrived to the one from which they would leave. Yet another nuisance.

The Civil War markedly changed the situation. Chicago was the beneficiary of the Mississippi River's being closed by Union forces and other limitations on North-South exchange. The Union Army contracted for processed pork and live cattle. Packing houses developed along the North and South branches of the Chicago River. Just under four hundred thousand live hogs were sent to Chicago in 1860; three years later, at the peak of the war, the number was almost five times larger. Meatpacking underwent an almost sixfold increase. Chicago packed 6 percent of western pork in 1860, and three years later it was packing 25 percent. The statistics for cattle are less dramatic. Cattle receipts tripled, and the amount of beef packed almost doubled.[33] The figures for the final years of the war are somewhat lower, but Chicago's dominance of meatpacking was not seriously challenged for almost a century thereafter.

All this meant more and more animals in the streets, sometimes feeding and more often being driven between stockyards. As Margaret Walsh notes, "Drovers, commision [*sic*] merchants, packers, butchers, and railroad investors all wanted better handling and transit facilities in order to avoid injury to stock, delay in receiving shipments, and expense in switching cars from one yard to another."[34]

By 1864 the growth of the livestock trade was such that the large number of individual stockyards was considered a nuisance to the public and a costly burden to the railroads.[35] On Christmas Day 1865, the Union Stock Yards opened for business on Halsted Street in the Town of Lake, on land purchased from U.S. Representative John Wentworth.[36] Nine railroad companies subscribed the vast majority of the $1 million cost, but every railroad entering Chicago was connected to these yards. Five hundred railcars could be loaded or unloaded simultaneously.

The yards covered roughly 375 acres. The biggest problem was mud because the land, though it now was composed of prairie, once lay underneath Lake Chicago. Drainage pipes were installed to improve the situation. The property had a water supply and sewers, five hundred pens, and fifteen miles of track. Eventually, three miles of water troughs went through the property; five hundred thousand gallons of water were withdrawn daily from the Chicago River upstream of the yards' sewage

Fig. 11. The Union Stock Yard by Jevne & Almini. (Chicago History Museum, ICHi-062081.)

outfall. The wastes, including blood and offal, drained into the South Fork of the South Branch, a fetid pool of pollution that became known as "Bubbly Creek."

These yards, the largest in the world at the time, continued to grow for the next several years, and the introduction of refrigeration would accelerate that growth dramatically.[37] The number of pens grew to twenty-three hundred in 1868. A few years after the fire, they were annually handling between eight and nine million animals, this figure rising to twelve million by 1885. Because it expanded meat packers' operations beyond manufacturing into distribution and byproduct utilization, it contributed to a large increase in the operating scale of these firms.

The Exchange Building was the center of operations. Its great hall functioned for livestock dealers in much the same manner as the Board of Trade did for grain traders. Within the building there was a bank. Cronon reports that, in the late 1860s, this bank handled $500,000 in transactions daily.[38] It also contained telegraph facilities gathering information from other yards, in particular, prices. Next door was a hotel called Hough House. Rather than the drovers of old, the accommodation attached to these yards were for livestock dealers.

The expansion of rail facilities to the west reached into an area just east of the Rocky Mountains where the climate was drier and less well suited to grain production. For centuries, it was home to thousands of buffalo, so it was ideal land for grazing cattle. As grass-fed western cattle were shipped east, they would come into an area that grew corn, on which they could be fattened. And when refrigeration entered the picture in a meaningful way after the fire, the animals could be transformed en route. Western steers were shipped to Chicago to become dressed beef that was shipped to the East Coast. Gone were the days when the animals that produced fresh meat had to be close at hand.

In 1867 an Illinois livestock dealer, Joseph "Cowboy" McCoy from near Springfield, bought 250 acres of land in Abilene, Kansas, and established a stockyard near the Kansas Pacific Railroad depot.[39] Although the railway continued west, Abilene's location at the northeast end of the Chisholm Trail was the key. McCoy's success in getting Texas cattle men to drive their longhorns to Abilene meant that Chicago received millions of cattle from that source alone.

The increased number of animals arriving in Chicago after the fire is largely attributable to refrigeration, with Gustavus Swift's refrigerated car normally receiving major credit. But that is the outcome of "research" that began long before the fire. It was about 1857 when the Pennsylvania Railroad introduced the use of ice in order to continue operations during the summer. It is doubtful that summer packing was feasible outside the Great Lakes region, where sizable quantities of ice could be found.[40] Even then, summer packing as a major activity was a post-fire phenomenon.

The first American patent for a refrigerated rail car was issued in 1867 to J. B. Sutherland of Detroit. Sutherland's device provided for good air circulation, which would prove important; however the most widely adopted car was patented the following year by William Davis, also of Detroit, whose car did not have air circulation as good as Sutherland's. It was in one of Davis's cars that the first shipment of dressed beef was made from Chicago in 1869.[41] In essence, regular box cars were outfitted with bins at each end that could hold at least a ton of ice, meaning once again that Great Lakes ports had a locational advantage. The problem with these cars was getting the meat east fast enough to maintain its freshness. Initially the meat came into contact with the ice, discoloring the meat, which was avoided by suspicious consumers. In 1868 Detroit packer George H. Hammond hung the meat from the ceiling of a car designed for shipping fruit, but the movement of the train caused the meat to swing which, in turn, caused the car to swing, making railway companies reluctant to accept such cars. Hammond was nonetheless so confident of the technology's potential that he moved his operation to Chicago to be closer to the cattle market.[42] Swift resolved the major marketing problems associated with shipping dressed beef in refrigerated cars a decade after the fire.[43] It was then that Chicago entered the age when it truly was "Hog Butcher to the World" and much, much more with respect to meat production. Yet it is important to recognize that this success was based on a foundation laid before the introduction of refrigeration.

LUMBER

The lumber industry was the final piece of the triad that dominated trade in pre-fire Chicago. The forests of northeastern Wisconsin and northwestern Michigan were filled with lakes and rivers, almost all of which led to Lake Michigan. Those forests provided a large supply of a resource that the prairies lacked. Old-growth white pines were felled (most often during the winter), and the logs were hauled (on sleds over the ice) to where they could be floated downriver when the ice and snow melted. The key was that they floated.[44] Some old-growth pines could be two hundred feet tall and perfectly straight. The logs were marked by a "scalar," who would calculate how many board feet were in each log and stamp it accordingly, also marking the company's logo. They would be turned into lumber—boards of standard length and dimension—at a sawmill adjacent to the shipping point. Mill towns began dotting the Lake Michigan shoreline beginning in the 1830s. Ships, and later railroads, then brought the lumber to a rapidly growing Chicago, which soon became the largest lumber market in the world—and would remain so through the end of the nineteenth century.[45] The canal and railroad then would carry lumber from Chicago to the prairie where trees were scarce.

Fig. 12. The lumber district. Photograph by J. Carbutt. (Chicago History Museum, ICHi-021301.)

Chicago lumber dealers were involved in all phases of the operation, and northern lumber companies often had a partner located in Chicago. The city became an important labor market for the industry because the ships that brought the lumber to Chicago could take workers back to the mill towns. The industry was initially focused on building material as almost all of Chicago and vicinity was constructed of wood. The first known shipment arrived in Chicago from St. Joseph, Michigan, in 1833.[46] Lumber was one of the goods for which farmers would exchange their grain. Before 1848 they would have made the trip via wagon, but thereafter both the I&M Canal and the Galena and Chicago Union Railroad were moving lumber to grain-growing areas. In this manner, wood from Michigan and Wisconsin forests was marketed over an ever-widening area, with Chicago the transshipment point. That wood became houses, barns, fences, railroad ties, grain elevators, and many other items—the fixed capital of the Midwest.[47]

The seasonality of the lumber industry, like that of agriculture, meant credit was an important element of a firm's success. Winter was the time loggers went into the forest. Some of them undoubtedly worked in the mills the rest of the year, but many of them returned to farms after logging season. Winter was the down time at the mill; a time when old equipment could be repaired, and new equipment installed. The custom was to give mill workers a one-year contract, and the mill company often ran the store from which they obtained their food and supplies. There would be an inventory of logs to be milled, and that inventory, as well as the cash inflow, would begin shrinking in the late fall and winter. Winter, however, was a time when the cash outflow did not shrink. Thus, as Cronon notes, "when firms found themselves, as they regularly did each winter, having to spend money they did not possess, the most attractive solution was to spend money belonging to someone else."[48] And that someone else could be found in Chicago.

A "cargo market" emerged near Wolf Point at Franklin Street, and a "lumber district" developed along the South Branch. Lumber commission merchants and wholesale merchants gathered every morning during the warmer months on wholesale docks at the north end of the district, where lumber was purchased by the shipload and paid for in cash. Some of the docks were owned by mill owners, who also owned the ships, but most of the dock space was owned independently, as were the vast majority of the ships. There were several lumber markets in the Midwest, but lumber mill owners preferred Chicago, where there were a variety of other supplies (and credit, if needed).

After the sale, the buyers had to tow the ship containing their purchase to the lumber district to unload. Approximately twelve miles worth of dock space was constructed to handle the many ships that arrived daily during the shipping season.[49] The lumber district, on the west bank of the South Branch, contained little but docks and wood piled ten feet high for blocks.[50] The ships were unloaded by "shovers," who were often immigrants. Early on, the docks were the site of tension between Irish and Black laborers, as will be discussed in chapter 7.[51] Wholesalers maintained huge stockpiles in the district, including new shipments of green lumber that needed to dry out, as well as wood ready to be shipped as orders came in. Before it could be sold, lumber workers had to sort and grade it.

Just as sellers of lumber preferred Chicago, so did buyers, because the large amount of stock and numerous sellers helped hold prices down. Since most buyers were going to purchase a load sight unseen to be delivered by canal or rail, the development of grades for lumber, like grades for grain, became important for those remote buyers to have confidence in their purchases. In this grading system, lumber was divided into "clear" (the best-quality boards) and various levels of "common" (first, second, and so on) wood.

Chicagoans invested in lumber towns up and down the lake. The stately homes constructed by the lumber barons in towns such as Muskegon and Ludington, Michigan, are still prominent. Recall that in 1856, William Ogden purchased more than two hundred thousand acres of pineland on the Peshtigo River and constructed Peshtigo, Wisconsin. By the time of the Civil War, Peshtigo was producing more than fifty million board feet of lumber annually.

The Chicago Fire began during a dry period in the fall with many leaves on the ground and a stiff southwest wind. It started on the city's southwest side and jumped the river by the lumber district, giving it additional life. The river might have provided a natural barrier had the wind not been blowing quite so hard. As Carl Smith reports, "The first building set aflame was not on the near edge of the opposite bank but fully four hundred feet east of the river."[52]

Following the fire, agricultural production that had existed within the city limits mostly moved outside them, especially dairy farms and truck farms (fruit orchards and vegetable gardens). Horses became the only farm animals that could be stabled in the city. Hay, corn, and oats continued to be grown close to the city to provide feed for the thousands of horses that moved people and goods around the city and for the animals at the Union Stockyards, where one hundred tons of hay were consumed daily at its peak. The city created "fire limits" in which buildings had to be constructed of brick or stone rather than wood, but wood was still an important input into building construction in the city and its hinterland, both of which continued to grow. In brief, grain, meat, and lumber markets continued to be major contributors to Chicago's economy.

CHAPTER 5

Those behind the Growth

The growth of Chicago's commerce and the origins of its industry were the result of the contributions of people from many backgrounds in the years before the fire. While Wright and Ogden played leading roles in initiating Chicago's economic growth, there were other entrepreneurs who played principal roles.[1] Some were also pioneers, arriving before Chicago was incorporated. Others came later, when growth was under way and Chicago's future much clearer. And there are those whose notoriety is largely based on events that took place after the fire, but the contributions of those such as Marshall Field, George Pullman, and A. Montgomery Ward could be foreseen in the decade before the fire. Comparing Chicago's elite to those of four other U.S. cities, Frederic Jaher notes that the Chicagoans were "often labeled vigorous but vulgar and devoid of old families and traditions."[2] They typically were not the sons of Boston Brahmins or elites in another city in which they had a position in the family's enterprise. They were young men who moved west seeking opportunity and a chance to make their mark. Unlike their eastern counterparts, Chicago's entrepreneurs typically did not specialize but were involved in many activities, as was the case with Hubbard, Wright, and Ogden. Nonetheless, they are responsible for the growth of some of Chicago's most important industries and firms. They all had connections in the East that would prove important.

Chicago's first town census (1835) showed a population of 4,365 people living in 398 dwellings with four warehouses, twenty-nine dry goods stores, nineteen grocery and provision stores, five hardware stores, three drug stores, nineteen taverns, and seventeen law offices. There were seven hotels but no independent restaurants. Eating out meant visiting either a hotel dining room or a neighborhood tavern.[3]

The Meatpackers

Meatpacking has long been associated with Chicago, but production wasn't heavily concentrated in Chicago in its early years. Nonetheless, several of Chicago's notable pioneer businessmen were involved in meatpacking. We have met Gurdon Hubbard, who drove hogs from central Illinois into the city before he became a resident. One of his main competitors was Archibald Clybourn, born in Pearlsburg, Virginia, in 1802. He came to Chicago in 1823 with his father Jonas, his brother Henley, and his half-brother John Kinzie Clark, who, like Beaubien and Hubbard, traded with the Native Americans.[4] Following the most direct path to his later life, Archibald was a drover and a butcher who constructed the area's first slaughterhouse in 1827. In 1829 he opened the city's first stockyard near what is now Elston Avenue. Shortly thereafter, he built a twenty-room brick house adjacent to that stockyard.[5] He held a contract with the federal government to sell beef to Fort Dearborn, and during the Black Hawk War the Clybourns were one of two families of butchers supplying the prisoners held in the fort. Most of his butchering was for the local market, and by 1833 Clybourn was slaughtering between four hundred and five hundred hogs each week. He later became the government butcher for the Potawatomi. He and his heirs remained in the business even after the rise of Chicago's more famous meatpacking firms such as Armour and Swift.

Meatpacking, however, was but one of Clybourn's occupations. Like many of Chicago's pioneers, he was a jack of all trades. Sometime around 1829 brothers Samuel and John Miller opened a store on the north bank of the river at Wolf Point, where the river divided into the north and south branches. That same year, Samuel Miller and Clybourn received permission to operate the first ferry across the river, Clybourn being the ferryman. John Miller built a structure near the tavern that was used as a tannery: the city's first factory. The ferry service ended during the winter of 1831–32 when the bridge was constructed across the North Branch, and a second bridge was added the following winter across the South Branch. Historian Alfred Andreas notes that several early settlers, including lawyer John Dean Caton, wrote in the autumn of 1883 that these two log bridges were roughly ten feet wide and cleared the river by about six feet.[6] In his spare time Clybourn served as the Chicago region's first constable, justice of the peace, and school trustee.

Another pioneering businessman with an involvement in meatpacking was George W. Dole, who arrived from Detroit in 1831, the partner of Oliver Newberry of that city. Newberry had replaced John Kinzie as the main provisioner of Fort Dearborn, and Dole was to be his man in Chicago. The flow of goods between Chicago and Detroit meant that terminal facilities at Chicago had to be developed. In the summer of 1832 the firm of Newberry & Dole erected what is thought to be the first frame building in Chicago intended to be used for business at Dearborn and South Water Streets; that business was the slaughtering and packing of cattle and hogs. While Clybourn, Hubbard, and others had driven animals to the city for slaughtering, Dole was the first to pack them for export—to Newberry in Detroit. The building is believed to be the first forwarding and commission house in Chicago as well as Chicago's first grocery store. By the autumn 1832 Dole was butchering and packing 150 cattle and 138 hogs daily for Newberry. Consequently, Dole is generally credited with being the father of Chicago's meatpacking industry—and its shipping, warehouse, and elevator systems. In 1839 the firm began shipping wheat from Chicago's first grain elevator, located at the north end of the Rush Street bridge (see figure 9 in chapter 4).[7]

Well before the fire, Chicago emerged as "hog butcher to the world." In about 1854 Nelson Morris, a German immigrant born as Moritz Beisinger, began working for a man named John Sherman, who operated a stockyard. After two years, he went into business for himself. Morris speculated in disabled stock (animals considered unsaleable) until he entered the packing business in 1859. The demand for animals during the Civil War helped make him a rich man.

The most important of Chicago's pre-refrigeration packers was Craigin & Co. George Craigin of New York City was running a provisions enterprise in the early 1850s when he decided to hire John Hancock, a beef packer in Maine, make him a partner, and send him to Chicago to manage a branch house. The motive was to secure better control over supplies of meat. Hancock built a packinghouse that could handle three hundred to four hundred cattle or one thousand hogs daily. Hancock became one of Chicago's commercial leaders, a prominent member of the Packers' Association. He served as president of the Board of Trade between 1863 and 1864 and was part of the group that brought the Chicago Union Stock Yards to life in 1865.[8] At the end of its first year, Craigin & Co. had established itself as a major Chicago packer. Like many others, it perceived these operations as part of a broadly defined interest in western produce.[9]

Phillip Danforth Armour was born in upstate New York in 1832. He went to California during the gold rush and used the money he made there to invest in a Milwaukee grain receiving and warehousing operation in 1863. He next entered a partnership called Plankinton & Armour that was involved in pork packing at several spots in the Midwest, including Chicago. In the spring of 1865 pork was selling for approximately $40 per barrel, and many easterners, frustrated by the slow progress of the Civil War, foresaw that the price could reach as much as $60 per barrel. Armour, believing the war to be coming to an end, sold short at $40 and down. After the war he purchased pork at $18 per barrel to meet his obligation. The result was that he became a millionaire and invested the money in enlarging his operations in Kansas City and Chicago; Chicago, however, did not become his home until after 1875.[10]

The first cold storage room was built in 1865, and, after the fire, every Chicago packer had a refrigerated plant. The ammonia absorption machine was invented by Ferdinand Carré, a Frenchman, and received a U.S. patent in 1860. The machine used water as the absorbent and ammonia as the refrigerant to make ice. Meatpacking, which had been a seasonal business before the introduction of refrigeration, became a year-round one. Refrigeration tilted the competition between national packers and local slaughterers in the direction of the former.[11] It led to an increase in concentration in meatpacking after the fire, led by the "Big Five" (Armour, Cudahy, Morris, Swift, and Wilson), all Chicago firms by then. In brief, with the growth of vertical integration and refrigeration in the years after the fire, Chicago was the world's preeminent butcher, but almost all the ingredients were in place before the fire.

The Lieutenants: Scammon and Newberry

Finance, insurance, and real estate industry is another business that attracted early settlers. As we have seen, William Ogden was emblematic of the growth in almost all aspects of that industry, while John Wright specialized in real estate, but they were not alone. Two early settlers, Jonathan Young Scammon and Walter Newberry, both associated with many of Ogden's activities, were important city-builders in their own right.

J.(onathan) Young Scammon, a lawyer and financier, was born in Maine in 1812 and graduated from Waterville College, now Colby College, in 1831. He was admitted to the bar in Kennebec County, Maine, and immediately embarked on a tour of several states arriving in Chicago in September 1835, when many of the citizens were reported as having "bilious fever" (most likely malaria). He delayed leaving because the weather was miserable. On the night before he planned to depart, the deputy of the clerk of the courts of Cook County sought him out. The deputy told Scammon that he could no longer serve as deputy and that the person chosen to replace him was ill. Would he stay for the duration of the court's term and serve as deputy? Scammon not only stayed for the term; he became a Chicagoan.

Scammon was offered the deputy's job full-time with the right to use the clerk's office for his law practice. He first stayed at the Sauganash Hotel, but soon moved into one of the rooms of the building that contained his office. Given Chicago's relatively small population at the time, officials performed multiple tasks. Colonel Richard J. Hamilton, the clerk, was also judge of probate, clerk of the Circuit Court, clerk of the County Commissioner's Court, school commissioner, recorder of deeds, notary public, and bank commissioner. Hamilton performed all those tasks in their shared office, so Scammon would have learned many, if not all, of them.

In 1836 he entered a law practice with Buckner Stith Morris; their partnership lasted eighteen months. Morris was the founder of Chicago's first literary society, the Chicago Lyceum, and was Ogden's successor as mayor. In 1837 Scammon joined with Norman B. Judd in a partnership that was to last for ten years. At about this time Scammon became interested in the Galena and Chicago Union Railroad project, which would become his principal endeavor. As noted earlier, Scammon and Ogden sought out individual farmers' investment in the railroad. There were approximately fifteen hundred stockholders in the road, the majority of whom owned but a single share. Ogden and Scammon had given these farmers their personal pledge in exchange for a subscription to the stock issue. As time passed and the railroad remained unfinished, many of these stockholders surrendered their share to either Ogden or Scammon seeking recompense. These very-short-term investors bought the two promoters the time needed to demonstrate the railroad's potential to others.

Another of Scammon's major interests was the Chicago Marine and Fire Insurance Company, which was chartered in 1836 with banking privileges but suspended business as a consequence of the Panic of 1837. Scammon became a large stockholder of the suspended company in 1849. In 1851 Illinois passed a general banking law that regulated Illinois banks and their note issue. Scammon was largely responsible for this legislation. Under the provisions of this law, Marine Bank was newly organized, with Scammon as its president. On the eve of the Civil War, it was generally considered to be the Midwest's leading financial house with capital of $500,000 in 1857.

Scammon took his family to Europe that year. When he returned in 1860, it was revealed that one of the bank's employees had misappropriated funds. Scammon decided to suspend bank operations. He also considered leaving the bank altogether, but his associates convinced him to return. The directors thought a large share of the missing money would be repaid, but the value of the securities the bank owned to support its note issue dropped, and their optimism was quashed. Elected a state senator (1860–62), Scammon had to address the fact that the crash in the securities prices was attributable to the Marine Bank's and many other Illinois banks' basing their note circulation on the stock of southern companies.[12] After the end of his term, in 1863, Scammon and his associates reorganized the bank as the Marine Company of Chicago. They reopened the bank shortly after the Civil War and developed correspondent relationships with several important European banking houses.[13]

Scammon was active in many other pursuits.[14] It was in part through his effort that the Illinois legislature passed an act in 1836 whereby Chicago could establish public schools if a majority of the city's voters approved. They did not immediately do so because speculators outnumbered permanent residents at that time. A year later, when Chicago was incorporated as a city, its charter of incorporation included a clause calling for public schools. Scammon became president of the Chicago Board of Education in the 1850s.

Between 1865 and 1874 the conservative *Chicago Tribune* was edited by Horace White, who led the newspaper in a liberal direction. In 1872 the paper championed the Liberal Republican movement, which united with the Democrats to support Horace Greeley for the presidency.[15] When the Republican party dropped this splinter movement, Scammon and others established the *Chicago Inter-Ocean*, a paper with decidedly conservative Republican leanings. Scammon, who had held Whiggish views, became a Republican quite naturally in the late 1850s. Abraham Lincoln's son Robert Todd Lincoln studied for the law in Scammon's law office. When Robert's father had a law office in Chicago, it was in the same building as his friend Scammon.

The Chicago Historical Society was formed in Scammon's office in 1856. At about the same time, he joined with several others in the offices of Edmund Andrews to form the Chicago Academy of Sciences.[16] In 1863 the Chicago Astronomical Society decided to build an observatory tied to the first iteration of the University of Chicago. Scammon agreed to underwrite the construction of the observatory's tower and dome if the building was named for his late wife, Mary Ann Haven Dearborn.[17] He paid the director's salary until the Chicago Fire reversed his financial fortunes. Scammon died in Chicago in 1890.

The other member of the triumvirate (with Ogden and Scammon) was Walter Loomis Newberry, a real estate mogul involved with the Galena and Chicago Union Railroad. He served as a director for many years and as president shortly before the Civil War. Born in Connecticut

Fig. 13a. J. Young Scammon. (Chicago History Museum, ICHi-066074.)

Fig. 13b. Walter L. Newberry. (Chicago History Museum, ICHi-068173.)

in 1804, he received an appointment to the United States Military Academy but failed the entrance physical. Consequently, in 1830 Newberry went to work for his older brother Oliver at the brother's dry goods store in Detroit. Two years later he was elected to the Detroit City Council. Joining a syndicate including William Astor (John Jacob's son) and Lewis Cass, Walter invested in real estate in what would become Milwaukee, Green Bay, and Chicago. He ultimately acquired a tract of land on the north side that extended from Kinzie Street to Chicago Avenue and from LaSalle to Market Street. Together, Newberry, Ogden, and John H. Kinzie owned most of the North Division. When a fire destroyed the Newberrys' Detroit store in 1833, the two brothers moved to Chicago, where Walter actively promoted the sale of town lots. The dramatic increase in land prices over the course of the next several years made him a wealthy man. He also entered into business with George W. Dole, who had moved to Chicago as his brother's partner.

Walter Newberry and Ogden helped organize the Illinois Whig Party, and Newberry worked hard to get his friend elected mayor. He was involved in the financial sector through the Merchants' Savings, Loan, and Trust Co., which he helped found and served as a director for many years. Newberry served as the first president of the Young Men's Library Association (a group that evolved into the Chicago Public Library), as a member of the Chicago School Board, of which he was twice the chairman, as president of the Chicago Historical Society, and as city comptroller and acting mayor. An ardent abolitionist, he joined the Republicans in 1855 and actively supported Abraham Lincoln.

Walter Newberry is best remembered for his estate. In 1868, as death neared, he drew up a will that left everything to his wife and daughters during their lives, and the balance to their heirs. In the event that there were no heirs, a library would become the alternative inheritor of half the funds. Both daughters died unmarried and left their estates to their mother. When she died in 1885, the Chicago Public Library, her husband helped start, was well established. The trustees of Newberry's will decided to use the bequest of slightly more than $2 million to establish the Newberry Library as a noncirculating reference library.[18] It has become one of the world's foremost research centers.

The *Democrat* and "Long John" Wentworth

While Scammon and Newberry were among the city's leading Whigs (later Republicans), one of the city's leading Democrats, "Long John" Wentworth, became involved with the newspaper business shortly after his arrival. He was also actively involved in politics, serving for many years as Chicago's congressman, the person charged with looking after the city's interests in the U.S. House of Representatives. His nickname derived from the fact he was six feet, six inches tall and weighed approximately three hundred pounds. The grandson of one of New Hampshire's delegates to the Continental Congress, Wentworth was born in the Granite State in 1815 and graduated from Dartmouth College in the Class of 1836. Shortly after graduating, he left for the west with $100 in his pocket.[19] On arriving in Detroit, he advertised for a teaching position in that city and in Ann Arbor, but none was forthcoming. He then put his trunk on a ship to Chicago and purchased a ticket on the stagecoach to Michigan City, Indiana, from which he hiked the rest of the way to Chicago.

John Calhoun, a Jacksonian Democrat from New York, arrived in Chicago in 1833 and began publishing the weekly *Chicago Democrat,* the city's first newspaper. It appeared in 1833 but then disappeared in the winter of 1834–35, only to be resurrected a year later—presumably because the Whigs had started a paper. Daniel Brainard, a well-known surgeon, arrived in Chicago in 1836 and became editor of the *Democrat* the following year. Because Wentworth had written articles for newspapers supporting Jacksonian policies while in college, Brainard turned the job over to Wentworth shortly after his arrival. Within a couple of years Wentworth purchased the paper. He used his spare time to read for the law. In the summer of 1841 he took a leave from the *Democrat* to study law at Harvard and was admitted to the Illinois bar shortly thereafter.[20] Wentworth continued his involvement with the *Democrat* until 1861, just before the start of the Civil War.[21]

Concurrently, he entered politics. The growth of Illinois's population as reported in the 1840 census meant that there would be an increase in the number of U.S. Representatives from the state. Wentworth used the *Democrat* to promote his views. It was said that Wentworth published more news about himself than about the city. If so, it may well have contributed to a successful political career. Wentworth was elected to the U.S. House of Representatives six times, the first five as a Democrat (1843–1851 and 1853–1855). When first elected, his district, one of seven in Illinois, was huge: it included the area from the Wisconsin line south about 250 miles and from the Indiana line west about 100 miles. His motto was "Liberty and Economy," and he was intensely anti-debt and anti-repudiation, in addition to favoring payments in specie and low taxation. Fellow Chicagoans Stephen A. Douglas and John Wright were pressing for a land grant for the Illinois Central Railroad, and Wentworth strongly supported it. However, he quarreled

Fig. 14. John Wentworth. (Chicago History Museum, ICHi-012874.)

with Douglas's willingness to placate the interests of the South and found himself, an old Jacksonian Democrat, being drawn to the policies of the Republicans and of Abraham Lincoln. He served his final term as a congressman (1865–1867) as a Republican and wrestled with how to retire the debt accumulated during the war and how to resume specie payments, which had been abandoned during the war.[22]

Wentworth also served two terms as mayor of Chicago (1857–1858 and 1860–1861). At the start of each term, the city was saddled with debt that Wentworth retired while reducing taxes. Before his first term, the city had begun the task of raising itself from the mud as part of the project to install a sewer system. Shortly after he took office, a freshet flooded much of Chicago, leading Wentworth to endorse a controversial proposal to raise the level of the city an additional two to three feet. Despite its obvious cost, a compromise measure passed.[23] Among the buildings to be raised was Tremont House, where Wentworth lived while in Chicago. He had married Roxanna Marie Loomis of Troy, New York, in 1840, but she chose to remain in Troy. She occasionally visited Chicago, and he, Troy. They had five children, but only their daughter Roxanna (b. 1854) survived infancy. When Marie died in 1870, Roxanna moved west to join her father in Chicago.

Earlier in his life Wentworth had found himself in the middle of a peculiar proposition. As noted, the Northwest Land Ordinance of 1787 called for the division of the Northwest Territory into three to five states. If there were to be more than three, the north-south dividing line was to be a line drawn tangent to "the southerly bend or extreme of lake Michigan." When Illinois was granted statehood in 1818, its northern border was moved north so that the entire area benefited by the I&M Canal would be contained within a single state. The Indiana border had been moved north earlier, but by much less. Disputes over the Michigan-Indiana border led to Michigan's being awarded what is now its Upper Peninsula.[24] Wisconsin politicians, anxious for their territory to become a state, correctly argued that if the northern tier of Illinois counties were in fact part of Wisconsin, as the law called for, there would be sufficient population for statehood. This was not a pipe dream. The rate of settlement in northern Illinois, centering on the Galena lead-mining district, accelerated almost immediately following Illinois's statehood. Most of this district was to the north of the 1787 boundary line, but political power in Illinois was firmly in the hands of the more populous south. Consequently, in October 1828 residents of the Galena district petitioned Congress for the creation of a new territory. Basing their claim on the 1787 ordinance, they argued that people in the district had a "right to expect" that the entire district north of the 1787 boundary line "would remain together."[25] They argued that, as unrepresented people, their sovereignty had been transferred without their knowledge or consent.

Wisconsin politicians, in particular Governors Henry Dodge and James Doty, noted that Illinoisans residing north of "the southerly bend or extreme of lake Michigan" seemed anxious to sever their connection to Illinois. In most of the fourteen northern Illinois counties involved (Cook County was not), elections were held during 1842 that overwhelmingly favored union with Wisconsin.[26] Northern Illinoisans, mainly migrants from New York and New England, supported union with Wisconsin because they found they had much more in common with their neighbors to the north than with those to the south. Southern Illinoisans had a three-to-one advantage in the state government, and there was a large state debt from the overly ambitious program of internal improvements that, apart from completing the I&M Canal, would have benefited these northerners little, if at all.

Many promises were made in the attempt to lure northern Illinoisans to cast their lot with Wisconsin. Wentworth noted in his reminiscences:

> The disputed tract had two Congressmen, the Hon. Joseph P. Hoge, of Galena, . . . and myself. And Wisconsin offered to make us the first two Senators, and also offered to give the disputed tract the first Governor. It was proposed to enact a law submitting the binding force of the ordinance of 1787 to the Supreme Court of the United States. Our Chicago people were much divided upon the question, and I really believe serious consequences would have grown out of it but for the embarrassments that would be caused by having the Illinois and Michigan Canal owned by two states. As an original question, all the five states being out of the Union, there is no doubt but Congress would have enforced the provisions of the ordinance, and Illinois been saved from the annoyance of Chicago lobbyists. But might made right. Wisconsin being out of the Union she could only come into it with boundaries prescribed by a majority of the states in it, and I lost the honor of being a Wisconsin United States Senator.[27]

And Chicago and the canal remained part of Illinois.

When he died in October 1888, the conservative *Tribune* noted, "To the last he was the same self-reliant, self-assertive, colossal embodiment of defiant, intellectual egotism, unrelieved by sweetness or light . . . too flinty and rugged to admit of polish, too hard and tenacious to assimilate or blend with the human material about him."[28] Long John Wentworth's liberal *Democrat* had contributed to the rapid growth and shaping of Chicago's newspaper industry.

Merchant Princes: Palmer and Field

An industry that played a major role in the development of Chicago's commercial function was dry goods, as seen, in particular, in the person of the two "merchant princes" of the pre-fire years: Potter Palmer and Marshall Field. By the 1870s most goods arrived in the Chicago area by rail, and the city had developed a large cadre of wholesale traders because of its position on the rail line, a position that had emerged far earlier, in an age of water transport.

Potter Palmer was born into a Quaker farming family in Albany County, New York, in 1826. When he turned eighteen his parents allowed him to choose an occupation. He chose to become a merchant and, to that end, became a clerk at store in Durham, New York. His employer was a banker, and, by his third year, Palmer was managing the mercantile business while his employer focused on banking. When he turned twenty-one, Palmer opened his own store in Oneida, New York. He stayed there for two and one-half years before seeking a larger town. After moving to Lockport, New York, for a year, he moved to Chicago in 1852 and opened a dry goods store.

Fig. 15a. Potter Palmer, c. 1868. (Chicago History Museum, ICHi-027395.)

The wares in his Chicago store were aimed at women, and he encouraged their trade with several unorthodox practices. Other merchants largely rejected what came to be called the "Palmer system." Palmer insisted that his goods be displayed in an attractive manner, both in the store and in print advertisements. His store was large, with extensive window displays including price comparisons. He allowed customers to take merchandise on approval and offered generous exchange provisions including a full refund.[29] Perhaps just as important, he emphasized the continual introduction of new goods and, wherever possible, attempted to become the exclusive Chicago agent for those goods.

At the start of the Civil War, Palmer's store was fully stocked and remained so during the war.[30] After the war Palmer's doctor advised him to leave the dry goods business, so he brought in two partners, Marshall Field and Levi Leiter. In 1867 Palmer left the partnership to concentrate on his growing real estate interests. A year later, his former partners leased from him a new building at State and Washington Streets. Palmer owned a good deal of property along State Street and began to erect other buildings, all of which would burn in the fire. He would borrow $1.7 million to rebuild.[31]

Fig. 15b. Marshall Field. Photograph from the Matzene Studio. (Chicago History Museum, ICHi-010281.)

Before the fire, Chicago's main downtown street was Lake Street, given that with its east-west axis it was parallel to the harbor. Afterwards, with the need to rebuild and the railroad in ascendancy, Palmer aggressively promoted a reorientation of the downtown district. State Street, which ran north-south, became the new main street, with his Palmer House Hotel and the firm of Field & Leiter in "Palmer's Marble Palace" the anchors of the rebuilt downtown.

Marshall Field's route to succeeding Palmer as Chicago's primary merchant prince encompasses much of the industry's history in Chicago. Field was born in Massachusetts in 1834. At age seventeen he began working in a Pittsfield, Massachusetts, dry goods store. A year later, in 1852, he headed west looking for new opportunities. He ultimately came to Chicago, where his brother was living.

What was perhaps Chicago's first wholesale merchant firm, Hamlin & Day, had opened in 1845. Two years later, the firm of Wadsworth & Phelps began; it became Cooley, Wadsworth, and Phelps the following year. After another two years, it became known as Cooley, Wadsworth, & Co. following Phelps's departure. This firm would hire two of the major forces in the industry.

John V. Farwell was born in New York State in 1825. Thirteen years later he moved to Illinois with his family. At the age of twenty he arrived in Chicago after graduating from Mount Morris Seminary. At first he worked for Chicago's city clerk but ended up as a bookkeeper for the dry goods firm of Hamilton &

White. After a year he moved to the firm of Hamlin & Day, then, in 1847, went to work at Wadsworth & Phelps. He was made a partner in 1850.

In 1855 Cooley, Wadsworth & Co. hired Marshall Field.[32] In 1860, after a successful stint as a commercial traveler and an offer to return to Massachusetts as a partner in his former firm, Field elected to stay in Chicago and become a junior partner. Four years later, with Cooley's departure and Wadsworth's retirement, the firm became Farwell, Field & Co., and Levi Leiter, who had started as a bookkeeper in 1853, became a partner. The personalities of the two principals suggested that the partnership would be short-lived in an age when there would be considerable personal contact. Although Farwell valued Field's business judgment, Field's formality conflicted with his partner's more relaxed manner. The relationship lasted but a year as Field and Leiter left to join Potter Palmer.[33]

In 1865 Field, Palmer, and Leiter hired Aaron Montgomery Ward, who quit his job at a Michigan general store and moved to Chicago.[34] After two years he took a job as a traveling salesman for a similar firm in St. Louis.[35] Ward lived among the farmers and learned "their living habits, their likes and dislikes, their complaints about the high cost of goods bought at retail from the inefficient, obsolescent general store."[36] He conceived the idea that through direct mail marketing he could make the goods enjoyed by city dwellers accessible to people living in small towns and on farms. Ward hoped to keep prices competitive by buying direct from manufacturers for cash and saving the expense of retail outlets and salesmen. Ward recognized that the National Grange of the Order of Patrons of Husbandry, better known as the Grange, was becoming a potent economic and social force in the agricultural Midwest. The organization believed strongly in cooperative purchasing to reduce farmers' expenses. By structuring the business as he did, and by emphasizing the very things in which the Grange believed, Montgomery Ward & Co. became the official supply house of the Grange. But before the business could open, the fire intervened. Ward suffered serious losses, and the start of business was delayed until 1872. Despite opposition from wholesalers and retail merchants alike, his concept proved an immediate success. As one measure of this triumph, Pierce points to the fact that the initial circular advertising the company's existence and the products it offered was one page long. Fourteen years later, the *Buyers' Guide*, which illustrated just about every item with a woodcut, had grown to 304 pages.[37]

The Field and Leiter partnership with Palmer lasted only two years; Field and Leiter remained partners until 1881. By then, Marshall Field & Co. had become a leading dry goods firm and a pioneering department store, the most complete retail establishment west of New York City. Because of Chicago's location on the rail network, many western merchants obtained their wares from Field's wholesale division. The Palmer system was still, in Field's phrase, to "give the lady what she wants." Its success forced other merchants to copy the practice.

The impact of what Hamlin and Day begat was such that, at the close of the Civil War, Chicago was the leading dry goods market in the Midwest. Buyers from western cities came there seeking wares, and drummers from Chicago firms visited western cities seeking affiliations. What made Chicago the dominant Midwest node for this business was the railroad. There is a story of a St. Louis merchant who traveled west, intent on developing business in what was generally considered to be St. Louis's hinterland, only to run into the representatives of Marshall Field, with whom local merchants had been dealing for some time.

The Reaper and Cyrus McCormick

One of the most iconic goods to be produced in Chicago was the McCormick reaper, which occupies a particularly important place in the city's history. The first McCormick reaper was constructed by Robert McCormick in the Shenandoah Valley in Virginia. When Robert abandoned his device, his son Cyrus Hall McCormick (born in 1809) continued to work on the concept and patented his version in 1834.[38] He did little with it for several years, however. It was not until 1840 that Cyrus believed his reaper was ready to market.

Two of Chicago's most important boosters became involved with reaper production. As discussed above, John Wright was involved for a short time with Obed Hussey, while William Ogden became involved with Cyrus McCormick. Hussey patented a horse-drawn reaper in 1833 and immediately began to sell it. Because he was unwilling to make improvements, it never worked as well as Hussey hoped. As it turned out, Hussey's design proved far better for mowing grasses than for reaping grain; McCormick's, just the opposite. This meant Hussey's potential market was in the East; McCormick's, on the Prairies.

In 1845, when he realized the demand for his reapers would be much greater in the West than in Virginia, McCormick moved from Virginia to begin production in Cincinnati. Hussey, who did a good deal of work on his original machine in Maryland, also moved to Cincinnati but marketed his machine in the East.[39] McCormick moved his operations to Chicago in 1847.[40] In part, this was attributable to Chicago's position relative to the emerging wheat-growing region. McCormick believed Chicago would become the great city of the Midwest, and Chicago, in the person of Ogden, offered to finance the move. Cyrus and his brother Leander established the firm of Cyrus H. McCormick and Brothers in 1848.[41] McCormick entered into agreements with C. M. Gray to manufacture reapers and, with Ogden, to distribute them.[42] It was expected that the move and the new arrangements would benefit McCormick's firm, Ogden's railroad, and the city of Chicago.[43]

Fig. 16. Cyrus H. McCormick. (Chicago History Museum, ICHi-068139.)

The key was Chicago's position on midwestern trade routes. Raw materials could be shipped by water into the city, and, indeed, the McCormick factory in the pre-fire years was located on the north side of the river close to the lakefront. And, as noted, the finished product could be shipped by rail to customers all over the West. The infrastructure developed to serve Chicago's commercial needs required little modification to serve industry's needs.

McCormick adopted several business practices that make it appear more like a modern firm than most nineteenth-century firms. For example, the firm established agency relationships with local businessmen whose job it was to promote the use of reapers. It was one of the first manufacturing enterprises to offer a written guarantee on every machine, and it offered a free trial period during which dissatisfied customers could get a refund of the stated purchase price. In contrast to the normal selling procedure, in which the seller and buyer haggled over the price, McCormick widely advertised the price in farm journals, newspapers, and other print media.[44] It can be argued that McCormick's ability to mass produce and mass market his machines, rather than his skills as an inventor, underlay his success.

By 1860 there were perhaps one hundred companies selling reapers, but McCormick was by far the largest, producing four thousand annually. The explanation for this rapid growth seems to be the efficiency of mechanical reaping on flat terrain. Reapers were a key factor in the expansion of midwestern agriculture.[45] They removed a major bottleneck in production. Given grain's perishability, a family farm could only plant as much as the family could harvest. The reaper made it possible to do in one day what previously had occupied the entire harvest season.

Many agricultural implements, especially the reaper, were shared, rented, jointly owned, or otherwise acquired, and more so as the cash outlay for implements increased. The rapidly growing number of implements, including the reaper, allowed a family to farm more acres, thereby expanding their output. Adoption of machinery conserved labor, and the addition of plentiful land inputs in the West raised the productivity of both capital and labor. During the Civil

War the demand for reapers increased significantly. From the start, agricultural implements, which were much more widely disseminated in the North, became as important to northern farmers as slaves were to southern farmers.

When the Chicago Fire burned the McCormick factory, a larger facility was constructed at the corner of Blue Island and Western Avenues, on the north bank of the South Branch, that produced twenty-five thousand reapers annually.[46]

City Raising, Palace Cars, and George Pullman

The final entrepreneur and industrialist of the pre-fire era discussed here who exploited Chicago's commercial assets to further his industrial pursuits was George Pullman, whose Pullman Palace Car Company leased space on trains for its privately owned railcars. Pullman was born in New York in 1831. When he was fourteen, his family moved to a town on the Erie Canal to help with the work of widening the canal. His father had invented and patented (1841) a machine using jackscrews to raise buildings to new foundations. After a short stint working as a clerk for a country store, Pullman assumed responsibility for the family business. After his father died in 1854, he received a contract to raise twenty more buildings along the line of the Erie Canal.

Pullman arrived in Chicago in 1857 knowing that the city would have a demand for his services as it built its new sewer system and raised the city's level. He was a partner in a firm titled Ely, Smith & Pullman, which was one of several firms hired to lift buildings. The company got a good deal of favorable publicity when it raised the five-story brick Tremont House six feet, allegedly as the hotel guests remained inside.[47] It was clear to Pullman that as old buildings were raised and new buildings were built at the new level, there wouldn't be a continuing demand for his services. Looking for something new, he decided on the manufacture and leasing of railroad cars.

Fig. 17. George M. Pullman. Photograph by Horton Bros. (Chicago History Museum, ICHi-021773.)

Contemporary sleeping cars were a new and very uncomfortable feature on railroads.[48] The beds were too close together; the ventilation was poor at best. Pullman formed a partnership with Benjamin Field to make improvements.[49] They entered into a contract with the Michigan Central Railroad in 1859 to fit two old passenger cars as sleeping cars. Pullman's first car was like those on other lines; it consisted of a series of bunks and was used only at night. Four years later, in 1863, when he couldn't reach an agreement with a car manufacturer, he obtained the use of an old Michigan Central repair shed in which he produced the first "Palace" car, one that could be used by day as well as for sleeping. It was based on the packet boats that plied the Erie Canal of Pullman's youth. The car cost $18,000 to produce and took a year to complete. Pullman then entered into an agreement with the Michigan Central whereby it was to use the car for several years. The enterprise was successful, and, over the course of the next thirty years, another two thousand Pullman cars were constructed. In early 1865 President Lincoln commissioned a car, and it was in that car later that year that his body was carried from Washington to Springfield, Illinois.[50]

In the years before the fire, Chicago's businessmen exploited its location on both water and rail networks to extend the city's influence, in essence, from coast to coast. The national rail network centered on Chicago made the city competitive over much of the area east of the Rocky Mountains despite the presence of many nodal sites throughout the area. People on cattle ranches in western Kansas got their dry goods from Chicago and sent their animals to stockyards in Chicago. The same was true for grain farmers in western Iowa.

For all the years before the fire, and for many years thereafter, the transshipment point located at the mouth of the Chicago River, the old Chicago Portage, was the key factor in Chicago's success. In this chapter we have looked at a few industries and entrepreneurs who made use of that location and contributed to Chicago's growth. In the twentieth century, highways and, especially, airplanes weakened the attraction to such locations as the confluence of Lake Michigan and the Chicago River. Yet the basis for the first airmail routes was the rail network. Fiber-optic cable for modern communication systems was placed on railroad rights-of-way. Since Chicago was the break between eastern and western railroad routes, it became the break between eastern and western airmail routes. Since the railroads came to the I&M Canal and the port of Chicago, it turns out that the highways and air routes did, too. The tie remains unbroken; that "glacial afterthought" continues to impact the city's growth. Chicago can still be considered a canal town.

CHAPTER 6

Creating Position: Sanitation and Health

One of Chicago's most obvious features is its flatness, a result of its location on a glacial lakebed. As has been noted, this meant that mud would be a nuisance and drainage a challenge. This was tied to a second challenge, even if it was misunderstood at the time—the health of the population. This chapter discusses the development of the sanitation and health infrastructure in Chicago in the years before the fire. To Dean, "position" includes what must be done so that a site can accommodate commerce and industry. In early Chicago, this meant that sanitation infrastructure was needed. By 1871 Chicagoans had sanitation and health infrastructure equivalent to that of much more established places, but not until the application of germ theory near the turn of the twentieth century would cities in general would become healthier places in which to live.[1]

At the turn of the nineteenth century, there were other difficulties as well. A posting at the first Fort Dearborn was unpleasant at best. The normal diet for anyone on the frontier would have included poorly cooked meat, a few fruits and vegetables, and boiled coffee. Summer brought malaria and other fevers. Winter brought cold and isolation; contact with the rest of the world was difficult given that the lakes were frozen. The hastily constructed buildings that provided shelter were crowded and unventilated. The diseases that affected those not native to the Illinois country were those that laid settlers low everywhere: malaria, typhoid fever, pneumonia, and a loosely defined group of digestive ailments. Medical care was limited by the lack of supplies and equipment in the possession of Fort Dearborn's doctor.

Within a year of the fort's founding, the sick list was long and remained so. And the same was true after the fort was rebuilt.[2] By the early 1830s, supply problems were alleviated to the extent that Chicagoans could purchase a large variety of patent medicines, which likely had little positive effect on their health.

In July 1832 soldiers passing through the city to fight the Black Hawk War brought cholera to Chicago, a remote part of a worldwide pandemic.[3] Cholera would continue to be the area's most feared disease for many years to come.[4] Chicagoans looked to their city fathers and the state legislature for financial assistance to combat this scourge.

In Chicago's law of incorporation, health and sanitation are mentioned only in the context of giving the municipality's officials the right to remove nuisances. When the act of incorporation was modified in 1835, the trustees' powers were extended so that they could adopt regulations to help secure the general health, such as quarantine laws. But the threat of cholera led to a demand for more; hence the Charter of 1837, which incorporated Chicago as a city and set the pattern for how it would be governed. It authorized the City Council to appoint three commissioners to form a Board of Health. Among the board's first expenditures were improvements to the water supply. In addition, it was to appoint a health officer each year who was responsible for preventing the spread of disease. These provisions codified actions that were taken as early as the 1832 cholera epidemic. The trustees were given the power to make public the location of and restrain the activities of businesses harming the public health. They could abate nuisances. Quarantine regulations allowed the Board of Health to remove infected ships from the harbor and move nonresidents infected with a communicable disease out of the city. The health officer was to inspect food markets, prepare death certificates, visit residents with infectious illnesses, and board vessels to check for sickness.[5]

Drainage and Sewerage

Perhaps the most serious problem facing Chicagoans was mud. An old story tells of two women coming out of a downtown store and seeing an officer from Fort Dearborn in full dress uniform up to his waist in mud. They inquired if he needed assistance. His response was that, though he himself did not, he believed the horse he was riding did.

Public works aimed at improving sanitation predate Chicago's becoming a city. Drainage was only one dimension of the city's sanitation problem; water supply and waste disposal were the others. In 1834 the town dug a public water well, but Chicagoans preferred Lake Michigan water to that from underground wells. The sluggish Chicago River provided water for some, but it, too, was regarded as inferior in quality to lake water. Some people traveled daily to the lake with pails; others waited for a waterman and his horse-drawn cart to bring lake water to their door.[6]

In that same year (1834) the town borrowed $60 to dig a ditch down State Street to the river.[7] Given the flat terrain, instead of draining the street, the ditch did the opposite. Whenever the river rose owing to rain or melting snow, the ditch provided a channel by which the water could back up and flood the town. In 1837 the new city used its authority to tackle the drainage problem, but all efforts proved ineffective. In 1850 roadside ditches were still the main medium of drainage. There was no sewer system, and garbage was simply dumped in the ditches in the hope that the next rain would flush it to the river. Chicago's random waste disposal methods led to a succession of cholera and dysentery epidemics.

In 1852 the Illinois legislature created sewage commissioners to install sewers in the most densely settled areas of Chicago to combat what was generally conceded to be an intolerable situation.[8] In 1855, as president of the City of Chicago's Board of Sewerage Commissioners, William Ogden was instrumental in implementing the first comprehensive sewer system for an American city.[9]

The commissioners sought "the most competent engineer of the time who was available for the position of chief engineer."[10] Their selection, Ellis Sylvester Chesbrough, resigned his position as Boston's city engineer and came to Chicago.

Before the new engineer's arrival, Chicago's sewerage commissioners solicited thoughts and suggestions from the public. Thirty-nine proposals were received, and, although the board claimed that Chesbrough utilized many of these suggestions, he did not use any of the proposals in their entirety.[11] His report was submitted almost immediately after he accepted the position. In it, he outlined his plan for a sewerage system designed to solve Chicago's drainage and waste-disposal problem.[12]

Chesbrough's task was to construct a sewerage system whose main objective was to "improve and preserve" the city's health. In his opinion, the existing privy vaults and drainage sluices were "abominations that should be swept away as speedily as possible," and "to construct the vaults as they should be, and maintain them even in a comparatively inoffensive condition, would be more expensive than to construct an entire system of sewerage for no other purpose, if the past experience of London and other large cities was any guide for the future of Chicago."[13]

Ellis Sylvester Chesbrough was born in Baltimore County, Maryland, in July 1813.[14] An unsuccessful business venture exhausted the family's means and suspended young Sylvester's education. Between his ninth and fifteenth birthdays he spent only a year in a classroom, but he did find time outside his countinghouse duties to pursue his studies. Most of his basic education was obtained without the benefit of formal training or a regular teacher, and the same was true of his engineering education.

Fig. 18. Ellis Sylvester Chesbrough, c. 1870. Photograph by Wallis Brothers. (Chicago History Museum, ICHi-009793.)

In 1828 Chesbrough was employed as a chainman engaged in preliminary surveying work for the city in and about Baltimore.[15] Most of the engineers were army officers, many of them graduates of the U.S. Military Academy's engineering course. Chesbrough was fortunate in being affiliated with several of the army's most prominent engineers. In 1830–31 he worked as an assistant engineer to Colonel Stephen H. Long.[16] Near the end of 1831, Chesbrough joined the engineering corps of Captain William Gibbs McNeill, where he served immediately under Lieutenant George W. Whistler.[17]

The Panic of 1837 and the resulting depression had dealt a hard blow to the country's internal improvement bubble, and Chesbrough, like many other engineers, found himself out of work as the flow of funds dried up in the early 1840s.

In 1846, after a brief stint as a farmer, Chesbrough was offered a position with the Boston Water Works.[18] Up to this time, all his experience was related to railroad engineering. He was reluctant to accept the Boston position because he considered himself unacquainted with hydraulic engineering. He assented after being assured of John Jervis's counsel. An association with Jervis was valuable because Jervis had been active in every phase of engineering, particularly those dealing with hydraulics. He was a product of the New York canal system and had learned hydraulic engineering on the job by working on the Erie Canal. In 1846 Jervis was appointed consulting engineer on the Boston Water Works, with Chesbrough the chief engineer.[19] Jervis was responsible for designing both the Cochituate Aqueduct and the Brookline Reservoir; Chesbrough, for supervising the execution of Jervis's plans.[20] In 1850 Chesbrough became sole commissioner of Boston's waterworks, and a year later, he became Boston's first city engineer, the position he occupied when Chicago's Board of Sewerage Commissioners hired him. Having learned about sewer construction, grading, and "building-raising," he now merged them and "pulled Chicago out of the mud."

Chesbrough's plan called for an intercepting combined sewer system that emptied into the river.[21] Combined sewers collected sewage from both buildings and streets, consistent with the best contemporary thinking and practice. He realized that this was a potential health hazard, particularly during the warmer months, and might obstruct river navigation if debris made the waterways shallower.[22] Drainage was to be accomplished by gravity, but Chicago's flatness created a problem. This was resolved by the simple but costly expedient of having the city raise its level.[23] As construction progressed away from the river, the sewers were laid at the level necessary to accomplish gravity flow. Earth was then packed around them, entirely covering them. The packed-down fill provided roadbeds for new, higher streets. These streets were slightly higher in the center, with gutter apertures leading to the sewer. Such streets would stay dry and could be paved—in contrast to the mud that had plagued the city.

Much of the fill was obtained by dredging the Chicago River. The river had been dredged previously, but it was still too small to handle the anticipated sewage load. Chesbrough planned to widen and deepen the river, as well as to straighten its meandering course.

The city council decided to raise the grade to ten feet on streets adjacent to the river, which was lower than what Chesbrough advocated.[24] Where vacant lots existed, they were filled to the new level. A few old frame buildings were torn down, and the lots filled. It proved relatively easy, albeit expensive, to raise frame buildings to the new level. The city's newer buildings, however, also constructed on the old level, were of brick and stone. These newer buildings would not be torn down, and so many of Chicago's homes and offices were to be left "in the

Fig. 19. Clark Street in 1857. (Chicago History Museum, ICHi-031690.)

hole." Because new buildings and sidewalks had to be constructed at the higher level, Chicago increasingly became a city built on two levels.[25] Legal attempts to maintain the lower level were uniformly settled in favor of the city and the higher level.[26]

After the work on Lake Street had begun, the Couch family, owners of the Tremont House, the city's largest hotel, requested an injunction to stay the work. John Dean Caton, chief justice of the Illinois Supreme Court, returned to Chicago to deal with the case, which was concerned with the raising of the city streets and buildings. Given Caton's position, he was permitted to hold a special term of the circuit court. The two opposing lawyers expected a long proceeding, but Caton began asking questions about the facts and about the relevant law. When he finished, he requested the papers in the case be given to him and adjourned the court. Ironically, he then returned to his room at the Tremont Hotel. By the time he turned in for the night, he had written his opinion. He carried that opinion and other documents to the clerk's office the next morning. Arriving before it opened, he put the papers through the transom above the door and returned to the Tremont. Encountering the contractor, he told him that he could start work and was on the train returning to Springfield when the clerk's office opened. His decision supporting the city was not appealed.[27]

The Tremont found a contractor willing to raise the hotel building, one who was able to do the work without interrupting its business. As discussed in chapter 5, that contractor was George Pullman, whose father's technique for raising buildings was used during the enlargement of the Erie Canal. Chesbrough would have known that the problems concomitant with raising the city's grade were surmountable.[28] Pullman was aware that his skills were in demand in Chicago. The Tremont's cellar was emptied, and huge timbers were placed to take the weight of the sustaining walls. Five thousand jackscrews were then placed under the timbers, and 1,250 men were hired to turn them. At a signal, each man turned one screw one-half turn. Chicago folklore says that guests in the hotel were unaware of the activity. The well-known picture of the raising of the Briggs House suggests that people looked out the hotel's windows to watch the work progress. Bricklayers constructed the new outside wall as quickly as there was spare space to lay brick. In the end, the Tremont was raised about six feet; other buildings were raised as much as fourteen feet. One can get a sense of how dynamic Chicago was in those days by considering that no one questioned the expense of building-raising as being far greater than its benefits.

Inevitably, the Chicago River became heavily polluted as a result of the new sewer system. The pollution spread into the lake until it reached the water supply intake. By 1860 Chicago's sewerage commissioners, concerned with the offensive

Fig. 20. The raising of Briggs House, c. 1857. (Chicago History Museum, ICHi-000698.)

condition of the Chicago River, called Chesbrough's attention to the "possibility and probability of an enlargement and deepening of the I&M Canal to such an extent as to create a constant current from the lake to the Illinois River."[29] They understood the consequences of reversing the river. Chesbrough had rejected the idea of a "through steamboat canal" when first considering a wastewater disposal strategy, and he still considered it "too remote" in the late 1850s.[30] And the water supply was a more pressing need.

Water Supply

In 1836 the Illinois legislature incorporated the private Chicago Hydraulic Company.[31] The company was given a seventy-year charter with the proviso that the necessary works be constructed within the first four years. The Panic of 1837 caused construction to be postponed until 1840, and it was not until 1842 that the works were finally operative. This delay led some Chicagoans to hope that the newly chartered city would take advantage of new powers and care for its own water supply. When the Chicago Hydraulic Company's initial supply proved pure and transparent, debate over public ownership was deferred.[32]

Problems with the company's supply arose within a short time. The intake was too near the shore, and occasionally low water levels in the lake left the intake above water. Storms increased turbidity; fish and debris clogged the intake pipe. Even worse, the intake was within reach of sewage discharged into either the

Chicago River or Lake Michigan. During the fall of 1847 the Hydraulic Company's supply was particularly polluted, and most Chicagoans believed the intake pipe needed to be extended farther into the lake.[33] Moreover, the company supplied only about 20 percent of the population. The remainder was dependent on private wells, the waterman, or, in the case of the poor, a bucket dipped in the sewage-befouled Chicago River.

Publicly owned waterworks appeared in 1851 when the Chicago City Hydraulic Company was incorporated; voters approved a $400,000 bond issue the following year.[34] A Board of Water Commissioners was appointed, and a new waterworks was constructed. The water intake was a wooden pipe that extended a few hundred feet out into Lake Michigan, a half-mile north of the Chicago River's mouth. Chicago was growing rapidly by 1850, and soon there were complaints about the offensiveness of the public company's polluted water supply. Furthermore, Chicago's demand for water remained greater than the company's supply capabilities. Although a second pumping station was added in 1857, the average Chicagoan was still not connected to the city supply.

Continued population growth through the decade of the 1850s, the new sewerage works, and the expansion of packinghouses and distilleries had increased the number of pollutants draining into the Chicago River. The "population equivalent," the number of humans it would take to produce all the city's wastes (human, industrial, and so on), was growing much faster than the human population. Lake Michigan soon became fouled by the river's influx, and Chicagoans complained about the public water supply's offensiveness and pollution. In 1859 one of Chicago's water commissioners "proposed to sink a wrought iron pipe . . . one mile out into the lake, to obtain the supply from a point which could not be affected by the river."[35] Chesbrough was asked to study and report on the commissioner's plan, as well as a plan for "erecting additional pumping works, in such locality as shall secure a supply of pure water."[36] Chesbrough's report discussed several methods without making a specific recommendation. Even at this early date, however, he considered a tunnel under the lake to be the most desirable alternative.

Shortly after its formation in 1861, the Board of Public Works, a merging of the sewer and water boards, adopted as its goal the acquisition of an unpolluted water supply. Chesbrough dismissed existing filtration methods as inadequate; his studied opinion was that the tunnel method was the most suitable.[37] When he had worked out the details, which called for a tunnel five feet in diameter extending two miles into the lake and protected by a crib (a structure that houses and protects offshore water intakes) that could also be used during construction, the proposal was submitted to several engineers, all of whom considered the plan to be feasible. Nevertheless, the 1861 board was against adopting the project. After a new board was elected and additional soil examinations were made, Chesbrough's plan for a water-supply tunnel was adopted.[38]

Chesbrough concerned himself only with plans that would bring water from a point two miles east of the existing Chicago Avenue Water Works, and there were two of these: one, an iron pipe with flexible joints, and the other, a tunnel under the bottom of the lake.[39] Although the iron pipe project cost slightly less than would the tunnel project, Chesbrough chose between them on a basis other than the initial cost:

> In consequence of the possibility of such a pipe being injured by anchors, by the sinking of a heavily loaded vessel over it, or by the effect of an unusual current in the lake moving it from its place, it has been thought preferable to attempt the construction of a tunnel under the bottom of the lake.[40]

His research had convinced him that the tunnel's construction would be less difficult than was generally supposed.[41] Lill and Diversey's brewery, adjacent to the waterworks, was the site of artesian borings that showed that, between a depth of twenty-five to one hundred feet, the ground at the lake shore was a clay which was also found on the lake bottom where the water was twenty-five feet deep. A tunnel could easily be constructed in this type of clay, if it were continuous. Chesbrough was confident that the clay was continuous, but he admitted that beds of sand might be interspersed with the clay.

The engineering achievement involved in constructing the water-supply system was no less significant than that represented by Chesbrough's sewer system. As conceived, the task was to dig a shaft near the lake shore to a depth significantly below the lake bottom, sink iron cylinders to the desired depth, then burrow two miles beneath the lake.[42] A similar shaft was to be dug at the lake end, protected by a crib. The engineering problem was to connect the shore end and the lake end by a straight line sixty-nine feet below the surface of Lake Michigan. Contemporary compasses could not be used since, below ground level, local attraction rendered them inaccurate. To a worker in the tunnel, the only place where the direction of the line drawn between the two shafts could be observed was at the top of either shaft. Consequently, when the engineers attempted to run the tunnel's axis parallel to this imaginary line on the lake's surface, they ran into difficulties affecting the turn from shaft to tunnel.

When the lake shaft was completed, workers were lowered in order to begin burrowing westward to meet with the workers burrowing eastward. The tunnel was sloped two feet per mile from the lake end to the shore so that it could be emptied should repairs prove necessary; the water would be shut off at the lake end. Although the methods were primitive—the tunnel was dug entirely by

Fig. 21. The Chicago water tower and the pumping station immediately after the fire. (Chicago History Museum, ICHi-002792.)

hand—it was claimed that the workers caused the two tunnel sections to meet within one inch of achieving a perfectly smooth wall.[43]

In spite of many difficulties, the water tunnel project got under way in 1863 in the midst of the Civil War; the last stone was laid in 1866. At the time of the fire, Chicago's continued rapid growth had created a demand that exceeded the tunnel's capacity; however, provision for a second tunnel had been made when the first was constructed. The policy of attempting to avoid pollution by extending the water intake point had its genesis in the first lake tunnel and continued until it was not feasible to extend the intake further into the lake.[44] Although the waterworks themselves were affected by the fire, the tunnels and mains were not.

Reversing the River

Chesbrough's 1863 report contained a section on "plans for improving the Chicago river."[45] Chesbrough knew that moving the water-supply intake farther into the lake would not improve the river's offensive condition. In the 1855 sewerage report, he had argued that flushing canals would be necessary in both the north and south branches to purify the river, and he restated this position in several reports thereafter. By raising the issue once again, Chesbrough demonstrated that he understood the interdependence between the sewage disposal, drainage, and water supply strategies. He argued for flushing canals because they were "undoubtedly feasible, would be completely under the control of the city, and there is every reason to believe [they] would be effectual."[46] He correctly assumed that "drainage southwest into the Illinois River Valley" would be the ultimate solution to separating the sewage outfall from the water supply intake, but he rejected it as "requiring much larger means than the Board can at present control."[47]

Once lake water reached the shore, it was distributed through a system of mains and pipes. The system's force was obtained from standpipes into which water was pumped.[48] As the city grew, several additional pumping stations were required in order to increase the pressure in areas inland from the shore. With continued growth and the annexation of suburban areas, Chicago constructed additional pumping stations, dug new lake tunnels with intakes protected by cribs, and finally in 1898 began the task of combining the several tunnel and pumping systems into an integrated whole. This system, with improvements, is the basis for Chicago's present supply.

Urban growth of the type Chicago experienced in the pre-fire years meant the river's condition worsened independent of the infrastructure that had been, and was being, built. An 1865 report recommended a reduction in the summit level of the I&M Canal below the lake level, and the project was approved shortly thereafter. It was hoped this would draw enough lake water through the Chicago River to create a purifying current and to keep much of the sewage from the water supply intake. The technology is known as the "dilution method." The canal was deepened over the twenty-six-mile stretch between Bridgeport and Lockport, and additional pumps were added at the Bridgeport end. It is customary to date the formal reversal of the Chicago River from the completion of these works in 1871 though, under certain conditions, the river had been reversed for more than a decade. When the I&M Canal plan was changed to make it a shallow-cut canal, the summit level of the canal had to be fed by pumps. Several summers in the 1850s were hot and dry, so the pumps had to be run almost continuously. Because the Chicago River was an open sewer, it was clear when the river's current was reversed.

In recent years it has become common to date the river's reversal to the opening of the Chicago Sanitary District's Main Channel in 1900. Those who are aware of the earlier works argue that they "didn't work as planned." Two factors explain the major problems with the works that opened in 1871. First, the Ogden-Wentworth ditch, dug in 1871, created a countervailing current. Second, and more important, the city's consistent economic growth and increasing industrialization dramatically increased the population equivalent, a trend that continued into the twentieth century.

In the 1860s, William Ogden owned land just north of where the I&M Canal passed through Mud Lake, where the Stevenson Expressway now crosses Harlem Avenue. To the southwest, John Wentworth had a farm retreat in the town of Summit. Drainage was a problem for much of the area's land, as its proximity to Mud Lake would suggest. Beginning in the mid-1860s, Ogden dredged a five-mile channel from the West Fork of the Chicago River's South Branch to the Des Plaines River near Summit, a ditch that paralleled the canal. The purpose was to drain the North Arm of Mud Lake.[49] Wentworth's land bordered the project for approximately a half mile, and he gave his consent to it. Consequently, the project became known as the Ogden-Wentworth ditch.[50] Spring floods in 1872 enlarged the ditch, diverting the Des Plaines River toward the Chicago River and compromising the latter's reversal, which had just begun. The ditch has been blamed for the reversal's not having its desired effects. When cholera struck again in 1873 (along with continuing smallpox and dysentery epidemics), the ditch was held to be the cause.[51] In 1874 Ogden consented to the construction of a dam (the Ogden Dam) at the west end to keep the Des Plaines River from emptying into the ditch unless there was a flood.[52] It caused the Des Plaines to overflow south of Summit. The dispute continued for years, and since Wentworth outlived Ogden, much of the anger was aimed at him. The controversy didn't end until the Sanitary and Ship Canal opened in 1900.

While the construction of the Ogden Dam solved the first problem, Chicago's continued economic growth produced so much waste that the city's population equivalent grew at a much faster rate than its human population and exceeded the newly dredged I&M Canal's capacity to oxidize wastes. The resulting growth of pollution in the Chicago River and, following large storms, Lake Michigan led to the creation of the Sanitary District of Chicago (1889) and the construction of the Sanitary and Ship Canal, which increased both the capacity of the channel and the capacity of the pumps. The old system worked well enough that it was kept in operation while the new, larger channel was dug next to it with a capacity designed for a population equivalent of 3.3 million. There was no alteration of the basic strategy. There was little consideration of the fact that continued economic and population growth would lead the population equivalent to exceed the Sanitary District's capacity in short order.[53] The ability of the dilution method to successfully execute the city's sanitation strategy on its own would have been short-lived. The new works would have been overwhelmed by the district's domestic wastes alone, and the industrial wastes were growing rapidly as well.[54]

As a consequence, the Sanitary District immediately began experiments with emerging sewage treatment technologies, especially with respect to the wastes from the stockyards. The adoption of sewage treatment made the Sanitary

District's canal system appear to be more successful than its 1871 predecessor. Without the new treatment technologies, the same criticisms would have been leveled at the new canal as its predecessor. Dating the reversal of the Chicago River to the opening of the 1871 works, not the 1900 works, is the proper thing to do.

Doctors and Hospitals

By 1871 Chicago's sanitation infrastructure was on a par with that of cities that had been established much earlier. Given that it was sited on a freshwater lake, the city had to come to grips with the problem of interdependency between water supply and wastewater disposal. That was one of the reasons why Chicago was the first city to install a comprehensive sewer system. The health of its citizenry was a major reason for the wastewater disposal strategy that reversed the flow of the Chicago River and conserved the city's Lake Michigan water supply. But health required a good deal more than a first-rate sanitation system.[55]

William Egan, who moved to Chicago in 1833, was one of the first physicians to arrive on his own account rather than being assigned to work at Fort Dearborn. Shortly thereafter, two other doctors, Josiah C. Goodhue, who arrived in 1835, and Daniel Brainard, who arrived the following year, formed a partnership and addressed the need to augment the supply of physicians by lobbying for a medical college. Brainard, it will be recalled, was also editor of the *Chicago Democrat* before relinquishing the job to John Wentworth. On March 2, 1837, the Rush Medical College was incorporated.[56] It was named in honor of Benjamin Rush, the only physician to sign the Declaration of Independence.[57] Brainard became president; Goodhue, a trustee. William Ogden was the president of the Board of Trustees. Two days after Rush's incorporation Chicago became a city, and Goodhue was elected alderman for the First Ward.[58] In the autumn of 1838, however, he moved to Rockford. Brainard, who remained president of Rush until his death in 1866, also lobbied for the first county hospital and helped organize the county and state medical societies.[59]

Rush Medical College was yet another victim of the Panic of 1837; the first course of lectures was not offered until 1843, when the school had its first graduate. The following year a building was opened at Dearborn and Indiana (now Grand) Streets on the north side of the river; Newberry and Ogden donated the lot.[60]

By 1848 the school had graduated seventy-one physicians. Like most medical schools at that time, there were two sixteen-week terms, with four lectures daily. The second term was largely a repeat of the first. Pierce reports:

> For graduation, students were required to have had three years of study with "a respectable physician," two courses of lectures, one of which had to be in Rush, or, in lieu of one course of lectures, two years of practice. Furthermore,

> the candidate had to be "of good moral character"; he must present a thesis on some medical subject in his own handwriting to be approved by the faculty, and must pass "a satisfactory examination on all branches taught" in the college.[61]

Like most other medical schools at the time, Rush was proprietary in nature. The faculty were essentially independent entrepreneurs who collected fees directly from medical students. Students were then issued tickets for admission for a course of lectures; ticket fees at Rush were $60. The professors paid the school for rent and the like, then kept the balance as their compensation.

In 1855 the building was enlarged so that it could accommodate 250 students (with the cost paid by the faculty). An even larger building was erected in 1867 on a vacant lot adjacent to the old building, the new building incorporating the old. Four years later, the fire consumed both.

Rush Medical College confronted the ever-present problem of recruitment of students by making it the responsibility of each faculty member. In consequence, Brainard sought out doctors who were ambitious and enthusiastic salesmen to become members of the faculty. One such hopeful would have an impact far beyond Rush. John Evans was born outside Waynesville, Ohio, south-southeast of Dayton, in 1814. As a youth he worked in his father's hardware store. Yet, much against his Quaker parents' wishes, he wanted to study medicine. They ultimately

Fig. 22. The first building occupied by the Rush Medical College, c. 1849. (Courtesy of the Rush University Medical Center Archives, Chicago.)

relented, and he began his studies at Clermont Academy in Philadelphia, graduating from Cincinnati College in 1838. Five years later, after practicing in Attica, Indiana, southwest of Lafayette, he moved his family to Indianapolis because he had successfully lobbied Indiana's legislators for a state insane asylum. He was named to the commission charged with building the asylum and was selected to be the first superintendent of the Indiana Central State Hospital. As a result, he came to Brainard's attention. Evans began teaching at Rush before he moved to Chicago in 1848. His enthusiasm helped publicize the school and attract new students from all over the Old Northwest.

Chicago's first medical journal, established by Professor James Blaney of Rush, appeared in 1844. It was called the *Illinois and Indiana Medical and Surgical Journal* in order to promote circulation in as wide an area as possible. Four years later, the editorship fell to John Evans, who changed its name to the *North-western Medical and Surgical Journal*. He saw it as a public relations vehicle; he wrote another professor, "You must see that the character, usefulness and success of our school must depend upon the reputation of its teachers. Then it becomes important for each of us, not only to teach well and profoundly, but to write well and extensively."[62] He wrote about and developed a quarantine program for cholera, a program he explained to Congress. In order to reduce the trauma caused by forceps during delivery, he invented an obstetrical extractor. In order to reduce seasickness, he patented a suspended bed for ships.[63] Evans was much more than a medical practitioner. He became involved in education, real estate, railroading, and politics. He invested his savings in Chicago land and buildings; his increasing wealth would cause him to leave the practice of medicine in the mid-1850s.[64]

Because of the competition between a large number of relatively small medical schools, raising standards would require a cooperative effort. Rush Medical College sent representatives to the first meeting of the American Medical Association in 1847, and Evans was sent to be its representative to the third meeting. It was there that Evans met Nathan S. Davis, founder of the AMA, and with Brainard's blessing, recruited him to the chair of physiology and pathology at Rush.

The first call for an Illinois state medical convention appeared as early as 1840 with an announcement stressing how competent physicians needed to band together to weed out irregular practitioners. But the need to serve patients, the dearth of good transportation, and low incomes (most Illinois physicians had a second source of income) meant that there was little urgency on the part of physicians to attend state meetings, much less national ones. It was not until 1850 that the first meeting of the Illinois State Medical Society was held in Springfield, with Evans among the founders.[65]

Additional health infrastructure appeared in the form of Chicago's first "hospital," which was authorized and constructed in 1843 to isolate victims of epidemics.

It burned two years later but was quickly rebuilt as a result of outbreaks of smallpox and scarlet fever.

The city's first general hospital opened in 1847 because of Rush's faculty. Tippecanoe Hall, which contained one hundred beds, closed in just a few years, leaving no place for the homeless to be treated when they were ill. Many consider this to have been the first Cook County hospital, since most of the supplies were furnished by the county. The city's poor were cared for when they became sick, perhaps because the poor lived on land that the miasma theory of disease would have considered a source of disease. It was believed that the probability that the general population would be afflicted by disease was lessened by minimizing the spread of disease among the indigent. The poor were generally treated in their unhealthy homes. Thus, both humanitarian and economic arguments were used to promote the construction of a new hospital. It was thought that the county tax that paid to treat the sick poor could be halved if they were brought together in one place.

That hospital, Chicago's second, the Illinois General Hospital of the Lakes, opened in the fall of 1850 in a series of rented rooms at the Lake House Hotel. This was largely a result of Davis's efforts to obtain clinical material for his course.[66] He determined that only a hospital could generate the needed data, and he delivered a series of public lectures on medicine and sanitation to fund the project. The county's patients were seen by special agreement. Rush's medical students were initially assigned to nurse the patients, but, in 1851, when this proved unworkable, an agreement was reached with the Sisters of Mercy, the city's first religious order, to assume the nursing and managerial duties.[67] Rush faculty reserved the right to make use of the hospital's clinical facilities in exchange for the promise of free medical care for the indigent.

Davis advocated a "graded curriculum": a medical course in which the second term built on and extended the learning accomplished in the first. When Davis was unable to establish such a curriculum at Rush, he left and established a competing school, the Lind University Medical School, formed in 1859. It was renamed the Chicago Medical College in 1863 and became affiliated with Northwestern University in 1870.[68] Davis also increased the length of each term and established entrance requirements, a significant improvement on the complete lack of such requirements in most U.S. medical colleges.

The Illinois General Hospital of the Lakes became Mercy Hospital when the Sisters of Mercy assumed responsibility for its administration. It moved from the Lake House Hotel into rooms at Wabash Avenue and Van Buren Street, then in 1863 it moved to Twenty-Sixth Street and Calumet Avenue, somewhat south of the majority of the city's population. It expanded to the east in 1869, adopting an address on prestigious Prairie Avenue. This was fortuitous two years later when the Great Fire passed it to the north, but it was close enough to help treat the victims. By 1877 it had grown to a five-hundred-bed operation, with Davis still the medical director.

Cook County Hospital, which opened 1857, was used by Rush as its teaching hospital until the Civil War, when it was converted to a military hospital. After the war, it resumed its role as a teaching hospital and founded the first medical internship program in the United States in 1866.

None of these hospitals admitted women as patients, and so Mary Harris Thompson, M.D., opened her own hospital. After receiving her degree in 1863 from New England Female Medical College in Boston, she moved west to work for the Northwestern Sanitary Commission's Chicago branch, where she cared for the wives, widows, and children of Union soldiers. When she was unable to obtain a hospital affiliation on account of her gender, in 1865 she founded (with the fund-raising help of Reverend William R. Ryder) the fourteen-bed Chicago Hospital for Women and Children, which provided medical care to indigent females. It was located at Rush Street and Indiana Street (now Grand Avenue), three blocks east of Rush Medical College. Support for the hospital came from wealthy Chicago women plus some male doctors. In addition to helping raise funds, the women managed the administrative work. The men aided Thompson in her medical and surgical practice, giving the hospital legitimacy in an era strongly prejudiced against women doctors. In 1871, Thompson and William H. Byford opened a medical school affiliated with the hospital to train women doctors. Given the lack of job openings elsewhere, many became attending physicians at the hospital.[69]

The Health of Chicagoans

In 1850 Davis noted that for every sick male in Chicago, there were five women and children who were ill. He blamed the illness on the density and lack of ventilation in the city's housing; it was stuffy and often windowless. He explained his statistic by noting that the men generally left home to work, so they spent less time in the slums and crowded rooming houses that provided accommodation in the rapidly growing city.[70]

An examination of Chicago mortality rates reveals the effectiveness of empirical sanitary measures undertaken before the fire. Beginning in the 1850s, and continuing past 1871, the death rate per thousand population generally fell except during the years when cholera appeared.[71] It was often accompanied by typhoid, but deaths attributable to typhoid were not recorded before 1855. As table 6.1 documents, the highest rates were during visitations of cholera, which made its last recorded appearance in the outbreak of 1866–67.

Cholera was common when the Sisters of Mercy took responsibility for running the Illinois General Hospital of the Lakes. The 1854 epidemic resulted from a trainload of Norwegian immigrants arriving in the spring. By the summer,

Table 6.1. Mortality in Chicago, 1843–1871

Year	Reported mortality	Population	Rate/ 1,000	Cholera	Dysentery	Scarlet Fever	Smallpox	Diptheria	Erysipelas
1843	129	7,580	17						
1844	306	10,170	30						
1845	313	12,088	26						
1846	359	14,169	25						
1847	320	16,857	19						
1848	580	20,023	29						
1849	1,547	23,047	67	678					
1850	1,334	29,963	45	420					
1851	843	34,000	25	216					
1852	1,652	38,734	43	630					
1853	1,205	59,130	20						
1854	3,834	65,872	58	1,424	242				
1855	1,983	80,023	25	147					
1856	1,897	84,113	23		305				
1857	2,170	93,000	23		465				
1858	2,050	84,000	24		224	233			
1859	1,826	94,000	19			253			
1860	2,059	109,260	19			125		154	
1861	2,072	120,000	17						
1862	2,578	137,030	19			335			
1863	3,523	150,000	23			405	115		15
1864	4,044	161,288	25				283		34
1865	3,663	178,492	21				57		
1866	5,931	200,418	30	990					
1867	4,648	225,000	21	10					
1868	5,984	252,054	24						
1869	6,488	280,000	23						
1870	7,323	298,700	25						
1871	6,976	334,270	21						

Source: Andreas, *History of Chicago*, 2:555. The population figures reported by Andreas differ somewhat from those reported elsewhere.

immigrants were leaving the city during a wave of hysteria. Seven of the nuns died during the epidemic. Cholera was responsible for almost 37.5 percent of the reported mortality that year; more than 2 percent of the population died from the disease. The *Chicago Tribune* attributed the death toll to "the foreign population."[72]

What may account for the dearth of information about typhoid fever in these years is the difficulty of differentiating typhoid from other fevers, particularly malaria, which was prevalent in the first half of the nineteenth century. Few early settlers would have escaped a bout of malaria. It probably accounted for a significant portion of illness within the city in the 1850s, with an epidemic occurring in 1854. Beginning in the 1860s typhoid gradually disappeared, the mortality rate falling from around seventy per 100,000 to fewer than six by the end of the century.[73]

The other major infectious disease that visited nineteenth-century Chicagoans was smallpox; the first serious scare was in 1848. The city marshal was asked to call on all the local physicians to determine how many were available to perform free vaccinations for the city's unvaccinated, who were asked to protect themselves immediately. Smallpox returned in December 1850, and it appears to have made an appearance most winters thereafter.

A hospital was built in the early 1850s, but it was not until 1864, when a major increase in the number of cases occurred, that a reliable "Pest House" (as the Smallpox Hospital was known) was constructed, though many victims were understandably reluctant to be admitted. Concurrently, when health matters were assigned to the police department, several officers were assigned to be health workers. By the end of 1865, more than two thousand cases had been reported. The disease abated for a while, but another outbreak arrived after the fire. By this point, health workers went house-to-house offering vaccination with what appeared to be good results.[74]

In addition to exposure to infectious diseases, a major health hazard faced women in particular: the many risks associated with childbearing. During the second half of the nineteenth century, puerperal (or postpartum) infection, which occurs when bacteria infect the uterus and surrounding area, was the cause in 13 percent of the deaths of women between twenty and fifty years of age. A greater risk faced infants and children. In the period before the fire, children under the age of five accounted for about 50 percent of all deaths in Chicago, reaching a peak of 70.7 percent in 1871. The Board of Health reported in 1874 that the six leading causes of death in this cohort were *cholera infantum*, convulsions, diarrhea, dysentery, *tabes mesenterica* (a form of tuberculosis), and teething.[75] More than any other cohort, these young children were victims of the crowded, unventilated, and unclean environment in the typical tenement inhabited by the poor.

The sanitary infrastructure had to have played some role in lowering the death rates of the late 1850s and 1860s, but it didn't prevent the occasional outbreak of waterborne disease such as the spate of cholera deaths in 1866. These numbers are high by contemporary standards, but, by 1871, after thirty-three years as a city, Chicagoans were benefiting from their sanitation and health infrastructure.

One important element of Dean's concept of position is that it involves what must be done in order for a site to accommodate commerce and industry. At a basic level, this includes a healthy environment so that the labor force can perform up to its potential. A population burdened with illness is a less productive population. In the case of Chicago, this meant dealing with the mud and with the interdependence between the wastewater disposal and water supply technologies. At the time of the fire a strategy was in place, but the necessary infrastructure had to grow as the city grew.

CHAPTER 7

Population and Labor

The first Europeans to live in Chicago were generally stationed there, perhaps by a Montreal trader or later by the U.S. government. In the early 1830s many came of their own volition, perhaps because of the land boom or the promise of the canal. For whatever reason, Chicago's population, and thus its labor force, grew rapidly throughout the pre-fire years. Like the entrepreneurs we have discussed, they came from a wide variety of socioeconomic backgrounds and geographic places. They came from overseas. Some immigrants may have been pushed by circumstance to leave their native countries, but they elected to come to Chicago. Without their labor, Chicago would not have grown as quickly as it did. It should be recalled that the labor force is one component of Dean's notion of nodality, one of the properties of a site that contributes to its command of the area where trade routes converge. This chapter looks at the composition of Chicago's population and labor force as those are revealed in the U.S. censuses (plus a few local ones) between 1840 and 1870. It then focuses on the two groups at the bottom of the socioeconomic scale, the Blacks and the Irish. The various censuses show that Chicagoans worked in a variety of occupations and most faced relatively few barriers to entering the labor force.[1] But how did the growth that benefited so many affect these two groups that faced job market (and other) discrimination during this period?

Chicago's Population

Chicago first appears in the U.S. Census of Population in 1840.[2] In addition to the federal census, however, there are several estimates of Chicago's population in non-census years. Most of them are quite similar, but it is important to remember that these are estimates, particularly in the early years. The population data presented here as table 7.1 are taken from Homer Hoyt's classic study, *One Hundred Years of Land Values in Chicago*. Hoyt took them from the U.S. Census as well as state and city censuses.[3]

Altogether, these data suggest that, over the period 1830–1871, Chicago's population doubled every four years, an average annual growth rate of 18.8 percent, but that includes the first few years of extraordinary growth, in part because the numbers were so low in the early 1830s. Beginning when Chicago incorporated as a town (1833) to 1871, the growth rate was 15.9 percent. Beginning when Chicago

Table 7.1. Population of Chicago, 1830–1871

Year	Population	Year	Population
1830	50	1851	34,000
1831	100	1852	38,734[b]
1832	200	1853	59,130
1833	350	1854	65,872
1834	2,000	1855	80,023
1835	3,265	1856	84,113
1836	3,820	1857	93,000
1837	4,170	1858	91,000
1838	4,000	1859	95,000
1839	4,200	1860	109,260
1840	4,470[a]	1861	120,000
1841	5,000	1862	138,186
1842	6,000	1863	150,000
1843	7,589	1864	160,353
1844	8,000	1865	178,492
1845	12,088	1866	200,418
1846	14,169	1867	220,000
1847	16,859	1868	252,054
1848	20,023	1869	272,043
1849	23,047	1870	298,977
1850	29,963	1871	325,000

Source: Hoyt, *One Hundred Years of Land Values*, table 93, p. 483.

[a] The 1850 census reports that it was 4,853. Data from IPUMS (formerly Integrated Public Use Microdata Series) aggregates the 1840 Chicago population to 4,834. https://www.ipums.org/usa.

[b] Hoyt's figure for 1852 is one person more than that reported by the Illinois Secretary of State.

became a city (1837), the growth rate was 15.0 percent. Even after the city became a bit more fully established, say, from 1848 through 1860, the growth rate is 15.7 percent. These figures all suggest a doubling in roughly 4.5 years. From the end of the Civil War in 1865 to the fire in 1871, the growth rate remained at an impressive 10.6 percent, a doubling in just under seven years.

The 1840 federal census reveals that the 4,470 people living in Chicago were relatively young and predominantly male—in the prime working years of life. Just how young they were can be seen by evaluating the data in table 7.2. Using the midpoint of the age range for each cohort, the average white Chicagoan in 1840 was 21.1 years old. For the 53 free Blacks then living in Chicago, the average age was 24.7. The imbalance in the male population in the prime working years, ages twenty through sixty, explains why the total is predominantly male. At earlier ages, there is much more balance.

To see how this compares to different locations, a similar calculation was made for three other cities, all established before Chicago. Boston was an older eastern city, while Cincinnati and St. Louis were both frontier cities. As table 7.3 documents, Chicago's White population was quite young, a half-year younger than the U.S. average. The city's free Black population, small as it was, was typical of those in the other cities, and the numbers suggest that, of the total of 386,000 free Blacks counted in the 1840 U.S. census, somewhat older Blacks lived in cities.

One reason for the higher average age for both Whites and Blacks in Boston is that 6.3 percent of its population was fifty years of age or older. In Cincinnati, 5.3 percent was in that age range. In St. Louis, the figure was 3.2 percent, but in Chicago it was only 2.5 percent.[4] All four cities had larger cohorts of young people

Table 7.2. Age and sex distribution of Chicago's population in 1840

	White			Free Black	
	Male	Female		Male	Female
Under 5	367	395	Under 10	9	5
5 and under 10	198	239	10 and under 24	5	4
10 and under 15	167	176	24 and under 36	15	7
15 and under 20	174	178	36 and under 55	3	2
20 and under 30	809	597	55 and under 100	2	1
30 and under 40	487	284	100 and older	0	0
40 and under 50	136	99	Total	34	19
50 and under 60	43	33			
60 and under 70	10	18			
70 and under 80	6	1			
80 and under 90	0	0			
90 and under 100	0	0			
100 and older	0	0			
Total	2,397	2,020			

Source: United States Department of State, *1840 Census.*

Table 7.3. Median age of populations of some U.S. cities, 1840

	White	Free Black
Boston	23.7	28.6
Chicago	21.1	24.7
Cincinnati	22.2	24.6
St. Louis	22.8	26.6
U.S.	21.6	24.3

Source: United States Department of State, *1840 Census.*

than did the nation as a whole (8.3 percent) in 1840. Boston, as a major port of entry into the United States, had a large surplus of males between twenty and forty years of age, as did the three frontier cities.[5]

Ten years later, in 1850, the average age of Chicago's White population was 22.3 years, whereas that of the free Black population was 23.7 years. The ratio of White males to White females twenty to forty years old had fallen from 1.47:1 to 1.395:1, while 4.5 percent of the White population was now over the age of fifty. Chicago's population growth was still rapid, still because of an influx of young adults, and still heavily male.

The federal census did not ask a question concerning place of birth until the 1850 census. The city census of 1843 and the state census of 1845, however, contain a little information, not necessarily consistent with any other census.

According to the 1843 city census, there were 2,256 foreign-born persons in the city, making up just under 30 percent of the population.[6] The largest groups of immigrants were the Germans and Norwegians, who were counted together. They totaled 816 individuals in 1843, increasing to 1,056 two years later.[7] Irish immigrants, the second-largest group, constituted 773 members of the 1843 population and 972 two years later. Many of the Irish were attracted by canal construction—and in particular, by the resumption of canal construction.

Beginning in 1845 the potato famine began pushing people out of Ireland. Revolution in Germany, which began in 1848, caused more Germans than Irishmen to enter by 1860. Together, these forces would contribute to the fact that, by 1850, foreign-born Chicagoans outnumbered the native-born, as can be seen in table 7.4. In 1860 and 1870, they were just about even. The large number of miscellaneous countries in 1850 no doubt is the result of the absence of entries for Wales, British America (Canada), the Low Countries, and Scandinavia.

With respect to the native-born, the largest share came from the Old Northwest—the states of Ohio, Michigan, Indiana, and Wisconsin, in addition to Illinois—people from the extended hinterland moving to the dominant node. Those from the Mid-Atlantic states were always more than double those from New England. Together, they never comprised as large a number as those from the Old Northwest.

Table 7.4. Population of Chicago by place of birth, 1850–1870

Chicago population	1850	1860	1870		1850	1860	1870
Total native-born	14,281	54,636	154,420	Total foreign-born	15,682	54,624	144,557
New England	1,861	6,574	13,752	England	1,883	4,354	10,027
Mid-Atlantic	4,683	13,906	30,410	Ireland	6,096	19,889	39,988
Old Northwest	6,635	31,462	101,284	Scotland	610	1,641	4,197
South	495	1,939	7,303	Wales		222	565
West	19	138	1,589	British America		1,867	9,648
Other	588*	617	82	Germany	5,094	22,230	59,299
				France	234	883	1,418
				Belgium		152	392
				Holland		305	1,640
				Denmark		150	1,243
				Norway		1,313	6,374
				Sweden		816	6,154
				Switzerland		503	1,226
				Italy	4	104	552
				Poland		109	1,205
				Russia		37	118
				Miscellaneous	1,761	49	511
				Grand total	**29,963**	**109,260**	**298,977**

Source: United States Bureau of the Census, Censuses of 1850–1870.
*The 588 people recorded here as "Other" in 1850 were reported in the census as unknown. See DeBow, *Statistical View of the United States.*

Information published at the county level in the 1850 census provides additional insights into the population at mid-century given that Chicago accounted for a large share of Cook County. For example, there were just over 5 people per household and 6.7 people per dwelling unit in Cook County. It was a time of large families and significant population density. Twenty-nine of the county's thirty-eight houses of worship (76 percent) were in the city. They contained 85 percent of the capacity and 99 percent of the value of Cook County's church property. Episcopalians, Presbyterians, Roman Catholics, and Methodists were the four largest denominations with respect to both capacity and value. There were sixty-eight schools and nine academies in Cook County. One hundred four teachers taught 4,387 pupils. By the time of the 1870 census the school population had increased to just over 50,000, 80 percent of them native-born and 274 of them Black. The numbers of males and females were just about even. There were no universities in 1850 (Northwestern University would be founded in Evanston in 1851 and the first University of Chicago in 1857). There were three libraries containing 6,400 volumes. Twenty-one newspapers were published with an average circulation of just over 110,000, but their readers would include residents from beyond Cook County.[8]

Table 7.5. Total population and population growth in major U.S. cities, 1830–1870

Year	Boston	Cincinnati	St. Louis	Chicago
1830	61,392	24,831	14,125	100
1840	93,383	46,338	35,979	4,470
1850	136,881	115,435	104,978	29,963
1860	177,840	161,044	190,524	109,260
1870	250,526	216,239	351,189	298,977
Population Growth (in percentage per annum)				
1830–70	3.52	5.73	8.09	21.17
1840–70	3.28	5.08	7.43	14.92

Source: Census of Population, 1830–1870.

In sum, table 7.5 lists the total population of Boston, Cincinnati, and St. Louis, as well as Chicago, for the census years between 1830 and 1870. As would be expected, Boston, the established East Coast city, was much larger than the other three in 1830, but by 1850 Cincinnati and St. Louis were gaining ground. Chicago in 1850 was only slightly larger than Cincinnati had been twenty years earlier. By 1860 St. Louis, the second-youngest, had become the largest of the four. Chicago was somewhat larger than St. Louis had been in 1850. In 1870 St. Louis was still the largest, but Chicago had grown larger than Boston and Cincinnati.

The population growth rates shown in the bottom panel of table 7.5 tell a similar story. These rates, calculated from the census data, are reported for both the full period, 1830–70, as well as 1840–70, given the way the extremely small number of people living in Chicago in 1830 affected its growth rate. Boston had the slowest growth, no matter which way you measure it. Cincinnati, the next-oldest city, had the second-lowest growth rates, with the difference between the two rates wider (0.65) than those for Boston (0.28). The difference for St. Louis was similar to that of Cincinnati (0.66), but, while St. Louis's rates were the second-highest, they were only about half those of Chicago.[9] If the rates for Chicago are calculated to 1880, almost a decade after the fire, they remain high—17.5 percent beginning in 1830 and 12.5 percent beginning in 1840. With this many new settlers, a logical question is whether the city was able to provide work for all its residents.

Chicago's Labor Force

The 1870 census provided a breakdown of occupation by place of birth. The occupations were divided into four groups: agriculture, professional and personal services, trade and transportation, and manufacturing and mining. Table 7.6 shows the percentage breakdown of those categories with respect to the occupations of Chicagoans.

Table 7.6. Occupations of Chicagoans in 1870

	Number	Percentage
Agriculture	533	0.47
Professional and personal services	42,063	37.24
Trade and transportation	29,806	26.39
Manufactures and mining	40,558	35.90
Total	112,960	100.00

Source: United States Bureau of the Census, *Ninth Census*, table 32, p. 782.

The presence of agriculture in 1870 Chicago, although negligible, is a reminder that there were still many farms within the city limits. With respect to the other three categories, trade and transportation would have been smaller had slightly different definitions been used. For example, all the officials and employees of transportation companies are in that category, including lawyers and laborers. People performing those functions in all other industries are included in the services group.

Table 7.7 shows the nativity for the entire population using the numbers reported in table 7.4. The percentage of the population that was U.S.-born is much larger than the percentage U.S.-born in the labor force. There are two obvious reasons for this. First, immigration usually takes place in young adult cohorts at a time when they are just beginning to earn their own livelihood. The working-age cohorts contained a far greater percentage of immigrants than other cohorts. Second, many (if not most) of the offspring of those young immigrants would be U.S.-born.[10] Since this was in an age when large families were

Table 7.7. Nativity of Chicagoans in 1870

	Population	%	Labor force	%
U.S.-born	154,420	51.65	39,755	35.19
Foreign-born	144,557	48.35	73,205	64.80
Germany	59,299	19.83	25,778	22.82
Ireland	39,988	13.37	22,337	19.77
England & Wales	10,592	3.54	5,688	5.04
Scotland	4,197	1.40	2,066	1.83
Sweden, Norway, & Denmark	13,771	4.61	7,213	6.39
France	1,418	0.47	747	0.66
Other northern Europe	3,258	1.09	762	0.67
Italy	552	0.18	298	0.26
Other southern Europe	1,323	0.44	3,694	3.27
British America	9,648	3.23	4,065	3.60
Miscellaneous	511	0.17	557	0.49
Total	298,977	100.00	112,960	100.00

Source: United States Bureau of the Census, *Ninth Census*, Table 32, p. 782.

common, it is noteworthy that 37.8 percent of the population was in the labor force.

The 1870 census also provides a breakdown of the labor force by age and sex. More than 95.8 percent of Chicago's labor force was between the ages of sixteen and fifty-nine. Those younger than sixteen made up 2.6 percent, while 1.6 percent were age sixty or older. The city's labor force was 83.8 percent male and 16.2 percent female. Men made up only 74.1 percent of those aged ten to fifteen, but they were 87.7 percent of those sixty and older, just as one would expect of a world in which married women were not expected (or not allowed) to be in the labor force.

Unfortunately, the occupational data are not broken down by age and sex. Table 7.8 reports the complete picture for the four major groups of occupations and some selected occupations within each group. These were selected for inclusion based on their absolute size compared to the other occupations reported by the census.

To help illustrate what people of different nativities did to earn their livings in Chicago, the numbers in each row and each column of table 7.8 were divided by the total reported for that row or column. This calculates two percentages (not shown in the table) for each item in the table. Those percentages were compared to the percentage of the total that each place of nativity made up and the percentage that each occupation made up of the total. For example, the 6,631 Irish laborers constituted almost 30 percent of the 22,337 Irish working in Chicago and more than 37 percent of the 17,717 individuals identified as laborers. As a reminder, the specific occupations do not add to the percentage for the group, as many occupations within the group were not selected for reporting.

Agriculture was far and away the smallest source of employment, with less than 0.5 percent of the labor force. No country, not even the United States, had as much as 1 percent of its population working in agriculture. Germans constituted more than a third (34.9 percent) of the agricultural labor force, more than any other group, including those born in the United States (28.3 percent). Native-born persons accounted for almost half of those working as farmers (49.6 percent), while Germans accounted for almost half of those working as gardeners (47.7 percent). England and Wales, as well as Scotland, had much larger shares of their émigrés working as farmers and gardeners than their shares of Chicago's labor force.

More than half of the Irish and Italians in the Chicago labor force, and almost two-fifths of the Scandinavians, were employed in personal and professional services. There were almost as many Irish-born persons working in this group as native-born Americans.[11] Among the Irish, 29.7 percent worked as laborers, while 15.7 percent worked as domestic servants. The Irish comprised 25.6 percent of the boardinghouse keepers, 28.5 of the domestic servants, 26.4 percent of the

Table 7.8. Occupation and nativity in Chicago, 1870

	Total	U.S.	Germany	Ireland	Nativity England & Wales	Scotland	Sweden, Norway, Denmark	France	Other northern Europe	Italy	Other southern Europe	British America	Unknown
Agriculture	533	151	186	84	42	17	21	3	1	0	18	9	1
Farmers/planters	131	65	17	22	11	4	4	0	0	0	4	4	0
Gardeners/nurserymen/vinegrowers	327	53	156	49	28	10	13	2	1	0	9	5	1
Personal & Professional Services	42,063	12,656	8,678	12,351	1,359	615	2,776	237	164	164	1,426	1,172	465
Barbers/hairdressers	604	295	204	9	14	3	7	9	6	14	25	14	4
Boarding/lodging house keepers	550	171	88	141	33	9	38	14	6	1	17	31	1
Clergymen	254	146	33	22	10	4	14	2	1	1	16	5	0
Domestic servants	12,279	3,753	2,064	3,503	330	117	1,524	69	52	8	454	389	16
Hotel/restaurant keepers and employees	3,741	1,180	970	988	99	30	109	40	25	84	124	89	3
Laborers	17,717	3,522	4,307	6,631	560	356	887	55	58	30	645	451	215
Launderers/launderesses	709	169	92	338	17	11	42	1	1	1	19	18	0
Trade & Transportation	29,806	14,915	5,424	4,312	1,453	475	1,094	173	389	63	580	883	45
Traders/dealers	7,466	3,926	1,724	726	350	107	153	55	44	19	212	146	4
Hucksters/peddlers/ commercial travelers	1,969	927	430	136	87	20	36	19	195	23	60	34	2
Clerks/salesmen/ accountants (in stores)	7,835	4,937	1,057	531	430	142	145	34	103	11	105	320	20
Officials and employees of railroad companies	2,744	1,531	243	578	132	49	53	11	1	1	22	87	36
Carmen/draymen/teamsters, etc.	2,996	314	917	1,325	152	34	68	19	12	1	55	97	2
Sailors/steamboatmen/ watermen, etc.	1,959	450	160	452	141	86	516	15	11	2	27	92	7
Manufacture/Mechanical/Mining	40,558	12,033	11,490	5,590	2,834	959	3,322	334	208	71	1,670	2,001	46
Blacksmiths	1,574	285	485	390	81	64	122	8	5	0	71	62	1
Boot/shoe makers	1,752	481	686	333	68	28	6	14	20	0	86	29	1
Brick and stone masons, marble and stone cutters	2,077	247	702	546	231	79	104	19	2	5	74	66	2
Carpenters and joiners	6,210	1,315	1,824	756	436	171	797	60	29	7	236	571	8
Machinists	1,336	412	216	180	181	105	89	12	1	1	41	95	3
Milliners/dress and mantua makers	1,924	1,013	165	276	135	33	63	16	5	2	39	174	3
Painters and varnishers	2,295	797	595	199	199	31	222	17	6	7	60	159	3
Tailors, tailoresses, and seamstresses	4,236	850	1,322	563	140	32	825	30	45	1	247	173	8
Total	112,960	39,755	25,778	22,337	5,688	2,066	7,213	747	762	298	3,694	4,065	557

Source: United States Bureau of the Census, *Ninth Census*, Table 32, p. 782.

hotel and restaurant workers, 37.4 percent of the laborers, and 47.7 percent of the laundry workers in Chicago's labor force. Among the Italians, 28.2 percent were hotel and restaurant workers, but they accounted for only 2.25 percent of the workers in that occupation. With regard to Scandinavians, 21.1 percent were domestic servants, the largest share of any nativity group. Note also that native-born Americans comprised nearly three-fifths of Chicago's clergymen, and Americans and Germans together comprised five-sixths of the barbers and hairdressers.[12]

Turning to the trade and transportation group, native-born Americans accounted for more than half the total employed. Specifically, they made up more than half of the traders, dealers, and clerks, more than half of the employees of railroad companies, and almost half of the hucksters. The Irish made up 44.2 percent of the teamsters. The Scandinavians comprised more than a quarter of the sailors, with the Irish just under a quarter. The total number of Irish sailors is two greater than the number of native-born Americans. More than half of the immigrants in the group designated "Other Northern Europe" were employed in this sector; half of that group were listed as hucksters, although their total numbers were quite small.

Finally, the manufactures and mining group consisted essentially of manufactures because only seventeen members of Chicago's labor force were identified as miners. Between 40 and 50 percent of the Germans, English and Welsh, Scots, Scandinavian, French, other southern European, and British American (Canadian) immigrants were in this sector. They were spread across the enumerated occupations and not concentrated in one or two. A little over 10 percent of the Scandinavians in the Chicago labor force worked as carpenters or as tailors. Native-born Americans were a smaller proportion of each of the enumerated occupations than they were of the total labor force except for the millinery trade, where they represented a majority of the workers. Germans, the largest single immigrant group in Chicago's population and labor force, accounted for 28.3 percent of the employees in this group. Germans comprised 30.8 percent of the city's blacksmiths, 39.2 percent of its boot- and shoemakers, 33.8 percent of its masons, 29.3 percent of its carpenters, 25.9 percent of its painters, and 31.2 percent of its tailors and dressmakers. The Irish, the second largest group, accounted for about 19.8 percent of Chicago's labor force but only 13.8 percent of this group, and they were generally a much smaller percentage of the labor force in the enumerated occupations. Only with respect to blacksmiths and masons was their share of that occupation's labor force greater than 20 percent. Finally, Scandinavians comprised almost a fifth of the city's tailors and an eighth of the city's carpenters.

Table 7.8 does not tell us how these occupations were divided by sex, although it is clear from the job titles that women were employed in many of these occupations; laundresses and seamstresses are but two examples. The table also does not tell us how these occupations were divided by race. Black Americans were included in the U.S.-born group. They were working as laborers, teamsters, even tailors. Blacks competed with the Irish for many of the jobs held by people at the lower tail of the income distribution. Although these data suggest how middle- and upper-class White workers fared, whether native- or foreign-born, a closer look at the Irish and Black Americans in Chicago's pre-fire labor market is warranted in order to better understand those in the lower class who not only performed menial tasks but faced discrimination.

The Irish

Histories of the Irish in Chicago concentrate on groups such as "canallers," those who worked on the I&M Canal. They focus on neighborhoods and parishes and shy away from discussing individuals. This is somewhat surprising because the Irish were the largest immigrant group in the city in 1850 and the second-largest in 1860 and 1870. That they were at the bottom end of the socioeconomic scale suggests that it was no accident that the cow of an Irishwoman, Catherine O'Leary, was falsely alleged to have been the cause of the fire.[13] Catherine and Patrick O'Leary were natives of Ireland; they married young and immigrated to Harrisburg, Pennsylvania, because of the potato famine. He served in the Union Army. After the war, as they approached their forties, they relocated to Chicago. He was an unskilled laborer; she, a housewife with a small neighborhood dairy business. They and their five children lived in two rooms of a quickly built wooden structure that they owned; their two other rooms were rented to another Irish couple. On their lot was a similar building plus the barn in which Catherine kept her four cows, a calf, and the horse that pulled her dairy wagon. Their neighborhood was densely packed with such wooden buildings. From all indications, this was a couple pursuing "the American dream." But they were Irish people living in a neighborhood of some disrepute. Who better to pick as the scapegoat for the fire than an entrepreneurial Irish mother of five whose barn caught fire through no fault of hers?

Chicago's first St. Patrick's Day parade dates from 1843, when the Irish constituted 10 percent of Chicago's population of 7,589. This was before the famine greatly increased their numbers; in 1850 they made up 20 percent of a population of 29,963. They lived along the Chicago River in three major clusters: Kilgubbin to the north, Hardscrabble-Bridgeport to the south, and near Adams and Desplaines Streets to the west.[14] William J. Quarter, born in Ireland, was appointed in 1844 as Chicago's first Roman Catholic bishop. Saint Patrick's parish was formed in 1846, and what is now known as Old St. Patrick's church opened in 1856 with largely Irish parishioners. In the late 1850s, under the leadership of Dutchman

Arnold Damen, Irish immigrants built Holy Family Church in the neighborhood into which the O'Learys would move. Damen became the father of Jesuit education in Chicago; he started both St. Ignatius College Prep and Loyola University Chicago, which remain major educational institutions. The Sisters of Mercy, who ran the city's first hospital, were headed by Agatha O'Brien, an Irish immigrant with a working-class background. The sisters also taught school, operated an employment bureau for Irish women, and established Chicago's first orphanage. In the first half of the nineteenth century, however, most of the Irish migrated to Chicago to build the canal.

James William Putnam's economic history of the canal has surprisingly little to say about the labor that built it. Given the small size of Chicago's population at the start of construction, everyone expected wages to increase in the hope of drawing laborers to the Illinois frontier. Putnam reports that, in 1837, advertisements in eastern newspapers promised monthly wages of $20 to $26.[15] It was reasonable to expect all the resources required to build the canal to cost somewhat more in what was still a frontier outpost, but the initial bids in 1836 well exceeded the engineers' estimates. Indeed, some were so high that they were not accepted. The hope was that the experience of the contractors whose bids were accepted would prove that the engineers' estimates had been realistic, and the fact that work was under way would attract enough labor to reduce wages. That did not happen until the late summer of 1837, after the panic of that year hit the East Coast, so most of the first two construction seasons were lost owing to a labor shortage.[16]

The saying that "to build a canal you needed a shovel, a pick, a wheelbarrow, and an Irishman" supposedly reflected the reality of the early nineteenth century. The immigration of Irishmen to North America began as the "transportation revolution" hit the United States.[17] Three thousand Irish laborers were employed in digging the Erie Canal by 1818. By 1826, 5,000 were at work on four other canal projects. By the end of 1836, 350 laborers worked on the I&M, and by the following autumn the number was close to 1,000. Even this number, however, was too small. By 1838, Irishmen, some Germans, and other immigrants who had been recruited in the eastern states and Canada began to appear along the canal line. In Chicago, the Roman Catholic population swelled to one thousand in a total population of roughly four thousand.[18]

The labor shortage was a continual problem.[19] By the time work resumed in 1845 the I&M Canal project faced competition from other canals and from the railroads. The result was that the labor shortage persisted, and this tended to raise the wage level for all workers from the low of 1843. Bessie Pierce reports that by the summer of 1846 the canal's chief engineer requested that agents in New York, Boston, and Montreal recruit immigrants to come work on the canal. And come they did, as they had in the early years of construction, particularly the Irish.[20]

The I&M also employed agents who made contacts with emigration societies to direct workers to Illinois. Workers were promised "bountiful" compensation and the chance to purchase land near the canal when the project was complete. The work was appalling. Unskilled labor was used (and misused) to dig canals by hand. Men stood in oozing channels from sunup to sundown (4:30 a.m. to 7:45 p.m. in 1847) before going home to a shanty that housed too many others.

That there would be worker complaints should have been evident from the start; after all, many of those who arrived to work on the I&M Canal had worked earlier on the Erie and other canals. The first recorded conflict came on the day of the ceremonies to mark the beginning of construction, July 4, 1836. The steamboat *Chicago* had taken participants from near the mouth of the Chicago River to Bridgeport for the groundbreaking. On the return trip, a group of Irish canallers stationed at a quarry along the river yet excluded from the ceremony hurled rocks at the dignitaries aboard the *Chicago*. The captain made a quick landing, and a reported fifty people disembarked with bludgeons, quickly bloodying many of the Irishmen and apprehending a dozen of them. The newspaper report of the event referred to "the heroes of the Emerald Isle," a reflection of the low esteem in which the Irish were held in spite of the fact that it was they who would do the work of making the canal a reality through their sweat, strain, and, all too often, deaths.[21]

Living conditions were abysmal. Wood was forbidden in the construction of workers' shanties because it was relatively scarce on the proposed route across the prairie, but this prohibition was often ignored. Shanties came in all shapes and sizes and were constructed of a variety of materials, especially sod and straw. A single shanty might house as many as fifty canallers. There were small shanties for married workers with families. In some cases, canal contractors supplied shanties; in others, the state or canal company sold them to contractors. In all cases, the rent was deducted from wages and was not adjusted at the same rate as wages.[22] Although most of the literature focuses on the downstate region, shanties were built in the Chicago area as well. Poverty remained in Irish communities long after the canal was completed.

From such conditions came health problems, with sporadic flare-ups of devastating diseases. The work took place in an environment where workers were exposed to malaria from mosquitoes that bred in the seething groundwater, cholera from the lack of effective sanitation in the shanty villages, and overexertion given the work schedule.[23] All three proved fatal to many canallers.

Ague, a form of malaria, was prevalent throughout the Old Northwest. It was hard to avoid in the marshes and swamps around Mud Lake, but the muddy and marshy depressions that dotted Illinois's prairie were also prime breeding grounds for mosquitoes. The canal's chief engineer noted that such summer illnesses "discouraged laborers abroad from coming here (for exaggerated reports of the unhealthiness of the country were everywhere circulated)" as well as driving off men already hired.[24]

Cholera, much more likely to kill, arrived with troops and the immigrants of the 1830s and 1840s. As the death toll rose, one federal official reported that all families had fled, "gone in different directions to escape from this malignant disease."[25]

Finally, in addition to the extremes of temperatures experienced in the Middle West, the immigrants' work involved unfamiliar processes and new machinery; it was dangerous. That morbidity and mortality were part of the job was understood. Unfortunately, although it was clear that these were new, even unprecedented, conditions, centuries-old common law precedents prevailed, so the laborers' rights were severely limited if they were injured on the job.

Regardless of location, work on the canal was spasmodic, subject to the vagaries of state and local finance, the caprices of contractors and their companies, and especially the weather. The workforce expanded in the summer to as many as 1,700 workers, then contracted in the winter to as few as 350. During the winter some of the workers were employed in Chicago's pork-packing industry and some worked cutting trees in the North Woods as part of the lumber industry.

Labor paid a heavy price following the Panic of 1837 and the ultimate cessation of construction. In May 1837 the State Bank of Illinois suspended specie payments, and other financial institutions soon followed suit. Payments to contractors were late, leading them to roll back wages from $26 a month to $22, causing a work stoppage.[26] By March 1839 the state treasury was exhausted, and the state was unable to pay in April and May. Workers and contractors were distressed, and the workers threatened to leave. This led the canal commissioners to issue scrip due on the state bank in ninety days. Workers were paid in this currency, which was accepted at par value for a while, but it ultimately depreciated as expected. By early 1840 the canal fund was exhausted, but contractors took on $1 million in canal bonds at par and agreed to bear the discount, which proved to be about 17 percent. As construction ground to a halt, workers' wages fell once again, to about $14 per month.[27] By June 1841 the discount on scrip reached 50 percent, and its value with respect to goods and services continued to fall. As canallers were laid off, a good number moved to Chicago, where they became a burden on relief agencies. A privileged few used saved scrip to buy land and become farmers.[28] And then work on the canal was suspended.

When work resumed in November 1845 many of the old contractors returned, but many had failed. Many of the canallers returned, but they were still being paid in scrip, and there was still a labor shortage. Unfortunately, just as work resumed, illness was widespread, causing another stoppage. The canal secretary was soon calling for hiring agents to "go thro' New York, and among the emigrant ships" to secure a thousand more laborers as well as running advertisements in New York, Boston, and Montreal newspapers.[29] The result was that hundreds of workmen arrived, many Irish. Two thousand people were employed on the Chicago end of the canal by late 1847. In that same year, with work well behind schedule, several contracts were transferred to the state. When contractors tried to increase the workday to fifteen hours (with no increase in wages), the workers struck. An oft-quoted excerpt from a petition the strikers sent to a canal trustee read: "So as not to have white Citizens Drover Even worse than Common Slave Negroes."[30]

On April 16, 1848, navigation was opened on the I&M Canal. The *Chicago Weekly Journal* called it "the wedding of the Father of Rivers to our inland seas."[31] Before the canal's completion, it took roughly three weeks for merchants to travel from the Chicago Portage to Starved Rock. The canal reduced the journey to a day on a boat towed by mules. Goods that once headed to the East via St. Louis and the Mississippi River now headed east via Chicago and the Great Lakes. A good deal of the traffic on the Mississippi began to travel north, bolstering the North and weakening the South in the years before the Civil War. In the end, however, "the I & M Canal's most visible accomplishment" was Chicago.[32] The city's population grew from near forty-five hundred in 1840 to almost thirty thousand a decade later, and the Irish remained Chicago's largest immigrant group in the latter year.

The municipal election of 1855 was a low point for Chicago's Irish. They normally supported the Democratic Party, but many (Irish and non-Irish) had abandoned the party over the question of slavery. Consequently, the anti-Catholic Know-Nothing Party was victorious and immediately passed a law that banned immigrants from applying for city jobs. It also raised the price of beer licenses. Both policies were rescinded the following year when a coalition of Irishmen, Germans, and others voted the Know-Nothings out of office. This opened positions in the public sector, but the private sector still held to the notion that "No Irish Need Apply," although historian Richard Jensen has argued this was largely a myth.[33] Despite the fear, largely of Catholicism, the United States made no attempt to exclude Irish immigrants, many of whom, not surprisingly, gravitated toward political careers.[34]

The Free Blacks

The city census of 1837 recorded 77 free Blacks (41 males, 36 females), almost all adults, living in Chicago.[35] They had come to Chicago from elsewhere in the Northwest and the upper South. With the panic of that year and the ensuing business downturn, the Black population in the 1840 Census of Population had decreased to 53 (31 of whom were between the ages eleven and thirty-five).[36] It is unclear where the others went; perhaps they moved to Canada, which was emerging as the end of the line on the Underground Railroad. The Black population had rebounded to 65 by the time of the second city census, which was taken in 1843, and the Illinois census of 1845 reported a total of 140. It should also be noted that the reported sex ratio (males:females), which had been relatively even in 1837, was much greater than one in 1840 and 1843, but returned to roughly even numbers in 1845. This population growth continued throughout the remainder of the 1840s; the federal census of 1850 reported 323 Blacks living in Chicago (181 males, 142 females). These numbers suggest both that young free Black males were being attracted to the city and that there were enough young free Black females for many of them to form families. While most of the Black population lived to the south of the downtown district, on both sides of the river, most scholars find that they lived among the White population; there was nothing that could yet be considered a "ghetto."[37] By 1860 the Black population had grown to 958, and after emancipation, it swelled to 3,691 (3,559 native- and 132 foreign-born). Nevertheless, the proportion of Blacks in Chicago's population was below 1 percent in the 1850s and rose only to about 1.25 percent during and after the Civil War.

White Chicagoans, according to Bessie Pierce, showed "kindliness and intolerance" toward their Black neighbors.[38] Although the Whites were protective of the rights Blacks were allowed under the law, they were not supportive of allowing them the same rights as Whites. Lewis Isbel, who arrived in the city in about 1838 and became Chicago's premier barber, with a shop in the Sherman House and a clientele that included William B. Ogden, was pickpocketed by a White man at an Emancipation Day celebration in the mid-1860s.[39] The thief was quickly caught, but the court disallowed Isbel's testimony against him. In February 1863 the all-White Illinois legislature (still dominated by downstate interests) reaffirmed what were known as the Black Laws or Black Codes (dating from 1819, immediately after Illinois became a state) stipulating that Blacks could not testify in court against White people, serve on juries, vote, or bear arms. In addition, they were required to register with the local authority. Segregation was supported in theaters and potentially in schools. America's nascent labor unions were reluctant to recruit Blacks because their White membership preferred not to work with them. Historian Kate Masur has skillfully documented what she terms "America's first civil rights movement" as the effort to eliminate such laws.[40]

What became the state of Illinois was first settled by people from Maryland and Virginia who came through the Cumberland Gap and down the Ohio River to southern Illinois. Over time, people from Kentucky and elsewhere south of the river moved with their families and slaves into southern Illinois. Throughout the antebellum years, the possibility of re-enslavement was a constant threat. Although the Northwest Ordinance of 1787 prohibited slavery in the Northwest

Territory, the Constitution of 1818 recognized the slaves that were already in the state as well as the practice of indenture.[41] Given the prohibition of slavery, adult Blacks would sign long-term personal service contracts, called indentures, with their "former owners."

Illinois law prohibited Whites from bringing enslaved persons into the state. Free Blacks were forbidden from emigrating to Illinois or residing in Illinois for longer than ten days. (Clearly, much, but not all, of this was ignored in Chicago.) If a White brought a legal complaint against a Black, and if the latter was found to be in the wrong, he or she could be fined up to $500. If the defendant did not, or was not able to, pay the fine, he or she could be jailed and sold at public auction.[42]

Such "legal" practices were often superseded by extralegal ones. Free Blacks could be, and were, kidnapped from the streets of Chicago and taken back to the South. In the absence of photographs, fingerprints, and the like, they had little to prove their freedom. And as time passed, the slave catcher seeking fugitive slaves proved an ominous presence. The Fugitive Slave Act of 1850, which intensified the efforts of the slave catchers, caused several of Chicago's Black families to sell their property at a loss and move to Canada.[43] (Blacks did, indeed, own property in Chicago. The city census of 1837 showed only one Black property owner, and it was evidently commercial property that was owned. By 1844 there were five property owners; there were ten in 1847 plus two Black-owned churches.)

Chicago's Blacks organized against the Fugitive Slave Law, as well as the Black Laws, which they defied by means of such devices as the Underground Railroad. Joanna Hall, wife of Reverend Abram Hall, became well known for her involvement with that institution; Abram Hall was one of the organizers in 1847 of Quinn Chapel African Methodist Episcopal Church, which played a major role in the abolitionist movement.[44] Most of Chicago's Blacks were born in the United States. Many were free, but some fled the South without obtaining their freedom. Elijah and Nancy Clary are but one example of what proved to be a large number of slaves seeking freedom during the Civil War. They were living near Tuscumbia, Alabama, in 1862 when Union and Confederate forces engaged in battle. Nancy Clary and several of her children fled to Chicago with the assistance of a White Chicago minister.[45] Elijah and his son Louis arrived seven months later because they had been impressed into a Union Army labor battalion.[46] Father and son both went to work as stevedores on Chicago's docks, a position which was highly seasonal given the reduction of shipping in winter. Louis enlisted in the U.S. Colored Troops a year after arriving in Chicago.[47]

Many achieved emancipation by purchasing it for themselves and their families. Christopher Reed, a historian of Black Chicago, relates the story of merchant-tailor John Jones.[48] He was born in 1816 on a North Carolina plantation to a mulatto

Fig. 23. Mary Jane (Richardson) and John Jones, shortly after their marriage in the 1840s. (https://en.wikipedia.org/wiki/Mary_Jane_Richardson_Jones#/media/File:John_and_Mary_Jones_in_the_1840s.jpg.)

mother and a father of German stock. From birth, he was free, but being biracial, he did not enjoy the liberties and opportunities available to White North Carolinians. His mother, afraid that his father's family might try to enslave him, was led to apprentice John to a White tailor. Thus, he spent the next years of his life much as those who were indentured servants once had done. As he was turning twenty-one, he came to understand that the tailor's heirs planned to claim him as part of their inheritance and sell him into slavery in Texas, which at the time was an independent republic. Consequently, Jones obtained his certificate of freedom and crossed the Mason-Dixon Line. He found his way to Alton, Illinois, where Elijah Richardson, a free Black and a blacksmith who had befriended him during his apprenticeship, now lived. Jones married Mary Richardson in Alton, and the two of them came to Chicago in 1847, becoming one of the city's first Black families. John Jones became one of Chicago's leading Black abolitionists.[49] In time, he was able to erect a two-story building on Dearborn Street from which his tailoring services were sought by a Black and White clientele.[50]

Jones's business met with success, but he faced increasing hostility from Whites. Such was especially true for young Black men who did not have Jones's work experience. The most common employment opportunities for Black men in early Chicago were associated with the ships that used the Chicago River as a harbor, where they were in direct competition with Whites (often Irish) for jobs. Blacks such as the Clarys served as stevedores and sailors, cooks, and watchmen. Several became watermen, delivering water to homes from a cart they filled directly from the lake. Joseph Hudlin, for instance, had worked as a stevedore on steamboats out of St. Louis. In 1855 he married Anna Lewis in Chicago, got a job as custodian at the Board of Trade, and built a five-room clapboard house where Plymouth Court now stands. During the Chicago Fire, Anna Hudlin opened their home to anyone, while he raced to the Board of Trade building and rescued valuable documents from the vault.

A major problem facing most Blacks arriving in Chicago was that they were uneducated; many southern states held that educating a Black was a crime. Most adult Blacks taught themselves to read and write, in many cases so that they could read the Bible. From an early date young Blacks were able to attend Chicago's public schools. The 1850 federal census reports that there were 29 Blacks in Cook County's schools in a total school population of 5,257. The fact that Philo Carpenter, a noted abolitionist, was on the first school board had to have played some role, as did the relatively small numbers. When the Democrats came into control of the city in 1862, a law was passed providing for segregated schools. Two hundred seven Black children could have been affected by this law, but some remained in integrated schools while their parents protested. The Hudlins were among those who insisted their children attend integrated schools. A new city charter passed in 1865 repealed the law, and the separate school which had been constructed—and boycotted—was abolished.[51]

The Civil War brought the question of race to the forefront. When the Democrats gained control of the city, pro-Confederate, anti-Black attitudes became much more apparent. Nowhere was this more in evidence than in the relations between the Irish and the Blacks. The Black Laws made clear that the races were not equal. In the summer of 1862, when Blacks competed with the Irish for jobs, at least two riots broke out between the two groups. With the Emancipation Proclamation the following year, anti-Black sentiment grew worse. The anti-Irish, anti-Catholic mindset of the Protestants that formed the majority had set up the competition between Black and Irish for jobs, housing, and many other things at the bottom of the social hierarchy. Thus it was that in 1864 a mob of Irishmen estimated at between four hundred and five hundred gathered to attack any Black who happened by Clark and Eighteenth Streets. The *Tribune* reported, "The Blacks had committed no offense whatsoever, except wanting to support themselves through honest labor."[52]

This situation changed after the Civil War. With emancipation, abolitionists were no longer part of a support structure. Blacks were "free" to compete for jobs in a world where racial prejudice was increasing. As more and more former slaves migrated north, that competition intensified. From a total of 958 in the census of 1860, Chicago's Black population increased to 3,691 in 1870. The path was not smooth, as about 300 Chicago Blacks emigrated to Canada and almost 50 emigrated to Haiti during the 1860s.[53] Of the Blacks living in Chicago in 1870, two-thirds of those who were native-born were born in the South, mainly in Kentucky and Virginia. Roughly one-quarter (955) came from the Old Northwest, with Illinois accounting for two-thirds of that group.[54]

The great influx of Black refugees in the 1860s was composed largely of people who recently had been plantation slaves. They were used to hard physical labor, but most lacked any of the special skills in demand by Chicago employers. Consequently, they ended up competing for unskilled positions with the odds stacked against them. Many entered domestic service or performed manual labor, a continuation of what they had done in slavery. Men continued to find seasonal work on the docks as stevedores and teamsters. Government employment was another possibility; more than six dozen worked for the postal service.[55] With the growth of the city, restaurants and taverns proffered employment as waiters, bus boys, dishwashers, and so on. Women became laundresses as well as housemaids. At the other extreme, there were Blacks who could be found in the professions. In addition to John Jones the tailor, there were Black doctors, dentists, barbers, and the like. James David Peck earned his MD from Rush Medical College in 1848, the first person of African descent to do so. The medical practice of J. H. Hutchinson was on the near South Side, at Harrison and Clark Streets. Beginning in 1861 he was assigned by the U.S. Army to examine both White and Black men to ascertain their fitness for military service. More middle-class employment awaited the Pullman company's decision to employ Blacks as porters on its Palace cars.

The census of 1870 showed that the vast majority of Chicago's Blacks were tenants and lived between the lake and the river south of Sixteenth Street. Blacks owned thirty-nine properties (residential and business structures), and there were four Black churches.[56] Much of the South Side was untouched by the fire, but the rebuilding of Chicago did nothing to change the relative status of the city's Black population.

Chicago on the eve of the fire was growing rapidly and attracting immigrants mainly because of the availability of jobs. These were the people who produced a growing output of goods sold in a national market and beyond. This chapter has discussed what can be learned about Chicago's population and labor force in these years from multilevel census data and has looked at the two groups at the bottom of the socioeconomic ladder, the Irish and the Blacks, to see whether the growth that benefited so many others trickled down to them. This chapter has not attempted to tie labor to the firms employing it; the census information reported in this chapter is from that obtained from individuals, not companies.

In the long run, the conflagration wouldn't change the social hierarchy that found White Protestant New Englanders at the top and Irish and Blacks at the bottom. In the short run, the need to prepare the land for new construction following the fire would provide employment opportunities for many, and a good number of those who came because of the job opportunities would stay. In 1880 Chicago's population was just over a half million, a greater than 67 percent gain over what it was in 1870. Chicago's nodal significance continued to increase.

Following the fire, the O'Learys moved to Michigan for a short time, but returned to Chicago—taking up residence on the South Side. Catherine O'Leary remained the scapegoat for the fire throughout her lifetime despite overwhelming evidence that she was blameless. Chicago's Committee on Police and Fire finally exonerated her in 1997, more than a century after her death in 1895.[57]

CHAPTER 8

The Lubricant of Growth: Money and Finance

A financial system that facilitates commerce and industry is the final component of Dean's notion of nodality. Business today requires a well-functioning financial system of banks, money, and credit, but that does not describe the situation in Illinois in general or Chicago in particular during most of the pre-fire period. Chicago became a city in 1837, the year after the charter for the Second Bank of the United States expired and, as luck would have it, the year of a severe financial panic. It wasn't even incorporated as a town when the fate of the Second Bank was decided by the 1832 presidential election between Andrew Jackson and Henry Clay.[1] A relatively well-functioning national financial system did not return until eight years before the fire, in the midst of the Civil War. The passage of the National Bank Act in 1863 provided that system, one that would prove useful in Chicago's recovery from the fire.

The fundamental unit of an economy is the transaction. In the absence of a medium of exchange, transactions involve the direct exchange of goods—barter. This requires what economists refer to as "a double coincidence of wants," in which each party owns something the other wants and values equivalently. Such a quid pro quo is relatively rare. As we have seen, fur trading on the frontier was primarily barter. Commonly, the two sides of an exchange are not valued equivalently; the problem becomes one of making "change." A farmer brings a steer ready for slaughter to the general store to exchange for a variety of staples, but he has no way of storing the barrels of flour, sugar, and salt that are equal in value to the steer. This is where money in its role as a medium of exchange helps facilitate trade, either when it helps equilibrate the value of what's exchanged or when the exchange itself becomes goods for money. At the eastern end of the fur trade, credit was required to outfit traders going west, and money was needed to compensate them on their return.

Banks help people manage their finances. They create accounts in which people deposit money over and above what is needed for current transactions. They provide loans to people who need to borrow for the purpose of purchasing a home, starting a business, and so forth.[2] Banks earn interest on the latter and pay interest on the former. The wages and salaries of employees, the rental of office space, and all the other costs of a bank come from the fact that the interest rate on what it lends is greater than the interest rate it pays on it accounts.

Until 1863 most of the banks operating in Chicago were state banks, meaning they had received a charter from the state. When people borrowed money from a bank during this period, they generally received the funds in the form of bank notes, pieces of paper signifying the bank's promise to pay the holder of the note. When a transaction exchanged goods for bank notes, ownership of goods passed from seller to buyer, and ownership of the notes passed from buyer to seller. In short, paper bank notes were part of the money supply. What's more, they were often legal tender, meaning that, if they were tendered in payment for goods or in payment of debt, the legal system regarded that as acceptable payment, and the party to whom the notes were tendered was obligated to accept them. In order to limit the amount of bank notes issued, most states required that they be redeemable in specie, that is, gold and silver coins. A person who chose not to hold a $20 bank note could take it to the issuing bank and exchange it for a $20 gold piece or twenty $1 silver pieces. Should a bank be unable to redeem its notes in specie, its charter would be forfeited. This provision proved difficult to enforce when a severe panic hit the financial system.[3]

For present purposes it is important to understand that one of the major activities of mid-nineteenth-century banks was the issuance of bank notes, and this currency was an important component of the money supply.[4] The vast majority of the money supply was specie in the form of coins minted by the federal government (cash) and bank notes issued by local banks (currency) that were required to be convertible into specie. It is difficult today, when the only legal currency is that issued by the Federal Reserve, to imagine what life was like when there were hundreds of different kinds of paper in circulation, issued by different entities, all purporting to be exchangeable for a given amount.

Assume that you held a $1 note, $1 per day being a little less than the average wage for nonfarm labor in 1860.[5] How much was it really worth? That depended on many things. First, if the issuing bank was a long way from Chicago, it was costlier to go there to request redemption in specie, so the note would be discounted to account for that cost. If the issuing bank was less well known and a greater risk was assumed with respect to redemption, it would be discounted. How much was the discount? Merchants could not be expected to know the proper discount for every possible bank note they might receive, so they relied on large books with pictures such as *Thompson's Bank Note Reporter* that listed bank note issuers as well as the discount on their notes.[6]

Before the 1850s, a group of investors seeking to establish a bank required the approval of the state's legislative and executive branches in the form of a charter granted through an act of incorporation. Banking was a very political activity. Supporters of a minority party were unlikely to receive state charters.

The major alternatives to state banks were private banks. Like state banks, they accepted deposits, made loans, and bought and sold bank notes; unlike state banks, they could not legally issue notes of their own. They did, however, issue certificates of deposit, pieces of paper acknowledging the deposit of funds, which were used as a medium of exchange. These were analogous to the certificates issued to those who owned grain in an elevator.

In the years preceding the passage of the National Bank Act of 1863, the history of banking in Illinois was characterized by four cycles (the first of which took place before Chicago's incorporation) that all followed a similar pattern. The initial upturn of each was triggered by an increase in the demand for money and credit. The state then passed a law permitting the formation of a bank allowed to issue notes, typically notes that proved inadequate in number and safety. This led to an initial period of prosperity followed by a downturn in which banks suspended the redemption of the notes into gold and silver, hurting those who held the notes, and ultimately the banks failed. At the bottom of the cycle, hard times were coupled with a strong anti-bank sentiment until such time—usually a short interval—as the demand for money increased once again.[7]

In brief, banking was a risky but necessary business if an economy, no matter how small, was to experience growth. Bank notes were the major part of the money supply and crucial for the purpose of exchange. Money and banking provided financial lubrication to the process of growth.[8] This chapter focuses on the link between Chicago banks and the supply of money in the city, but what was true of Chicago banks in particular was true of Illinois banks in general.

The First Cycle

The first cycle had just ended (1832) when Chicago was incorporated as a village in 1833. Its importance for Chicago history is its impact on what happened thereafter. Before 1833 the vast majority of exchanges on the frontier took place via barter, so there was little need for money. Afterward, immigrants from the East brought cash instead of goods, hoping to purchase what they needed on arrival. This was a major source of what little money circulated in the area.

The initial settlement of Illinois occurred in the south as potential pioneers traveled through the Cumberland Gap, down the Ohio River, and in some cases up the Mississippi River. Much of this was happening at the same time as the expiration of the charter of the First Bank of the United States in 1831. The consequence of allowing the federal bank's charter to lapse was an increase in the demand for state-chartered banks, banking being viewed as a state function.[9] What followed was an increase in the number of new banks all over the country, including southern Illinois, all anxious to issue bank notes. And with more money in circulation, prices increased. Money was especially in demand for the purchase of land, and government sales of Illinois land began in 1814.

At the time, parcels not sold at auction were priced at $2 per acre. A buyer was required to make a down payment of 5 percent, with an additional 20 percent to be paid within forty days. The balance was due at the rate of 25 percent each at the end of the second, third, and fourth year. Thus, for $16 down and $64 within forty days, a family could acquire a quarter section of land (160 acres).[10] In order to facilitate such a transaction (and others), new Illinoisans demanded that banks provide individual loans, lines of credit, and a medium of exchange.

The first Illinois banks were established by the territorial legislature in the 1816–17 session. All were in the southern part of the territory. For example, the Bank of Illinois was located in Shawneetown, on the Illinois side of the Ohio River just west of the mouth of the Wabash River.[11] Other banks were chartered in Cairo, Edwardsville, and Kaskaskia. None would have had much, if any, impact in the Chicago area where Fort Dearborn had just been rebuilt and only a few fur traders and frontier farmers resided.

When Illinois became a state in 1818, its constitution included a provision that stated, "There shall be no other banks or money institutions but those already provided by law, except a state bank and its branches which may be established and regulated by the general assembly of the state as they may think proper."[12] Although the territorial banks were grandfathered, all eventually failed, so the practical effect of this provision was that the state had control of banking and issuing of notes, even though there was nothing that legally limited ownership to the state; however, the state bank referenced in the constitution was to be owned by the state, not by private investors. The first State Bank of Illinois was located in Vandalia, with four branches also located in southern Illinois.[13] A resident of a northern Illinois county desirous of banking services would be directed to the branch assigned to that county, but most looked elsewhere. There was no provision that the notes the bank issued had to be redeemed in specie if so requested. Consequently, people lacked confidence that these notes were worth their face value, and they began depreciating almost immediately. The depreciation ultimately reached thirty cents on the dollar.

Another problem was that because coins were extremely scarce, those notes, issued in dollar amounts, were the smallest denominated part of the money supply in general circulation. As a result, in 1823 the State Bank's directors sanctioned the practice that had developed of tearing $5 bills or smaller into halves, quarters, and the like for the purpose of making change. They approved accepting the torn portions of their bills in payment of all obligations to the bank.[14]

The State Bank became an issue in the 1830 gubernatorial race. Jacksonian Democrats opposed the bank (and any note-issuing bank, for that matter); they believed that transactions should involve gold or silver exclusively. The Democrats won the election, and the bank was closed in 1831. The closing triggered a business depression in Illinois because the basic medium of exchange (i.e., the State Bank's notes) vanished. For the next two sessions of the Illinois legislature, the Whigs introduced a bill to replace the State Bank, and the Democrats voted it down, albeit by a single vote in 1833. This event marks the end of the first cycle. As historian of early Chicago banking F. Cyril James notes, people considered money and capital to be synonymous, and both became more pressing needs as business conditions improved all over the country and the westward migration increased.[15]

The Second Cycle and the Panic of 1837

The second cycle began with the move toward a second State Bank of Illinois, a move that was tied to the imminent demise (1836) of the Second Bank of the United States, whose fate had been decided in the 1832 presidential election.[16] Illinoisans expected the closing of the federal second bank to exacerbate the monetary shortage caused by the absence of the first State Bank of Illinois. Accordingly, in 1835 the legislature created the second State Bank of Illinois, with a twenty-five-year charter, one year before the charter of the Second Bank of the United States was to expire. As a reflection of the population growth in the north of the state, the bank's principal office was located in Springfield, with a branch in Vandalia, the state capital until 1839. A large number of additional branches were opened, including one in Chicago, with John H. Kinzie its president.

The second State Bank's charter attempted to adjust for the lessons learned from the first bank. In particular, the bank notes it issued, while still not guaranteed by the state, were now limited to a multiple of 2.5 times the bank's paid-in capital and were to be redeemable in specie at all times. Should the bank not redeem its notes in specie within ten days of their being presented, its charter was forfeit, and the bank was to be liquidated as expeditiously as possible. As time passed, the state would have to revisit this provision whenever a business downturn developed.

Two of the banks chartered by the territorial government and grandfathered by the 1818 constitution were technically still in existence. The Bank of Illinois at Shawneetown had gone out of business in 1823, and the Bank of Cairo had never accepted its charter. The prosperity of the early 1830s brought both back to life. The Bank of Illinois was reorganized and opened for business with an amended charter in 1834. The Bank of Cairo's charter was used to open a bank at Kaskaskia. As Bessie Louise Pierce states, notes issued by both these banks circulated in Chicago, such was the demand for money.[17]

By the time the second State Bank opened in 1835, the economy was in the midst of an upswing. The real estate boom was under way, and the lands granted to the I&M Canal were about to go on sale.[18] Land speculation was rampant in Chicago and spreading to the rest of the state. The demand for loans was far in excess of what the State Bank could supply given its limited supply of specie.[19]

Before 1835, the needs of trade were often handled through pioneer merchant Gurdon Hubbard, who kept an account in Buffalo and provided other merchants and traders with drafts.[20] One of the first private (not state-chartered) banks in Chicago was the firm of Hubbard and Balestier, which opened in 1835 with the intention of lending money for mortgages on unimproved (and unencumbered) land throughout Illinois. They charged 12 percent interest on their mortgages. Other early private banks included ones that were formed for the purpose of buying and selling bank notes, to facilitate foreign trade, to extend the operations of a pawn shop, and to facilitate a forwarding and commission business.[21]

Bessie Pierce comments that, in these early years, most of the capital invested in Chicago came from the East, from relatives and friends, or from banks and other financial intermediaries such as the one Hubbard used.[22] This also accounted for much of the money in circulation. These sources of capital, however, were not going to provide a satisfactory solution for the city's needs as it grew.

John F. McDonald compiled data from Homer Hoyt's path-breaking 1933 book *One Hundred Years of Land Values in Chicago* to provide a statistical view of the boom connected with the sale of canal lands. As McDonald notes, in 1830 the price of land was $1.25 per acre, and the highest price paid for a lot eighty feet by one hundred feet was $100. These prices persisted through 1832. By that November, a lot that had sold for $42 in 1830 brought $800. The following year prices were sharply increasing almost daily. A lot that sold for $100 in 1832 brought $3,500, and later in the year it was resold for $67,000.[23]

While this was happening, the federal government was contemplating what to do with a budget surplus. In 1836, as has been discussed, the Jackson administration elected to distribute the money among the states, most of them planning to spend it on internal improvements.[24] Illinois's plan was unrealistic. The decision to authorize the borrowing of $8 million represented eight times the sum of the revenues Illinois collected in the first nineteen years of its existence as a state and more than sixteen times the amount it received from the federal distribution.[25]

Enthusiasm for internal improvements joined the frenzy for real estate, with landowners growing wealthier by the day, if only on paper. The market, however, had all the earmarks of a bubble, one which peaked in 1836. The value of the land within Chicago had grown from $168,000 in 1830 to $10.5 million six years later. But then the bubble was burst by the Panic of 1837. In 1839, when the land on which the second Fort Dearborn stood was sold, it brought $100,000, one-ninth of what it had been worth three years earlier. This was a typical drop in land values. When the real estate market hit bottom in 1842, the total value of the land within Chicago had fallen from $10.5 million to $1.4 million.[26] Much of the money financing the boom in Chicago had come from the East and from Europe, and many of those investments were trapped when the bubble burst.

With the bust, anti-bank sentiment became stronger. It was an ever-present force during the Jackson administration. About a year into his first term, Jackson revived the constitutional objections that Jefferson and others had raised against the First Bank of the United States and argued that, if a bank large enough to cover the nation were to prove necessary, he would prefer one exclusively owned by the federal government.[27] Although the Whigs were able to gain sufficient congressional support to pass a bill rechartering the Second Bank of the United States in 1832, they lacked the votes to overcome Jackson's veto. Further, in that November's presidential election, in which the bank's rechartering was a main issue, Jackson won a decisive victory and began the withdrawal of federal deposits from the Second Bank, redepositing them in favored state-chartered banks.[28]

In July 1836 Jackson issued what is known as the "Specie Circular," an executive order requiring gold and silver in payment for government land. Its impact took some time to be felt. Ostensibly, the motivations for this order were to discourage excessive speculation in land in the West and to curtail the increasing amount of paper money (bank notes) in circulation.[29] Before this order was issued, payment for Illinois land would have been made in bank notes, with the notes redeposited into the banking system.[30] Following this order, buyers had to pay in specie. A loan taken out to pay for government land would be converted to specie, and rather than the specie being redeposited in the banking system, it would be deposited in a U.S. Treasury vault. With the removal of the notes issued by the Second Bank of the United States and the removal of specie as a result of land sales conducted after the promulgation of the Specie Circular, the money supply was significantly diminished.[31] The Panic of 1837 followed.

Jacksonians had done little to moderate the inflation that preceded the panic, especially in such places as Chicago, where the banks' lending policies helped inflate the bubble. In January 1837 several of the stronger New York banks refused to grant immediate credit to those depositing in their accounts either the notes of weaker banks or checks (whose use was generally limited to business at that time). The public remained generally unaware of impending difficulties until March 4, when a drop in cotton prices led to the sudden bankruptcies of several New Orleans commission houses (businesses that sold a planter's goods on commission).

These bankruptcies seriously weakened the position of the New York bankers (and merchants) who were involved in the cotton trade. Little was done to prevent the situation from deteriorating, and on May 8 the failure of a New York bank led to runs on several other banks. Two days later, specie payments were suspended in New York, and the following day they were suspended in Philadelphia. The rest of the country soon followed suit.

Illinois banks voted to suspend specie payments on May 29. Though this was a violation of the charter of the second State Bank of Illinois, its directors had to know that the enormity of the situation would preclude the legislature from closing it. In particular, the bank had become one of the largest holders of the state's internal improvement bonds.

All Chicago businesses came to a standstill. Capital funding became practically unobtainable; the few eastern lenders with available funds demanded exceptionally high interest rates. Chicago's chief governing body, the unicameral Common Council, now unable to obtain a loan from the State Bank of Illinois, issued $5,000 in scrip to cover its obligations.[32] Shortly thereafter, the commissioners of the I&M Canal, forced to do the same, issued more than $150,000 worth of scrip. The Chicago Marine and Fire Insurance Company, which was not a bank, sensing the demand for money, issued certificates of deposit that it believed would be circulated as a medium of exchange.[33] Chicagoans quickly began using these certificates in transactions, even though they did not have legal status as bank notes did and were inconvertible. Too few certificates were issued to prevent the money supply, and therefore prices, from falling. The deflationary circumstances created a major problem for the debtor classes, especially those who were unable to repay their (fixed-interest) loans.

Banks in New York and New England bit the bullet and resumed redeeming their notes in specie. Banks in Pennsylvania and states to the west continued with inconvertible paper, thinking this would counter the deflation necessitated by the resumption of specie payments by the New York banks.[34] After a brief respite in late 1838 and early 1839 (during which time Illinois banks resumed specie payments), the economy turned down again. By August, eastern and southern banks were again abandoning specie payments. When in October 1839 the former Second Bank of the United States failed, state banks in Pennsylvania suspended specie payments. Illinois banks did likewise.

Once again, the second State Bank of Illinois concluded that abandoning specie was necessary though that meant violating its charter. This time, however, with an anti-bank Democrat as governor, the result was a full-scale investigation into the bank's activities.

In his 1913 doctoral dissertation on early Illinois banking, George Dowrie detailed how the investigation found excessive loans to speculators, and in particular land speculators.[35] With respect to the Chicago branch, the bank's president (John H. Kinzie) and directors were found to be negligent in their oversight. The cashier and clerk, in conjunction with two commission men, had financed speculation in the pork market with $26,000 of the bank's funds.[36] Simultaneously, they had refused to provide funds for the city's legitimate needs.

The State Bank of Illinois was allowed to continue in operation, but several changes were mandated by the state. In particular, because of its speculation in pork, the Chicago branch was to be closed and moved to Lockport, 36.5 miles away. In economic terms, this made no sense. During its nearly four years of existence, the Chicago branch had contributed to the city's growth by making Eastern funds available to merchants; about $0.5 million worth of commercial loans had been made. So, shortly after the Lockport branch opened, the legislature restored the Chicago branch because it came to understand that Chicago's commercial needs were much greater than Lockport's.

Although the economy began to show signs of improvement in 1841, the reputation of the State Bank continued to wane. As its notes were increasingly discounted, the real cost of goods to Illinoisans continued to rise.[37] In February 1842 the bank's directors revealed that the bank had suspended operations indefinitely as required by the state. As a result, its notes, which remained in circulation, depreciated rapidly; by April the rate had fallen from 85¢ on the dollar to 44¢. By May, the Chicago branch and two others were closed. The bank itself was liquidated in February 1843.[38]

Cyril James is clear in attributing blame for the fate of these two institutions:

> In part, the responsibility for the failure of the Banks of the State of Illinois rests upon the shoulders of their directors and officers, who were responsible for the adoption of policies that were both unwise and unsound; in even larger proportion, it rests upon the shoulders of the legislators who had attempted continuously to use the banks for political ends. Banking . . . as an instrument for the promotion of internal improvements and public works was disastrous. In both cases, a lack of wisdom on the part of the politicians had combined with the inefficiency of politically appointed banks to bring about conditions of financial chaos and economic depression.[39]

With the closing on the second Bank of the United States and the weakened condition of the local branch of Illinois's "official" bank, Chicago turned to what Dowrie called "illegal banking operations" to finance its growth. He was referring to institutions that were not legally chartered as banks, many of them unincorporated and unchartered private banks. While it existed, the Chicago branch of the State Bank of Illinois provided a small portion of the paper money that circulated in the city; the majority consisted of notes issued by financial institutions throughout the country as Chicago was becoming the area's main commercial node.

Just about the only state bank in what were then the West and the South that proved a success was the State Bank of Indiana, which provided many of the notes in circulation (outside Indiana as well as within) that were lawful and sound.[40] Notes from the wildcat State Bank of Michigan were lawful, but not sound. They created problems; farmers and laborers accepted such notes at face value without being aware that they were subject to a heavy discount. The certificates of the private Wisconsin Marine and Fire Insurance Company were sound, but not lawful, and they were widely accepted in Chicago.[41]

Private banks, also known as "brokerage houses," issued certificates of deposit, which filled a vacuum in the money supply. Naturally, some brokerage houses failed, but overall, their history is much more positive than the history of official banks. Following Gresham's Law, the discounted bills of the weaker official banks drove the sparse supply of specie out of circulation.[42]

The most important of Chicago's early private banks was the Chicago Marine and Fire Insurance Company, mentioned above, which was incorporated by the Illinois legislature in 1836 as an insurance company and did business from January 1836 to January 1840. Capitalized at $100,000, it was allowed to receive deposits and lend money. It, however, was not allowed to issue notes, though this limitation was easily overcome. Its power to finance shipping ventures enabled the firm to issue certificates of deposit. During the Panic of 1837, in the wake of Jackson's Specie Circular, the company gave depositors certificates ranging from $100 to $500 redeemable in specie on demand. Although these certificates did not physically resemble bank notes, they circulated at par value. When the company underwent a voluntary liquidation three years later, the vast majority of these certificates were redeemed and retired without loss to those who held them. When the company was revived in 1849 under Chicago financier J. Young Scammon, the certificates that remained in circulation were augmented by a new issue.[43]

Perhaps the company's most important contribution was that it provided the model for George Smith's Wisconsin Marine and Fire Insurance Company. In the years before the panic Smith, of Aberdeen, Scotland, visited Chicago and was impressed by the city's prospects and by the quality of the land that surrounded it. On his return to Scotland he formed the Scottish Illinois Land and Investment Company, which did quite well until the panic. In 1836, Smith visited Chicago with Patrick Strachan and William Scott, who were to act as the company's agents.

Smith was also impressed by the success of Chicago Marine and Fire. He went to the territorial government of Wisconsin in 1839 and obtained a charter for the Wisconsin Marine and Fire Insurance Company, whose shares were purchased by a small cadre of Scotsmen. The business was run from Chicago in spite of the fact that the head office was in Milwaukee. Like the original firm in Chicago, Wisconsin Marine and Fire was forbidden to issue notes, but its certificates of deposit, which were intended to circulate as money, were widely accepted. Smith guaranteed that they would be redeemable in specie.[44] While active, these certificates proved a reliable currency at a time when the city needed a widely accepted medium of exchange. By 1851 almost $1.5 million was in circulation, with numerous agencies facilitating redemption.[45]

The trough of the second cycle was reached in 1841, with the promise of the canal as dormant as construction on it. Improvement was in the offing, but not until passage of the National Bank Act of 1863 would there be some order to the money circulating in Chicago.

The Third Cycle

Well into its recovery from the Panic of 1837, with the canal completed and the railroad expanding, Illinois adopted a free banking law in 1851 based on the experience of New York and other states. This meant that any small group with a little capital could obtain a state bank charter by applying to a designated state official; legislative approval was no longer required. James refers to the idea of these "free banks" as "revolutionary."[46] After the governor unsuccessfully attempted to veto it, the Illinois law still required the approval of the state's voters, who ratified it; Chicago voters overwhelmingly were in favor.[47] Banks had been the subject of partisan debate, but Jacksonian Democrats found that their anti-bank rhetoric was not received as well on the upswing of the cycle as it had been on the downswing. As the editors of the *Illinois Journal* asked in 1850, "Does not necessity and self-preservation call upon us to doff our scruples about banking for the present—make our own banks, use our own money, and pay the profit to our own State?"[48] Chicago businessmen had demanded a new banking law for some time. The private banks were small relative to Chicago businesses' demand for capital, and the state of the local currency had dissuaded capitalists from making loans in Chicago.

It is important to keep in mind that in the aftermath of the previous downturn no legally issued Illinois bank notes—and precious little specie—were in circulation. Businessmen had to cope with a wide variety of paper from the legally issued bank notes of other states, the certificates of private banks, various forms of scrip, and even counterfeit notes, which were not easy to spot given the variety of currency in circulation. Recall, as well, that negotiable warehouse receipts were in circulation that were used as collateral for the issuance of credit in the grain marketing system centered on Chicago. Though not part of the money supply, they helped augment the supply of credit for that industry.

Almost all this miscellaneous currency was subject to discount, if not in Chicago, then in whichever eastern market it was proffered as payment. The costly consequence of the lack of a bank was that Chicagoans had to borrow from out-of-state banks and in-state nonbanks, which meant higher interest rates and a higher price for credit—and slower growth than otherwise might have been.

Under the new law, any group that could assemble a minimum capital stock of $50,000 was permitted to open a general banking business. Shareholders' liability was limited to their share of the capital stock. In order for bank notes to be issued, securities (largely federal and state bonds) had to be deposited with the Illinois state auditor as backing for the issue. Notes were to be honored as legal tender at the bank's place of business; failure to do so required closing the bank. The interest on loans was limited to 7 percent. There was a system of oversight in that quarterly reports were to be sent to the state treasurer, state auditor, and three bank commissioners, who together supervised the system.

Scammon's Marine Bank was the first Chicago bank to organize under the new law. Scammon and the other directors acquired the Marine Bank in 1852 in order to profit from its ability to issue a circulating medium, as would be the case for most of the other nine Chicago banks created under the new law before 1860. Like the Marine Bank, most of them were organized by those who had been private bankers. In general, the notes were issued to agents who reloaned the notes at 10 percent interest, the added step being necessary because the market interest rate was greater than the 7 percent legal rate. Under the law, the notes that these banks could legally issue had to be redeemable in specie. This did not stop many from continuing to issue illegal notes, which would be subject to a discount when redeemed.

As has been noted, roughly $1.5 million worth of George Smith's Wisconsin Marine and Fire Insurance Company certificates commonly circulated in Chicago. They were subject to a 1 percent discount since they were not legal notes; free banker's notes were required to be redeemed at par. This meant, again in keeping with Gresham's Law, that Chicago's free banks were losing specie to Smith's nonbank firm. James characterizes the situation as a "Bank War" between the issuers of legal free-bank notes led by Scammon and the issuers of illegal certificates of deposit led by Smith.[49]

Clearly, any institution chartered as a bank, in Illinois or elsewhere, would view Smith's issues as unlawful competition. In particular, it would have been galling that Smith's certificates were much more popular than their own notes. And, as a group, chartered bankers did not wait for government to act. In late November 1849 a coalition of Chicago and Michigan bankers had presented $100,000 in

Smith's certificates for redemption at the firm's Milwaukee office in the hope that it would lack sufficient specie. In addition, they spread a rumor that the company was about to fail. This led to runs in Milwaukee and at the other agencies that redeemed the certificates. Smith met all requested redemptions without problem.

This led Smith to gain a controlling interest in a Washington, DC, bank, and he then obtained a charter for the Bank of America in Chicago under the free banking law.[50] Smith's Bank of America in Chicago began issuing notes, but its note issue never amounted to much. Instead, Smith issued in Chicago the notes of his Washington bank, which looked almost like those of the Chicago bank. He was taking advantage of the fact that, unlike Illinois, the District of Columbia did not require securities to be deposited to back note issues. Further, he purchased a controlling interest in two banks in Georgia: the Atlanta Bank and the International Bank of Griffin (in the Atlanta metropolitan area). Georgia's requirements for note issue were as lax as those in Washington, so Georgia notes were sent to George Smith and Company in Chicago, where they were put in circulation. Taken together, Smith's note issue, largely based on his spotless reputation, accounted for 75 percent of the paper money in circulation in Chicago.[51]

This did not sit well with the legal bankers. Scammon and other free bankers amassed as many of Smith's Georgia notes as they could find and sent a representative to Georgia to present them for payment in specie. Again Smith paid them in full. Every one of Smith's notes that came into the Scammon group's hands in Chicago was presented for payment at George Smith and Company, often at what James termed "the most inopportune times."[52] These runs stopped when Scammon learned how many of Scammon's notes were held by Smith. Pierce refers to an "armed truce" between the two—neither would interfere with the other's note issue or attempt a run on the other's bank.[53]

The "war" then moved to the courts, where in December 1852 a Cook County grand jury recommended that an indictment be issued against Smith and a few others stemming from their illegal note issue. Nothing seems to have come from the subsequent suits, so the next step was for Scammon and other legal bankers to plead their case to the Illinois legislature. In February 1853, as the economy approached a downturn, an act was passed making it illegal to issue or receive paper money that was not legally issued by a state-chartered bank per the banking law of 1851.[54]

It now became illegal to issue in Illinois any medium of exchange other than those approved under the free banking law. Paper issued outside Illinois could circulate within the state if it was denominated $5 or higher and issued by regular specie-paying banks. Given the amount of the circulating medium for which Smith alone accounted, this implied a large drop in Chicago's money supply. As a result of the 1853 act, George Smith sold Wisconsin Marine later that year to Alexander Mitchell, the company's secretary, who converted it to a Wisconsin-chartered bank. Over the course of the next few years Smith sold his other banks and returned to Scotland a man of great wealth.[55]

Although it takes us on a bit of a tangent, a discussion of Chicago banking in this cycle would be remiss not to recount the peculiar adventures of Seth Paine and his private Bank of Chicago (a.k.a. the "Spiritual Bank"), whose actual capital never exceeded $6,000 and whose note issue was less—and entirely illegal. The bank opened in October 1852. It did not open under the free banking law; it was not operated as a normal bank; but it did issue a large number of notes in making loans in support of its spiritualist principles. Notably, the loans were made at 6 percent interest, considerably below the market rate.

Seth Paine was a gifted speaker and writer who made his ideas known with an evangelical zeal. In addition, he was a believer in the utopian socialism of Charles Fourier, which led him to establish a commune on land he owned in what he named Lake Zurich, Illinois, about forty miles northwest of Chicago, where today there is a school that bears his name.[56] He was an abolitionist and became an ardent spiritualist, holding the belief that the living can communicate with the deceased.[57] And as senior partner in Seth Paine and Company, he believed he could reform banking.

The bank was housed in a Clark Street building owned by Ira Eddy, another ardent spiritualist and the principal investor. The bank's prospectus made clear that loans would not be made to "aid in making or selling intoxicating liquors, or tobacco," and they would not be made to "gamblers or usurers who borrow to loan again."[58] Loans for real estate or for speculation in general were also on the prohibited list. It approved only loans "aiding the natural exchange between the producer and consumer, whether of body, soul or spirit, and for the time necessary to produce the exchange."[59]

To Paine, it was important to combine spiritualism and banking; thus he created "Harmony Hall," a group of spiritualists who met in a room above the bank. He and Eddy brought in one Mrs. Herrick as the group's "High Priestess," a medium who was believed to have the ability to directly contact spirits. But that wasn't her only duty. When one of the bank's customers requested a loan, Paine would invite Mrs. Herrick down to the bank's parlor, where she would consult the spirit of Alexander Hamilton as to whether the loan should be granted. Hamilton's spirit was generous with women, children, Blacks, and spiritualists; it had no trouble rejecting drinkers, smokers, gamblers, and bankers.

Paine, never content to stop partway, began publishing the weekly *Christian Banker*, in which he took issue with many of his "competitors." As the bank's

Fig. 24. A $3 banknote from the Bank of Chicago (a.k.a. the Spiritual Bank). (Chicago History Museum, ICHi-183706A.)

business practices became known, friends of Ira Eddy, including his brother Devotion C. Eddy, a Chicago lawyer and financier, petitioned the court to "protect" Ira Eddy's interest in the bank. Ira was brought before a judge, testimony was heard, and the court ruled that he was committing lunacy and was, therefore, incapable of managing his affairs. Devotion was appointed conservator of his brother's estate. The news of this decision caused a run on the bank, but Paine and the High Priestess were prepared.

The following day, Devotion attempted to take possession of the bank as ordered by the court. Ira threatened to shoot, and the priestess refused to allow the court-appointed bookkeeper to do his job. That gentleman complained to the court of attempted intimidation by personal violence. Consequently, all the bank's employees were arrested and taken before a judge. At the ensuing trial, a few were summarily discharged; $500 was paid in bail for all the others save the High Priestess, who had been taken to jail during the trial for becoming unduly demonstrative, to say nothing of resisting arrest en route.[60] The fact of the matter is that the Bank of Chicago was doomed once Ira Eddy's deposits were gone, but the customary story is that its doors were closed by the police—presumably once all of the bank's personnel were in the paddy wagon.

A minor panic in 1854 led to the trough of the third cycle and caused many in Chicago to present for redemption notes issued by Chicago banks. Half of the free banks in Chicago closed their doors; only one ultimately reopened. However, by the end of 1854, with Smith's departure as a result of the 1853 act (and Paine's exit), Chicago had a rapidly growing population and a money supply that was for the most part legal, albeit small.

The Fourth Cycle and the Panic of 1857

The fourth and final pre-fire cycle was marked by the Panic of 1857. After receiving news of the failure of several eastern banks, Chicagoans began runs on the city's banks. The discount on suspect bank notes and nonbank paper became so high that the bills themselves were virtually worthless, especially those from out-of-state banks. When St. Louis merchants discredited Illinois currency and returned it for redemption, Chicago firms experienced problems, though the St. Louisans were persuaded to change course within a few days.[61] Pierce reports that during the panic more than two hundred firms failed, with debts in excess of $10 million.[62] By the autumn of 1856, only three incorporated banks were still operating, and only one, Scammon's Marine Bank, was still in business in 1860, but it, too, experienced problems, as discussed in chapter 5.

Incorporated banks were not the only financial intermediaries operating in Chicago in the 1850s. There were perhaps twenty-five private banks ranging from large firms that functioned much the same as the incorporated banks to small firms that functioned much like pawnbrokers. Chicago also participated in two innovations of the 1850s: trust companies and savings banks.[63] Even before the Civil War, Chicago had an interconnected financial network composed of a wide variety of institutions focused on increasingly specialized tasks. Given the rapid rate at which Chicago continued to grow, however, an overall capital shortage remained. Whereas the nation's financial system was better integrated owing to improvements in transportation and communication during the decade, a result of the spending spree made possible by the discovery of gold in California, the advent of the telegraph meant that financial contagion could spread much faster than it once did.[64]

In the spring of 1857, when the national economy approached the peak of the upswing, money was extremely tight. The breaking point came in August with the failure of the Ohio Life Insurance and Trust Company's New York office because of bad investments in businesses related to agriculture.[65] This company, as its name suggests, was involved in both insurance and banking. It had handled a good portion of the domestic exchange business between New York and the west and, at the time, was in debt to several New York banks. Its failure caused panic in the East and the subsequent failure of several eastern banks. A month later the panic headed west. James noted that between August 15 and October 17, deposits in New York City declined 42.7 percent; specie reserves, somewhat less.[66] As the economy began its collapse, firms that sold produce and goods on commission failed; railroads were at risk of going into receivership.

As summer gave way to fall, things remained quiet in Chicago. Yet the correspondent accounts that New York City banks held for banks in other cities helped the downswing spread. On October 13, in order to replenish their monetary stocks, banks across the country withdrew $4 million in specie from correspondent accounts in New York City banks, and a suspension of specie payments followed immediately. The impact this had in Chicago was related to the fact that the Illinois banking legislation of February 1857 had not addressed the quality of the bonds deposited by state-chartered banks for the purpose of issuing notes. As it turned out, by the fall of 1857 more than half of the deposited bonds were from the state of Missouri, whose internal improvement projects had caused a large debt to accumulate. The price of those bonds began to fall as early as February, and Illinois banks were having to reduce their circulation of notes. This contraction in the money supply led to the closing of several Chicago financial firms before the panic hit with full force in late August, causing Chicago banks to suspend specie payments.

The panic was short-lived, but painful. New York banks were able to resume specie payments in mid-December, and the rest of the country followed by year's end. In Chicago, there were roughly 204 failures accounting for $10 million in liabilities. Compounding the situation was the fact that the 1857 Illinois harvest was poor. The Chicago economy was hard hit. As the economy recovered, the use of checks spread from business use to individual use in New York, but in Chicago bank notes remained the primary medium of exchange, and Illinois bank notes remained suspect. Businesses and other affected parties demanded banking reform in Illinois and in many other states.

As the Civil War approached, southern securities began to decline in value, while the price of eastern notes rose relative to Illinois currency. Fearing the repercussions of a continuation of this trend as secession became more likely, Illinois changed its banking law in 1861 so that only U.S. government and Illinois securities were acceptable as backing for notes issued.[67] In his examination of the financial condition of all Illinois banks in the aggregate and of several individual Illinois banks, Dowrie somewhat sarcastically concluded, "The stock bank system, instead of providing the state with adequate and dependable facilities for all lines of banking, had created a machine for the issue of paper money."[68] In other words, instead of facilitating the greater good, Chicago's economic growth, the banks were focused on their own selfish ends.

Because the new law could not go into effect immediately without having a major effect on securities markets, people holding paper money were suddenly faced with a good deal of uncertainty as to the value of the various pieces of paper in their possession. Banks began to hoard bills based on the securities of northern states and leave in circulation bills based on southern securities. A bill could face a 50 percent discount from the amount at which it had been accepted. In short, the banking system seemed headed for another collapse. Altogether, the value of

Illinois notes in circulation fell from $3.5 million in October 1861 to $0.57 million at the end of 1862.[69] The only solution appeared to be a return to specie backing.

The drop in the price of southern securities created problems for several specific banks. In particular, the Marine Bank, the remaining bank incorporated under the Free Banking Act, proved unable to repay funds deposited by Chicago's Board of Education and by the Sewerage Commissioners. The Chicago Marine and Fire Insurance Company decided to suspend operations at the same time the Marine Bank closed, July 8, 1861. Both were to be liquidated by Scammon, who once again became a private banker, to the consternation of many who thought an independent receiver (a court-appointed individual unrelated to the bank who "receives" the institution to manage) was a more appropriate alternative.

When the Civil War began in April 1861, near the end of the fourth cycle, there was not a single incorporated bank in Chicago; what financial services were available were supplied from entities elsewhere. For example, the Bank of Montreal had opened an agency in the city as a result of the recent panic. In July the federal government issued "Demand Notes" to help finance the war. Though not legal tender (until March 1862), they were exchangeable for specie on demand. Unlike state notes and bank notes, they were printed on both sides, which led to the name "greenbacks." In December 1861 New York banks stopped redeeming bills in specie, and the federal government did likewise a month later. To be clear, this meant that the United States abandoned the international gold standard; this action would cause problems at the war's end. Not until the end of February 1862 did the federal government first issue United States Notes, also called greenbacks. Although they were not redeemable in specie, they were legal tender. A goodly number circulated in the West, where their value (with respect to gold) fluctuated with the successes and failures of the Union Army.

The *Chicago Tribune* commented that the new law did not live up to expectations. Scammon and others did not believe it went far enough. They proposed to create the Union Bank of Illinois, modeled on the Bank of the State of Indiana. Like the earlier State Banks of Illinois, it would have branches throughout the state but have a central board of directors. The state legislature passed a law chartering the Union Bank in February 1861, but a referendum on the bill was defeated decisively in the November 1862 election. There are several reasons why voters rejected it. Between the time the act passed the legislature and the time the vote was taken, the trough of the fourth cycle was reached and the banking system collapsed, so there was a good deal of anti-bank sentiment. Greenbacks had been issued, and the need for an ample supply of money was less pressing. Finally, a new Illinois state constitution was under discussion, and it was felt that banking issues were better addressed there. Dowrie argued that the Illinois state banking system as amended in 1861 would have worked "had it had a fair trial."[70]

The National Banking System

The banking and currency problems that extended through the four major cycles were diminished by the passage of the National Bank Act in 1863. That Chicago had grown as it did under the previous regime, which generally restricted the amount of available capital, was a notable achievement. The new act envisioned a system of nationally chartered banks that would establish a uniform national currency. The fact that, in order to issue national bank notes, a national bank had to deposit U.S. Treasury securities with the Treasury, helped finance the Civil War.[71] When the federal government received fewer applications than expected, however, the act was revised the following year. A new office was established, that of the Comptroller of the Currency, which actively supervised commercial banking. Under the revised act, national banks had capital requirements that depended on the population of the cities in which they were located (initially they ranged from $50,000 for a city with a population of six thousand to $200,000 for a city of fifty thousand or more). A 15 percent legal reserve requirement was imposed on the national banks. If a bank purchased U.S. bonds equal to at least one-third of its required capital and deposited those bonds with the Comptroller, it received national bank notes (with that bank's name embossed on them) equal to 90 percent of the face value of the bonds it deposited.[72] Such features were supposed to attract deposits to national banks because they would be perceived as much safer institutions than their smaller, state-chartered competitors.

Chicago was named a National Bank Act reserve city, and under the 1864 revision, national banks outside such cities were allowed to count deposits in those cities toward their reserve requirement. This designation demonstrates the city's growing nodality. A system of correspondent arrangements emerged across Chicago's trading area, enhancing the city's position and nodality. At the time of the fire, there were 245 national banks in its trading area, and it is likely that almost all had correspondent relationships with at least one bank in Chicago.

The hope was that national bank notes would become the standard currency, but state bank notes remained in circulation. And since state bank notes were traded at a discount, national bank notes were hoarded rather than circulated, as Gresham's Law would predict. In June 1864 the federal government levied a tax of 2 percent against state bank notes in an attempt to drive them out of circulation.[73] That tax was raised to 10 percent the following year, then to 20 percent. Because many of the state banks existed mainly to profit from their note issue, a great number simply closed rather than become national banks or try to compete against them.

The First National Bank of Chicago opened in July 1863.[74] Edmund Aiken, a man well known in banking circles nationally, had invited several key Chicago businessmen to his office in the Board of Trade building to discuss forming a national bank as the act was being debated in Washington. Aiken was the surviving partner of Aiken and Norton, a small private banking house. In early May, this group had applied for a charter and received the eighth charter to be granted. Aiken was selected to be president and Samuel Nickerson, vice president. The bank began its operations in the space formerly occupied by Aiken and Norton. The incorporators had paid in the requisite $100,000 capital a month before its opening, and the directors increased that amount to $250,000 before the bank opened. By January 1865 the bank's capital had been boosted to $1 million, the maximum allowed by the charter.

There clearly had been a demand for such an institution. These increases in capitalization reflected Chicago's demand for money; the supply of greenbacks circulating in the city was inadequate. By September 1863 the directors of First National ("The First," as it was known) had increased the amount of securities they had deposited with the Comptroller to $200,000 in order to increase their note issue, although the notes did not arrive in Chicago until early 1864. The existence of national bank notes from First National and the other Chicago national banks contributed to the city's strong support for the elimination of state bank notes. By the fall of 1863, First National had deposits of $273,000; a year and a quarter later that amount had grown to just under $1.3 million.[75]

Such growth required the bank to seek ever larger quarters. In early 1864 it moved out of the space in which it began, and shortly after the war, it erected its own building at the southwest corner of State and Washington Streets. Aiken died in January 1867 and was replaced by Nickerson. Lyman Gage, who joined

Fig. 25. The First National Bank of Chicago before and after the Chicago Fire. (Chicago History Museum, ICHi-064266.)

the bank as cashier in 1868, eventually replaced Nickerson. He would be an important part of the Chicago banking community for several decades and serve as Secretary of the Treasury under Presidents William McKinley and Theodore Roosevelt, having turned down an earlier offer from President Grover Cleveland.

The Union National Bank opened in January 1865 under the leadership of William Coolbaugh, who in 1862 had moved from Iowa, where he had been a politician, to Chicago to become a banker. By the middle of 1866 Union National had become Chicago's largest bank, with correspondent accounts with banks across the area.[76]

There were other banks that remained in business following the institution of the national banking system. First were the legally authorized state-chartered banks. In 1867 the Illinois legislature allowed them to continue their banking activities, but they had to retire their notes and reduce their capital stock. Under the law, it was to be the case that thereafter "no more banks with power to issue notes . . . shall be organized."[77] Some of the remaining state banks were commercial banks, others were savings banks, and a few combined elements of the two. There were sixteen such banks left in Chicago in 1871. In particular, the Illinois Savings Institution, chartered in 1857, was, as its name implies, a savings bank. It was sponsored by Gurdon Hubbard, John H. Kinzie, and William Ogden. At one point it had as much as $4 million in deposits. Pierce commented that these banks helped undermine the dominance of the private banks before the war.[78]

Second, private banks continued to exist. There were thirty-one when the war began, but only twenty-one at its end. Although they performed a wide variety of services, they tended to specialize in one. The national banks, being much larger, tended to take over the business of these banks.[79]

The large number of financial institutions and the ever-widening use of checks contributed to the forming of a cooperative organization to coordinate the clearing of checks. History suggested it also would be prudent to have a forum for Chicago bankers to discuss their problems. Consequently, the Chicago Clearing House Association was formed. It was largely a copy of such associations in eastern cities. In March 1865 seven men from national banks gathered and concluded that they would meet again the following week with a larger group. Sixteen institutions (ten national, three state, and three private banks) were represented at the next meeting. William Coolbaugh was elected president, and shortly thereafter rooms were acquired in Scammon's building. Gage was appointed manager, but he was too valuable to his bank to take on the job permanently. The first clearings took place in April 1865 among nineteen member banks.[80]

The end of the Civil War initiated a question concerning the currency that would continue to be debated for most of the rest of the century. Inflation during the war set the stage for what would prove to be a half-century of tinkering with the currency. With few exceptions, deflation predominated for roughly thirty years following the end of the Civil War, ultimately prompting William Jennings Bryan's famous "Cross of Gold" speech in Chicago.[81]

The Treasury Department's primary objective in the immediate postwar years was to return to the international gold standard, that is, to resume specie payments, as soon as possible. Other nations had not experienced wartime inflation in the early 1860s, so a return to pre-war competitive conditions required that U.S. prices fall. This meant that issues of paper money had to be limited. To that end greenbacks (U.S. Notes) were retired, but it proved expedient to freeze the amount in circulation. National bank note issues were tied to Treasury bonds, and when those bonds began to be retired after the war, the base for note issue and the money supply shrank. So, the first "money revolt," the Greenback movement, developed to defeat the deflation that hit debtors exceptionally hard, including those in Chicago.[82] The fact that the falling prices also reflected rising productivity and produced rising real wages and incomes was irrelevant to advocates for inflation. They favored paper money in addition to silver (and gold). Thus, they opposed the arguments of the "sound money" folks who were arguing for gold. The conflict delayed resumption of redemption in specie until 1879.

After the war, national banks lost some of their attractiveness. The restrictions of the system and the discovery of ways to become profitable in the absence of note issue, especially checking accounts, meant that some relinquished their national charters and became state banks, which enjoyed greater freedom. That was a common story in the East, but in Chicago and the West there were very few conversions.

Instead, following the Clearing House model, they created the National Banking Association in order to try to improve the system. Coolbaugh was a key member of its executive committee for many years, and Chicago bankers were stalwarts of the association. They had numerous grievances. The bills were physically deteriorating. Of some $315 million in bills that had been issued, only $16 million had been exchanged for new notes. The bills were described as "filthy," which is one reason why people expected that the right to issue notes would be restored.[83] The Illinois Constitutional Convention of 1869 did just that. The Constitution was adopted, but the federal prohibition on issuing of notes by state banks remained. Before this matter could be resolved, the fire intervened.

Most of Chicago's major banks and financial institutions were in the downtown area, and most burned in the fire. The heat was such that not even bank vaults always provided reliable protection. Although the safes of many of the larger banks preserved their contents, not all did. Anticipating their loss, several bankers attempted to move their assets to a safer place. Officers of the Merchants

Loan and Trust Company, whose records ended up being destroyed, fled the fire carrying bundles of notes and securities worth hundreds of thousands of dollars. The president of the Union Trust Company brought his horse and buggy to the bank, removed the currency and securities from the vault, carried them home, and hid them in his barn. The head of the Second National Bank packed $600,000 in currency from the vault in a trunk and offered a worker $1,000 to get it west to the Milwaukee Railroad station. On the way, he lost sight of the man with the money, was forced eastward by the flames, and reached the station several hours later. There was the man, sitting on the trunk, patiently waiting to collect his fee. A less fortunate banker trying to escape the flames encountered thieves who took the money.[84]

Because national bank notes were now the principal form of currency, the adjustment to the losses from the fire were less confusing than would have been the case had the variety of state bank notes still been in circulation. The new banking system did not alter the business cycle. The four cycles discussed were typical business cycles, but the last three occurred during an atypical time, the wildcat banking era—the period between the closing of the second Bank of the United States and the passage of the National Bank Act. In all four, as the business cycle entered an upswing, the demand for money and credit increased. This led to the creation of new banks issuing their own notes. The process reversed itself once the peak of the cycle was reached, with the banks first suspending specie payments, then failing. Because the notes issued by these banks comprised a significant portion of the money supply, the supply moved with the cycle, constituting a pro-cyclical monetary policy.[85] As a consequence, the amplitude of the cycles, up and down, was augmented, adding to economic instability. Nevertheless, Chicago grew, with only the Panic of 1837 causing a prolonged problem. Like the fire, the panic interrupted growth but did not extinguish it. Chicago's banks, with their supplies of money and credit—the lubrication for the city's economy—would finance the resumption of growth.

CHAPTER 9

Where Things Stood

Days after the fire destroyed much of Chicago, including his home, William Bross traveled east to meet with potential investors and current trading partners to spread the word that Chicago would rebuild. Born in New Jersey in 1813, Bross graduated from Williams College in 1838, then a decade later arrived in Chicago, where he prospered. One of his early projects was a newspaper, the *Democratic Press*, which merged with the *Chicago Tribune* in 1858. The purpose of his trip was, in part, to purchase equipment needed by the *Tribune*, but he also spoke to several groups such as the Buffalo Board of Trade and the Chicago Relief Committee of the New York Chamber of Commerce.[1] His message was that it was in the financial interest of his listeners to invest in Chicago. Moreover, he suggested that their sons begin their careers in Chicago because "they would be under the tutelage of the city's exceptionally capable entrepreneurs at the most exciting of moments."[2]

Many of those entrepreneurs were in mid-career when the fire struck (Marshall Field, Cyrus McCormick, George Pullman, Montgomery Ward). Others were reaching the end of their careers (Gurdon Hubbard, William Ogden, J. Young Scammon). And many others were just getting started who would promote Chicago's growth well after the fire (Phillip Armour, Samuel Nickerson, Richard Sears, Gustavus Swift). The city's entrepreneurial spirit had accelerated its growth in the 1830s, had seen it through the Panic of 1837, and had guided it through the Civil War. Bross was one of many who saw opportunity in rebuilding Chicago. Many historians such as Frederic Jaher have concluded that Chicago's entrepreneurs exploited its natural advantages: "Chicago emerged as the colossus of the West because its hinterland contained the world's most productive agricultural area and because it was the terminus of the world's greatest internal waterway."[3]

These attributes, which were unaffected by the fire, reflect what Bross recognized, namely, that Chicago's growth was anchored by William Dean's three key variables: its trade routes, position, and nodality. A summary of what evolved with respect to each of those three helps focus our understanding of how Chicago grew.

Dean's Concepts

TRADE ROUTES

While there were several portages over the divide between the Great Lakes and the Mississippi River drainage systems, the Chicago Portage became the favored one when the Americans assumed control of the area late in the fur trade era. These portages were the main east-west trade routes when travel was via canoe. This portage may not have been the route of Marquette and Jolliet, but it was an oft-used route (as well as an oft-avoided one) by the time of Point de Sable, Ouilmette, Kinzie, and Hubbard. And though neither the French nor the English saw fit to protect access to the portage by building fortifications near the mouth of the "inconsequential" Chicago River, it was the Americans' intent from the Treaty of Greenville in 1795 to protect access to that trade route and to improve it by building a canal across the Chicago Portage. The promise of a canal drew people to Chicago; it accelerated growth at the minor node on what would become a major trade route.

Given that the fur trade took place in an era when transport via water was more efficient than via land, the principal alternative trade route that could have been developed was the Calumet River. Before the natural waterways were altered, the Grand Calumet River emptied into Lake Michigan near Miller Beach, Indiana, just to the east of Gary, at the southernmost part of the lake. Had the Americans built a canal across the Chicagoua Portage, the likely site of the nodal point would have been almost exactly where it would have been had improvements to the area's trade routes been delayed until after the railroad became the primary transport mode. This counterfactual exercise helps emphasize how much the location of Chicago depended on the Chicago Portage and the transportation technology at the time of the first major improvements to that trade route.

The proposed canal was responsible for Chicago's becoming part of Illinois. It was supposed to have been part of Wisconsin. The Land Ordinance of 1787, the Northwest Ordinance, called for the dividing line between the two westernmost states in the territory to be at the bottom of Lake Michigan. The plan to build a canal across the Chicago Portage was under discussion well before Illinois became a state in 1818. Because President Madison vetoed a bill for federal funding of the Erie Canal in 1817, the bill for Illinois statehood moved the proposed state's border roughly sixty miles to the north of the line defined in the Northwest Ordinance. This, it was thought, would mean the entire area benefited by the canal would be included in the state that would have to pay for the canal's construction. Thus, Chicago became part of Illinois, not Wisconsin.

The second major trade route present during the fur trade era, the Great Lakes themselves, is a much less often discussed part of Chicago history than the route across the Chicago Portage. Early on, the French used the Ottawa River to reach the western Great Lakes in order to avoid the Iroquois and the portage around Niagara Falls. By the end of that era, the Iroquois were no longer a threat, and the Welland Canal of 1833 eliminated the need to portage around the falls. Indeed, the opening of the Erie Canal in 1825 provided a new and faster east-west route, one that avoided the northeastern journey on the St. Lawrence River.

LaSalle's barque *Le Griffon* was the first large sailing ship on the lakes and the harbinger of the steamboats that appeared on Lake Michigan in 1826. Six years later, a government steamboat carrying troops and supplies for the Black Hawk War from Buffalo to Chicago also brought cholera, a scourge that would bedevil Chicagoans for many years to come; "bads" as well as goods traveled on trade routes. As late as the River and Harbor Convention of 1847, ships arriving in Chicago would anchor about a half mile from shore, but the Chicago River was a federal harbor and facilities were under construction so that, only a few years later, one-hundred-ton ships could dock in the Chicago River. The infrastructure for a large port there appeared in the form of a growing number of wharves, docks, warehouses, elevators, and the like. McCormick built his first factory on the north side of the river near the lake. As the Supreme Court noted in 1877 in *Munn v. Illinois*, the river's mouth had become "the gateway of commerce."

Once under way, construction on the long-hoped-for canal proceeded by fits and starts. By the 1830s, railroads in the East had proved their superiority. Nevertheless, Illinois proceeded with the canal until the Panic of 1837 brought everything to a halt. Fortunes were lost when the land-price bubble burst. Banks closed when they were unable to redeem notes in specie. Construction on the canal stopped when loans could not be arranged to keep it going. In retrospect, there was one silver lining to these dark clouds. The I&M Canal had been designed as a deep-cut canal, one that would allow lake boats to navigate it. When construction resumed, the plan was changed to make it a shallow-cut canal because its lower cost meant that loans could be arranged to complete construction and open the route.

The shallow-cut canal created a clear break-in transport point. At first, cargoes had to be shifted from canal boats and railcars to lake boats and vice versa. As railroads were built in all directions as spokes centered on Chicago, the number of trade routes coming into Chicago grew rapidly. As these spokes were combined into rail networks, the volume of commerce handled in the city continued to grow. As the railroad network was completed, Chicago emerged as the western terminus of eastern roads and the eastern terminus of western roads. In short, the city became a break-in transport between western and eastern railroads as well as between rail and water. Further, several of those western roads took advantage of the lower construction costs across the low divide that was the Chicago Portage to begin their westward journeys. Had the canal been built as a deep-cut one, the impact of the break-in transport might have been postponed because lake boats could have entered it. Nevertheless, technological change in the form of railroads and larger lake boats would have caused a break eventually.

William Dean emphasized that the economic importance of trade routes is primarily a function of population density, the size of the tributary area, and the area's dependence on trade per capita. This is far easier to grasp conceptually than to document empirically.

The population density of Chicago rose dramatically before 1871. The total population was growing rapidly, but then the city's boundaries were also expanding, especially in the 1850s and 1860s. The area occupied by the city of Chicago when it was incorporated was more than four times that occupied by the town of Chicago when it was incorporated four years earlier. Chicago today now covers 227.4 square miles as compared to 35.8 square miles in 1871, due in large part to annexations in 1889. Its population density today is 11,783 persons per square mile, which is not much more than the figure of 9,089 per square mile for 1871 or 10,381 in 1868, prior to the annexations and extensions of 1869.

As more and more land was brought into cultivation on a growing number of farms east of Chicago in the years before the fire, and as the frontier west of Chicago filled, the population density in Chicago's hinterland also increased. Once the voyageurs crossed the Chicago Portage, they had access to more than a million square miles of territory. The area of the Louisiana Purchase in 1803 alone was 828,000 square miles. A few years later, Chicago entrepreneurs, assisted by the railroads, were anxious to trade with as much of that area as possible. Cyrus McCormick's reapers were produced where they could be transported easily to grain farmers on the prairies. Marshall Field's wholesale business stocked the shelves of many western merchants.

The final factor that Dean listed was the area's dependence on trade per capita. Table 9.1 repeats the per capita growth rates of receipts and shipments of selected items in Chicago's commerce between 1854 and 1871, rates that were first reported in chapter 4. These figures are taken from the Chicago Board of Trade's *Annual Reports*, and the fact that there is a Board of Trade indicates that the commerce

Table 9.1. Per capita receipts and shipments in Chicago, 1854–1871

	Receipts (%)	Shipments (%)
Barley, bu.	9.771	13.819
Corn, bu.	-0.408	-0.260
Oats, bu.	3.707	1.304
Wheat, bu.	-3.858	-4.201
Flour, bbl.	4.006	6.609
Cured meats, lbs.	-3.689	11.826
Cattle, no.	4.743	8.453
Live hogs, no.	6.944	8.477
Dressed hogs, no.	0.745	7.974
Beef, bbl.	4.238	-6.294
Pork, bbl.	-3.083	-0.832
Hides, bbl.	6.151	2.540
Wool, lbs.	10.566	12.760
Coal, tons	6.803	4.949
Lumber, feet	-0.483	-2.004

Source: Chicago Board of Trade, Annual Reports, 1854–1871. These rates are those reported in table 4.8 table minus the population growth rate.

moved on Chicago's trade routes was an important component of the city's economy. That some of these rates are negative emphasizes the growing consumption of goods by Chicagoans and those in its hinterland. For example, corn was used to feed people and animals, and as the animal population in the hinterland grew, less corn per capita was received and shipped in Chicago. In the days before refrigeration, the animals arriving at the stockyards left as either live animals or cured meat. It is quite clear that for such agriculturally based industries as meatpacking the receipts and shipments reflect the receipt of raw materials and the shipment of final products. Because industry was attracted to a commercial site, the site would become more dependent on its trade routes as production increased.

POSITION

The Americans were drawn to the Chicago River's mouth by the economic activity attendant on the fur trade as well as their belief that there had once been a fort at the site. It has been argued that people in Philadelphia, the nation's capital at the time, knew Point de Sable's farm was the source of fresh produce in the area. But why was he there? It appears that he was doing in Chicago something similar to what he had done earlier for Pierre Durand in Michigan City, Indiana, but there is no known link between Point de Sable and a trader like Durand in Chicago. There *is* a person who receives little mention in early Chicago history, a man who deserves a more prominent place in that history, because he may well have played a crucial role in establishing economic activity at Chicago, that is, in Dean's terms, in establishing Chicago's position. William Burnett seems to have supplied the financing that underwrote the efforts of those who are better known in Chicago history (e.g., John Kinzie), but the nature of his business relationship with Point de Sable is unclear. From all indications, the house in which the Point de Sables lived at the turn of the nineteenth century also functioned as a trading post for multiple fur traders, one of whom most likely would have been Burnett. He may also have controlled the land that the Point de Sables farmed. It does seem more likely that a fur trader would have spurred this economic activity, but exactly who chose the site remains a mystery. This activity appears to have been a factor in the Americans' demand for title to that land in the Treaty of Greenville.

The historian Richard Wade called cities such as Pittsburgh, Cincinnati, Louisville, and St. Louis the "urban frontier." These cities preceded the line of western settlement. Had he extended his analysis to the north, cities such as Chicago and Milwaukee would have been included. All six were founded as commercial settlements.[4] Chicago's major economic growth began shortly after its 150-year involvement with the fur trade came to an end. The occasion was the start of the third attempt to build the I&M Canal. In anticipation of the canal, enough people arrived in Chicago to warrant incorporation as a town in 1833. When, in 1836, the U.S. Congress began discussing rebating the federal budget surplus to the states, canal construction appeared to be assured. Chicago was incorporated as a city in 1837, at the height of a land-price bubble. Migrants arrived to help construct the canal, to open entrepreneurial ventures, or to speculate on land. This rapid growth would come to a literal halt when the bubble burst a couple months after incorporation and the depressing effects of the Panic of 1837 reached the new city. Despite its new political trappings, Chicago was still very much on the frontier.

To Dean, the primary qualities of position had to do with a city's location with respect to the convergence of trade routes. During the era of water transportation, the site at the southwest corner of the Great Lakes was both a terminal and an intermediate node on a major trade route for passengers and freight. Later, with railroad networks, the Chicago terminals remained near the confluence of river and lake. Chicago's unique position on the railroad network—it was a terminal node for both eastern and western roads—contributed to the city's growth far into the future, but it must be remembered that it was the canal that was responsible for locating the city at the mouth of the Chicago River, the site of Point de Sable's farm.

Position also involves what must be done so that a site can accommodate commerce and industry. Given that the area developed atop what once was a glacial lakebed, the most pressing problem was to reduce the mud. Two of the earliest public works were the digging of a public well and a drainage ditch. Given the city's flatness, the ditch failed because it proved more a conduit for bringing water into the city than for taking it out. In the early 1850s Chicago began constructing the nation's first comprehensive sewer system to drain the city. That system required raising the city's level by several feet, significantly raising costs in the short run. Costs also rose because the sewers emptied either directly into Lake Michigan or indirectly through the Chicago River and despoiled the city's water supply. The success of the new sewer system led to a demand for improvements in the water system long before the germ theory of disease was widely accepted. This forced the city to face the interdependency problem that confronts cities located on a freshwater lake: Its logical water supply source was simultaneously the logical place to dispose of its wastewater. A new water system went into effect during the Civil War that attempted to separate the water intake from the wastewater outfall. The continual growth of the city rendered that strategy ineffective because heavy storms could push wastes to the intake point. The quest to supply Chicagoans with high-quality water would continue long after the fire.[5]

Although the I&M Canal was not part of the city's initial sanitation strategy, it proved essential to establishing Chicago's position. In the 1850s, when the sewer works were being constructed and the waterworks were being planned, dry, hot summers required that the pumps at the Chicago end be run continuously to maintain the canal's summit level. This, in turn, resulted in the canal's drawing water from the lake, informally reversing the flow of the river. Since the river was thought of as an open sewer (implicitly beginning with the first drainage ditch and explicitly once sewers drained into the river), it would have been obvious to anyone looking at the river that objects floating on it were moving away from the lake, not toward it. Hence, some Chicagoans began lobbying for both the canal and its pumping capacity to be enlarged in order to formally reverse the river, so as to protect the city's water supply from its wastes. This serendipitous discovery became the solution to the interdependency problem. What was happenstance in the 1850s was adopted as policy in the 1860s. These works were completed in 1871, the year from which it is customary to date the reversal of the river, but Chicago's continued growth made it necessary to enlarge them by the end of the nineteenth century and supplement them with sewage treatment soon thereafter. Chicago's strategy of drawing its water from Lake Michigan and flushing its wastes into the Illinois River Valley has been unchanged for over 150 years now. Not only did this reduce the threat posed by waterborne diseases such as cholera, it also significantly reduced the mud and reinforced Chicago's position as a site where commerce and industry could thrive.

NODALITY

Dean's third variable is nodality, "the marketing significance of a site emerging from its properties at an intersection of trade routes." When Chicago was incorporated as a town, it was located adjacent to a low divide on an important trade route to what was still frontier. Both the canal and the railroads developed that and other trade routes, with Chicago as a terminus, as the frontier was settled. As such, those who moved to the frontier through Chicago looked to it to supply much of what they demanded from a market, either directly or indirectly, through one of the city's many wholesalers. Among the many places that still call themselves "Gateway to the West" is Lyons, Illinois, just outside Chicago. Lyons is the site of the Chicago Portage National Historic Site, which commemorates the major trade route over the divide.[6] As Dean noted, "the technology of the system, the locus of population and the nature of traffic are socioeconomic phenomena."[7] The canal and the railroads moved thousands of people westward, many over what had been the Chicago Portage, and the traffic flows increased throughout the period before the fire.

Dean also argued that routes competed with routes for traffic, regions with regions for position, and sites with sites for nodality. The key to nodality is how a site commands what we would now consider its metropolitan area. William Ogden, who played an entrepreneurial role with respect to both the canal and the railroads, seemingly understood the importance of this competition in building a city. From his childhood, when his family supplied lumber to Philadelphia, he recognized the importance of establishing trade routes to bring resources into a city and to ship its production out. He recognized that cities were more than just ports and terminals. He attracted and supported firms whose production would provide jobs for the citizenry. He helped develop educational and cultural institutions. And he was one of many who founded the Chicago Board of Trade in 1848 to facilitate and regulate commerce. While most know its role today as a futures market, its initial role was defined in terms of promoting uniformity in the behavior of the city's merchants, speedily adjudicating disputes, collecting and disseminating information, and the like. The board appointed committees on the grading of commodities, appointed inspectors for those commodities, and promoted improvements to the harbor. All this was to inspire confidence that Chicago was a market where sellers and buyers wanted to do business, to encourage the use of the trade routes that led to the city. Because Chicago was a frontier city, its hinterland was largely agricultural, and the three major markets that developed in Chicago were grain, meat, and lumber. When the new Board of Trade opened at the foot of LaSalle Street in 1930, it came as no surprise that a statue of Ceres, Roman goddess of grain, adorned the top.

It should also be no surprise that the first industries attracted to Chicago were associated with agriculture. Cyrus McCormick arrived in 1847 having been convinced by Ogden that Chicago's transportation facilities would give him easier and less expensive access to his customers than would Cincinnati. The Union Stock Yard and Transit Company was built and operated by the railroads themselves when the city made clear that it wanted to minimize the problems the industry created (e.g., driving cattle between railroad terminals) by prohibiting stock yards within the city limits. The number of animals greatly increased during the Civil War with the military demand for meat and the Union Army blockade of the lower Mississippi River—blocking north-south trade on the river, blocking St. Louis, and directing more animals to Chicago. By 1865, pork receipts were 360 percent and beef receipts 290 percent of what they had been in 1860. By-product utilization led to additional industries locating in Chicago such as those making use of the hides to produce leather and those producing leather goods. All this boosted Chicago's nodality with respect to rival frontier cities such as Cincinnati and St. Louis.

Ogden, Newberry, and other early settlers fundamentally were real estate developers, so anything that helped Chicago grow had a potential private benefit for them. Yet there was, potentially, an even greater public benefit from enhancing Chicago's nodality. This included such activities as Ogden's becoming the first president of the Union Pacific Railroad, which had its eastern terminus at Omaha, Nebraska. By 1869 a railroad headed for Chicago, a line that came to be known as the Chicago, Rock Island, and Pacific, was waiting across the Missouri River in Council Bluffs, Iowa. The most direct connection to the East, it meant that the first transcontinental railroad included a Chicago terminal, growing its nodality further, especially with respect to its Midwestern rivals, St. Louis, Milwaukee, and Minneapolis–St. Paul.

Four Growth Factors

In sum, four crucial factors explain Chicago's growth.

PLACE

Chicago's location near a low divide between two of the country's main watersheds put it on a trade route well known to the Native population long before Europeans "discovered" the area. Occasionally, there is an element of geographic determinism in discussions of Chicago's evolution, in particular the notion that a large city was inevitable at a site adjacent to such a low divide (the Chicago Portage). But that alone is neither necessary nor sufficient to explain Chicago's growth. After all, there were several other portages in the area, and the historical significance of the Chicagoua Portage remains to be determined.

TIMING

That Chicago began its growth at the conclusion of the canal era and the beginning of the railroad era provided several benefits. Just before actual construction began on the I&M Canal, the promise of the canal was understood in the context of the success of the Erie Canal, and that attracted people to the area. One of those people, William Ogden, delivered a speech to the New York legislature on the wisdom of building a railroad along the line of the Erie Canal just before he came to Chicago. In the aftermath of the Panic of 1837, he advocated for completing construction of the I&M Canal and commencing railroad construction. That Chicago began railroad construction when it did, at a time when St. Louis remained tied to steamboats, gave Chicago first-mover advantages with respect to becoming the principal node for much of the West. And by starting when railroads were built as spokes from a node, Chicago found itself in a unique situation when those spokes were assembled into networks—it was the terminal point for the most important eastern and western railroad networks. There was a break-in land transport as well as that in water transport and that between land and water.

PEOPLE

Those attracted to Chicago included far-seeing entrepreneurs who made the trek from the East to an outpost on the far western frontier in the 1830s. They also included the individuals whose labor would help make dreams reality. Together, they built the infrastructure that made Chicago the logical marketplace for farmers in the surrounding area and, eventually, for those many hundreds of miles away. These were entrepreneurs who understood what needed to be done to assure the city's growth and who invested in transport facilities that brought people and goods to Chicago from all directions. And they recognized that a good location and investments in trade routes were not enough. A growing city required workers to build the canal and railroads, the docks and wharves, and the homes. It required people to do the often back-breaking work of moving cargoes from one mode of transport to another. It required those who could see the advantage of producing in Chicago. It required those involved in financial services to provide the funds needed for all these activities. And it required those who addressed the other concomitants essential to urban life (e.g., newspapers, schools, and saloons). All played their role, for better and sometimes for worse, in Chicago's evolution and growth.

SANITATION

The key to making the site fit for economic growth was drainage. An imaginative and expensive plan made Chicago the first U.S. city with a comprehensive sewer system to drain surface water from what once was a glacial lakebed and remove other wastes. The success of the sewer system necessitated improvements to the water system. By recognizing the interdependency problem created by using Lake Michigan as both the water supply and the sewage discharge, and by ultimately reversing the Chicago River, the city adopted a sanitation strategy that conserved its water supply and significantly reduced the incidence of waterborne disease. That strategy has been unchanged since before the fire, but numerous capital improvements have since been required. It should come as no surprise that Chicago has one of the largest sewage treatment plants in the world.

Final Thoughts

The results speak for themselves. In 1831 Chicago was a small hamlet of about 100 with an uncertain future as the fur trade was ending. Two years later, it was incorporated as a village with a population of 350. Four years after that, it was incorporated as a city of just over 4,000 amid massive real estate speculation. In 1871 it was a major city of 325,000 people.

Amid all the success, it should not be forgotten that a great deal of luck and serendipity were associated with Chicago's growing to become the principal node of the Midwest. We may never be able to resolve the route of Marquette and Jolliet from the Des Plaines River to Lake Michigan, but it doesn't matter. It may well remain a mystery why Jean Baptiste Point de Sable came to run a trading post and to farm at the mouth of the Chicago River, but he did. We may never know why the Americans chose to focus on the mouth of the Chicago River, but they did. And they planned to construct a canal a long time before the means to do so materialized. What is clear is that the Americans believed the Chicago Portage was the way west from the Great Lakes and that, in an era of waterborne transport, the commerce that developed with the fort in place would multiply many times over with the canal.

There are two important "what ifs" from the 1830s. First, what if William Ogden's fiancée hadn't died? Would the family have sent him to Chicago to look after the land his brother-in-law owned? While it would be foolish to attribute Chicago's growth to one person, Ogden seems to be the key individual behind Chicago's initial growth. It was he who advocated for building a railroad while simultaneously pushing to finish the canal. And it was Ogden and Scammon who visited farms on the proposed railroad's route, selling shares one at a time.

Second, what if completing the canal hadn't required shifting from a deep-cut to a shallow-cut canal? Although this was of little consequence to the long-term development of Chicago's commerce, it could have been of tremendous consequence to its drainage, the conservation of Lake Michigan, and the health of Chicagoans, all part of what Dean termed position. Had the canal been deep-cut, would the possibility of reversing the Chicago River been as readily demonstrated? As with Ogden's hypothetical absence, the answer is perhaps, but, in both cases, Chicago was in luck.

The fact that Chicago's railroads competed against the I&M Canal from the start kept rates lower than they otherwise might have been and gave Chicago a competitive advantage in making the West part of its hinterland. The trade routes centered on Chicago attracted McCormick from Cincinnati. He might have moved to St. Louis had the entrepreneurs of that city embraced railroads earlier.

The impact of reversing the river would not be felt until after the fire, but that possibility was introduced in Chesbrough's plan for Chicago's sewage scheme in the 1850s. And here's a final "what if." What if Chicago's city fathers had rejected as beyond the city's means, and as too much hassle, the notion of raising the city and installing sewers on top of the ground? Would the city's position have been the same? Would commerce and industry have grown as they did? Could such a city ever have grown from mud-filled lots and streets to become a metropolis?

Notes

Introduction

1. This story is retold in Quaife, *Chicago and the Old Northwest*, 14–15.

2. The date of Chicago's incorporation as a city is March 4, 1837; the panic is usually dated from a bank run in New York City on May 10, 1837.

3. An excellent book on Cincinnati's early years is Binford, *From Improvement to City Planning*. For St. Louis see Primm, *Lion of the Valley.*

4. Dean, "Theory."

5. Morrissey, *People of the Ecotone*, discusses the area as "the forest-prairie mosaic," a non-homogeneous mixture of forest, grassland, and wetland. The land is the subject of his chapter 1. His theory about how all this came together historically is on page 52. See also Nelson, *Muddy Ground.*

6. See, e.g., Sells, *History of the Chicago Portage*, a well-researched, comprehensive study of the portage.

7. Cronon, *Nature's Metropolis.*

8. Pierce, *History of Chicago*, 2:12. Interested readers should visit https://coloredconventions.org/black-illinois-organizing.

9. *Munn v. Illinois*, 94 U.S. 113 (1876).

10. Alfred Weber, *Theory of the Location of Industries*. The quotation is from Fales and Moses, "Thünen, Weber, and the Spatial Structure of the Nineteenth Century City," 130.

11. Cooley, "Theory of Transportation."

12. Von Thünen, *Der isolirte Staat in Beziehung auf Landwirtschaft*. Von Thünen's work led to two branches: central place theory and industrial location theory. Dean's work is on the latter branch. For more, see Cain, "Urban Growth."

13. Cooley, *Transportation*, 14.

14. Vidal de la Blanche, *Principles of Human Geography*, 473.

15. Dean, *Theory*, 134. Dean was the second African American to receive a Harvard PhD in economics. Although he graduated as one of Harvard's top students, he faced discrimination in his search for an academic position following commencement. He taught at Atlanta University until 1942, then served during the war as the chief economist for the Office of Price Administration in the Virgin Islands and Haiti. After the war he served as acting chief of the United Nations Africa Unit, Division of Economic Stability and Development. In early 1952, shortly after returning from a four-month mission to Italian Somaliland, he committed suicide.

16. Dean, *Theory*, 144.

17. Dean, *Theory*, 179.

18. Dean, *Theory*, 179.

19. This is consistent with the "mercantile model" of Vance, *Merchant's World*. The model assumes trade in staples between a frontier and a developed area. As population and the volume of trade increase, "points of attachment" become necessary. These are settlements on the frontier's edge with ready access to transportation routes. Some of these settlements will grow faster than others and become entrepôts in which it proves profitable for the merchant to invest in processing staple goods and in distribution centers for manufactured goods shipped from older centers, which once were similar entrepôts. The process then repeats itself.

20. The economic significance of gradients is most easily seen in regard to canals. Locks are utilized to rearrange an incline into a series of level steps, but the greater the gradient, the greater the number of locks needed. Gradient problems were also important to railroads, but railroads could be less concerned with the character of natural drainage.

21. Dean, *Theory*, 130.

22. "Relations of Father Dablon," quoted in Andreas, *History of Chicago*, 1:165. See also D. Miller, *City of the Century*, esp. chap. 1.

23. The present-day St. Louis River is more than 190 miles long and flows into the western end of Lake Superior. Before c. 1750, it was known as "Rivière du Fond du Lac."

24. The Friends of the Chicago Portage believe it's the Des Plaines River (http://drupal.library.cmu.edu/chicago/node/93), while Sells states that it's the Illinois River (*History of the Chicago Portage*, 1).

25. There are many other portages, such as that between the Fox and Wisconsin Rivers, that Marquette and Jolliet used on their way south. Nelson, *Muddy Ground*, refers to Chicago's portages but generally focuses on the Chicago Portage.

26. Keating, *Chicago Neighborhoods*, 254.

27. Sells, *History of the Chicago Portage*, explains where he believes Jolliet's "half a league" was on the Chicago Portage at 142.

28. Goode, *Geographic Background of Chicago*, 30.

29. Notable exceptions include places like Blue Island and Stony Island.

30. The water reached fifty feet above today's Lake Michigan in what is termed the Glenwood Stage. During the Calumet Stage it was thirty-five feet above the lake, and during the Tolleston Stage, twenty feet above the lake.

31. By comparison, the next lowest divide, near Fort Wayne, Indiana, is roughly 190 feet above lake level.

32. Bilek, "Old Chicago Portage."

33. Nelson, *Muddy Ground,* 61. De Liette was a relative of Henri de Tonti, La Salle's lieutenant.

34. Nelson, *Muddy Ground,* depicts the Portage des Perches as being to the north of what Swenson calls the Chicagoua Portage, and thus, according to Nelson, they were two different portages. This book follows Swenson, who identifies them as the same portage.

35. Currently the most complete discussion of Swenson's hypothesis can be found in the first three episodes of the Windy City Historians podcasts (http://windycityhistorians.com). Sells, *History of the Chicago Portage,* does not address Swenson's hypothesis.

36. Chicagoua was named for what today are called "ramps" (*Allium tricoccum*) or "wild leeks" and were known as "wild garlic" to early travelers. This plant still grows throughout the Chicagoua area, but not as much at the mouth of the Chicago River.

37. Morrissey discusses the end of the Cahokia chiefdom in the late twelfth century in *People of the Ecotone,* 44f.

38. The park is administered by the Olympia Fields Park District.

39. On old French maps, both Butterfield Creek and Hickory Creek are labeled as "Chicagoua River," which Swenson interprets as waterways on which one can reach Chicagoua. On the other hand, what is now called the Chicago River is labeled as "Chicagoumema" or "False Chicago," which Swenson interprets as not a route to Chicagoua.

40. If there was a journal of the Marquette-Jolliet expedition from the previous year, it was lost when Jolliet's canoe overturned shortly before he returned to Québec. Jolliet's "relations" of the expedition to Fr. Dablon leave unanswered the question of whether they came north via "downtown Chicago" or via "Chicagoua." If Marquette went south via "Chicagoua" the following year, it seems likely that that was the route he took north with Jolliet.

41. The journal covers the La Salle Expedition of 1684–1688.

42. Quaife, *Chicago and the Old Northwest,* 5.

43. Quaife, *Chicago and the Old Northwest,* 8.

44. Quaife, *Chicago and the Old Northwest,* 15.

45. The Potawatomi lived on the south and west shores of Lake Michigan and in what is now southern Michigan and northern Indiana as far east as Lake Erie. The Odawa lived on the north and east shores of Lake Michigan and were predominant in western Michigan. The Ojibwa lived in eastern Michigan and western Ontario. The largest Native community was that of the Illinois, the Grand Village of the Kaskaskia, near Starved Rock.

46. Nelson, *Muddy Ground,* 34.

47. A twenty-mile cession from Chicago to the Illinois River and safe passage for surveyors was negotiated in 1816. Keating, *Rising up from Indian Country,* 199; Nelson, *Muddy Ground,* 159.

Chapter 1. The Fur Trade and Chicago

1. White, *Middle Ground.*

2. Saunt, *Unworthy Republic,* xiii; Nelson, *Muddy Ground* (183), refers to "government-backed dispossession" and "environmental degradation."

3. Between the demise of the Cahokia and the coming of the French, Morrissey (*People of the Ecotone,* 43ff.) relates how the Oneonta moved into the area surrounding Chicago and adapted to the habitat.

4. John Cabot arrived in Newfoundland in 1497 searching for a northwest passage on behalf of England. By the first half of the sixteenth century, England, France, and Portugal were fishing the Grand Banks.

5. Dugua was a French merchant and colonizer who traveled to Canada for the first time in 1599. He made several trips, including one with Champlain in 1604. Henry IV granted Dugua exclusive right to colonize lands in North America between 40° and 60° North latitude in 1603. For his part, Dugua promised to send sixty colonists per year to his territory. New France started as a proprietary colony initially run by the Compagnie des Cent-Associés, which was granted monopoly privileges. A proprietary colony was a grant of land in the form of a charter, or a license to rule, to an individual or group, but the ultimate land holder remained the Crown. In order to maintain their privileges, proprietors were to recruit settlers and encourage the conversion of the Natives to Roman Catholicism. A 1648 battle in which the Iroquois defeated the Wendat led to difficulties that ultimately bankrupted the company. Other companies followed. Most failed. When the Company of Habitants went bankrupt in 1663, Louis XIV converted Quebec to a crown colony. A crown colony was land directly administered by the Crown through its government, usually via a governor appointed by the Crown. See MacBeath, "Dugua de Mons, Pierre."

6. Given that the ships that brought furs from the New World to the Old were the ships that carried the trade goods from the Old to the New, there was little room for migrants. Fortunately, the fur trade does not require the same manpower as do more agricultural pursuits, so French migration was small relative to English migration, and the demand for privately held land was significantly less.

7. They were also known as the Haudenosaunee, or People of the Longhouse. After 1722 they absorbed the Tuscarora to the southeast and were known as the Six Nations. Norton, *Fur Trade*, argues that the Iroquois's desire for independence caused them to trade with the English; missionaries were not part of the story.

8. Norton, *Fur Trade*, 222, argues that the British were fortunate that Dutch traders settled Albany. If English farmers had settled the New York frontier, they likely would have caused the Iroquois to ally with the French, but the Dutch traders had little desire to occupy Indian lands. Prior to the Dutch, people from the Plymouth colony actively engaged in the fur trade.

9. Following the Wendat (Huron) defeat in 1648 (see note 5), the French attempted to develop direct trade relations with the distant tribes.

10. The Wendat came to play an important role in the system as trade expanded outward from Quebec. They became middlemen, both collecting furs and delivering them to Quebec, then delivering French trade goods back to the Natives. Hunter, *God's Mercies*.

11. The shift from a competitive organization toward monopoly was a gradual one with fluctuations over time according to the demands of the trade. Easterbrook and Aitken, *Canadian Economic History*, 76. Champlain established a trading post in Montreal, and the settlement grew as the fur trade moved west.

12. Sleeper-Smith, *Indian Women and French Men*, 4, discusses the kinship structure of exchange. It is a main theme of her book.

13. Marr and Paterson, *Economic History*, 58.

14. Foster and Eccles, "Fur Trade."

15. Much of this is discussed in Morrissey, "Kaskaskia Social Network," and Sleeper-Smith, *Indian Women and French Men*.

16. Morrissey discusses why Illinois women might have been interested in marrying French men in *People of the Ecotone*, 118.

17. Morrissey, "Kaskaskia," 109–10.

18. Innis, *Fur Trade in Canada*, 42.

19. Innis, *Fur Trade in Canada*, 44. The Ottawa River (from the Algonquian "to trade") led from Montreal to Lake Nipissing, then into Georgian Bay. Innis erred in identifying the Sauk, Fox, and Illinois as beaver hunters. They primarily hunted bison, but they could have trapped beaver in the winter. The beavers from the "warmer" Illinois River valley were less desirable because they grew less hair than beavers living in more northerly climes. See Morrissey, *People of the Ecotone*, chaps. 2–5.

20. Marr and Paterson, *Economic History*, 58.

21. Innis, *Fur Trade in Canada*, 61.

22. In the mid-1600s a French crown was worth about 3.75 British shillings. There was nothing like a U.S. exchange rate until the end of the 1700s, when one British pound was worth about $4.50. Using those two figures, a French crown was worth $0.85 in 1790s U.S. dollars. Using the Consumer Price Index, that is equivalent to just under $20 today.

23. Foster and Eccles, "Fur Trade."

24. Easterbrook and Aitken, *Canadian Economic History*. The English required the Natives to come to the site of their factory; the French were in the Native's villages.

25. They tried to limit the number of traders by requiring them to have a license and to control prices by forcing the partnerships to sell furs at prices set by the colonial government.

26. It should be clear in what follows that using a state name to identify a place is to use a name that was not associated with the place at that time.

27. The initial fort was built by Louis de Buade and called Fort De Buade.

28. Hernando de Soto is credited with being the first European to discover the mouth of the Mississippi in 1541. Marquette and Jolliet traveled on it for a much greater distance.

29. Currently the most complete discussion of Swenson's hypothesis can be found in the first three episodes of the Windy City Historians podcast, http://windycityhistorians.com.

30. His brother Jean made the trip the previous year. Jean was a Sulpician priest, but René-Robert had yet to take his final vows when he left for New France.

31. The name *Lachine* is said to be attributable to the fact that, when La Salle returned without having found a passage to Asia, he and his men were mockingly referred to as *les Chinois*. The name was officially adopted in 1676 when the parish of Saints-Anges de Lachine was created; it was shortened to Lachine in 1829 when a post office was opened. See, e.g., https://montreal.ca/en/about/lachine.

32. Colbert to Jean Talon, April 5, 1666, in W. J. Eccles, *The Canadian Frontier* (Albuquerque: University of New Mexico Press, 1983),104, quoted in Skinner, *Upper Country*, 13.

33. Skinner, *Upper Country*, 25.

34. Innis (*Fur Trade*, 44) marks this as the beginning of navigation on the Great Lakes.

35. La Salle, Louis Hennepin, and a crew of thirty-two left to sail west in August. In September La Salle sent the ship back toward Niagara with a load of furs and a crew of six. The ship and crew vanished, and its whereabouts remain unknown.

36. The fort was destroyed four months later by members of the expedition when the Beaver Wars extended into the area and the Iroquois were on the attack. De Tonti built the more substantial Fort St. Louis du Pimiteoui nearby the following year.

37. This "fort" is often described as being in New Lenox, Illinois, which is on Hickory Creek. Yet New Lenox's "Old French Fort" in Higinbotham Woods is thought to be Fort Le Pouz, built in the fall of 1729 by the commandant of Fort St. Joseph in southwest Michigan. See Karen Meyer, "French Left Their Mark in Higinbotham Woods," *Chicago Tribune*, December 26, 1993.

38. See Morrissey, *People of the Ecotone*, especially chap. 5, which discusses the life and death of Grand Village. Sleeper-Smith (*Indian Women and French Men*, 16) describes the area's population as diverse.

39. Morrissey notes that the French often commented on the Illinois's prowess as runners. *People of the Ecotone*, 64–65.

40. See Morrissey, *People of the Ecotone*, 119, 124. Morrissey comments that bison hides were at the heart of La Salle's grants as well as his ambition (148).

41. Six years later, in 1691, Fort St. Louis itself was abandoned because of the risk the Iroquois posed to the French. There also was a short-lived French fort at the mouth of the Grand Calumet River near present-day Gary, Indiana. Neither this fort nor the one discussed in note 37 seem consistent with the one that would be referenced in the Treaty of 1795.

42. Holt, "Birth of Chicago," 83, mentions evidence of a French fort at the mouth of the Chicago River in the late seventeenth century. This evidence was from a French map reflecting a planned, but never constructed, fort. See Nelson, *Muddy Ground*, 63–64.

43. These wars, including mourning war, are given a fresh interpretation by Morrissey throughout *People of the Ecotone*. To the Illinois, the main antagonists of the Fox War, "the most important material circumstance" was the bison (174).

44. Quaife, *Chicago and the Old Northwest*, 39. Morrissey, *People of the Ecotone*, esp. chap. 7, provides a detailed discussion of the Fox War (1712–30), a war between the French and the Fox Indians, who were once trading partners of the French but then allied with the Iroquois against the French; Morrissey refers to their "alienation from the Great Lakes alliance" (16). This conflict disrupted commercial traffic over the Chicago portage.

45. See Lebeau, "Fur Trade."

46. After the war, the tribes that had been aligned with the French moved westward away from the triumphant English. Pontiac, an Odawa chief from Detroit, led a resistance movement to prevent the ceding of former French forts in the west to the English. Whereas the French had been content to limit their economic involvement with the Natives to trade, the English were anxious to obtain the Natives' land. In broader terms, Pontiac was part of a movement with little chance of success but which hoped to drive out all the Europeans in order to secure their land and maintain their way of life.

47. Widder, "Cartography of Dietrich Brehm."

48. Dankers and Meredith, *Early History*, 278.

49. See Lebeau, "Fur Trade."

50. Dankers and Meredith, *Early History*, 7, 128.

51. Dankers and Meredith, *Early History*, 177. Until Chicago was incorporated, the North Branch was known as the Guillory River.

52. The most recent biography of Point de Sable is Swenson, "Jean Baptiste Point De Sable." It should be noted that references to Point de Sable as simply "du Sable" appear after his death; Swenson argues persuasively that he should be referred to as "Point de Sable." Keating, *Rising Up*, is a superlative comprehensive account of this mostly forgotten period of Chicago history. Nelson, *Muddy Ground*, is a detailed history of the Indigenous people who lived in the vicinity of Chicago's portages with an emphasis on the 1700s.

53. Many have guessed that he came from Haiti given his French name. Juliette Kinzie, who arrived in Chicago long after Point de Sable left, wrote in her 1856 memoir that he was "a native of St. Domingo." Kinzie, *Wau-Bun.*

54. The town of Bourbonnais, Illinois, is named for him. In a 1726 census of Kaskaskia the couple is reported to own 150 arpents (about 127.5 acres) that were being cultivated, two Black slaves, five Indian slaves, twenty-one head of cattle, and three horses. See Morrissey, "Kaskaskia," 140. The Illinois Country and the rules of slavery there are discussed in Skinner, *Upper Country*, chap. 5.

55. Whether or not he was born there, Point de Sable's trading ventures took him there well before 1778, and there was no Roman Catholic priest in Chicago until much later.

56. The Quebec-based theory is discussed at https://drloihjournal.blogspot.com/2021/09/an-in-depth-history-of-jean-baptiste-pointe-de-sable-chicagos-founder.html.

57. They were financed and bonded by the aforementioned Jean Orillat, who had been trading in Illinois since the 1760s.

58. Some sources refer to "pro-American" sentiments but, since he was French, "anti-British" seems more accurate.

59. Keating, *Rising Up*, 28; Sells, *History of the Chicago Portage*, 70.

60. Whicker, *Historical Sketches*, 10–12. That his sympathies might have changed is explained in Kelley, "William Burnett." Both pieces share the biases of the time, especially Kelley's.

61. Sleeper-Smith, *Indian Women and French Men*, claimed that Point de Sable "was initially a Lake Peoria trader supplied by Burnett" (92). Burnett, too, was arrested by the British. According to Kelley, "William Burnett," he had been working independently when he was called to Mackinac and asked to work with other British traders. When he refused he was told he would not be allowed to return to St. Joseph, so he agreed to a one-year trial. When he refused to continue the arrangement, his former partners reported that he had had dealings with the U.S. Indian agent. He was then arrested and sent east to Montreal as a prisoner. Making good his escape, he returned to St. Joseph, where much of his property had been confiscated by his clerks. His arrest was the event that led to his marriage and the support of his in-laws. Frank E. Ross, "The Fur Trade of the Western Great Lakes Region," reported that Burnett was arrested in 1791, but he likely meant 1781.

62. Well after the fact, Juliette Kinzie wrote in *Wau-bun* that Burnett died in the battle following the U.S. Army's abandoning Fort Dearborn during the War of 1812. Though Burnett was known to have been in Chicago at about that time, the date and circumstances of his

death remain a mystery. Whicker (*Historical Sketches*, 14–17) reports that there is a legend that Burnett and his eldest son died in the Battle of Kickapoo. The key role played by Kakima Burnett is discussed in Sleeper-Smith, *Indian Women and French Men*, 90–92.

63. Morrissey, *People of the Ecotone*.

64. Sleeper-Smith (*Indian Women and French Men*, chap. 8) discusses how the Potawatomi women developed agriculture in southwestern Michigan. She notes that some fields were as large as three hundred acres (78). Nelson (*Muddy Ground*, 65) cites a contemporary as stating, "The Indians, and particularly their wives, are excellent canoe makers."

65. Vierling, "Where Was the du Sable Farm of 1790?" argues that the Point de Sable family moved onto the Guillory site near Wolf Point and lived there from 1788 to 1798. The soil inland was much more suitable to the type of farming in which the family was engaged than was the sandier soil nearer Lake Michigan.

66. Nelson, *Muddy Ground*, 133.

67. Matters initially continued much as they had in the western Great Lakes as, after the Revolution, Great Britain refused to cede control of Forts Detroit and Michilimackinac; see Sleeper-Smith, *Indian Women and French Men*, 74.

68. Sleeper-Smith, *Indian Women and French Men*, 16, reports that Ouilmette spoke for La Salle in the Illinois Country.

69. Her three sisters also married traders.

70. Grosse Pointe encompassed what would become Rogers Park, Evanston, and Wilmette. The French referred to that area as "Grosse Pointe" after the large point of land which is now marked by the Grosse Point Lighthouse in Evanston.

71. A transcript of the treaty can be found at https://www.docsteach.org/documents/document/treaty-greenville.

72. Similar to the situation described in note 42 above, a fictitious fort was included in a prospective French map. The known forts in the area were Fort Miami (1679) at the mouth of the St. Joseph River in Michigan, Fort Crèvecoeur (1681) at the confluence of the Kankakee and Des Plaines Rivers, and Fort Saint-Louis-des-Illinois (1683) at Starved Rock. It is thought that an unnamed fort (1683) was built near New Lenox, Illinois, as well as a French army post (not a fort) on the South Branch near Damen Avenue (1685) that lasted less than a year. One possible source is the 1788 map of Thomas Hutchins, which noted: "River Chikago, Indian village and fort at the entrance." See Karrow, "Mapping Chicago."

73. Nelson, *Muddy Ground*, 130.

74. La Lime replaced Point de Sable as the government's interpreter, ultimately working for Captain Whistler at the fort, Charles Jouett at the Agency House, and Matthew Irvin at the factory. The figure of $1,200 in 1800 is the equivalent of a little more than $30,000 today if the CPI is used as the comparator and a little more than $1 million if the production worker's wage is used. See MeasuringWorth.com.

75. See Quaife, "Property of Jean Baptiste Point Sable."

76. Point de Sable obtained a license to operate a ferry across the Missouri River.

77. In 1800 the American governor of the Northwest Territory visited Chicago. It is not clear whether Point de Sable was still in residence, but, given that his (former?) home was

the largest in Chicago, one with guest accommodations, it is reasonable to surmise that the governor stayed there. Had Point de Sable still been living there, it seems inevitable that the two men would have talked. The governor might have confirmed that a fort was planned.

78. Quaife, *Chicago and the Old Northwest*, 129.

79. Swenson, "Jean Baptiste Point De Sable," 393–94.

80. In 1841 the U.S. Congress passed the Preemption Act, which allowed "squatters" who were living in a structure built on federal land to purchase up to 160 acres at a price not less than $1.25 per acre before the land was to be offered for sale to the public. In earlier years, preemption rights had been granted in response to local demands. In Chicago, between May 28 and June 30, 1835, the government sold land to bona fide settlers who had filed claims earlier. Dankers and Meredith, *Early History*, 296.

81. It was named after Henry Dearborn, Jefferson's secretary of war.

82. Quoted in Kirkland (1892), *Story of Chicago*, 51.

83. Quoted in Nelson, *Muddy Ground*, 136.

84. See Norton, *Fur Trade in Colonial New York*, 207ff.

85. There is no known image of John Kinzie. Most of those purporting to be of him are of his son, John H. Kinzie.

86. Keating, *Rising Up*, 18.

87. In 1785 John Kinzie and his partner John Clark helped rescue two sisters from Virginia who had been kidnapped by the Shawnee ten years earlier and adopted into the tribe. One of the women, Margaret McKinzie, married Kinzie, while her sister married Clark. Margaret and John had three children. She eventually took the children and returned to Virginia; he remarried in 1800. As adults, all three children moved to Chicago.

88. In addition to Chicago, Kinzie and Forsyth operated trading posts in Milwaukee, the Rock River area, the Illinois and Kankakee River areas, and Sangamon County.

89. Initially engagés rowed the traders' canoes.

90. The female helped with household chores while her husband and two other males helped with the trading business and agricultural pursuits. Keating, *Rising Up*, 69. In addition, Kinzie and his half-brother are known to have sold "by Indenture" a "negro wench" and to have purchased the "indenture" of one Jeffrey Nash, who worked with Forsyth at the Peoria trading post. See Pierce, *History of Chicago*, 1:19.

91. In 1805 Burnett felt betrayed by Kinzie and Forsyth, and their relationship suffered.

92. Keating, *Rising Up*, 74.

93. Colleen Connolly, "Flashback: Did 'Bad Blood' on the American Frontier Lead to Chicago's First Murder?" *Chicago Tribune*, June 18, 2017.

94. Vierling, "Fur Trade in Illinois," 2. Other theories are that La Lime was informing the fort about corrupt economic activities or was about to expose Kinzie's real estate dealings.

95. There also was a long-standing feud between Kinzie and John Whistler Jr., son of the man who built and initially commanded Fort Dearborn. When their partnership dissolved, Kinzie lost the privilege of supplying provisions to the fort, while the Whistlers were responsible for enforcing regulations with respect to traders such as Kinzie who supplied liquor to the Indians.

96. Keating, *Rising Up*, 117. Nelson, *Muddy Ground*, views this as symbolic: "Kinzie's attack on La Lime demonstrated that the struggle at Chicago broke down not along lines of racial distinction but rather between those who actively promoted a state-designed approach to controlling the local landscape [La Lime] and those who remained determined to maintain an older model of interpersonal and geographic fluidity at the portage [Kinzie]" (147).

97. Neil Gale discusses the incident in the Digital Research Library of Illinois History Journal, https://drloihjournal.blogspot.com/2017/04/john-kinzie-chicago-founding-father.html. A slightly different take on this point can be found at Hub Pages, August 14, 2024, https://discover.hubpages.com/education/john-kinzie-father-of-chicago-chicago-a-history.

98. As noted, one line of thinking is that Burnett died in the battle on the shores of Lake Michigan when the U.S. Army abandoned Fort Dearborn.

99. Billy Caldwell (also known as Sauganash, "one who spoke English") was the son of a Mohawk mother and a British officer. Educated in Detroit, he was fluent in French and English. In 1803 he became one of Kinzie's clerks in Detroit. He also served as Tecumseh's interpreter until Tecumseh's death in 1813. He moved to Chicago in 1820. He learned Algonquian and was considered a chief by the Potawatomis. Mark Beaubien's Sauganash Hotel bore his name.

100. Chandonnai was a métis, a nephew of Potawatomi leader Topinbee, and therefore related to Burnett's wife. He was Kinzie's chief clerk in Chicago by 1812. After the battle, he took the commander of Fort Dearborn, Captain Nathan Heald (whose release was negotiated by Kinzie), and his wife Rebecca (whom Chandonnai ransomed) to St. Joseph, where Topinbee lived. He rejoined Kinzie in Detroit where, while, working for the British, they were urging the Potawatomi to negotiate with the United States.

101. This is the subject of chap. 16 of Keating, *Rising Up*, "Kinzie's Retreat to Chicago, 1816–1828."

102. Their grandfather Naunongee was a warrior who lived near Lake Calumet and opposed American expansion into Indian Country. He died in hand-to-hand combat during the battle.

103. Robinson is discussed in greater detail in chapter 2. It suffices here to note that he ultimately married one of Archange and Sheshi's sisters.

104. Both citations are from Grover, *Antoine Ouilmette*, 25.

105. Schultz and Hast, *Women Building Chicago*, 653–54.

106. Much of this section is based on Haeger, "American Fur Company"; Quaife, *Chicago and the Old Northwest*; and Dankers, "French Chicago."

107. The principal motivation for forming the South West Fur Company was to sidestep U.S. regulations. See Ross, *Fur Trade of the Western Great Lakes Region*, 301. Only after the fact did they learn the Nonintercourse Acts applied to them, but they were able to function, remarkably so during the War of 1812.

108. Varnum was the son of Joseph Bradley Varnum, a U.S. representative and later a senator, from Massachusetts, who served as factor from 1816 to 1822, at which point he left government service. Dankers and Meredith, *Early History*, 345.

109. Liquor was expensive and heavy, and it reduced the Indians' desire to hunt. See Haeger, "American Fur Company," 125.

110. Quaife, *Chicago and the Old Northwest*, 304–9, discusses the factor system and Benton's role in it. Benton was elected as one of Missouri's first two senators. He had been an aide to General Andrew Jackson in the War of 1812 and was elected to Congress at the time Jackson became president.

111. D. Miller, *City of the Century*, 51. During his indenture he received $120 annually and often complained of what he saw as inadequate wages. He even considered joining the Chouteau firm in St. Louis.

112. Haeger, "American Fur Company," 127–29.

113. A year later Antoine Deschamps resigned, and Gurdon Hubbard was appointed to replace him as agent in the Illinois River valley.

114. Wolcott married Kinzie's daughter Ellen, and Kinzie's son John H. married Wolcott's niece Juliette.

115. Kinzie moved out of his home in 1827, a year before his death. The house passed to Anson Taylor, who is thought to have used it as a store, and later to Jonathan Bailey, who was Chicago's first postmaster. Dankers and Meredith, *Early History*, 219.

116. Antoine Ouilmette was also involved with the negotiations for this treaty, which made provisions for Chiefs Alexander Robinson and Billy Caldwell, Ouilmette's children, and others as well as paying Ouilmette $800 in compensation. The Treaty of 1833 is discussed in Quaife, *Chicago and the Old Northwest*, 348–66.

117. A dollar in 1833 is equal to $37.48 today if the CPI is used and $621.58 if the production worker wage is used. See MeasuringWorth.com.

118. See Haeger, "American Fur Company," 135–37.

119. Quoted in Quaife, *Chicago and the Old Northwest*, 281.

120. Pierce, *History of Chicago*, 1:31.

121. East, "Inhabitants of Chicago," 131.

122. Nelson, *Muddy Ground*, 167.

123. Pierce, *History of Chicago*, 1:44.

Chapter 2. Pioneers and Boosters

1. Quoted in A. Wright, "In Memoriam," 6.

2. His parents were reputed to have had ten children, and his father had fifteen additional children from a previous marriage.

3. Robinson, born in Mackinac in 1789, was the son of a Scots-Irish trader and an Odawa mother. While at Bailly's post in St. Joseph, Michigan, he met John Kinzie and maintained a long relationship with him. Although he spoke many languages, unlike Beaubien, he never learned to read or write.

4. See Keating, *Rising Up*, 68–69. Shabbona fought with Tecumseh against the Americans in the War of 1812. Shabbona was an Odawa married to a Potawatomi from a village just southwest of Chicago.

5. Most accounts have the Beaubiens joining her family in Milwaukee. Keating, however, reports that Josette was in the Kinzie family boat on the day of the Battle of Fort Dearborn. Keating, *Rising Up*, 142.

6. Mark Beaubien plays a prominent role in D. Miller, *City of the Century*, chap. 2, "Didn't Expect No Town."

7. Also in 1830, a plat of Chicago was completed by surveyors for the I&M Canal.

8. Alexander Wolcott, Indian agent at the fort, arranged for Robinson and Billy Caldwell to be elected Potawatomi chiefs by 1829. Robinson succeeded his father-in-law. Caldwell ultimately moved out of Chicago with his band, while Robinson, who also moved, elected to return and live on his land. Dankers and Meredith, *Early Chicago*, 93, 301, 364.

9. Like the Treaty of Greenville, the Treaty of 1833 is on the National Archives website: https://catalog.archives.gov/id/155390860.

10. Dankers and Meredith, *Early Chicago*, 296.

11. Roden, "Beaubien Claim."

12. D. Miller, *City of the Century*, 100–101. The commissioners were William Archer, Gurdon Hubbard, and William Thornton.

13. Josette died in 1845; Louise would survive him. Dankers and Meredith, *Early Chicago*, 68.

14. The route became Illinois Route 1. See Hubbard, *Autobiography of Gurdon Saltonstall Hubbard, Pa-pa-ma-ta-be, "The Swift Walker."* The phrase in quotation marks is a reference to his Indian name, which he earned by walking seventy-five miles in a single night to warn Danville of a potential Indian raid. He began work on the autobiography in the late 1860s and produced an eight-hundred-page manuscript that was destroyed in the Great Fire. Before his death, he was only able to reproduce what he had written about his life up to 1829.

15. Five years later he married Mary Ann Hubbard, who was not a direct relation.

16. As will be discussed in chapter 8, Hubbard used his financial connections in Buffalo to help provide early financial services in Chicago. The most infamous of Hubbard's steamships was the *Lady Elgin*, which sank in 1860 near Winnetka, Illinois, and was discovered in 1989. Hubbard accepted insurance money for the loss, but he never abandoned ownership of the ship.

17. As will be discussed in chapter 6, the hotel would host what would become Mercy Hospital. John H. Kinzie was the second president of the Town of Chicago, serving from 1834 to 1837.

18. Pierce, *History of Chicago*, 1:58. The boom is discussed in chapter 8.

19. The Wigwam was built on the site of Mark Beaubien's Sauganash Hotel in the hope of attracting the 1860 Republican Convention. The attempt was successful, and it was there that Lincoln was nominated for the presidency. Much of this is discussed in H. Hamilton, "Biographical Sketch of Gurdon Saltonstall Hubbard." Hamilton does not claim he saw combat; that assertion is from the website of Chicago's Hubbard High School: https://www.hubbardhighschool.org/apps/pages/index.jsp?uREC_ID=1252393&type=d&pREC_ID=1477034.

20. Andreas, *History of Chicago*, 1:111.

21. Wendt, *Swift Walker*, 378.

22. Chester Dewey was a professor of mathematics and natural philosophy who was a widely respected naturalist and botanist. Another of young Wright's teachers was Mark Hopkins, who became president of Williams College a decade later.

23. Lewis, *John S. Wright,* 15.

24. Carpenter, who also arrived in 1832, was Chicago's first pharmacist and a staunch abolitionist.

25. Quoted in A. Wright, "In Memoriam," 11.

26. MeasuringWorth.com calculates that $300,000 in 1836 is $10.15 million today if the CPI is used and $204.4 million if the production worker wage rate is used.

27. A. Wright, "In Memoriam," 13.

28. This was a prestigious organization. John Dean Caton, soon to be chief justice of the Illinois Supreme Court, was elected president, and William B. Ogden was elected treasurer. It's not clear how well versed in agriculture either of those two worthies were.

29. The basis for the veto was this: Because the expenditures did not relate directly to national defense or foreign commerce, it was the states' responsibility to finance such internal improvements.

30. A. Wright, "In Memoriam," 17.

31. A. Wright, "In Memoriam," 16.

32. The earliest was the one by the Cairo (Illinois) Company. The official name for the 1850 Act is "An Act Granting Right of Way, and making a Grant of Land to the States of Illinois, Mississippi, and Alabama, in Aid of the Construction of a Railroad from Chicago to Mobile" (9 Stat. 466), signed by President Fillmore on September 20, 1850.

33. Lewis, *John S. Wright,* 114.

34. Lewis, *John S. Wright,* 140. The occasion was Caton reminiscing about antebellum Chicago.

35. The usual conclusion regarding the competition between Hussey and McCormick is that the former's reaper worked better as a mower of eastern grass while the latter worked better on the western prairies.

36. See Moore, "Largely Forgotten Role of Jearum Atkins."

37. J. Wright, *Chicago: Past, Present, and Future.* For the description of it see A. Wright, "In Memoriam," 25; Lewis, *John S. Wright,* 204.

38. Andreas, *History of Chicago,* 1:136.

39. During his hearing to be confirmed as Eisenhower's secretary of defense, Wilson, a former head of General Motors, was asked if he could make a decision adverse to the interests of GM. He replied in the affirmative but added that such a situation was unlikely because "for years I thought what was good for our country was good for General Motors, and vice versa." See https://history.defense.gov/Multimedia/Biographies/Article-View/Article/571268/charles-e-wilson/.

40. Jack Harpster wrote two books about his relatives: *John Ogden, the Pilgrim* (2006) and *Railroad Tycoon* (2009). Other books about the family are in the works. Much of the following is based on Wheeler, *Ogden Family in America.* This book is available online through Heritage Quest Online. One of the motivations for Harpster's first book is that the family hired an unreliable English genealogical researcher to assist Wheeler; Harpster attempts to correct the errors.

41. Dickerson had lived in Morris County, New Jersey, and would later become both governor of New Jersey and a senator from that state.

42. Ogden's mother was the daughter of a military officer from New Canaan, Connecticut, who, at the end of the Revolution, was out of cash and out of business. He and other officers built a new town on the Delaware near Walton.

43. Andreas (*History of Chicago*, 1:444) notes that Ogden was admitted to the Illinois Bar on February 6, 1841. It is not clear exactly how he qualified, but one could "read for the law" in Illinois at that time.

44. According to his friend Isaac Arnold, Ogden told many stories of his experiences running these rafts down the swollen Delaware River. Arnold, "William B. Ogden." This is the text of an address that Arnold, president of the Chicago Historical Society, gave on December 20, 1881, when Ogden's widow donated a portrait of Ogden to the society.

45. Washington was a friend of Abraham's and used his Morristown home as a headquarters for several weeks. Three of Abraham's sons became distinguished lawyers and land speculators like their father.

46. This must have had a great deal to do with the influence of his brother-in-law Charles Butler, a member of the Albany Regency led by Martin Van Buren. Butler was married to William's older sister Eliza and was well connected. He studied law with Van Buren and began his legal practice in Geneva, New York. Indeed, it is thought that Van Buren was responsible for William Ogden's making the speech on behalf of the New York & Erie Railroad. Jack Harpster, pers. comm., June 27, 2008.

47. Quoted in Downard, "William Butler Ogden," 50.

48. See R. Miller, "Transportation Innovation."

49. The company would administer and sell real estate in western Michigan, northern Indiana, and Wisconsin, as well as Illinois. There is some thought that Sarah North's death was a factor in the family's asking and Ogden's accepting this task though more than five years had passed since her death.

50. Charles Butler, "William B. Ogden and Early Chicago," December 17, 1881, a copy of which is in the Chicago History Museum. Quoted in Downard, "William Butler Ogden," 51.

51. The American Land Company had to have been Ogden's major client, but Pierce suggests he had perhaps another one hundred nonresident clients. Pierce, *History of Chicago*, 1:151.

52. Ogden to John J. Baily, June 7, 1836, in *Ogden Letter Books*, 1:1, quoted in Pierce, *History of Chicago*,1:62, n100.

53. His first responsibility was to negotiate a loan, the proceeds of which were used to purchase two additional fire engines. Andreas, *History of Chicago*, 1:142.

54. It was Ogden who convinced Van Osdel to move to Chicago; he is now considered the first member of the Chicago School of architecture and built many of the public buildings that perished in the fire.

55. McLear, "William Butler Ogden," 283. The Chicago land market during this first boom, and bust, is discussed in detail in Hoyt, *One Hundred Years of Land Values*, 23–44.

56. For more on the election see Pierce, *History of Chicago*, vol. 1, chap. 11, esp. 375–77.

57. Binford, "Multicentered Chicago."

58. See Keating, *World of Juliette Kinzie.* Given the panic, Ogden's mayoral achievements were limited. A permanent Board of Health was appointed (with Ogden serving as president ex officio), a Board of School Inspectors was elected, and the first census was authorized.

59. He also wrote the city's first charter. Holli, "Mayors." After his term as mayor, he was elected alderman of the Sixth Ward in 1840 and alderman of the Ninth Ward in 1847.

60. This episode is presented in *Biographical Sketches of the Leading Men of Chicago,* 15–16.

61. Ogden to Butler, June 17, 1839, *Ogden Letter Books,* 2:106, quoted in Pierce, *History of Chicago,* 1:69.

62. Kirkland, *Story of Chicago,* 119.

63. Newberry and Ogden also gave land to several other churches. The first iron bridge was erected in 1856 at Rush Street; one at Madison Street was erected the following year. See Pierce, *History of Chicago,* 1:341–42.

64. See Scammon, "William B. Ogden," 46.

65. Ogden to D. Hugunin, March 22, 1841, *Ogden Letter Books,* 3:204, quoted in Pierce, *History of Chicago,* 1:72, n154.

66. Ogden to D. Gold, February 2, 1842, *Ogden Letter Books,* 3:436, quoted in Pierce, *History of Chicago,* 1:72, n154.

67. See Williams, "Chicago River and Harbor Convention." Ogden was one of a committee of nine appointed the previous year in New York to arrange the affair.

68. The federal government had announced it was going to distribute the surplus it had accumulated to the states. Most states planned to use the funds for internal improvements. Illinois planned on far more projects than its share of the surplus could finance. This is discussed in chapter 8.

69. The *Pioneer* now resides in the second-floor galleries of the Chicago History Museum.

70. It should be noted that Gurdon Hubbard, George Dole, John H. Kinzie, and others obtained a charter for the Chicago and Vincennes Railroad in 1835 to tap the area in which Hubbard once lived. The company did not materialize. See Pierce, *History of Chicago,* 1:114.

71. His brother Mahlon and brother-in-law Charles Butler were named directors. See Grant, *North Western.*

72. Tilden served as governor of New York beginning in 1874 and was the Democratic candidate for president of the United States running against the Republican Rutherford B. Hayes in the disputed election of 1876.

73. Pierce, *History of Chicago,* 2:51–54. The merger was not without opposition. For example, John Wentworth, also a former mayor of Chicago and a stockholder of the Galena, believed the line was stronger on its own than as part of the Chicago and North Western. Elliot Anthony, the Galena's attorney, filed a suit on behalf of Julius Wadsworth, a stockholder who held that the merger was illegal. He charged that the consolidation meetings were not called or held in a proper manner and that the stockholders' interests had not been properly protected. His arguments were upheld in court in 1865.

74. Through the 1860s, the Cedar Rapids and Missouri River Railroad, a part of the Chicago and North Western network, pushed westward across Iowa. The destination was Council Bluffs, across the river from Omaha, the eastern terminus of the Union Pacific. The

North Western became the eastern segment of the trip from Chicago to San Francisco, but it soon had competition from the Rock Island Line and the Burlington Route. See Grant, *North Western*, 30.

75. Grossman, Keating, and Reiff, *Encyclopedia of Chicago*, 348.

76. More than a century later, in 1988, the building was renovated into a commercial and retail complex. It is located near McClurg Court and Illinois Street.

77. Andreas, *History of Chicago*, 1:121.

78. Cited in McLear, "William Butler Ogden," 288. Shortly thereafter, Lill entered a partnership with Michael Diversey, and Ogden ended his involvement. By 1857 the Lill and Diversey brewery had grown to be the largest establishment of its kind in the Old Northwest.

79. Ezra Butler McCagg, a law partner of J. Young Scammon, married Ogden's widowed sister in 1854. It is not clear whether the firm produced rail ties.

80. Arnold, "William B. Ogden," 21.

81. Cain, "A Canal and Its City."

82. It was Ogden who suggested that McCormick exhibit his reaper at the London Exhibition of 1851; McCormick won a Council Medal, the exhibition's highest award.

83. Andreas, *History of Chicago*, 2:678.

84. There were several hundred people living in the village of Peshtigo at the mouth of the river on Green Bay. Scammon ("William B. Ogden," 55) estimated that the company produced forty million feet of lumber annually for the Chicago market.

85. Quoted in Andreas, *History of Chicago*, 1:464.

86. This was across the street from Douglas's home, Oakenwald.

87. Ogden was a trustee of the Dearborn Seminary, which was organized in 1854, and financially supported the Theological Seminary of the Northwest.

88. Pierce, *History of Chicago*, 2:397; Andreas, *History of Chicago*, 3:815–17; and Grossman, Keating, and Reiff, *Encyclopedia of Chicago*, 845. The second (and current) University of Chicago opened in 1892 in Hyde Park on land donated by Marshall Field with initial funding from John D. Rockefeller.

89. See chapter 4.

90. There are few histories of the Board of Trade. An early three-volume history is C. Taylor, *History of the Board of Trade*. A more academic approach can be found in Lurie, *Chicago Board of Trade*. A popular approach emphasizing the personalities involved is Ferris, *Grain Traders*. Also see Cronon, *Nature's Metropolis*, and D. Miller, *City of the Century*.

91. See Andreas, *History of Chicago*, 2:626–27.

92. Pierce, *History of Chicago*, 2:400.

93. In the same year, Ogden was appointed to the executive committee of a group of Chicagoans who planned to provide relief for needy Irishmen at the height of the famine; a similar group was established for needy Scots. Harpster, *Railroad Tycoon*, 103.

94. Andreas, *History of Chicago*, 1:384.

95. Andreas, *History of Chicago*, 1:390.

96. The latest, and one of the best, books about the fire is Smith, *Chicago's Great Fire*.

97. Arnold, "William B. Ogden," 34. Alternatively, that translates to at least $610.9 million today if the production worker wage is used, according to MeasuringWorth.com.

98. Christ Church in Walton has stained glass windows donated by Ogden's estate in the memory of the Ogden and North families. Arnold ("William B. Ogden," 28) claims that Ogden's will made provision for Sarah North's nearest surviving relatives.

Chapter 3. Assembling Trade Routes and Establishing Position

1. When Indiana became a state two years earlier, its northern border was moved twenty miles to the north. See Cain, "Carving the Northwest Territory into States."

2. Meese, "Nathaniel Pope," 11–12.

3. Pierce, *History of Chicago*, 1:37; see, e.g., http://www.connectingthewindycity.com/2017/02/february-8-1861-description-of-first.html.

4. Fort Dearborn was closed shortly before the Black Hawk War, but it reopened during the war. In 1837, when Chicago was incorporated as a city, the federal government deeded it to the city, and the superintendent of harbor works used it.

5. Larson, *Those Army Engineers*, is a factual account of the work of the Army Corps of Engineers in this district.

6. Andreas, *History of Chicago*, 1:166–67; Putnam, *Illinois and Michigan Canal*, 4–6.

7. This section is largely based on the first chapter of Cain, *Sanitation Strategy for a Lakefront Metropolis*. In *Muddy Ground*, John William Nelson argues the construction of internal improvements and the removal of Indigenous people should be considered two parts of the same process: "a fundamental alteration of the interior geography, backed by state investment and authority, that served to undercut Indigenous power on the continent and eventually transformed spaces like Chicago's portage from a site of Native hegemony to a place of American authority and settler prosperity" (156). To Nelson, obtaining land for critical internal improvements as opposed to the demand for land by settlers is what drove U.S. policy toward Native populations.

8. An early example is Cooley, "Theory of Transportation," 223–371.

9. Andreas, *History of Chicago*, 1:166.

10. Andreas, *History of Chicago*, 1:167.

11. Putnam, *Illinois and Michigan Canal*, 21. Readers interested in a more detailed account of the canal's economic history should consult Putnam's book.

12. "Report of the Illinois and Michigan Canal Commissioners," 1844, reported in Andreas, *History of Chicago*, 1:168.

13. Pierce, *History of Chicago*, 1:31. See also Andreas, *History of Chicago*, 1:168.

14. Putnam, *Illinois and Michigan Canal*, 31ff.

15. Pierce, *History of Chicago*, 1:80.

16. Putnam, *Illinois and Michigan Canal*, 35.

17. See Wyman, *Immigrants in the Valley*, and McMahon, "Canal Diggers, Church Builders," 43–81.

18. Pierce, *History of Chicago*, 1:61.

19. Pierce, *History of Chicago*, 1:74, notes that Gurdon Hubbard in 1842–43 even wrote to the American Fur Company about re-employment when his own business was at its nadir.

20. In April 1839 the canal commissioners decided to issue a large amount of ninety-day scrip based on the canal fund with which they would pay contractors. The May 1839 issue was $266,237; the August issue, $128,317. Andreas, *History of Chicago*, 1:168.

21. Hoyt, *One Hundred Years of Land Values*, 45.

22. Putnam, *Illinois and Michigan Canal*, 58.

23. Putnam, *Illinois and Michigan Canal*, 58.

24. Andreas, *History of Chicago*, 1:170.

25. Putnam, *Illinois and Michigan Canal*, 58. The three feeders were (1) from the Fox River at Dayton to Ottawa; (2) from the Kankakee River to the Dresden level, and (3) from the Calumet River through the "Sag" to the Summit level.

26. Belcher, *Economic Rivalry*, 35 (emphasis in original).

27. The canal experienced significant passenger traffic in the years before the opening of the railroad.

28. Monkkonen, *America Becomes Urban*, 45.

29. Young, *Iron Horse*, 3. With respect to the railroads operating before the fire, Young focuses on the Galena and Chicago Union Railroad, the Rock Island Line, and the Illinois Central.

30. Young puts considerable emphasis on the back haul. Chicago, he notes, was in a better position on the Great Lakes to develop relatively equal traffic in all directions, and he analyzes the components of that traffic.

31. Belcher, *Economic Rivalry*, 40.

32. Galena and its environs were the only known American source for lead, which was in demand in the east for paint and glass, and transport costs were a significant proportion of the price in eastern markets. See Mahoney, *River Towns*, 182–87.

33. The history of the Galena and Chicago Union Railroad is told by Scammon, "William B. Ogden," 63–72, and by Andreas, *History of Chicago*, 1:247–63.

34. See McLear, "Galena and Chicago Union," 17.

35. McLear, "Galena and Chicago Union," 24.

36. Ogden reportedly raised $20,000 in one day from farmers selling their fall crop in Chicago. See Cronon, *Nature's Metropolis*, 65–66. As they went, Ogden and Scammon also touted the virtues of McCormick reapers and John Deere plows.

37. Scammon, a lawyer, was the financial manager behind many of Ogden's enterprises (see chapter 5). Smith is discussed in some detail in chapter 8. In 1853 the Galena and Chicago Union reached Freeport, Illinois, between Rockford and Galena; the remainder of the route was completed in 1854 by the Illinois Central Railroad.

38. The impact of the railroad on the competition between St. Louis and Chicago is discussed in Mahoney, *River Towns*, 159f.

39. Andreas, *History of Chicago*, 1:251.

40. The classic reference is Gates, *Illinois Central Railroad*. The Illinois Central also had a great deal to do with the decision to locate the University of Illinois in Champaign-Urbana.

41. The decision to end the other branch at Dunleith altered the western terminus of the Galena and Chicago Union Railroad. As many in Galena feared, the promises of Ogden and Scammon were ignored by their successors.

42. Belcher, *Economic Rivalry*, 63.

43. Belcher, *Economic Rivalry*, 54.

44. See Stover, *American Railroads*, 87.

45. See Gordon, "Illinois Railroad Legislation," especially the introduction by H. B. Hammond.

46. Corliss, *Main Line of Mid-America*, 46.

47. Brownson, *History of the Illinois Central*, 51–54, quoted in Pierce, *History of Chicago*, 2:48.

48. See Kirkland, *Story of Chicago*, 220–21. The railroad spent $2 million on the project.

49. Roswell Mason, president of the railroad and chief negotiator of the arrangement, later became the city's mayor.

50. Parenthetically, it was not until 1857 that the eastern network was completed when a railroad was built connecting Toledo and Buffalo. Before then, that stretch of the trip normally involved a Lake Erie steamboat.

51. Pierce, *History of Chicago*, 2:58.

52. There were also street railroads. The contract for the first one was awarded in 1857, but the project fell victim to the financial panic of that year. Another contract was awarded the following year, and construction began in November 1858.

53. Pred, *Urban Growth and City-Systems*, makes a general case for the "important" role played by the telegraph. The minimum value MeasuringWorth.com reports for the value today of $2 in 1848 is just under $80.

54. Belcher, *Economic Rivalry*, 69.

55. Ackerman, *Early Illinois Railroads*, 54. Ackerman served successively as secretary, treasurer, vice president, and president of the Illinois Central.

56. Mahoney, *River Towns*, 219.

Chapter 4. How Chicago Grew

1. The figures for the canal area are from Putnam, *Illinois and Michigan Canal*, 96–97, 106–7; those for Chicago are from Hoyt, *One Hundred Years of Land Values*, table 93, p. 483.

2. Putnam, *Illinois and Michigan Canal*, 106.

3. The technique of examining four years in this manner is questionable: Variations between years and between commodities make it doubtful that one year could be used to represent a period of several years. The primary concern of the analysis, however, is related to the change in magnitudes. The figures given for these four years are not out of line with the figures for surrounding years. Also, each year came during an expansion of the business cycle.

4. There are some differences between data sources. These differences may result from miscopied numbers in the Chicago Board of Trade reports. Receipts and shipments are given for the lake, the canal, and each railroad separately. The sum of these does not always correspond to the reported total printed elsewhere in the report. The growth rates were calculated from the summary.

5. A. C. Cole, *Era of the Civil War*, 367.

6. Andreas, *History of Chicago*, 3:342.

7. See, e.g., A. H. Cole, *American Wool Manufacture*, 1:291, 2:141.

8. Cronon, *Nature's Metropolis*, chap. 3, "Pricing the Future: Grain," is the best single discussion of the growth of Chicago's grain market.

9. United States Census Office, Eighth Census, 1860, *Agriculture of the United States in 1860*, cxxxv (Washington, DC, 1864), quoted in Lee, "Chicago Grain Elevator System," 16.

10. Cronon, *Nature's Metropolis*, 109.

11. See W. Brown, *American Colossus*, 56–60.

12. Cronon, *Nature's Metropolis*, 111.

13. Whereas the unit used for grain remained a bushel, the number of bushels in a sack was a measure of volume that became a measure of weight with the grain elevator.

14. Currey, *Chicago*, 3:231.

15. The Welland Canal connected Lakes Erie and Ontario, paralleling the Niagara River.

16. Andreas, *History of Chicago*, 1:585.

17. Lee, "Chicago Grain Elevator System," 19.

18. It was not until 1878 that the annual report of the Board of Trade listed quotations for transactions in futures. That activity grew as the number of goods benefiting from futures transactions grew.

19. Lee, "Chicago Grain Elevator System," 20.

20. Along with the development of futures markets came the attempt of some traders to corner the market. Cronon has an excellent description of this practice as well as "the year of the corner" in 1868. See Cronon, *Nature's Metropolis*, 127–32. With the demise in the 1970s of the Bretton Woods system for managing a fixed exchange rate system, the development of a futures market in foreign exchange introduced similar predictability to international trade. In short, the Chicago Board of Trade has grown from a group primarily concerned with matters of local trade at its inception to a body that plays a crucial role in the global economy today.

21. Founded in 1867 and still active, the National Grange of the Order of Patrons of Husbandry encourages farm families collectively to foster their community's economic and political well-being as well as to advocate for agricultural interests.

22. Pierce, *History of Chicago*, 2:81. Munn and Scott received grain from the Chicago and North Western, the Chicago & Alton, and the I&M Canal.

23. Both Munn and Scott were expelled from the Board of Trade owing to "irregularities" in their elevators. See Pierce, *History of Chicago*, 3:77.

24. See *Munn v. Illinois*, 94 U.S. 125 (1877).

25. Hughes, *Governmental Habit Redux*.

26. Cronon, *Nature's Metropolis*, 145–46, emphasis in original.

27. See Aduddell and Cain, "Location and Collusion," and Aduddell and Cain, "Public Policy."

28. See Walsh, *Midwestern Meat Packing Industry*. Chicago also became the nation's primary lumber market in 1856.

29. Hill, "Development of Chicago."

30. Walsh, *Midwestern Meat Packing Industry*, 53.

31. Pierce, *History of Chicago*, 2:92. As in many other cities, cattle, pigs, and sheep regularly roamed the streets feeding on household scraps. Meatpackers drew their supply from these animals as well as those driven into the city.

32. Before the coming of the railroad, a packing center's tributary area had a radius of no more than 150 miles.

33. Hill, "Development of Chicago," 262–63.

34. Walsh, *Midwestern Meat Packing Industry*, 73.

35. Among those closely identified with the livestock trade of the 1860s are Samuel Allerton and Nelson Morris. At first, buyers and sellers dealt with each other directly, but, by 1865, there were eight commission houses in Chicago.

36. John Wentworth is discussed in the chapter that follows.

37. See Aduddell and Cain, "Location and Collusion."

38. Cronon, *Nature's Metropolis*, 211.

39. He is the McCoy of "It's the real McCoy." See https://buckarooleather.com/blogs/buckaroo-johns-blog/joseph-g-mccoy-the-real-mccoy.

40. Aduddell and Cain, "Location and Collusion," 92.

41. Clemen, *American Livestock and Meat Industry*, 218–29.

42. Given his need for large quantities of ice, he located near an ice-harvesting firm on the banks of the Calumet River in what is now Hammond, Indiana. See Cronon, *Nature's Metropolis*, 233.

43. Swift, a New Englander, did not arrive in Chicago until 1875 and recognized that this task would require a large increase in the firm's size. When Swift was ready to try his car in the early 1880s, he found that most railroads would not accept it, but the one that did proved it worked. Swift and other packers began shipping refrigerated dressed beef east, often in Swift-built cars. It went to refrigerated branch houses in the major cities. Smaller municipalities were served by refrigerated rail cars known as "peddler cars." The cost saving over the shipment of live animals was significant; a dressed steer weighed approximately 55 percent as much as a live steer.

44. Logging generally took place in winter for two reasons. A source of labor was available during down times on farms, and the heavy trees could be moved more easily across ice. Part of the success of the venture depended on the amount of snow. A year with too little snow might lead to too little water in the streams and rivers to get the large logs to the mill. See Cronon, *Nature's Metropolis*, chap. 4.

45. David Carver, who arrived in Chicago (probably from St. Joseph, Michigan) on an eponymic vessel in 1833, established a lumberyard on the south bank between LaSalle and Wells and is normally given credit for undertaking the first lumber shipment.

46. Chicago also had a sawmill a short distance up the North Branch. Regarding the lumber shipment, see http://www.encyclopedia.chicagohistory.org/pages/767.html.

47. It was believed that the balloon-frame house was invented in Chicago, but that is not true. It is a much older invention. It was widely adopted in the Midwest, however, being relatively easy to construct (and move). One explanation for why this falsehood gained some traction is that Chicago factories produced ready-made houses with balloon frames that were sold in the Midwest.

48. Cronon, *Nature's Metropolis*, 168.

49. See http://www.encyclopedia.chicagohistory.org/pages/767/html.

50. The lumber district also housed industries that made use of large amounts of lumber: furniture and piano factories, wagon makers and shipbuilders.

51. After the fire, Bohemian shovers spearheaded the railroad strike of 1877, during which there were battles with the police, with the result that Chicago workers were radicalized. See Karamanski, "Lumber."

52. Smith, *Chicago's Great Fire*, 39. The building was the newly constructed three-story stable for Franklin Parmelee's omnibus and stagecoach company, which took passengers from one rail station to another or to a hotel.

Chapter 5. Those behind the Growth

1. The primary sources for the biographies in this chapter are the histories of Chicago by Alfred Andreas (1884, 1885), Bessie Louise Pierce (1937, 1940), and *Biographical Sketches of the Leading Men of Chicago, written by the best talent of the Northwest* (1868), plus various online reference sites such as Wikipedia.com and Britannica.com.

2. Jaher, *Urban Establishment*, 453.

3. See Kirkland, *Story of Chicago*. Of the dining rooms, the grandest was at Lake House Hotel on Kinzie Street, the first in Chicago to have menus, napkins, and toothpicks. John H. Kinzie was the primary owner; Gurdon Hubbard also had an interest. The Chicago Census of 1835 was reported in the *Democrat* of November 26, 1835.

4. Jonas and Henley ultimately settled in Westville, Indiana. John Clark (a.k.a. Nonimoa or Prairie Wolf) visited Fort Dearborn in 1818. By 1830 he carried the mail by horseback between Chicago and Milwaukee and ultimately settled along the route in Deerfield, Illinois. Prairie Wolf Slough, a forest preserve in Deerfield, is named for him.

5. The bricks were made by F. C. Sherman, who later constructed the Sherman House Hotel. That name would be attached to a downtown hotel until 1973. In the 1830s Archibald Clybourn built the Washington House hotel in Milwaukee.

6. Andreas, *History of Chicago*, 3:632. Caton served on the Illinois Supreme Court.

7. Charles Walker made the first shipment of wheat the previous year. Jared Gage established the first flour mill in 1836, and, by 1839, Chicago had become a net exporter of flour. In 1838 the steamship *Great Western* carried seventy-five bushels of wheat as subsidiary cargo from Chicago; by 1848 the city would become the world's largest grain depot. In June 1832 the first shipment of coal arrived in the city because of Newberry & Dole.

8. See *Biographical Sketches*, 157–61.

9. Although the Chicago plant concentrated on meat production, the firm had many other interests. Walsh, *Midwestern Meat Packing*, 52–53. Walsh also discusses the firms of Culbertson, Blair & Co. and A. E. Kent & Co. as the other important early packing firms. Gurdon Hubbard, she notes, preferred to remain a general merchant rather than becoming a full-time packer.

10. A Chicago branch was created in 1867 and run by Phillip's brother, Joseph Armour. Another brother, Herman, who started working in Chicago as a livestock commission merchant in 1862, moved to New York in 1865 to head Armour, Plankinton, and Company. See D. Miller, *City of the Century*, 211–216.

11. The Pennsylvania Railroad began to experiment with refrigeration in 1857, but the first U.S. patent went to J. B. Sutherland of Detroit.

12. He also found the currency severely depreciated and addressed that problem as well. It is a problem discussed in chapter 8.

13. Meanwhile, he opened a private bank in his own name that was then merged into the Mechanics National Bank, of which he was president. See *Biographical Sketches*, 29.

14. In 1837 he was selected to be the attorney of the State Bank of Illinois. Two years later, he started six years of service as reporter of the Illinois Supreme Court.

15. See Dante, "Chicago Tribune's 'Lost' Years," 139–64.

16. It was officially formed in 1857, was chartered in 1865, and had one of the best natural history collections in America, which was destroyed in the Great Fire.

17. His wife died in 1860 on the family's European trip and was buried in Germany.

18. This is roughly equivalent to just under $65.5 million today using the CPI to make the comparison. See MeasuringWorth.com.

19. This was a somewhat substantial amount; it is roughly equivalent to the value of GDP per capita in 1836. In 2019 U.S. GDP per capita was $65,297.50, according to the World Bank. See https://data.worldbank.org/indicator/NY.GDP.PCAP.CD?end=2023&start=1960&view=chart.

20. Fehrenbacher, *Chicago Giant*, 18, 37.

21. There were several reasons for this. He claimed that he was tired from his second term as mayor and handicapped by David Bradley's death in 1857. It was Bradley, Wentworth's longtime assistant, who ran the *Democrat* while the owner was away attending to his elected offices. It was also the case that the expenses of more modern equipment and expanding so that the paper could adequately cover the expected war were quite high. Finally, Scammon sued the *Democrat* for libel after Wentworth published a cartoon depicting Scammon as a wildcat banker (a fat cat was pictured wearing a pair of Scammon's distinctive spectacles). After closing the paper, Wentworth gave his subscription list to the *Chicago Tribune*.

22. He retained his Locofoco Democrat belief in sound money. The Democrat who ran against him was Cyrus McCormick.

23. The area south of Madison Street would be lifted by an additional two feet or so. Fehrenbacher, *Chicago Giant*,144.

24. The political dispute between Michigan and Ohio concerned which side of the extended Michigan-Indiana line the city of Toledo, Ohio, was located. See Cain, "Carving the Northwest Territory into States."

25. Radebaugh, "Boundary Dispute," 123. Today, with the political power reversed, it is the southerners who are looking for a way to reduce the influence of northern Illinoisans.

26. Votes such as 570 for union, 1 against in Stephenson County, 495 to 11 in Boone County, and 971 to 6 in Winnebago County were typical. See Radebaugh, "Boundary Dispute," 136.

27. Quoted in Andreas, *History of Chicago*, 1:171.

28. *Chicago Tribune*, October 17, 1888, quoted in Fehrenbacher, *Chicago Giant*, 226.

29. Wendt and Kogan, *Give the Lady What She Wants!*, 62.

30. He lent the government $0.75 million during the war. *Biographical Sketches*, 61.

31. According to MeasuringWorth.com, that is equivalent to $43.8 million today if the CPI is used for the adjustment and $519.2 million if the production worker's wage is used. See https://www.palmerhousehiltonhotel.com/about-our-hotel/.

32. Wendt and Kogan, *Give the Lady What She Wants!*, 62.

33. The firm they left became John V. Farwell & Co., which was purchased by Carson, Pirie & Co. in 1926.

34. Another former employee was Harry Gordon Selfridge, who worked at Field's for twenty-five years before opening his eponymous London department store.

35. See Cronon, *Nature's Metropolis*, 334.

36. Emmet and Jeuck, *Catalogues and Counters*, 19.

37. Pierce, *History of Chicago*, 3:182. Success breeds imitation, and soon Ward had a formidable competitor in his own backyard, but Sears and Roebuck did not come to Chicago until 1887. Indeed, at the time of the fire, Richard Sears was eight years old and living in Minnesota.

38. Cyrus was assisted by Jo Anderson, a family slave. He returned his attention to reaper production to pay off the debts incurred in another business. In 1836 he and his father purchased an iron foundry called Cotopaxi, which was never successful. The foundry's problems, exacerbated by the Panic of 1837, provided an excellent schooling in business for young Cyrus. Hower, "Cyrus Hall McCormick," 70–71.

39. Both men initially licensed others to also produce their reapers. McCormick moved in order to produce all his reapers himself; Hussey never stopped licensing production to others.

40. In part, this was due to his not being satisfied with the financial arrangements he had made in Cincinnati. Like Hussey, he found he had to license his patent in order to produce sufficient volume; some machines were constructed in Brockport, New York, as well as in Cincinnati. On the other hand, Hussey, who tested his reaper in Hamilton County, Ohio, moved to the east and continued to allow others to produce his machine under license.

41. William McCormick arrived in Chicago a year later to take charge of the company's finances. It became McCormick Harvesting Machine Company in 1879 and formed part of the International Harvester Company in 1902.

42. Gray was a former licensee. He also enlarged the factory. Seven hundred reapers were produced the first year and fifteen hundred in the next.

43. The area included all but four counties of Illinois, Indiana, Michigan, Kentucky, and Tennessee. Although their partnership formally expired in 1850, Ogden encouraged McCormick to go to the London Exhibition of 1851, where his reaper received a Council Medal, the exhibition's highest award. Royal Commission, *Reports by the Juries*, 231, 232, 241. See also Moser, "What Do Inventors Patent?" and French, *Great Exhibition*.

44. See Cronon, *Nature's Metropolis*, 313–18, and D. Miller, *City of the Century*, 103–6.

45. David, *Technical Choice Innovation*, 89.

46. This figure is taken from the *Chicago Tribune*, October 9, 1872, cited at https://chicagology.com/rebuilding/rebuilding151/. In 1886 the infamous Haymarket Riot was tied to a strike against the firm over the $9 per week salary it paid its workers. Those interested in reading more about the Haymarket Riot should consult Avrich, *Haymarket Tragedy*, Smith, *Urban Disorder*.

47. A similar claim that there was no interruption of business was made about the raising of Scammon's Marine Bank building.

48. The idea of a sleeping car was not Pullman's; the first was built in 1857.

49. Field was a friend and former New York state senator.

50. Beginning in 1880, Pullman planned and constructed his eponymous model town, where Palace cars were built and repaired.

Chapter 6. Creating Position: Sanitation and Health

1. See, e.g., Cain and Hong, "Survival in 19th Century Cities." Much of this chapter's first section is based on Cain, *Sanitation Strategy.*

2. See Pierce, *History of Chicago*, 1:20, 30.

3. It has been estimated that cholera and desertion explain why only 350 of the 950 men who left Buffalo headed for Fort Dearborn actually arrived in Chicago. Hamilton, "Epidemics of Chicago," 75–76, cited in Sells, *Tunnel Under the Lake*, 11.

4. Chicago's leaders required all men aged twenty-one to sixty to spend three days each year cleaning streets and alleys or face a penalty ranging from seventy-five cents to five dollars. This reflected the then-current miasmatic theory of disease, which was that filth caused cholera. That cholera was waterborne was first documented by the English physician John Snow in 1854, and the exact cause of the disease was discovered by the German physician Robert Koch in 1883.

5. A quarantine hospital was constructed early in the spring of 1845 that helped limit the spread of smallpox.

6. Cain, *Sanitation Strategy*, 38.

7. Cain, *Sanitation Strategy*, 20.

8. The board was empowered to (1) supervise the drainage and sewage disposal of Chicago's three natural divisions, (2) plan a coordinated system for the future, and (3) issue bonds, purchase lots, and erect buildings to implement their plan. The board's actions were made subject to the Chicago City Council's approval. The act is summarized in several works including G. Brown, *Drainage Channel and Waterway*, 50.

9. Ogden had visited Europe for approximately eighteen months beginning in 1853. In particular, he examined the public works of the cities he visited, especially the Amsterdam ship canal. This suggested to him the desirability of the initial deep-cut plan for the I&M Canal, which would allow for unbroken steamboat navigation between Chicago and the Mississippi River. To that end, the Illinois River Improvement Company was incorporated in 1857 to produce a navigable channel. Ogden was one of the incorporators. Pierce, *History of Chicago*, 2:39.

10. Andreas, *History of Chicago*, 1:191; Pierce, *History of Chicago*, 2:330. For the quotation see Soper, Watson, and Martin, *Report to the Chicago Real Estate Board*, 69, hereafter referred to as the *CREB Report.*

11. Although the commissioners' report mentions the public's proposals, it does not indicate what they were or even which parts of Chesbrough's plan were adapted from these suggestions. Board of Sewerage Commissioners, *Report and Plan of Sewerage*, 20.

12. To be clear, most cities had some sewers, but Chicago was the first American city to adopt a plan that encompassed the entire city. Chesbrough's report is at https://digirepo.nlm.nih.gov/ext/mhl/2546005R/PDF/2546005R.pdf. See Cain, *Sanitation Strategy*, chap. 2. See also Cain, "Raising and Watering a City," 353–72.

13. G. Brown, *Drainage Channel and Waterway*, 53.

14. The material about Chesbrough is largely derived from Cain, "Raising and Watering a City."

15. His engineering education began in this setting, and he quickly proved an apt student. See *Biographical Sketches*, 192; see also "Memoirs of Deceased Members."

16. Of particular interest to Chesbrough's later career is the fact that Long had carried out extensive exploratory surveys in the West. In 1816 Long was asked to report to the federal government on the physiographic features in the region of a proposed canal between Lake Michigan and the Illinois River. Although it is only speculation, one wonders how much knowledge of Chicago's topographical peculiarities Long passed on to Chesbrough. It is known that Long prepared detailed reports of his visit to Chicago. See Wood, *Stephen Harriman Long*.

17. George Washington Whistler was the son of Major John Whistler, the builder of Fort Dearborn. George Whistler's first wife died young; his second wife was the sister of Captain William Gibbs McNeill. The oldest of their five sons, James Abbott McNeill Whistler, painted his mother in Paris while his father was building the St. Petersburg–Moscow Railroad for Czar Nicholas I.

18. See Cain, "Raising and Watering a City," 355–56.

19. It is quite possible that Jervis played a significant role in Chicago's selecting Chesbrough, for during the early 1850s Jervis was professionally engaged in the Chicago area. The city fathers would have been aware of Jervis's reputation as an engineer, and it is probable that he was consulted regarding candidates for the chief engineer's position. Because he had worked with Chesbrough just before this, it is likely that Jervis gave Chesbrough an excellent recommendation. In 1881 Chesbrough, serving as consulting engineer of the New Croton Aqueduct, employed Jervis, who discussed the work with Chesbrough daily. This indicates the esteem in which Chesbrough held Jervis, for Jervis was then eighty-six years old. Chesbrough, at sixty-eight years of age, belonged to another generation.

20. Chesbrough's role in the Cochituate works is mentioned in Blake, *Water for the Cities*, 210–16.

21. Board of Sewerage Commissioners, *Report and Plan of Sewerage*; also quoted in *CREB Report*, 71.

22. Chesbrough planned to pump sufficient lake water into the north and south branches of the Chicago River to flush offensive solid pollutants. He proposed flushing the sewers, as well. See Pearse, "Chicago's Quest for Potable Water," 3.

23. Chesbrough emphasized that a higher grade was necessary in order to have dry streets. Chicago lacked this high grade, and thus, the decision to raise the city's level, concomitant with sewer installation, was one that solved the sewage disposal and drainage problems in the context of Chicago's existing topography and future necessities.

24. Chesbrough's grade was rejected because the city fathers felt there would be difficulties in locating sufficient fill. See *CREB Report*, 70.

25. Randolph, "History of Sanitation in Chicago," 229. For many years, some sewers lay wholly above the ground, at the same level as or higher than adjoining buildings. Randolph was the chief engineer of the Sanitary and Ship Canal.

26. Workers of the Writer's Program, "Up from the Mud." The raising of cities was relatively common.

27. Kirkland, *Story of Chicago*, 232–33. Caton, who was elected Chicago's corporation attorney in 1833, was the first person to make a living as a practicing attorney in the city. Caton's first case was tried in John Miller's tannery, with the witness "box" a chair placed

on a small riser. There was no proof of the charges against a man accused of stealing money until Caton, the prosecutor, observed a lump in the defendant's sock. He took $10 from the roll of stolen bills as his fee and returned the balance to the court.

28. D. Miller, *City of the Century*, 124–26. At the time when his firm raised the Tremont, Pullman himself was at the Pike's Peak gold rush.

29. Cain, *Sanitation Strategy*, 61–62.

30. This alternative reflects the strategy Chicago would adopt with an additional decade of economic and population growth, but Chesbrough believed in 1855 that the city's population of eighty thousand did not warrant incurring the large expense that would be involved. Board of Sewerage Commissioners, *Report and Plan of Sewerage*, 8.

31. Pierce, *History of Chicago*, 1:342.

32. In 1845 the state chartered a second private firm, the Lake Michigan Hydraulic Company, to supply that part of Chicago north of the Chicago River. The company never erected works and never supplied water. Smith, *City Water, City Life*, provides an excellent comparison of the waterworks histories of Chicago, Boston, and Philadelphia.

33. Andreas, *History of Chicago*, 1:186.

34. Andreas, *History of Chicago*, 1:186.

35. G. Brown, *Drainage Channel and Waterway*, 32.

36. G. Brown, *Drainage Channel and Waterway*, 32

37. G. Brown, *Drainage Channel and Waterway*, 33.

38. Board of Public Works, *Second Annual Report of the Board of Public Works*, 5, hereafter referred to as *1863 Report*.

39. *1863 Report*, 39. This tunnel is the subject of Sells, *Drainage Channel and Waterway*.

40. *1863 Report*, 41.

41. Cain, *Sanitation Strategy*, 45.

42. Wing, *Tunnels and Water System*, 33. See also Cain, "Raising and Watering a City," 369.

43. Wing, *Tunnels and Water System*, 76.

44. By 1915 the desirable depth for a water intake was fifty feet, but this would have required a ten- to fifteen-mile lake tunnel.

45. Cain, "Raising and Watering a City," 369–70.

46. *1863 Report*, 57.

47. *1863 Report*, 57.

48. The famed Water Tower contains the standpipe for Chesbrough's water supply system.

49. Bilek, "Old Chicago Portage." The Nickerson ditch drained the South Arm.

50. See Fehrenbacher, *Chicago Giant*, 212–14.

51. See Harpster, *Railroad Tycoon*, 140.

52. The Ogden Dam, built directly on the west line of Harlem Avenue during 1876–77, eradicated Mud Lake by holding back the waters of Portage Creek that flooded it periodically.

53. This was true even after additional canals were built on the North Shore and in the Calumet region.

54. See Cain, "Unfouling the Public's Nest."

55. The two major histories of Chicago are the basis for much of this material and they treat medical history in very different ways. Andreas has a separate chapter in each volume,

whereas Pierce has integrated the material with other subjects. Andreas, in volume 1 (1884), discusses the city's medical history at 459–67 with a separate section on homeopathy at 467–71. The chapter in volume 2 (1885) can be found at 521–56. In Pierce (1937), readers interested in medical history should consult the index in volume 1; hospitals are discussed at 330–32. The same advice holds for volume 2 (1940), but there are three discrete sections to note. Hospitals can be found at 448–51; medicine, at 397–98; and health in general at 334–37. The most specific study is Bonner, *Medicine in Chicago.*

56. There is a rather winding road to the modern Rush University Medical Center. Members of the Rush faculty established Presbyterian Hospital, a teaching hospital, in 1883. Rush Medical College became affiliated with the University of Chicago in 1898 and remained so until 1941, when Chicago organized its own medical school. The college was closed from 1942 until 1969. Saint Luke's Hospital, founded in 1864, merged with Presbyterian Hospital to form Presbyterian–St. Luke's Hospital in 1956. Following the reactivation of the Rush Medical College charter in 1969, the college merged with Presbyterian–St. Luke's Hospital to form Rush-Presbyterian–St. Luke's Medical Center. Rush University was established in 1972 and changed its name in September 2003 to Rush University Medical Center.

57. Benjamin Rush of Philadelphia, who died in 1813, was an advocate for education in general and medical education in particular. A graduate of Princeton (at age fourteen), he later earned the M.D. at the University of Edinburgh. He was the Surgeon General of the Continental Army and afterwards taught chemistry, medical theory, and clinical practice at the University of Pennsylvania.

58. He is considered the founder of the city's public school system and served on the committee to raise funds for the Galena and Chicago Union Railroad.

59. He, too, dabbled in politics, unsuccessfully running for mayor of Chicago in 1858. A lengthy discussion of Brainard can be found in Hyde, *Early Medical Chicago*, 25–30.

60. They also contributed $500 in exchange for a promise that the building would be on the north side, where, the donors hoped, the presence of the school would raise property values.

61. Pierce, *History of Chicago*, 1:284. The quotations are referenced in Norris, *General Directory*, 74. See also Bonner, *Medicine in Chicago*, 47.

62. Quoted in Bonner, *Medicine in Chicago*, 49.

63. Evans was one of a group of Methodists who founded Northwestern University in Evanston, where he lived, and served as the first president of Northwestern's Board of Trustees.

64. Although it is only tangentially related to questions of health, a short digression on Evans's political career is instructive. He first served as a Chicago alderman between 1853 and 1855 with a focus on public health, education, and urban development. He helped found the Illinois Republican Party because of his conviction that slavery was wrong. As a result, he became friends with Abraham Lincoln, who in 1862 appointed Evans to be the second governor of the Colorado Territory. In Denver, he helped found what became the University of Denver in 1864 and served as chairman of its Board of Trustees until his death in 1897. He was a founder and president of the Denver Pacific Railroad, which connected Denver with the Union Pacific Railroad in Cheyenne, Wyoming. Evans hoped to be sent to Washington

as a U.S. senator, but it was not to be. He served as Colorado's Superintendent of Indian Affairs and adopted policies that shifted resources, and land in particular, away from the Natives toward white settlers. Since this was still during the Civil War and many men were away, Lincoln himself approved an Evans order to shoot Natives on sight because Denverites perceived them as a dangerous enemy. Friendly Natives were to put themselves under the "care" of the U.S. government at designated forts for their "safety and protection." Although few tribes accepted these terms, one that did was a group led by Black Kettle. When the fort to which Evans ordered them did not provide all they were promised, they moved to an area known as Sand Creek in treaty-approved territory. It was there in 1864 that troopers under the command of a colonel of the Colorado Volunteers massacred Black Kettle's group. Evans decorated the colonel and his troopers. Two congressional committees and one military committee investigated the Sand Creek Massacre in 1865 and found the government at fault. Evans was forced to resign as governor with his legacy forever tarnished.

65. In 1852 Davis revitalized the Chicago Medical Society.

66. Davis was responsible for the medical side, Brainard for the surgical side. Additional hospital staff came from Rush's faculty.

67. The Sisters of Mercy were founded in Dublin in the 1830s and came to the United States in the 1840s. In 1846 six sisters arrived in Chicago.

68. It became the Northwestern University Medical College (now the Northwestern University Feinberg School of Medicine) in 1906. When Davis and others left Rush in 1859, the agreement with Mercy Hospital switched from Rush to Lind.

69. The fire destroyed the hospital and medical school buildings, but Thompson soon reopened in a private home tending to men and women burned in the fire; her hospitalized patients were placed in the homes of friends. Her enterprises received $25,000 from the Relief Aid Society of Chicago and reopened in a new location at Adams and Paulina Streets in 1872. Thompson was admitted to the Chicago Medical Society in 1873.

70. Bonner, *Medicine in Chicago*, 6.

71. A cholera epidemic broke out in April 1849 when a canal boat arrived with a sick captain and passengers.

72. See Sells, *Tunnel Under the Lake*, 31.

73. Bonner, *Medicine in Chicago*, 28.

74. The last major outbreak of smallpox in Chicago occurred just after the Columbian Exposition, likely the result of the arrival of unvaccinated immigrants.

75. All these statistics are reported in Bonner, *Medicine in Chicago*, 29–30.

Chapter 7. Population and Labor

1. In consequence, separate sections were not thought necessary for those such as the Germans, who generally did quite well. See Jentz and Keil, *German Workers in Industrial Chicago*.

2. A map drawn for the 1830 census simply notes "Pottawatomie Indians" at the bottom of Lake Michigan. United States Census Office, *Distribution of the Population East of the 100th Meridian*, plate 6.

3. There are also data points that are derived from the Chicago school census.

4. One woman living in Boston and one man in Cincinnati were more than one hundred years old, but there was no one in St. Louis or Chicago who reported being over the age of eighty.

5. The ratio of males aged twenty to forty to females in that age range was 2.5:1 in St. Louis, 1.47:1 in Chicago, 1.41:1 in Boston, 1.40:1 in Cincinnati, and less than 1.08:1 in the total U.S. population. The different age cohorts reported for the Black population do not allow direct comparisons.

6. Fergus, *Directory of the City of Chicago*.

7. The 1845 data are from a state census. Norris, *General Directory . . . for the Year 1845–46*. See also Norris, *Business Directory*.

8. United States Bureau of the Census, *Seventh Census*; United States Bureau of the Census, *Ninth Census*.

9. The numbers reported here are only for census years, whereas the numbers reported at the beginning of this chapter are based on estimates for all years. The patterns for intercensal years reduce the rates by a relatively small amount. They are still quite high.

10. The census included a column for China and Japan, but there were none reported as working in Chicago.

11. It should be noted that until 1910 the census did not classify many workers, especially those called laborers, into the industries in which they were employed. The census lumped them together and arbitrarily put them into one of the industries, in this case, services.

12. The other cases in which the calculated percentage is 1.5 times or more than the average for that occupation or nativity group all involve fewer than twenty people.

13. See Smith, *Chicago's Great Fire*.

14. See McCaffrey, Skerrett, Funchion, and Fanning, *Irish in Chicago*, 3.

15. Putnam, *Illinois and Michigan Canal*, 38, n. 1. This was above the $19 per month that agricultural workers received in Philadelphia in 1837. Manufacturing workers there received $20.84 per month in 1837. See Carter et al., *Historical Statistics of the United States*, Series Bz4222–23.

16. Putnam, *Illinois and Michigan Canal*, 38. In fact, some of the contractors whose bids were accepted ended up abandoning their work, forfeiting a performance bond.

17. Quoted in McMahon, "Canal Diggers, Church Builders," 46. Even before the potato famine increased their numbers, Irish people were motivated to immigrate by overpopulation, an oppressive land system, and general dissatisfaction with the political situation. The phrase "transportation revolution" reflects George Rogers Taylor classic, *Transportation Revolution*.

18. See Wyman, *Immigrants in the Valley*, 80. The previous year, a petition to retain Fr. St. Cyr as parish priest was signed by 141 individuals, 117 of them Irish. See Pierce, *History of Chicago*, 1:180.

19. The Illinois Central Railroad, which also would be built on the frontier, faced a similar labor problem. It, too, would attempt to lure workers from similar transportation infrastructure projects in states to the east.

20. Pierce, *History of Chicago*, 1:195. Pierce reports that "a number of Germans" arrived in the late 1830s to work on the canal (1:181).

21. This story is told in Way, *Common Labour*, 173; Dearinger, *Filth of Progress*, 58; and Harris, *Prairie Passage*, 45. Good mortality statistics are not available for the I&M Canal, but, of the approximately fifty thousand who worked on the Erie Canal project, one thousand died. Kimberly Hegeman, "Looking Back on the World's Deadliest Construction Projects," August 28, 2019, https://www.forconstructionpros.com/blogs/construction-toolbox/blog/12096401/looking-back-on-the-worlds-deadliest-construction-projects.

22. In some cases, workers put down a deposit for their equipment. Dearinger (*Filth of Progress*, 62) reports a 94¢ deposit for shovels.

23. See Dearinger, *Filth of Progress*, 67–73.

24. Wyman, *Immigrants in the Valley*, 95.

25. Wyman, *Immigrants in the Valley*, 94. Cholera made intermittent appearances in Chicago for the following half-century.

26. Wyman reports that wages were cut from $26 per month to $20 per month by late 1837. In addition, contractors raised the board charge above the $2 per week amount that had been stipulated, which had to contribute to the workers' strike. Wyman, *Immigrants in the Valley*, 82.

27. Wages recovered to about $16 per month by 1843. Putnam, *Illinois and Michigan Canal*, 61.

28. Way, *Common Labour*, 210, 270.

29. Wyman, *Immigrants in the Valley*, 83. Wyman notes that many who responded to the call were not hired.

30. See, e.g., Wyman, *Immigrants in the Valley*, 230, and Dearinger, *Filth of Progress*, 96. Details of the strike can be found in either book.

31. Quoted in Dearinger, *Filth of Progress*, 57.

32. Harris, *Prairie Passage*, 26.

33. Jensen, "'No Irish Need Apply,'" 405–29.

34. The man who has been termed Chicago's first Irish politician was Billy Caldwell, Sauganash, who was an early arrival. He was a justice of the peace in the late 1820s.

35. See Reed, "Early African American Settlement of Chicago," 212.

36. Fergus, *Directory*; Norris, *General Directory . . . for the Year 1845–46*; United States Bureau of the Census, *Sixth Census*; United States Bureau of the Census, *Seventh Census*.

37. See Reed, "Early African American Settlement of Chicago," 214. Pierce, *History of Chicago*, refers to the "concentration" of the Black population on the South Side (2:11), but Charles N. Zucker (1972), "Free Negro Question," found no evidence of a ghetto.

38. Pierce, *History of Chicago*, 2:2.

39. See Reed, *Black Chicago's First Century*, 73f.

40. Chapter 7 of Masur, *Until Justice Be Done*, is a discussion of the Black Laws in Illinois (and elsewhere) as well as the more general question of whether free Blacks were U.S. citizens under the Constitution. Masur is involved with a website (https://coloredconventions.org/black-illinois-organizing) that addresses many of the issues raised by her book and the history of Blacks in Illinois.

41. See Pierce, *History of Chicago*, 2:393. The census of 1840 recorded 331 slaves and about 3,500 free Blacks in all of Illinois; none of the slaves were in Cook County.

42. If the fine was paid, it was split evenly between the jurisdiction and the accuser, which gave Whites an incentive to "police" Blacks.

43. Reed, *Black Chicago's First Century*, 227–28, notes that in Chicago Whites and Blacks rioted together against slave catchers, in contrast with places like New York and Philadelphia, where there were riots against Blacks as "refugees or workers."

44. Reverend John Brown Dawson, trained as a barber like many of the Black men in early Chicago, opened a grocery store in 1857 and was the owner-operator of Dawson's subdivision (which is now known as Avondale). He was particularly active in attempting to repeal the Black Laws.

45. The Clarys lost six of their twelve children to "cholera, measles, tuberculosis, typhoid fever, and lung disease." Garb, *Freedom's Ballot*, 38.

46. Both sides made use of Black labor to build fortifications and other tasks.

47. Reed, *Black Chicago's First Century*, 234.

48. Reed, *Black Chicago's First Century*, 218–19. See also Garb, *Freedom's Ballot*, 218.

49. When Frederick Douglass visited Chicago, which he did often, he usually stayed at the Jones's home. In 1866 Jones accompanied Douglass to Washington, DC, as a member of a committee to urge President Andrew Johnson to grant voting rights to former slaves. In 1871 Jones began serving the first of two terms as a Cook County commissioner, the first Black to hold elected office in Illinois.

50. The fact that Jones was biracial and light-skinned must have been to his advantage. See Bodenhorn, *Color Factor.*

51. Reed, *Black Chicago's First Century*, 240.

52. "Mobbing Negroes," *Chicago Tribune*, July 15, 1864, https://www.proquest.com/docview/175416163/BE1CFA27A3F04024PQ/2?accountid=12861&sourcetype=Historical%20 Newspapers.

53. Pierce, *History of Chicago*, 2:34.

54. Pierce, *History of Chicago*, 2:11–12.

55. Reed, *Black Chicago's First Century*, 254.

56. Pierce, *History of Chicago*, 2:11–12.

57. The story is found at https://www.chicagotribune.com/news/ct-xpm-1997-10-06-9710070022-story.html.

Chapter 8. The Lubricant of Growth: Money and Finance

1. The Second Bank of the United States had been chartered for a twenty-year-year term by Congress in 1816. It provided financial services to the federal government and private parties through branches located throughout the country. The branches closest to Chicago were in Cincinnati, Louisville, and St. Louis; the branch at Buffalo was at the eastern end of the Great Lakes shipping route.

2. This chapter focuses on Chicago banks; it does not discuss the New York and London banks that lent money to Chicago and Chicagoans for various purposes, including infrastructure. That type of finance is discussed in terms of the financing of the I&M Canal and the Galena and Chicago Union Railroad in chapter 3. It continued to be an important part of the total financial picture throughout the period.

3. Chicago grew to late adolescence, if not maturity, during what is known as the "wildcat bank" era. There are many theories and no single answer for what that term means. One theory concerning the origin of the term *wildcat bank* is that such banks were located out where the wildcats lived, places where note holders were unlikely to go seeking redemption. Easterners might have thought Chicago such a place had not so many of them started moving there.

4. In simplest terms, the money supply is customarily defined as the sum of cash, currency, and demand deposits that can be used almost as easily as cash. Economists refer to assets that be easily converted to cash as liquid. Today, demand deposits (checking accounts) are the most liquid type of bank deposit and are an important part of the money supply termed M_1. They were almost exclusively used by businesses (but not all businesses) in the mid-nineteenth century. The term M_2 also includes time deposits (savings accounts).

5. See Lebergott, "Wage Trends, 1800–1900."

6. It is not surprising that, with so many notes in circulation, counterfeiting was rampant.

7. See Dowrie, "Development of Banking," 3. There is no precise dating of the early business cycles in American economic history. The group responsible for dating business cycles today, the National Bureau of Economic Research, has only pushed its methodology back to a trough in economic activity in 1854. The four cycles to be discussed can be associated with troughs in 1832, 1841, 1854, and 1861. Troughs in 1848 and 1858 fall in the middle of longer cycles. In these years there were two large downswings, the Panics of 1837 and 1857, the former having the greater impact.

8. It should be noted that several other institutions provided some of the services of a financial intermediary that nurtured the processes of saving and borrowing. These include fraternal orders, professional societies, labor organizations, religious organizations, social clubs, and the like. See, e.g., Emery, "Fraternal Sickness Insurance."

9. Federally chartered and state-chartered banks differ by the level of government that charters them; they can be publicly, privately, or jointly owned. The first two Banks of the United States were federally chartered, but they were jointly owned (20 percent public and 80 percent private). In general, state-chartered banks were privately owned, but most of those titled "State Bank of [name of state]" were publicly owned. All chartered banks were able to issue notes.

10. Clarence Danhof estimated that ten to fifteen acres might be cleared in the first year; clearing two hundred acres could be considered the work of a lifetime. See Primack, "Land Clearing," 484–97. Danhof's calculations are reported in his unpublished manuscript titled "Enterprise in American Agriculture," cited by Primack.

11. A detailed discussion of this bank can be found in James, *Growth of Chicago Banks*, 1:10–12.

12. *Illinois Constitution* (1818), art. 8, sec. 21.

13. The history of this bank is the subject of chapter 2 of James, *Growth of Chicago Banks*, "Banking as an Instrument of Social Welfare." At the time, Vandalia was the new state capital; the four branches were to be in Edwardsville, Shawneetown, Palmyra, and Brownsville. The latter two did not survive.

14. Dowrie, "Development of Banking," 21.

15. James, *Growth of Chicago Banks*, 81. *Capital* is a much broader term than *cash*, encompassing a wide variety of financial assets in addition to money (e.g., marketable securities).

16. The Bank of the United States was chartered by the federal government for a twenty-year term in 1816. The State Bank of Illinois was chartered by the State of Illinois in 1835. The notes issued by both banks were part of the money supply.

17. Pierce, *History of Chicago*, 1:153. Just to be clear, these two banks were, in effect, chartered by the state but not owned by the state; the State Bank of Illinois was both chartered and owned by the state. Save for these two banks, after the closing of the Bank of the United States, the State Bank of Illinois would have had a monopoly of banking in Illinois.

18. This land grant was discussed in chapter 3.

19. Bank loans involved the lendee's receiving bank notes. A lack of specie limited the creation of bank notes given that the notes had to be redeemable into specie, and this, in turn, limited the bank's ability to make loans.

20. A bank draft is essentially a check drawn by a bank on funds it had deposited in another bank (e.g., a Chicago bank that maintained an account with a New York bank).

21. Pierce, *History of Chicago*, 1:157–62, discusses these firms in some detail.

22. Dowrie, "Development of Banking," 149.

23. McDonald, *Chicago*, 27; Hoyt, *One Hundred Years of Land Values*.

24. Illinois planned to use it not only to complete the I&M Canal but also to build seven new railroads and to dredge all of the state's important rivers.

25. Illinois received $477,919.14 as its share of the distributed revenues. Bourne, *History of the Surplus Revenue*, 59.

26. McDonald, *Chicago*, 27. The CPI fluctuated much less. Between 1832 and 1837, consumer prices rose 11.7 percent, then fell 14.8 percent between 1837 and 1842. See MeasuringWorth.com.

27. The first and second Banks of the United States were joint public-private ventures. Jackson's argument implies a monopoly bank owned exclusively by the U.S. government and a prohibition on state-chartered banks. Early in his life Jackson had accepted what proved to be worthless bank notes in payment for a large amount of land and had become anti-bank for the rest of his life.

28. Because the second State Bank of Illinois was run by Whigs, the Jacksonian Democrats chose to bypass that bank and deposit government funds in the downstate Bank of Illinois.

29. Ten years later, in 1846, the Independent Treasury Act required all payments made to or by the federal government be in specie or Treasury notes. All federal funds were to be deposited in the Treasury and not in the nation's banks. In essence, the federal government was to handle its affairs in specie, while business handled its affairs with bank notes. This proved to be one of the most oft-violated laws in history. It was completely unworkable, but it was not repealed until the passage of the Federal Reserve Act in 1913.

30. Not only was it not in the banks, it was not in the state. The closest federal government depository was in St. Louis. However, by the late 1830s, the Secretary of the Treasury had begun to deposit funds in the Chicago branch of the state bank. See Dowrie, "Development of Banking," 87.

31. This was a contractionary monetary policy that caused a major downturn.

32. See James, *Growth of Chicago Banks*, 121. In this case, it was nonredeemable paper money.

33. These certificates of deposit were pieces of paper of a size similar to that of bank notes indicating that a given amount of money had been deposited in the institution for the benefit of a particular party, but they allowed for endorsements, so the holder of a suitably endorsed certificate could receive payment from the institution. This allowed them to be used as a substitute for bank notes.

34. Since the amount of specie in circulation had been decreased, the amount of money that could be issued had decreased, and this put downward pressure on prices. The leader of the Pennsylvania group was the former Second Bank of the United States, now a state-chartered bank based in Philadelphia.

35. Dowrie, "Development of Banking," 89–95.

36. See James, *Growth of Chicago Banks*, 197–98, and Pierce, *History of Chicago*, 1:154–55.

37. The real cost is the cost adjusted for price changes. Assume you earn $1 a day and receive a $1 bank note as compensation. That day, you can buy a good that costs $1 with your note. If, however, the note depreciates, if merchants believe the note is now worth only $0.95, then you will have to offer more than the note to get that $1 item; the real cost of the item has increased.

38. Although the bank was scheduled to become a private institution in March 1847, the closing sale of the bank's property did not occur until November 1862 (see Dowrie, "Development of Banking," 122). Similarly, the Bank of Illinois in Shawneetown survived until 1853.

39. James, *Growth of Chicago Banks*, 160. James is referring to the fact bank charters had to be approved by a state's legislature, which made the process very political. In a state controlled by one party, it was quite likely that it would charter a bank for the purpose of accumulating funds that could be lent to the party.

40. In fact, in early 1842 they carried a premium of 1–2 percent. James, *Growth of Chicago Banks*, 165.

41. Given the wide variety of notes and certificates in circulation, of varying degrees of soundness, the publication of "bank note reporters," "counterfeit detectors," and the like were necessary in order to conduct business; the public relied on money tables published in newspapers.

42. In its common form, Gresham's law says that "bad money drives out good." The idea is that if there are two types of money in circulation, the less valuable one (discounted $1 bills) will cause the more valuable one ($1 in specie) to disappear from circulation as people hold on to them. Because coins were minted from specie, they, too, disappeared. This meant that once again there was a small change problem.

43. In 1844 it was reorganized under a different name, and Scammon later resurrected its charter. See *Industrial Chicago*.

44. James, *Growth of Chicago Banks*, 203.

45. George Smith and Company in Chicago also dealt in foreign exchange and real estate, operating as a private bank until 1862. Smith also organized banks in Washington and Atlanta to issue and redeem notes in the Old Northwest. See Dowrie, "Development of Banking," 146; Pierce, *History of Chicago*, 1:125–26.

46. James, *Growth of Chicago Banks*, 183. James traces the idea to John McVickar's *Hints on Banking* (1827).

47. Pierce, *History of Chicago*, 2:120, reports that the vote in Chicago was 2,122 to 79. James, *Growth of Chicago Banks*, 211, reports that the vote in the state was much closer—37,578 to 31,321. Only four counties north of Springfield voted against the act; counties south of Springfield returned large majorities against it.

48. *Illinois Journal*, October 12, 1850, quoted in James, *Growth of Chicago Banks*, 208.

49. James, *Growth of Chicago Banks*, 226.

50. Recall that it was Smith who lent Scammon the money he and Ogden needed for the Galena and Chicago Union Railroad. On the eve of the Panic of 1857, a worldwide financial panic, he retired to Scotland with his good reputation intact.

51. Schweikart, "Banking, Commercial."

52. James, *Growth of Chicago Banks*, 229.

53. This is covered in some detail in James, *Growth of Chicago Banks*, 121–22.

54. In the fall session of 1853 the state legislature considered revising the banking law. Jacksonian Democrats advocated its repeal. Chicago's Board of Trade argued that such a step would wreak economic havoc.

55. Andreas, *History of Chicago*, 1:546, 2:617–18.

56. There is a second school bearing his name in Hawthorn Woods.

57. He ran a branch of the Underground Railroad that moved slaves from Chicago to Lake County.

58. The entire prospectus can be found in Andreas, *History of Chicago*, 1:540.

59. Quoted in James, *Growth of Chicago Banks*, 221–22.

60. James, *Growth of Chicago Banks*, 224. For more, see Pierce, *History of Chicago*, 2:122–24, and David Rutter, "In Search of Seth Paine." Paine later lived in Lake Zurich, Illinois, where, among other things, he ran a stop on the Underground Railroad.

61. See Dowrie, "Development of Banking," 152.

62. Pierce, *History of Chicago*, 2:128. MeasuringWorth.com reports that this sum would be $360 million in today's dollars if the CPI is used for the adjustment, $5.5 billion if GDP per capita is used, and $63.5 billion if the relative share of GDP is used.

63. A trust company acts as agent, or trustee, for a person or business; it manages the assets before their transfer to those benefiting from the trust. A savings bank (not to be confused with a savings and loan) primarily offered savings accounts on which interest was paid; the funds were invested in corporate and government bonds (not mortgages). Investment banks did not appear until after the Civil War.

64. The emerging transportation network enhanced the nodality of sites located on the network, and they grew. Trade between them increased, and the financial flows between sites increased. The financial markets that developed in major cities could send information via the telegraph across the country that people could react to much faster than they could earlier.

65. With the end of the Crimean War in 1856 European agriculture rebounded, and the need for American imports declined.

66. James, *Growth of Chicago Banks*, 263.

67. Dowrie, "Development of Banking," 164–68.

68. Dowrie, "Development of Banking," 162–63.

69. James, *Growth of Chicago Banks*, 284. Only 17 of the 110 banks chartered under the Free Banking Act were still operating.

70. Dowrie, "Development of Banking," 173. "A National Monetary System" is the subject of James, *Growth of Chicago Banks*, chap. 9.

71. It was originally titled the National Currency Act.

72. National bank notes were made legal tender for all transactions except customs payments.

73. James (*Growth of Chicago Banks*, 315) notes that Joseph Medill, editor of the *Chicago Tribune*, wrote to Salmon Chase, Secretary of the Treasury, urging him to implement a tax on state bank notes that would "eliminate the state 'debt factories' and their 'heterogeneous rags.'"

74. A year later Chicago had seven national banks, and it had seventeen by 1871. The National Banking System was intended to supply central banking services much as the First and Second National Banks of the United States had done. It was replaced by the Federal Reserve System. The First National Bank of Chicago was a member of the NBS.

75. James, *Growth of Chicago Banks*, 345. It should be noted that First National sponsored James's two-volume study.

76. The Union Bank and First National would merge in 1900.

77. *Laws of Illinois*, 1867, P-49, quoted in Dowrie, "Development of Banking," 173.

78. Pierce, *History of Chicago*, 2:133.

79. Recall that one of the largest private banks, that of George Smith, had closed the year before the National Bank Act was passed.

80. James, *Growth of Chicago Banks*, 370.

81. Interested readers should consult Rockoff, "*Wizard of Oz* as a Monetary Allegory," to appreciate the tie between the well-known book and the equally well-known speech.

82. See Unger, *Greenback Era*.

83. Dowrie, "Development of Banking," 154.

84. James recounts this incident in chapter 9 of *Growth of Chicago Banks*.

85. A counter-cyclical monetary policy would not prove to be a regular feature until after the Treasury–Federal Reserve Accord in 1951.

Chapter 9. Where Things Stood

1. Smith, *Chicago's Great Fire*, 135–37. Although the *Democratic Press* generally supported the Democratic Party, it differed on the issue of slavery. Consequently, Bross was an early supporter of the newly formed Republican Party and served as Illinois's lieutenant-governor from 1865 to 1869.

2. Smith, *Chicago's Great Fire*, 137.

3. Jaher, *Urban Establishment*, 454.

4. See Wade, *Urban Frontier*.

5. The Jardine Water Purification Plant, which opened in 1968, is the last large capital investment in Chicago's water supply.

6. The statue in the park is much less grand than the Gateway Arch in St. Louis, but what the two commemorate is quite similar. This park is the northeast end of the I&M Canal National Heritage Corridor, which follows the route of the canal from the park southwest to LaSalle, Illinois.

7. Dean, "Theory of Geographic Location," 130, 134.

Bibliography

Ackerman, William K. *Early Illinois Railroads*. Fergus Historical Series 23. Chicago: Fergus, 1884.

Aduddell, Robert M., and Louis P. Cain. "Location and Collusion in the Meat Packing Industry." In *Business Enterprise and Economic Change*, edited by Louis P. Cain and Paul J. Uselding, 85–117. Kent, OH: Kent State University Press, 1973.

Aduddell, Robert M., and Louis P. Cain. "Public Policy Toward 'The Greatest Trust in the World.'" *Business History Review* 55, no. 2 (Summer 1981): 217–42.

Andreas, Alfred T. *History of Chicago: From the Earliest Period to the Present Time*, vol. 1: *Ending with the Year 1857*. Chicago: A. T. Andreas, 1884.

Andreas, Alfred T. *History of Chicago: From the Earliest Period to the Present Time*, vol. 2: *From 1857 Until the Fire of 1871*. Chicago: A. T. Andreas, 1885.

Andreas, Alfred T. *History of Chicago: From the Earliest Period to the Present Time*, vol. 3: *From the Fire of 1871 Until 1885*. Chicago: A. T. Andreas, 1886.

Arnold, Isaac N. *William B. Ogden and Early Days in Chicago*. Fergus Historical Series 17. Chicago: Fergus, 1882.

Avrich, Paul. *The Haymarket Tragedy*. Princeton, NJ: Princeton University Press, 1984.

Belcher, Wyatt Winston. *The Economic Rivalry Between St. Louis and Chicago, 1850–1880*. New York: Columbia University Press, 1947.

Bilek, Edward T., Jr. "The Old Chicago Portage, 1673–1836." National Park Service, Park History Program, June 25, 1967.www.nps.gov/parkhistory/online_books/chpo/chicago_portage.pdf.

Binford, Henry. *From Improvement to City Planning: Spatial Management in Cincinnati from the Early Republic Through the Civil War Decade*. Philadelphia: Temple University Press, 2021.

Binford, Henry. "Multicentered Chicago." In *The Electronic Encyclopedia of Chicago*. Chicago: Chicago Historical Society, 2005.

Biographical Sketches of the Leading Men of Chicago, Written by the Best Talent of the Northwest. Chicago: Wilson & St. Clair, 1868.

Blake, Nelson M. *Water for the Cities.* Syracuse, NY: Syracuse University Press, 1956.

Board of Public Works. *Second Annual Report of the Board of Public Works to the Common Council of the City of Chicago*, April 1, 1863. Https://books.google.com/books/about/Second_Annual_Report_of_the_Board_of_Pub.html?id=FGMpAAAAYAAJ.

Board of Sewerage Commissioners. *Report and Plan of Sewerage for the City of Chicago, Illinois*, December 31, 1855. Https://www.commons.wikimedia.org/wiki/File:Report_and_plan_of_sewerage_for_the_city_of_Chicago_Illinois_adopted_by_the_Board_of_Sewerage_Comissioners_December 31_1855_(IA_2546005R.nlm.nih.gov).pdf.

Bodenhorn, Howard. *The Color Factor: African-American Well-Being in the Nineteenth-Century South.* New York: Oxford University Press, 2015.

Bonner, Thomas Neville. *Medicine in Chicago, 1850–1950: A Chapter in the Social and Scientific Development of a City.* Madison, WI: American History Research Center, 1957.

Bourne, Edward G. *The History of the Surplus Revenue of 1837*. New York: G. P. Putnam's Sons, 1885.

Brown, G. P. *Drainage Channel and Waterway: A History of the Effort to Secure an Effective and Harmless Method for the Disposal of the Sewage of the City of Chicago, and to Create a Navigable Channel Between Lake Michigan and the Mississippi River.* Chicago: Donnelley, 1894.

Brown, William J. *American Colossus: The Grain Elevator, 1843 to 1943*. Brooklyn, NY: Colossal, 2013.

Brownson, Howard Gray. *History of the Illinois Central Railroad to 1870*. Urbana: University of Illinois Press, 1915.

Cain, Louis. "A Canal and Its City: A Selective Business History of Chicago." *DePaul Business Law Review* 11, no. 1 (1998): 126–84.

Cain, Louis. "Carving the Northwest Territory into States." In *The Vital One: Essays in Honor of Jonathan Hughes*, edited by Joel Mokyr, 153–68. Greenwich, CT: JAI, 1991.

Cain, Louis. "Raising and Watering a City: Ellis Sylvester Chesbrough and Chicago's First Sanitation System." *Technology and Culture* 13, no. 3 (1972): 353–73.

Cain, Louis. *Sanitation Strategy for a Lakefront Metropolis.* DeKalb: Northern Illinois University Press, 1978.

Cain, Louis. "Unfouling the Public's Nest: Chicago's Sanitary Diversion of Lake Michigan Water." *Technology and Culture* 15, no. 4 (October 1974): 594–613.

Cain, Louis. "Urban Growth." In *Handbook of Cliometrics*, edited by Claude Diebolt and Michael Haupert, 987–1017. Berlin: Springer-Verlag, 2024.

Cain, Louis, and Sok Chul Hong. "Survival in 19th Century Cities: The Larger the City, the Smaller Your Chances." *Explorations in Economic History* 46, no. 4 (October 2009): 450–63.

Carter, Susan B., Scott Gartner, Michael Haines, Alan Olmstead, Richard Sutch, and Gavin Wright, eds. *Historical Statistics of the United States: Millennial Edition*. New York: Cambridge University Press, 2006.

Clemen, Rudolph A. *The American Livestock and Meat Industry.* New York: Ronald, 1923.

Cole, Arthur Charles. *The Era of the Civil War, 1848–1870*, vol. 3. Springfield: Illinois Centennial Commission, 1919.

Cole, Arthur Harrison. *The American Wool Manufacture*, 2 vols. Cambridge, MA: Harvard University Press, 1926.

Cooley, Charles H. "The Theory of Transportation." *Publications of the American Economic Association* 9, no. 3 (May 1894): 13–148.

Corliss, Carlton J. *Main Line of Mid-America: The Story of the Illinois Central.* New York: Creative Age, 1950.

Cronon, William. *Nature's Metropolis: Chicago and the Great West.* New York: Norton, 1991.

Currey, Josiah Seymour. *Chicago: Its History and Its Builders; A Century of Marvelous Growth*, vol. 3. Chicago: Clarke, 1912.

Dankers, Ulrich. "French Chicago During the 18th Century." In *A Compendium of the Early History of Chicago to the Year 1835 When the Indians Left*, edited by Ulrich Dankers and Jane Meredith, 383–87. River Forest, IL: Early Chicago, 2000.

Dankers, Ulrich, and Jane Meredith. *A Compendium of the Early History of Chicago to the Year 1835 When the Indians Left.* River Forest, IL: Early Chicago, 2000.

Dante, Harris L. "The *Chicago Tribune*'s 'Lost' Years, 1865–1874." *Journal of the Illinois State Historical Society* 58, no. 2 (Summer 1965): 139–64.

David, Paul. *Technical Choice Innovation and Economic Growth: Essays on American and British Experience in the Nineteenth Century.* Cambridge: Cambridge University Press, 1975.

Dean, William, Jr. "The Theory of the Geographic Location of Economic Activity." PhD diss., Harvard University, 1938.

Dearinger, Ryan. *The Filth of Progress: Immigrants, Americans, and the Building of Canals and Railroads in the West.* Berkeley: University of California Press, 2016.

DeBow, J. D. B., comp. *Statistical View of the United States . . . Being a Compendium of the Seventh Census.* Washington, DC: Beverly Tucker, 1854.

Downard, William L. "William Butler Ogden and the Growth of Chicago." *Journal of the Illinois State Historical Society* 75, no. 1 (1982): 47–60.

Dowrie, George William. "The Development of Banking in Illinois, 1817–1863." PhD diss., University of Illinois, 1913.

East, Ernest E. "The Inhabitants of Chicago, 1825–1831." *Journal of the Illinois State Historical Society* 37, no. 2 (June 1944): 131–63.

Easterbrook, W. T., and Hugh G. J. Aitken. *Canadian Economic History.* Toronto: Macmillan Company of Canada, 1956.

Emery, Herb. "Fraternal Sickness Insurance." *EH.Net Encyclopedia*, edited by Robert Whaples, March 26, 2008. Http://eh.net/encyclopedia/fraternal-sickness-insurance/.

Emmet, Boris, and John Jeuck. *Catalogues and Counters: A History of Sears, Roebuck & Company.* Chicago: University of Chicago Press, 1950.

Fales, Raymond, and Leon Moses. "Thünen, Weber, and the Spatial Structure of the Nineteenth Century City." In *Spatial, Regional, and Population Economics: Essays in Honor of Edgar M. Hoover*, edited by M. Perlman, B. Chinitz, and C. Leven, 137–68. New York: Gordon & Breach, 1972.

Fehrenbacher, Don E. *Chicago Giant: A Biography of "Long John" Wentworth.* Madison, WI: American History Research Center, 1957.

Fergus, Robert, comp. *Chicago River and Harbor Convention.* Fergus Historical Series 18. Chicago: Fergus, 1882.

Fergus, Robert. *Directory of the City of Chicago, Illinois, for 1843.* Fergus Historical Series 28. Chicago: Fergus, 1896.

Ferris, William G. *The Grain Traders: The Story of the Chicago Board of Trade.* East Lansing: Michigan State University Press, 1988.

Foster, John E., and William John Eccles. "Fur Trade." In *The Canadian Encyclopedia.* Https://www.thecanadianencyclopedia.ca/en/article/fur-trade.

French, Yvonne. *The Great Exhibition: 1851.* London: Harvill, 1950.

Garb, Margaret. *Freedom's Ballot: African American Political Struggles in Chicago from Abolition to the Great Migration.* Chicago: University of Chicago Press, 2014.

Gates, Paul W. *The Illinois Central Railroad and Its Colonization Work.* Cambridge, MA: Harvard University Press, 1934.

Goode, J. Paul. *The Geographic Background of Chicago.* Chicago: University of Chicago Press, 1926.

Gordon, J. H. "Illinois Railroad Legislation and Commission Control Since 1870." *University of Illinois Bulletin,* March 15, 1905.

Grant, H. Roger. *The North Western: A History of the Chicago & North Western Railway System.* DeKalb: Northern Illinois University Press, 1996.

Grossman, James R., Ann Durkin Keating, and Janice L. Reiff. *The Encyclopedia of Chicago.* Chicago: University of Chicago Press, 2004.

Grover, Frank R. *Antoine Ouilmette: A Resident of Chicago, A.D. 1790–1826; The First Settler of Evanston and Wilmette (1826–1838) with a Brief History of His Family and the Ouilmette Reservation.* Evanston, IL: Evanston Historical Society, 1908.

Haeger, John D. "The American Fur Company and the Chicago of 1812–1835." *Journal of the Illinois State Historical Society* 61, no. 2 (Summer 1968): 117–39.

Hamilton, Henry E. "Biographical Sketch of Gurdon Saltonstall Hubbard." Paper read before the Chicago Historical Society, April 15, 1907, and published by the society a year later, 249–50. Https://www.seekingmyroots.com/members/files/G003117.pdf.

Hamilton, John. "The Epidemics of Chicago." *Bulletin of the Society of Medical History of Chicago* 1, no. 1 (October 1911): 73–86.

Harpster, Jack. *John Ogden, the Pilgrim (1609–1682): A Man of More Than Ordinary Mark.* Cranbury, NJ: Fairleigh Dickinson University Press, 2006.

Harpster, Jack. *Railroad Tycoon: A Biography of William B. Ogden.* Carbondale: Southern Illinois University Press, 2009.

Harris, Emily. *Prairie Passage: The Illinois and Michigan Canal Corridor.* Urbana: University of Illinois Press, 1998.

Hill, Howard Copeland. "The Development of Chicago as a Center of the Meat Packing Industry." *Mississippi Valley Historical Review* 10, no. 3 (December 1923): 253–73.

Holli, Melvin. "Mayors." *The Electronic Encyclopedia of Chicago.* Chicago: Chicago Historical Society, 2005.

Holt, Glen E. "The Birth of Chicago: An Examination of Economic Parentage." *Journal of the Illinois State Historical Society* 76, no. 2 (Summer 1983): 82–94.

Hower, Ralph M. "Cyrus Hall McCormick: American Business Leader." *Bulletin of the Business Historical Society* 10, no. 5 (November 1936): 69–76.

Hoyt, Homer. *One Hundred Years of Land Values in Chicago.* Chicago: University of Chicago Press, 1933.

Hubbard, Gurdon S. *The Autobiography of Gurdon Saltonstall Hubbard, Pa-pa-ma-ta-be, "The Swift Walker."* Chicago: Lakeside, 1911.

Hughes, Jonathan R. T. *The Governmental Habit Redux.* Princeton, NJ: Princeton University Press, 1991.

Hunter, Douglas. *God's Mercies: Rivalry, Betrayal and the Dream of Discovery.* Toronto: Random House of Canada, 2007.

Hyde, James Nevins. *Early Medical Chicago: An Historical Sketch of the First Practitioners.* Fergus Historical Series 11. Chicago: Fergus, 1877.

Industrial Chicago: The Commercial Interests. Chicago: Goodspeed, 1894.

Innis, Harold A. *The Fur Trade in Canada.* Toronto: University of Toronto Press, 1962.

Jaher, Frederic Cople. *The Urban Establishment: Upper Strata in Boston, New York, Charleston, Chicago, and Los Angeles.* Urbana: University of Illinois Press, 1982.

James, F. Cyril. *The Growth of Chicago Banks*, vol. 1. New York: Harper, 1938.

Jensen, Richard. "'No Irish Need Apply': A Myth of Victimization." *Journal of Social History* 36, no. 2 (Winter 2002): 405–29.

Jentz, John, and Hartmut Keil. *German Workers in Industrial Chicago, 1850–1910: A Comparative Perspective.* DeKalb: Northern Illinois University Press, 1983.

Karamanski, Theodore. "Lumber." *The Electronic Encyclopedia of Chicago.* Chicago: Chicago Historical Society, 2015.

Karrow, Robert W., Jr. "Mapping Chicago." *The Electronic Encyclopedia of Chicago.* Chicago: Chicago Historical Society, 2005.

Keating, Ann Durkin, ed. *Chicago Neighborhoods and Suburbs: A Historical Guide.* Chicago: University of Chicago Press, 2004.

Keating, Ann Durkin. *Rising Up from Indian Country.* Chicago: University of Chicago Press, 2012.

Keating, Ann Durkin. *The World of Juliette Kinzie: Chicago Before the Fire.* Chicago: University of Chicago Press, 2019.

Kelley, Edward S. "William Burnett: A Representative Eighteenth Century American Trader, Pioneer, and Home Builder." *Michigan Pioneer and Historical Collections* 30 (1906): 855–95. Https://www.cmich.edu/library/clarke/ResearchResources/Native_American_Material/Excerpts_from_the_Michigan_Pioneer_and_Historical_Collections/Documentskelley,_edward_s_pg_85–95.pdf.

Kinzie, Juliette M. *Wau-Bun: The "Early Day" in the North-West.* Chicago: University of Illinois Press, 1992.

Kirkland, Joseph. *The Story of Chicago.* Chicago: Dibble, 1892.

Larson, John W. *Those Army Engineers: A History of the Chicago District, U.S. Army Corps of Engineers.* Washington, DC: U.S. Government Printing Office, 1980.

Lebeau, B. Pierre. "Fur Trade." *The Electronic Encyclopedia of Chicago*. Chicago: Chicago Historical Society, 2015.

Lebergott, Stanley. "Wage Trends, 1800–1900." In *Trends in the American Economy in the Nineteenth Century*. National Bureau of Economic Research, Conference on Research in Income and Wealth, 449–500. Princeton, NJ: Princeton University Press, 1960.

Lee, Guy A. "The Historical Significance of the Chicago Grain Elevator System." *Agricultural History* 11, no. 1 (January 1937): 16–32.

Lewis, Lloyd. *John S. Wright: Prophet of the Prairies.* Chicago: Prairie Farmer, 1941.

Lurie, Jonathan. *The Chicago Board of Trade, 1859–1905: The Dynamics of Self-Regulation.* Urbana: University of Illinois Press, 1979.

Mahoney, Timothy R. *River Towns in the Great West: The Structure of Provincial Urbanization in the American Midwest, 1820–1870*. Cambridge: Cambridge University Press, 1990.

Marr, William L., and Donald G. Paterson. *Canada: An Economic History.* Toronto: Macmillan of Canada, 1980.

Masur, Kate. *Until Justice Be Done: America's First Civil Rights Movement, from the Revolution to Reconstruction.* New York: Norton, 2021.

MacBeath, George. "Dugua de Monts, Pierre," *Dictionary of Canadian Biography*. http://www.biographi.ca/en/bio/du_gua_de_monts_pierre_1E.html.

McCaffrey, J., Ellen Skerrett, Michael F. Funchion, and Charles Fanning. *The Irish in Chicago.* Urbana: University of Illinois Press, 1987.

McDonald, John F. *Chicago: An Economic History.* New York: Routledge, 2016.

McLear, Patrick E. "The Galena and Chicago Union Railroad: A Symbol of Chicago's Economic Maturity." *Journal of the Illinois State Historical Society* 73, no. 1 (1980): 17–26.

McLear, Patrick E. "William Butler Ogden: A Chicago Promoter in the Speculative Era in the Panic of 1837." *Journal of the Illinois State Historical Society* 70, no. 4 (1977): 283–91.

McMahon, Eileen M. "Canal Diggers, Church Builders: Dispelling Stereotypes of the Irish on the Illinois & Michigan Canal Corridor." *Journal of the Illinois State Historical Society* 111, no. 4 (Winter 2018): 43–81.

"Memoirs of Deceased Members." *Journal of the American Society of Civil Engineers* 15 (November 1889): 161. Https://babel.hathitrust.org/cgi/pt?id=uva.x002207917&seq=166.

Meese, William A. "Nathaniel Pope." *Journal of the Illinois State Historical Society* 3 (1910–11): 7–21.

Miller, Donald L. *City of the Century: The Epic of Chicago and the Making of America.* New York: Simon & Schuster, 1966.

Miller, Roberta Balstad. "Transportation Innovation and Regional Development in 19th Century New York: The Case of the Erie Canal." In *Retrospective Technology Assessment—1976*, edited by Joel A. Tarr, 75–87. San Francisco: San Francisco Press, 1977.

Monkkonen, Eric. *America Becomes Urban: The Development of U.S. Cities & Towns, 1780–1980.* Berkeley: University of California Press, 1988.

Moore, Sam. "The Largely Forgotten Role of Jearum Atkins in Reaper Development." *Farm Collector*, June 6, 2018. https://www.farmcollector.com/equipment/jearum-atkins-reaper-development-zmlz18julzhur/.

Morrissey, Robert Michael. "Kaskaskia Social Network: Kinship and Assimilation in the French-Illinois Borderlands, 1695–1735." *William and Mary Quarterly* 70, no. 1 (January 2013): 103–46.

Morrissey, Robert Michael. *People of the Ecotone*. Seattle: University of Washington Press, 2022.

Moser, Petra. "What Do Inventors Patent?" Working paper. 2006. Http://web.mit.edu/moser/www/patrat603.pdf.

Nelson, John William. *Muddy Ground: Native Peoples, Chicago's Portage, and the Transformation of a Continent*. Chapel Hill: University of North Carolina Press, 2023.

Norris, James W. *Business Directory and Statistics of the City of Chicago for 1846*. Chicago: Eastman and Davidson, 1846.

Norris, James W. *General Directory and Business Advertiser of the City of Chicago for the Year 1844*. Chicago: Ellis and Fergus, 1844.

Norris, James W. *General Directory and Business Advertiser of the City of Chicago for the Year 1845–46*. Chicago: J. Campbell, 1845.

Norton, Thomas Elliot. *The Fur Trade in Colonial New York, 1686–1776*. Madison: University of Wisconsin Press, 1974.

Pearse, Langdon. "Chicago's Quest for Potable Water." *Water and Sewage Works* 102, no. 5 (May 1955): 183–91.

Pierce, Bessie Louise. *A History of Chicago*, vol. 1: *The Beginning of a City, 1673–1848*. New York: Knopf, 1937.

Pierce, Bessie Louise. *A History of Chicago*, vol. 2: *From Town to City, 1848–1871*. New York: Knopf, 1940.

Pierce, Bessie Louise. *A History of Chicago*, vol. 3: *The Rise of a Modern City, 1871–1893*. Chicago: University of Chicago Press, 1957.

Pred, Allan. *Urban Growth and City-Systems in the United States, 1840–1860*. Cambridge, MA: Harvard University Press, 1980.

Primack, Martin L. "Land Clearing Under Nineteenth-Century Techniques: Some Preliminary Calculations." *Journal of Economic History* 22, no. 4 (December 1962): 484–97.

Primm, James Neal. *Lion of the Valley: St. Louis, Missouri, 1764–1980*. 3rd ed. St. Louis: Missouri Historical Society Press, 1998.

Putnam, James William. *The Illinois and Michigan Canal*. Chicago: University of Chicago Press, 1918.

Quaife, Milo Milton. *Chicago and the Old Northwest, 1673–1835: A Study of the Evolution of the Northwestern Frontier, Together with a History of Fort Dearborn*. Urbana: University of Illinois Press, 1913. The original edition was published in 1913 by the University of Chicago Press.

Quaife, Milo Milton. "Property of Jean Baptiste Point Sable." *Mississippi Valley Historical Review* 15, no. 1 (June 1928): 89–96.

Radebaugh, William. "The Boundary Dispute Between Illinois and Wisconsin." Address read before the Chicago Historical Society at a special meeting held May 19, 1904. Chicago: Chicago Historical Society, 1904.

Randolph, R. Isham. "The History of Sanitation in Chicago." *Journal of the Western Society of Engineers* 44 (October 1939): 227–40.

Reed, Christopher Robert. *Black Chicago's First Century: 1833–1900*. Columbia: University of Missouri Press, 2005.

Reed, Christopher Robert. "The Early African American Settlement of Chicago, 1833–1870." *Journal of the Illinois State Historical Society* 108, no. 3–4 (Fall/Winter 2015): 211–65.

Rockoff, Hugh, "The *Wizard of Oz* as a Monetary Allegory." *Journal of Political Economy* 98, no. 4 (August 1990): 739–60.

Roden, Carl B. "The Beaubien Claim." *Journal of the Illinois Historical Society* 42, no. 2 (June 1949): 157–61.

Ross, Frank E. *The Fur Trade of the Western Great Lakes Region*. St. Paul: Minnesota Historical Society, 1938. Http://collections.mnhs.org/MNHistoryMagazine/articles/19/v19i03p271-307.pdf.

Royal Commission. *Reports by the Juries on the Subjects in the Thirty Classes into Which the Exhibition Was Divided*. London: Clowes, 1851.

Rutter, David. "In Search of Seth Paine." *Country: Barrington Style & Substance*, April 1, 2020. Https://jwcdaily.com/countrymag/2020/04/01/in-search-of-seth-paine/.

Saunt, Claudio. *Unworthy Republic: The Dispossession of Native Americans and the Road to Indian Territory*. New York: Norton, 2020.

Scammon, J. Young. "William B. Ogden." *William B. Ogden and Early Days in Chicago. Fergus Historical Series 17*. 5–72. Chicago: Fergus,1882.

Schultz, Rime Lunin, and Adele Hast, eds. *Women Building Chicago, 1790–1990*. Bloomington: Indiana University Press, 2001.

Schweikart, Larry E. "Banking, Commercial." *The Electronic Encyclopedia of Chicago*. Chicago: Chicago Historical Society, 2005.

Sells, Benjamin. *A History of the Chicago Portage Lake*. Evanston, IL: Northwestern University Press, 2021.

Sells, Benjamin. *The Tunnel Under the Lake*. Evanston, IL: Northwestern University Press, 2007.

Skinner, Claiborne A. *The Upper Country: French Enterprise in the Colonial Great Lakes*. Baltimore: Johns Hopkins University Press, 2008.

Sleeper-Smith, Susan. *Indian Women and French Men: Rethinking Cultural Encounter in the Western Great Lakes*. Amherst: University of Massachusetts Press, 2001.

Smith, Carl. *Chicago's Great Fire*. New York: Atlantic Monthly Press, 2020.

Smith, Carl. *City Water, City Life: Water and the Infrastructure of Ideas in Urbanizing Philadelphia, Boston, and Chicago*. Chicago: University of Chicago Press, 2013.

Smith, Carl. *Urban Disorder and the Shape of Belief: The Great Chicago Fire, the Haymarket Bomb, and the Model Town of Pullman*. Chicago: University of Chicago Press, 1995.

Soper, George, John Watson, and Arthur Martin. *A Report to the Chicago Real Estate Board on the Disposal of the Sewage and Protection of the Water Supply of Chicago, Illinois*. Chicago: Chicago Real Estate Board, 1915.

Stover, John F. *American Railroads*. Chicago: University of Chicago Press, 1961.

Swenson, John F. "Jean Baptiste Point de Sable: The Founder of Modern Chicago." In *A Compendium of the Early History of Chicago to the Year 1835 When the Indians Left*, edited by Ulrich Dankers and Jane Meredith, 388–94. River Forest, IL: Early Chicago, 2000.

Taylor, Charles. *A History of the Board of Trade of the City of Chicago.* Chicago: Robert O. Law, 1917.

Taylor, George Rogers. *The Transportation Revolution, 1815–1860.* New York: Rinehart, 1951.

Unger, Irwin. *The Greenback Era.* Princeton, NJ: Princeton University Press, 1964.

United States Bureau of the Census. *The Fifth Census of the United States: 1830.* Washington, DC: Duff Green, 1832.

United States Bureau of the Census. *The Sixth Census of the United States: 1840.* Washington, DC: Blair and Rives, 1841.

United States Bureau of the Census. *The Seventh Census of the United States: 1850.* Washington, DC: Robert Armstrong, 1853.

United States Bureau of the Census. *The Eighth Census of the United States: 1860.* Washington, DC: Government Printing Office, 1864.

United States Bureau of the Census. *The Ninth Census of the United States: 1870.* Washington, DC: Government Printing Office, 1872.

United States Census Office. *Distribution of the Population East of the 100th Meridian: 1830.* Prepared under the supervision of Henry Gannett, Geographer of the Twelfth Census. New York: Julius Bien, 1903.

United States Department of State. *1840 Census: Compendium of the Enumeration of the Inhabitants and Statistics of the United States.* Washington, DC: Thomas Allen, 1841.

Vance, James. *The Merchant's World: The Geography of Wholesaling.* Englewood Cliffs, NJ: Prentice Hall, 1970.

Vidal de la Blanche, Paul Marie Joseph. *Principles of Human Geography.* Edited by Emmanual de Martonne, translated by Millicent Todd Bingham. New York: Holt, 1926.

Vierling, Philip. "The Fur Trade in Illinois—3," *Chicago Portage Ledger* (newsletter) 7, no. 1 (January/April 2006). Http://drupal.library.cmu.edu/chicago/collections.

Vierling, Philip E. "Where Was the du Sable Farm of 1790?" *Chicago Portage Ledger* (newsletter) 13, no. 2 (May/August 2012). http://drupal.library.cmu.edu/chicago/collections.

von Thünen, Johann Heinrich. *Der isolirte Staat in Beziehung auf Landwirtschaft und Nationalökonomie.* Hamburg: Wirtschaft & Finan, 1926.

Wade, Richard. *The Urban Frontier: The Rise of Western Cities, 1790–1830.* Cambridge, MA: Harvard University Press, 1959.

Walsh, Margaret. *The Rise of the Midwestern Meat Packing Industry.* Lexington: University Press of Kentucky, 1982.

Way, Peter. *Common Labour: Workers and the Digging of North American Canals, 1780–1860.* Cambridge: Cambridge University Press, 1993.

Weber, Alfred. *Theory of the Location of Industries.* Translated by Carl J. Friedrich. Chicago: University of Chicago Press, 1929.

Wendt, Lloyd. *Swift Walker: An Informal Biography of Gurdon Saltonstall Hubbard.* Lake Bluff, IL: Regnery, 1986.

Wendt, Lloyd, and Herman Kogan. *Give the Lady What She Wants! The Story of Marshall Field & Co.* Chicago: Rand McNally, 1952.

Wheeler, William Ogden. *The Ogden family in America, Elizabethtown branch, and their English ancestry: John Ogden, the Pilgrim, and his descendants, 1640–1906, their history, biography & genealogy.* Philadelphia: Printed for private circulation by J. B. Lippincott Co., 1907.

Whicker, John Wesley. *Historical Sketches of the Wabash Valley*. Attica, IN: Reprinted from the *Attica Ledger* and Published for Private Circulation by the Author, 1916.

White, Richard. *The Middle Ground: Indians, Empires, and Republics in the Great Lakes Region, 1650–1815*. New York: Cambridge University Press, 1991.

Widder, Keith R. "The Cartography of Dietrich Brehm and Thomas Hutchins and the Establishment of British Authority in the Western Great Lakes Region, 1760–1763." *Cartographica* 36, no. 1 (April 1999): 1–23.

Williams, Mentor L. "The Chicago River and Harbor Convention, 1847." *Mississippi Valley Historical Review* 35, no. 4 (March 1949): 607–26.

Wing, J. M. *The Tunnels and Water System of Chicago*. Chicago: Crerar, 1874.

Wood, Richard George. *Stephen Harriman Long*. Glendale, CA: Clark, 1874.

Workers of the Writer's Program. "Up from the Mud: An Account of How Chicago's Streets and Buildings Were Raised." N.p.: Works Progress Administration in Illinois for Board of Education, 1941.

Wright, Augustin W. "In Memoriam: John S. Wright; An Address Delivered Before the Chicago Historical Society Friday Night, July 1, 1885." Chicago: Fergus, 1885.

Wright, John S. *Chicago: Past, Present, and Future*. Chicago: Horton & Leonard, 1868.

Wyman, Mark. *Immigrants in the Valley: Irish, Germans, and Americans in the Upper Mississippi Country, 1830–1860*. Chicago: Nelson-Hall, 1984.

Young, David M. *The Iron Horse and the Windy City: How Railroads Shaped Chicago*. DeKalb: Northern Illinois University Press, 2005.

Zucker, Charles N. "The Free Negro Question: Race Relations in Ante-Bellum Illinois, 1801–1865." PhD diss., Department of History, Northwestern University, 1972.

Acknowledgments

The summer following my second year in graduate school, I began to consider potential dissertation topics. Knowing I wanted to write my dissertation on an applied economics topic, I chatted with several potential advisers and concluded that Hal Williamson was my best choice. The "new economic history" (now called "cliometrics"), which merged economic theory and quantitative techniques with the study of the evolution of the economy and its institutions, was blossoming. It offered an area of application that promised to maintain my interest, and indeed it has. During my third year, with Hal's assistance, I developed a dissertation proposal. At that time Hal was approaching sixty-five and would be forced to retire; my oral exam on the proposal was delayed until Hal's replacement, Jon Hughes, got settled. Shortly after the exam began, Jon started to alter the topic. I left that exam having passed, but with an entirely different topic, one that involved looking at three technologies (sanitation, electricity, and gas) available to city dwellers at the turn of the twentieth century but not yet adopted in many rural areas. Chicago was to be a case study. Simply because sanitation was in the public sector, I began with that subject.

All of Hal and Jon's dissertation students were part of the Economic History Workshop, and we had to deliver a progress report once per quarter. When the time arrived for me to present, I reported that Chicago had laid its first sewers on top of the ground and voted to raise the level of the city. Jon became excited; another change was in the offing. I was to forget about electricity and gas. My dissertation was to address two questions: Does Chicago's location make economic sense? What had to be done to make that location viable for economic activity? A little over a half century later, this book addresses the question of how that worked out. What happened next? How did Chicago grow?

My dissertation research led me to read most of the two major three-volume histories of Chicago, the first by Alfred Andreas, published in the 1880s, and the other by Bessie Louise Pierce, whose first volume was published in 1937. They were the principal secondary sources for my dissertation, as were several other works such as *Biographical Sketches of the Leading Men of Chicago, written by the best talent of the Northwest*, published in 1868. Today there is a resource that was not available when I was in graduate school—the internet. An internet search for a topic in this book often leads you back to those volumes, either directly or indirectly through a citation on an online reference site. When the same facts appeared in multiple sources, I chose not to include them in an endnote, but there are general notes in several chapters indicating the principal resources for a section of that chapter.

Chicago has been a component of much of my research through the years. A two-year stint as a visitor at the University of British Columbia in the 1970s taught me much about Canadian economic history and the fur trade. I wondered then about Chicago and the fur trade, but it was not until I retired from teaching that I got around to doing any serious research. That research was the stepping-stone to this book.

Histories of Chicago often begin with a mention of Marquette and Jolliet, a nod to Jean Baptiste Point de Sable, and then a paragraph or so about the city's incorporation. Marquette and Jolliet passed through Chicago more than a century before Point de Sable arrived, and he left Chicago thirty-three years before (and died fifteen years before) it was incorporated as a town in 1833. Having skipped the fur trade years in my reading of Andreas and Pierce, I had lots of blanks in my knowledge. In particular, did the fur trade, which was the main economic activity involving Europeans from Marquette and Jolliet in 1673 through to 1833, have any lasting impact? If not, what was the relation between early Chicago and the four decades of growth that preceded the Great Chicago Fire? If not, what explains that growth? And that is how, in retirement, during COVID, I returned to research I began as a graduate student.

There are many people to thank, not the least of whom are Hal and Jon, who perforce receive their thanks posthumously. Joel Mokyr arrived at Northwestern in the mid-1970s and became a friend, colleague, and racquetball partner. Joel, Joe Ferrie, and Walker Hanlon direct NU's Center for Economic History and have kindly allowed me to be affiliated with the center since its inception; Joe commented on a couple of the chapters. The center generously contributed to expenses incurred in putting this book together. For that, and many other things,

I extend my thanks. The weekly Economic History Workshop (recently directed by Carola Frydman and Nancy Qian) has been a constant in my life since that second summer of graduate school. All the faculty and grad students who have attended the workshop over the years contributed in some way to how I think about economic history.

Three scholars who have been exceptionally generous with their knowledge of Chicago history and with their time over the years—and again for this volume—are Henry Binford, Ann Durkin Keating, and Carl Smith. All have read and commented on at least pieces of this work. In fact, Henry read and commented on most of this manuscript as he transitioned to retirement and all that involves. All three have the gift of being able to write more elegantly than I, and I thank them for having read what an economist has written and making suggestions that elevate what you have read.

Many other friends have read and commented on individual chapters. Bob Coen (Department of Economics, Northwestern University) and Frank Fennell (Department of English, Loyola University Chicago) form half of a golf foursome that extends well back into the previous century; both offered comments to help make the argument more accessible to non-economic historians. Don Paterson of the University of British Columbia provided materials concerning the fur trade that were otherwise unavailable during the COVID lockdown. Tom Weiss of the University of Kansas, a friend since my first cliometrics conference at Purdue, read several chapters from the perspective of one whose ties to Chicago are through his wife, a city native. George Harmon, a college classmate who is also a lifelong Chicagoan, a former newspaper editor, and a retired Northwestern journalism professor, read the entire manuscript, making innumerable suggestions that improved its readability. I should note that one of his ancestors, Elijah Dewey Harmon, MD, arrived in Chicago in May 1830 to serve as the tenth medical officer at Fort Dearborn. For a brief time, he lived and practiced in the same house where the Point de Sables and Kinzies once had lived.

The Center for Economic History at Northwestern made it possible for me to access four superb research assistants: Priyanka Panjwani, Michael Giordano, Xueyan Li, and Isabelle Hauf-Pisoni. Their ability to track down materials, especially during the pandemic, was invaluable.

Martha Bayne of the University of Illinois Press was enthusiastic—and patient—from the start. The anonymous readers she enlisted made numerous helpful suggestions throughout the process. Tad Ringo of the Press oversaw production; Jane Zanichkowsky was the adroit copyeditor. Mariah Schaefer and Gary Smith helped coordinate the illustrations that accompany the text. Jennie Fisher designed the cover.

Thanks are due Maggie Cusick and Natalie Sinclair of the Chicago History Museum, who went out of their way to help find those illustrations. They are carrying on a standard of service I first enjoyed as a graduate student working on my dissertation and have had occasion to revisit several times over the course of my career. Thanks are also due Nathalie Wheaton of the Rush University Medical Center Archives for providing the illustration of that institution's first home and to Northwestern's Kevin Leonard for connecting me with Nathalie.

Méch Frazier of the Northwestern Library did yeoman work creating the maps for this volume. Many readers of early versions of this manuscript strongly suggested that maps would be helpful, and I believe Méch has fulfilled their requests. Thank you.

Last, users of the book have Katy Balcer to thank for her incomparable job of producing the index.

Index

LOUIS P. CAIN is an adjunct professor of economics at Northwestern University and a professor emeritus at Loyola University Chicago. He is the coauthor of *The Children of Eve: Population and Well-being in History*.

The University of Illinois Press
is a founding member of the
Association of University Presses.

Composed in 10.75/13 Arno Pro
with Trade Gothic LT Std display
by Lisa Connery
at the University of Illinois Press
Manufactured by Versa Press, Inc.

University of Illinois Press
1325 South Oak Street
Champaign, IL 61820-6903
www.press.uillinois.edu